The Summer Slide

What We Know and Can Do About Summer Learning Loss

The Summer Slide

What We Know and Can Do About Summer Learning Loss

EDITED BY

Karl Alexander
Sarah Pitcock
Matthew Boulay

Foreword by Paul Reville

TEACHERS COLLEGE PRESS

TEACHERS COLLEGE | COLUMBIA UNIVERSITY
NEW YORK AND LONDON

Published by Teachers College Press, 1234 Amsterdam Avenue, New York, NY 10027

Copyright © 2016 by Teachers College, Columbia University

Cover by Laura Duffy Design. Dandelion image by Brian A. Jackson, Shutterstock.

Library of Congress Cataloging-in-Publication Data is available at loc.gov

ISBN 978-0-8077-5799-4 (paper)
ISBN 978-0-8077-7509-7 (ebook)

Printed on acid-free paper
Manufactured in the United States of America

23 22 21 20 19 18 17 16   8 7 6 5 4 3 2 1

Contents

PART II—DRIVERS OF DIFFERENTIAL SUMMER LEARNING: FAMILY ADVANTAGE AND FAMILY DISADVANTAGE

PART III—STEMMING SUMMER LEARNING LOSS: LESSONS FROM AND ABOUT RESEARCH

Foreword

One summer when I was Massachusetts secretary of education, I had an opportunity to visit a special summer learning program located on one of the islands in Boston Harbor. After a short ferry trip, I and other policy and philanthropy leaders had a tour of this STEM camp aimed at introducing young people, in this case a limited number of disadvantaged youngsters from the Boston Public Schools, to the wonders of the outdoor world while building their academic skills. We observed what one would see at high-quality camps elsewhere: children engaging in fun and challenging activities with bright, enthusiastic young counselors; discovering nature; forming new relationships; and building skills and knowledge about subjects that they were finding relevant and exciting.

At the end of our tour, the visiting group engaged in a discussion of just how the camp was achieving such positive results. When it came time for me to comment, I respectfully said that I wasn't surprised by the results, because I, like other people of privilege, routinely send my children to similar kinds of camps because they are such positive learning experiences. What interested me about this program was not why and how it was successful—that was self-evident—but rather how we might make programs like these broadly available to all disadvantaged children who didn't happen to get access to them through the accident of birth. The interesting and compelling question to me was, How do we make such programs the rule, an entitlement, for inner city kids rather than the luck of the draw?

It seemed to me then and even more so now, having read this compelling set of articles, that the answer to this question should be an urgent policy priority in our quest to build a 21st-century education system that prepares all of our children for success.

If you are concerned, as I am, about the failure of the last quarter century's school reform to achieve anything close to equity—let alone excellence—for all, you would be hard-pressed, after reading this book, not to conclude that we've grossly underinvested in increasing access to summer learning, to say nothing of out-of-school learning generally. The authors present powerful evidence suggesting that investments in such programs provide a very appealing return in terms of closing opportunity and achievement gaps. If we intend to renew our reform agenda, as we must, summer learning should be a top priority. This volume provides a clear rationale for investment in summer learning as well as a balanced analysis of the ways and means of assuring effective implementation.

This book offers more convincing evidence that learning which occurs in the 80% of children's waking hours that is spent outside of school, especially in summer, is every bit as important as any in-school learning in determining achievement gaps. With affluent families spending more than ever before on enriching the learning of their children virtually constantly during their out-of-school hours, while poor families find it harder than ever before to make ends meet and have dramatically less time and money to spend on their children's out of school enrichment, the gaps are growing.

This book makes it clear that if our education reform strategies, as they have to date, focus almost exclusively on improving what happens in school (as important as that may be), then we have little hope of closing persistent achievement gaps which are caused at least as much by the wide and growing opportunity gaps in access to high-quality out-of-school learning. In other words, if we focus reform solely on optimizing the 20% of waking hours that students spend in school, and if we expect improvements in that piece of their life experience to compensate for all the other inequities, we are missing the target while incidentally engaging in an exercise in magical thinking.

For these reasons, I believe we need a national campaign for a new concept: making summer learning, in effect, a third education semester each year. Every child should have access to high-quality learning, and disadvantaged children should be entitled to such access. The third semester should be seen as essential to each educational year. This concept is not about prescribing more formal schooling but rather about providing enrichment, stimulation, and learning opportunities that are often, though not always, aligned with academic goals. Summer enrichment should also be about developing new interests, relationships, social capital, social-emotional learning, and skills. Such an entitlement would not be a mandate forcing all kids to attend summer school but rather a guarantee that every child, irrespective of financial means, would have access to at least 6 weeks of high-quality summer learning and enrichment.

If we have any hope of realizing our education reform ideals and educating all students to the point where they are prepared to be successful in college and careers, then we have to create a third semester. We can no longer treat summer learning as incidental, an accident of birth; rather, we must see it as an essential ingredient in achieving student success at scale. It isn't something "nice to do" but something we must do, as this book so effectively illustrates. If we're serious about closing achievement gaps, summer enrichment must become an entitlement. Obviously, this will require more resources to support such additional learning opportunities, at least for those who don't ordinarily have access to them, but such an investment is one of several critical features of the pathway to "all means all." If federal, state, and local policymakers fail to make such investments, then we should just openly admit that our best efforts at school reform will be insufficient to close achievement gaps. We will need to be resigned to perpetual achievement gaps and all the attendant consequences.

My daughter attends a school that is part of an urban school system. She is a privileged child who enjoys a rich buffet of enrichment opportunities every summer. She is stimulated and connected to all kinds of valuable learning opportunities, from camps, to tutoring, to sports, to travel, and exposure to all kinds of interesting people. She attends school side by side with youngsters who, through no fault of their own, have no access to such opportunities. Her classmate may live in a dangerous neighborhood and have no access to affordable summer programs; his mother may insist that, to be safe, he must stay in the apartment all day until she returns from work. His summer enrichment opportunities will be severely constrained by isolation and the shortcomings of television and, even if he's lucky, video games. Is it any surprise, then, that his academic trajectory will typically differ widely from that of my daughter when these kinds of opportunity gaps persist, day after day, summer after summer, for the 13 years of K–12 education and throughout the 80% of their waking hours that students spend outside of school?

The contributing authors and editors of this book carefully show why such inequality of opportunity not only is unfair but is totally undermining our educational goal of preparing all of our children for success. We cannot continue to tolerate this. We must devise systems of educational opportunity that address the vast inequities that result from a society in which widespread and growing income inequality exists. A good place to start is summer learning. Only in this way will we get to our goal of preparing all of our students to be successful, and, as is frequently asserted in our reform rhetoric, "all means all."

Paul Reville
Francis Keppel Professor of Practice of
Educational Policy and Administration
Director, Education Redesign Lab,
Harvard University Graduate School of Education

Introduction

Karl Alexander, Matthew Boulay, and Sarah Pitcock

The summer months can be considered the most inequitable time for young people in this country. While schools and teachers have been under unprecedented scrutiny for over a decade as legislators and school administrators try to stem the expansion of academic achievement gaps, research suggests that young people of different income levels achieve at relatively the same rate (albeit not the same level) during the school year. It's the summer when the gap widens and the experience varies most widely based on income. Despite our collective ideal of summer "vacation," learning is not a 9-month endeavor for higher-income families.

The phenomenon of summer learning loss is well documented. But summer loss is about much more than reading and math skills. When not maximized, the summer months bring with them losses in learning, health and well-being, college and career opportunity, and support needed to break cycles of intergenerational poverty and move young people and their families forward. Alternately, when infused with high-quality learning opportunities, the summer months can be a lever for growth, safety, and prosperity for families, schools, and communities.

We are at an interesting point in the "time and learning" conversation. The influx of charter schools and the failure of many reform movements to move the needle on academic progress have led more cities and states to explore expanded definitions of when and where students can learn and earn credit. At the 2013 National Summer Learning Association (NSLA) conference, former Massachusetts secretary of education Paul Reville likened our K–12 education system to a 50-yard dash—we fire a gun in kindergarten and expect all young people to finish the race in 12th grade, despite the fact that some kids are starting 10 yards behind, some 10 yards ahead, and others everywhere between. He argues for a "new engine" for education, one that opens up alternatives to seat time and standard curriculum tracks. Today 80% of minority students in this country are not proficient in reading by the end of 3rd grade, making them at least four times as likely to drop out of high school. Knowing how far behind so many of our students are,

1

clearly the "new engine" should include a focus on learning opportunities year-round.

So, we ask, how are we organized to respond to this growing body of evidence? What does it mean for our collective ideal of summer "vacation"? Whose responsibility is it to keep young people safe, healthy, and engaged in learning during the summer, and what are the best ways to do it?

The literature on summer learning loss has not kept pace with the changing education and policy landscape to help us answer these critical questions. Until now, that is. The NSLA is the only national nonprofit exclusively focused on closing the achievement gap by increasing access to high-quality summer learning opportunities. As NSLA's leadership team, we determined that the time was right for a thoroughgoing survey of the landscape—to update the research (as noted below, the seminal studies in this area now are quite dated); to review advances in summer programming intended to stem summer slide; and to take stock of the policy, context, and prospects for advancing that agenda. Toward that end, we commissioned papers from leading authorities to review the current state of knowledge with respect to research, policy, and practice. These papers, presented here in chapter form, also are forward looking. They will help frame a summer learning agenda for the 21st century. *The Summer Slide: What We Know and Can Do About Summer Learning Loss* is tightly constructed and accessible by design but also rigorous and state of the art.

It is our pleasure to share this material with you. We hope it will raise awareness of summer learning loss and its impact, inspire those already committed to alleviating summer learning loss to redouble their efforts, and provide practical guidance on best practices in summer programming, including how to implement and evaluate strong summer programs.

BACKGROUND

Harris Cooper and his colleagues (1996) trace the history of research on summer learning loss to the turn of the 20th century, with studies revealing that many children lose ground academically in reading and math over the summer months. But that early research was rudimentary by contemporary standards and did not address the equity issues that today are so prominent: The learning of poor and minority children is most compromised by the long summer break.

In the modern era, Barbara Heyns's pathbreaking book *Summer Learning and the Effects of Schooling* (1978) was the first to demonstrate that the achievement gap across social lines widens when disadvantaged children are cut off from the learning resources available to them at school. Heyns compared the academic progress of 6th- and 7th-graders in Atlanta, Georgia, over an 18-month period. That time frame brackets 2 school years and the summer break between them. Her findings fundamentally altered our understanding of the forces that impinge on poor and minority children's learning. Atlanta schoolchildren from low-income families and African American children came close to keeping pace with their more-advantaged counterparts during the school year but fell back during the summer months.

Other studies followed. In Baltimore, Maryland, Entwisle, Alexander, and Olson (1997), in their Beginning School Study (BSS), found that the reading comprehension achievement gap separating low-income children from children of middle-class family background increased from 0.5 grade equivalents in the fall of 1st grade to 3.0 grade equivalents in the spring of 5th grade. To be reading at a 3rd- or 4th-grade level at that point in their schooling, as many poor children were, does not auger well. And sadly, those expectations held true: The poor children in their project were much less likely to pursue a high school college preparatory program of study, much more likely to drop out of high school, and much less likely to continue on to college. But here was the startling revelation: Almost all of the increase in the achievement gap over the elementary school years traced to differences across social lines in summer learning, and two-thirds of the reading comprehension gap separating children from low-income families and those from middle-income families in 9th grade (up to 3.5 grade equivalents at that point) likewise originated in differential summer learning over the elementary school years (Alexander, Entwisle, & Olson, 2007).

These are trends, not iron laws. For every "rule" there are exceptions, but the trends are quite real and quite powerful: The prospects are bleak for children who suffer summer learning losses.

National studies report similar patterns. Downey, von Hippel, and Broh (2004) document disparities across social lines in summer learning over the summer between kindergarten and 1st grade. Poor and disadvantaged minority children (on average) begin school already behind in the cognitive skills that support academic learning (Lee & Burkam, 2002), and over the course of their schooling, the disparity widens. What we now know is that much of the achievement-gap increase happens outside school and is rooted in family disadvantage.

Those conclusions also are borne out in literature reviews, the best known and still relevant being the 1996 study by Cooper, Nye, Charlton, Lindsay, and Greathouse, "The Effects of Summer Vacation on Achievement Test Scores: A Narrative and Meta-analytic Review." Their review of 39 studies dating back to 1978 (13 of which could be formally analyzed) concludes that, on average, students lose about 2 months of grade-level equivalency in mathematical computation skills over the summer months, whereas in reading achievement, low-income students typically lose more than 2 months, while those of middle-class background register slight gains.

This is a fair, if abbreviated, summary of our understanding of summer learning loss at the turn of the 21st century. The evidence is clear and compelling, and its implications for action hard to ignore, yet as recently as 2002, Gerald Bracey, in his "Research Briefs" column in the *Phi Delta Kappan* (2002), could identify summer loss as "The Phenomenon No One Wants to Deal With" (the title of his piece). Bracey continued:

> Schools whose poor children are learning over the year will suffer because summer loss will cause them to fall farther and farther behind their middle-class peers and fail to show much growth in reading and math. It will thus appear that the schools are failing, and they will be blamed for what is happening—or, more accurately not happening—in the family and the community.

But there has been a sea-change in recent years. In 2009 Secretary of Education Arne Duncan (2009) announced that, "Summer learning loss is . . . devastating. There is a ton of evidence . . . . [Children] get to a certain point academically in June, and over the summer they lose that. They come back in September further behind. It is literally a step backward."

In 2010, President Obama observed that "students are losing a lot of what they learned during the school year during the summer" (Interview, NBC Today Show, September 27, 2010).

Malcolm Gladwell, in his book *Outliers* (2011) carried the message to a broad readership beyond the research and policy communities:

> Virtually all of the advantage that wealthy students have over poor students is the result of differences in the way privileged students learn when they are *not* in school. . . . America doesn't have a school problem. It has a summer vacation problem. (pp. 258–260)

Finally, National Summer Learning Day 2015, an NSLA initiative, launched with an inspiring message from First Lady Michelle Obama:

> Summer shouldn't just be a vacation. Instead, it should be a time to get ahead, to branch out to acquire new skills, to have new experiences, like acting in a play and doing some outdoor learning. And for anyone who's fallen behind, it's a time to catch up on the lessons they missed. . . . And of course, you've gotta read, read, read!

The Summer Slide provides an up-to-date account of summer learning loss, of the conditions in low-income children's homes and communities that impede their learning over the summer months, and of best practices in summer programming, with lessons on how to strengthen program evaluations and the usefulness of program evaluations for informing policy. If we have done our job well, *The Summer Slide* will build on the impressive momentum now under way to help motivate additional initiatives to increase access to high-quality summer learning opportunities.

WHAT FOLLOWS

The Summer Slide contains three substantive sections and a wrap-up stock-taking, with 18 chapters total.

Part I, "Summer Learning and Summer Learning Loss: Theory and Research," updates the basic pattern of summer learning and summer learning loss across social lines and surveys the landscape of summer program availability for low-income children. What does the problem look like today, and is there an adequate infrastructure in place for combatting it?

In Chapter 1, Downey addresses what are perhaps the most fundamental questions regarding the seasonality of learning: Why is it that low-income children lose ground during the summer months when they lack access to school-based learning resources? Given that many low-income children attend high-poverty schools with the known challenges that entails, how is it they come closer to keeping up during the school year? Downey reviews how scholars have theorized about the question and assesses the adequacy of those accounts.

The next three chapters review and update the demographics of summer learning loss. Though the pattern itself is well established, the foundational studies are dated: Heyns's Atlanta study uses data from the 1970s, the Baltimore Beginning School Study (BSS) uses data from the 1980s, and the national Early Childhood Longitudinal Study is anchored in the 1990s. Alexander and Condliffe (Chapter 2) review the BSS research and update the Baltimore situation with current data on summer learning patterns in the city's public schools. Atteberry and McEachin present data in Chapter 3 on summer learning patterns for a single southern state from 2007 to 2012 across grades 2 through 9.

Davies, Aurini, and Milne add a comparative perspective in reviewing studies of summer learning and summer learning loss in Canada. Summer slide has yet to command much attention beyond our borders, in part because most other mature industrial economies have a much shorter summer recess than in the United States (our national template is for a school year of roughly 180 days; in other countries, students attend school for as many as 245 days). But as Davies, Aurini, and Milne establish in Chapter 4, this U.S.-centric focus is mistaken: Canadian children experience the same sort of summer setback as do disadvantaged children in the United States.

The last two chapters in Part I report what might be considered needs assessment research on the availability of summer programming for low-income children. Focusing on 16 states, Borman, Schmidt, and Hosp examine state mandates for summer school against best practice guidelines. In Chapter 5, Pitcock assesses the summer opportunity gap at the local level by examining program availability in cities throughout the country and the resources that support them. Observing that often policies are not well aligned with the import of evaluation studies, Chapter 6 formulates guidance for developing practical, research-based policy to promote effective summer school programs designed to achieve these goals. Her review concludes that the supply of high-quality summer programs for disadvantaged youth falls far short of the demand.

Part II, "Drivers of Differential Summer Learning: Family Advantage and Family Disadvantage," reviews the academic advantages typical of middle-class children and, correspondingly, the shortfall experienced by children of low-income families: What are the mechanisms that govern differences in summer learning across social lines?

In Chapter 7, Pallas surveys the bases of middle-class privilege at the interior of family life and in the communities where they live. Merry, Buchmann, and Condron (Chapter 8) interrogate shadow learning through the lens of the summer experience gap. *Shadow learning* refers to after-school, weekend, and summer fee-for-service schooling and tutoring. The practice originated in Asia, where socioeconomically advantaged parents use supplemental schooling to purchase academic advantages for their children. The implications of shadow education across lines of family income have yet to be assessed from a seasonal perspective.

Reporting new qualitative data from Baltimore, Condliffe examines issues in Chapter 9 at the other end of the family resource spectrum. Condliffe engages with a sample of low-income parents of 1st graders to learn how they navigate the summer programming landscape—what they know and how they engage with the marketplace of summer learning opportunities available to their children. This inquiry addresses a matter of great practical relevance, as even the best conceived programs are of little value if parents are unable to avail themselves of them.

Summertime isn't just about learning and summer learning loss. The final chapters in Part II take up two issues that are of great importance in their own right but also pose implications for summer learning. Children at greatest risk for summer learning loss also are most susceptible to weight gain over the summer and are exposed to high levels of stress in their daily lives (e.g., neighborhood crime). In Chapter 10, Bohnert, Zarrett, and Heard draw on developmental theories to inform why levels of childhood obesity spike during the summer months. They also review policy initiatives at the local, state, and federal levels that incorporate summertime in efforts to reduce obesity and promote healthy development. Bohnert, McLeod, Marshall, and Grant follow in Chapter 11 with a review of summer interventions geared to promoting youth's psychological well-being. Their chapter concludes with best practice recommendations.

Part III, "Stemming Summer Learning Loss: Lessons from and About Research," takes up summer program interventions. In Chapter 12, McEachin, Augustine, and McCombs review the results of a large, randomized trial that evaluates five different summer learning programs, using this field-test, along with their review of the broader evaluation literature, to sketch research-informed best practice principles for high-quality summer programming. Von Hippel surveys the landscape of year-round schooling in Chapter 13 and evaluates the effectiveness this calendar reform, which replaces the long summer break with shorter breaks spaced throughout the year. He asks whether it is superior to stand-alone supplementary summer programming.

Cheatham and Williams review the provision of summer programs for children in rural settings. With rural populations widely dispersed geographically, rural programming faces quite distinctive challenges, yet these communities are virtually absent in studies of summer learning loss. Chapter 14 reviews what is known and sets forth recommendations for an invigorated agenda for research, policy, and practice in rural settings.

Part III concludes with three chapters that interrogate the interrogators. In Chapter 15, Goetze provides an overview of the assessment of summer learning programs from an economic perspective, including cost analysis, cost-effectiveness analysis, and cost-benefit analysis. Illustrative data are presented to show how information on program costs can be combined with student outcome data to inform future planning and to establish program cost-effectiveness. Stein and Fonseca follow in Chapter 16 with suggestions for improved reporting practices in program evaluations. Part III concludes with recommendations from Ackman, White, and Kim in Chapter 17 for using program evaluations more effectively to inform policy.

While the pipeline from research to policy and practice can often be long and circuitous, the field of summer learning may provide a welcome counterexample. Findings and recommendations from research studies like the ones discussed in this book are now routinely cited by parents, teachers, principals, and a range of local, state, and federal policymakers. The past 15 years or so also have witnessed an increase in the number of programs specifically designed to curb summer learning loss, and we take it as a good sign that a number of foundations have made significant commitments to support such programs. Some of these programs are formal, enrollment-based programs offered by schools and school districts, whereas some are less intensive, more informal interventions such as book distribution and library-based reading programs. The range of program models suggests a certain level of innovation as providers create interventions that meet their particular needs and constraints. It is worth noting that beyond a simple increase in the number and type of programs, there also is widespread recognition that the *quality* of program design and implementation matters a great deal. In other words, we are making progress toward the goal of not only offering children a summer program but working hard as a field to ensure that it is a high-quality program.

What we haven't seen to this point is a significant and broad-based increase in public funding for summer learning programs. While a number of cities and even a few states have authorized new funding for summer programs, there has been little movement at the federal level. By drawing attention to the evidence and issues discussed in *The Summer Slide*, we hope to advance the conversation around summer learning and summer programming across the country and at all levels of educational policymaking and practice.

REFERENCES

Alexander, K. L., Entwisle, D. R., & Olson, L. S. (2007). Lasting consequences of the summer learning gap. *American Sociological Review, 72,* 167–180.

Bracey, G. W. (2002). Summer loss: The phenomenon no one wants to deal with. *Phi Delta Kappan, 84*(1), 12–13.

Cooper, H., Nye, B., Charlton, K., Lindsay, J., & Greathouse, S. (1996). The effects of summer vacation on achievement test scores: A narrative and meta-analytic review. *Review of Educational Research, 66,* 227–268.

Downey, D. B., von Hippel, P. T., & Broh, B. A. (2004). Are schools the great equalizer? Cognitive inequality during the aummer months and the school year. *American Sociological Review, 69*(5), 613–635.

Duncan, A. (2009). Retrieved from the U.S. Department of Education, www2.ed.gov/news/av/video/2009/06/interview.html

Entwisle, D. R., Alexander, K. L., & Olson, L. S. (1997). *Children, schools & inequality*. Boulder, CO: Westview Press.

Gladwell, M. (2011). *Outliers: The story of success*. New York, NY: Little, Brown.

Heyns, B. (1978). *Summer learning and the effects of schooling*. New York, NY: Academic Press.

Lee, V., & Burkam, D. T. (2002). *Inequality at the starting gate: Social background differences in achievement as children begin school*. Washington, DC: Economic Policy Institute.

Obama, B. Interview, NBC Today Show, September 27, 2010.

Obama, M. (2015, June 19). A summer learning day message from First Lady Michelle Obama. Retrieved from www.youtube.com/watch?v=cjfWycXggq8

Part I

SUMMER LEARNING AND SUMMER LEARNING LOSS: THEORY AND RESEARCH

CHAPTER 1

Schools, Families, and Inequality

Strong Empirical Patterns
in Search of Strong Theory

Douglas B. Downey

Seasonal comparison researchers consistently demonstrate that socioeconomic-based achievement gaps grow faster when school is out versus in, suggesting that inequality would be worse if not for schools. This remarkable pattern and its implications is not yet embedded in the public mind, however, perhaps because the ideas explaining the relationship between schools and inequality are undertheorized. In this paper I discuss some of the ideas scholars have presented so far, along with persisting theoretical challenges.

The traditional narrative about schools and inequality is straightforward: Children from advantaged families enjoy substantially better schools than their disadvantaged peers, and this inequity plays an important role shaping stratification outcomes. This is why parents spend resources to ensure their children's enrollment in good schools. It is why school reform is touted as a way to improve the conditions of the poor. This story has become so pervasive that it is now a cultural assumption largely unchallenged by policymakers, the general public, and even scholars.

But seasonally collected data produce two important patterns that undermine the traditional narrative. First, gaps in cognitive skills based on socioeconomic status (SES) grow faster when school is out versus in (Downey, von Hippel, & Broh, 2004; Entwisle & Alexander, 1992; Heyns, 1978). Second, schools serving high-SES children do not promote more learning than schools serving low-SES children (Downey, von Hippel, & Hughes, 2008). Combine these findings with the fact that SES-based achievement gaps are formed almost entirely prior to kindergarten (Brooks-Gunn, Cunha,

Duncan, Heckman, & Sojourner, 2006; Duncan & Magnuson, 2011),[1] and together, these patterns represent a significant challenge to the traditional understanding about schools' role in the stratification system.

But seasonal comparison research has yet to change the traditional narrative, in part because it raises more questions than it answers. Specifically, seasonal comparison research needs to address the following puzzle: How can low-SES children, with their poorer homes and schools, learn at roughly the same rate as high-SES children when school is in session? I consider three explanations: (1) The Faucet Theory, (2) Homes Vary More Than Schools, and (3) Schools Are Compensatory Institutions. I conclude that the compensatory view receives the strongest empirical support, prompting a rethinking of the assumption that schools are an engine of inequality.

THE FAUCET THEORY

One of the first attempts to make sense of the seasonal patterns was offered by Entwisle, Alexander, and Olson (1997), who introduced what they called the "faucet theory":

> When school is in session, the faucet is turned on for all children, the resources children need for learning are available to everyone, so all children gain. When school is not in session, children whose families are poor stop gaining because for them the faucet is turned off. The resources available to them in summer (mainly family resources) are not sufficient to promote their continued growth. (p. 37)

The faucet theory deserves credit for initiating the process of trying to understand seasonal patterns by targeting the appropriate question. Its explanation, however, is underdeveloped. For example, it acknowledges that high- and low-SES children learn at roughly the same rate during the school year, when the faucet is on yet glosses over this puzzling pattern too quickly. Two problems emerge with assuming that the resource "faucet" is simply on for all children during the 9-month school year. First, while there is a home faucet and a school faucet of resources, both continue to matter during the school year. Even during the 9-month school year, children spend nearly two-thirds of their waking hours outside of school. High-SES children should learn faster than low-SES children during the school year, therefore, because they enjoy parental inputs (e.g., provision of health care, educational resources, family stability, warmth, intellectual stimulation) more conducive to learning. While the resource faucet may be on during the school year for both high- and low-SES students, socioeconomic status continues to shape children's school experiences during the school year so that those faucets are unequal.

A second reason high-SES children should learn faster during the school year is because they enjoy better schools than low-SES children. When we talk about "better schools," we usually mean a wide range of factors such as better teachers, improved curriculum, more efficient administrators, fewer discipline problems, more academically inclined peers, more extracurricular activities, and better facilities. Better schools should have all of these advantages, and they should also promote more math and reading learning. It is widely assumed that high-SES children enjoy better schools than their low-SES peers by providing better opportunities to learn. The notion that a faucet of resources is on during the school year fails to confront the widely held view that high-SES children enjoy better schools than low-SES children. The faucet may be on for everyone, but shouldn't it be "more on" for high-SES children?

The faucet theory starts us on the path toward explaining seasonal results, but it leaves the most challenging question unanswered: Why do high- and low-SES children learn at roughly similar rates during the school year when high-SES children enjoy two advantages: (1) better homes and (2) better schools?

Homes Vary More Than Schools

Perhaps school environments really are advantageous to high-SES children, it is just that homes environments are even more advantageous. Figure 1.1, adapted from Downey et al. (2004), provides a useful visual for this perspective. It suggests that the inequalities children face outside of school are substantially greater than those in school. From this perspective, some school processes may favor the advantaged, yet achievement gaps grow even faster when school is out. As we wrote:

Figure 1.1. A Contextual View: Variation in Nonschool and School Environments

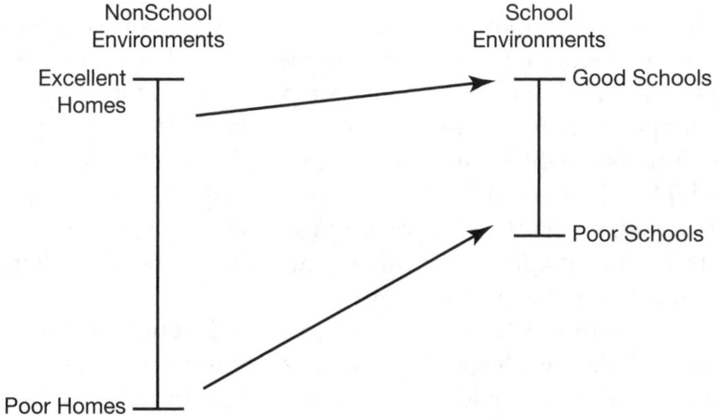

Because non-school environments vary more than school environments, a child from a disadvantaged non-school environment can attend a disadvantaged school and yet still enjoy a greater school benefit than a child from an advantaged non-school environment who attends an advantaged school. (p. 614)

In this way, schools could provide advantages to high-SES children in the way many suspect yet still be an environment that slows the growth of achievement gaps relative to summer.

The merits of this explanation depend, in part, on whether variation in home environments really is greater than variation in school environments. While this question has yet to be thoroughly explored, available evidence tends to find that variation in home environment is greater. Von Hippel (2010) reports greater variation among families than schools across income inequality, parent/teacher credentials, and class size/family size.

Focusing on financial resources is one of the more convenient ways of comparing variance in school and nonschool environments. Kozol's widely read 1991 book, *Savage Inequalities*, documented marked disparities in funding between inner city schools and their suburban counterparts. Looking broadly at school funding patterns, however, reveals a different view. The 1971 *Serrano v. Priest* ruling in California prompted a rethinking of the heavy reliance on local taxation, and since that time disparities in funding have declined. When adjusted for inflation, expenditures per student from 1995–1996 through 2006–2007 increased the most in high-poverty districts (35%) and increased the least in low-poverty districts (26%) (National Center for Education Statistics, 2012).[2] And in 2006–2007, expenditures per student were slightly higher in high-poverty ($10,978) versus low-poverty districts ($10,850) (National Center for Education Statistics, 2012). Although notable differences in resources exist across schools, these are mostly evident at the extremes and have been historically declining (Corcoran, Evans, Godwin, Murray, & Schwab, 2004). In contrast, household income disparities are substantially larger and historically increasing (Piketty, 2014).

If the explanation that homes vary more than schools is accurate, then schools are still culprits when it comes to inequality, they are just not as bad as homes. An attractive feature of this perspective is that it does not disrupt a key assumption about schools—that they are better learning environments for high- versus low-SES students. We can still maintain that schools advantage high-SES children in many ways (e.g., ability grouping, tracking, cultural capital, student/teacher racial mismatch, funding, teacher quality, administrator quality, and curriculum), and the assumption that schools promote achievement gaps can be preserved.

There is a problem with this view, however. It would be more persuasive if we had clear evidence that high-SES children enjoy better schools. One would think that would be easy to come by. On its surface it appears that there is substantial evidence for this position. Schools serving high-SES children enjoy better test scores, better teachers, less turnover, higher graduation rates, fewer disciplinary problems, and better morale. They look better in nearly every way that we can measure, which is part of why parents are willing to spend so much money on private schools or homes in wealthy districts with "good" schools.

But it is difficult to know if these outcomes are a result of better schools or simply because the schools serve advantaged children in the first place. Interestingly, when we employ methods that attempt to isolate schools' contribution to learning, there is surprisingly little evidence that differences in the school experiences of high- and low-SES children explain achievement gaps.

While a wide range of value-added models exist, most estimate school effectiveness (or sometimes teacher effectiveness) with models that predict children's test scores at Time 2 with a control for their score at Time 1 and perhaps other covariates (Reardon & Raudenbush, 2009). Some do so by comparing the difference between children's learning rates from summer to school (Downey et al., 2008).

There is not yet consensus over which kind of value-added model is most valid. For our purposes, however, it is important to note that as education scholars develop better techniques for isolating school from nonschool effects, one pattern stands out: Models that more persuasively isolate school effects suggest that the differences in effectiveness between schools serving high- and low-socioeconomic status children are modest or even nonexistent (Atteberry, 2011; Downey et al., 2008). For example, analyzing a nationally representative sample of 287 schools, we found no relationship between our measure of school quality ("impact") and the percentage of children in the school receiving free or reduced-price lunches (Downey et al., 2008). Along the same lines, some scholars have noted that public schools do not produce less learning than private ones (Lubienski & Lubienski, 2013). This remarkable conclusion—that the distribution of school effectiveness is unrelated to socioeconomic status—forces us to consider ways in which schools may actually serve low-SES children *better* than high-SES children.

Schools as Compensatory Institutions

When we introduced the "Homes Vary More Than Schools" perspective in 2004, I thought we were on to something, but if I were writing that article again, I would do it differently. Sure, homes vary more than schools and that may be part of why SES-based achievement gaps grow faster when school is out versus in, but the seasonal patterns suggest a more positive interpretation of schools—that they play a compensatory role.

Why do I say that schools are compensatory given that most seasonal research finds that high- and low-SES children learn at roughly the same rate when school is in session? Does that not suggest a neutral role? And in the case of my previous work, high-SES children even learned a little *faster* than low-SES children (Downey et al., 2004). If schools are not reducing achievement gaps in the absolute sense, or sometimes even allowing them to continue to grow a bit, how can schools be compensatory?

An analogy may help. Suppose I assess a year-long weight loss program by randomly assigning subjects to either treatment or control groups. And suppose that, upon completion, the treatment group has not lost any weight. On its surface this result suggests that the treatment failed—the subjects did not lose weight—but the proper way to assess the causal effect of the treatment is in *comparison to* the results for the control group. If the control group gained 5 pounds, on average, then the weight loss program had a positive effect, even if the treatment subjects lost no weight.

One can even imagine a scenario where the control group gained, on average, 5 pounds during the study while the treatment group gained 2. Even though the treatment group *gained* weight, we would still define the treatment as a success because it reduced the weight gain observed in its absence. Similarly, the proper way to assess schools' effect on achievement gaps is not to focus solely on the school year patterns but to compare the school year (treatment) and summer (control) patterns. If achievement gaps grow faster during the summer, then the treatment (schools) is reducing them.

An overlooked advantage of the seasonal research design is that all of the school processes that favor high-SES children and all of those that favor low-SES children are weighed against each other together at the same time. This important feature is distinct from most studies that target a single school characteristic, like class size. What does it mean if we find that class sizes are smaller for high- versus low-SES children and that class size is associated with greater learning? We have identified a single school characteristic that favors high-SES children, but that is insufficient for assessing the larger question: How does schooling affect achievement gaps? To gain an *overall* understanding of how schools matter, the magnitude of all school mechanisms exacerbating achievement gaps must be compared to that of their compensatory counterparts. By focusing on a single school characteristic or process, we may learn a lot about each tree but little about the forest.

Of course, the limiting aspect of seasonal research is that it does not identify the precise school mechanisms that influence achievement gaps but instead documents the broad patterns. It is sort of like learning that baseball team A ended the season with a better record than baseball team B, but knowing nothing about which team had better pitching or hitting or the scores of any of the games. Seasonal comparison research produces a compelling estimate of how schools influence achievement gaps—indeed a better estimate than other approaches produce—but we do not learn much about the mechanisms by which schools are compensatory.

Seasonal comparison research does not identify these mechanisms, but we can speculate. Admittedly, they do not readily come to mind, not like the school mechanisms that favor high-SES children, because compensatory processes have been undertheorized. Below I begin that process by introducing three school practices that might benefit low-SES children more than their high-SES counterparts.

Curriculum Consolidation. There are many ways schools can organize children, but students' chronological age is the default basis on which children are grouped. We organize children in this manner, but then we tend to forget this important decision. The result, however, is a powerful mechanism by which children of widely varying skills are exposed to the same curricular challenges. Critics of schools have focused on curriculum differentiation practices (e.g., ability grouping, tracking, gifted programs, and retention) that may advantage high-SES children, but this research tradition fails to address how grouping by chronological age consolidates the curriculum.

To understand how important this mechanism is for promoting equality, we can consider the distribution of cognitive skills among children in kindergarten, 1st, and 5th grades in the *Early Childhood Longitudinal Study-Kindergarten Cohort 1998–99*. It turns out that there is substantial overlap in cognitive skills across grades. Forty percent of kindergartners outperform the bottom 10% of 1st graders in reading (author calculation). A nontrivial number of kindergartners even read better than 5th graders. What do schools tend to do with these high-performing kindergartners? A few are accelerated through the system by skipping a grade, but even this practice is unlikely to expose them to challenging material. Some of these children are so far ahead of their age-based peers that they would need to be advanced multiple grades in order to find curriculum in their "sweet spot." That rarely happens. Most remain with their age-group peers, a practice that is likely compensatory because it is difficult for them to produce academic gains while exposed to material mostly below their level.

Targeting Resources Toward Disadvantaged Children. It is important not to overlook the many education policies designed to promote the school conditions of disadvantaged children. Title 1, Head Start, the Rehabilitation Act of 1973, and the Americans with Disabilities Act in 1990 were all intended (and to varying degrees have succeeded) in promoting the quality of school experiences for low-SES children. Most school funding comes from local and state sources, so a look at how resources are distributed across children with special needs versus honors students at the state level is also informative. As one example, in 2007 in Kentucky, the average child with special needs received an additional $11,970 in resources per year while the average child deemed "gifted" received $62 per year (Seiler et al., 2008). While disparities in funding are real and, in many cases, continue to favor those from advantaged backgrounds, we need to recognize that forces operating in the other direction exist and in some contexts counter the traditional forces producing unequal resources.

Egalitarian Teachers. In addition, there may be student/teacher interactions within the classroom that favor the disadvantaged. The kinds of people attracted to teaching are distinct from the general population—interested in helping others and endorsing relatively egalitarian views. For example, in the *1972–2014 General Social Survey data*, only 31% of elementary and secondary teachers agree that "lack of effort" explains why people are poor, compared to 47% of all other employees.[3] Teachers may employ a wide range of mechanisms, therefore, to "even out" the widely disparate skills they confront. A national survey of teachers found that, when asked who was most likely to receive one-on-one attention, 80% of teachers said "academically struggling students" while just 5% said "academically advanced" students (Duffett, Farkas, & Loveless, 2008).

CONCLUSION

Seasonal comparison research represents a formidable challenge to the dominant narrative about how schools matter. The story we typically hear is that the best way to improve the opportunity structure for the disadvantaged is to fix their broken schools. This perspective is endorsed by liberal politicians calling for smaller class sizes, higher salaries for teachers, a more inclusionary curriculum, and more equitably distributed resources across schools. It is also endorsed by conservative politicians, although they believe that market-based reforms are the way to improve schools—vouchers and charter schools, weaker teachers' unions, more testing, and greater accountability. While each side has a different approach to the problem, the common assumption—that the current school system is an engine of inequality—goes largely unchallenged.

But the assumption is probably wrong with respect to SES-based gaps in cognitive skills. While seasonal patterns fall short of a comprehensive analysis of the relationship between schools and inequality,[4] they merit special attention because they are revealed by a uniquely powerful method (seasonal comparisons). Prior to collecting data seasonally, most scholars would have anticipated that schools played a pernicious role regarding SES-based achievement gaps because they would assume that high-SES children attend schools that promote more learning. The seasonal method, however, reveals that when it comes to SES-based achievement gaps, schools are more part of the solution than the problem.

The traditional narrative about schools is constructed from methods dependent on incomplete information. For too long we have relied on studies describing how a single school characteristic (e.g., class size) advantages high-SES children. Even stitching together the results of several studies, all identifying various pernicious school processes, only provides us with one side of the story. The problem is that our critical view of schools has prompted us to carefully document school processes favoring high-SES children while overlooking compensatory ones. To address this challenge, it is important that we employ methods that consider all processes, both those increasing and decreasing achievement gaps, and compare their overall magnitude. Of course, it is very difficult to identify and measure perfectly all of these processes. The seasonal comparison method, while imperfect, provides an attractive strategy for overcoming that obstacle. For this reason current seasonal comparison evidence should trump previous work and prompt us to think seriously about how to reduce SES-based achievement gaps in a world where schools are already compensatory.

To be sure it is possible to make some progress reducing achievement gaps via school reform, even though the assumption about schools as the problem is wrong. Imagine someone who gained 10 pounds during a year while eating very poorly and exercising an average amount. Even though it would be possible to lose weight via additional exercise, physical activity is not the main problem or the most viable solution. Similarly, we can reduce achievement gaps somewhat via school reform even though schools are not its source. But reducing societal-level achievement gaps would not just require raising the quality of schools serving low-SES children up to the level of those enjoyed by high-SES children; in fact, we already live in a world where the average learning gains produced by schools serving high-SES children are similar to those produced by schools serving low-SES children. It would require providing low-SES children with substantially *better* schools while denying them to high-SES children, a politically infeasible position at the national level. In addition, while we have evidence that some school-based reforms can cut into achievement gaps among small samples, it is likely more efficient to prevent large gaps from emerging in the first place than remediating them later with school reform.

This shifts the policy attention away from school reform and toward the root cause of the problem—large inequalities in social conditions outside of schools. Americans have made a wide range of decisions differently than people in other countries with respect to health care, tax structure, the rights of organized labor, mass incarceration, immigrant status laws, low-income housing and public transportation, unemployment compensation, and the minimum wage. Often, Americans have chosen policies that lengthen the stratification ladder (Fischer et al., 1996) while those in other countries have chosen more egalitarian policies. It is these decisions that likely explain why income-based achievement gaps have increased by about 40% in the last 25 years (Reardon, 2011). And it is these decisions that likely account for why American children are so far behind Canadian children at 4–5 years of age, before kindergarten begins (Merry, 2013).

The best evidence supports a new narrative about schools and inequality. Inequalities in broader social conditions and achievement gaps are inextricably linked, and it is unlikely that we will reduce societal-level achievement gaps in a meaningful way without first reducing societal-level inequality. This is troubling news because it means that the problem is bigger than we thought and requires more fundamental change than school reform. But if we move away from the traditional narrative, we can at least start looking for solutions in the right place.

NOTES

1. Analyzing the *Early Childhood Longitudinal Study-Kindergarten Cohort of 1998–99,* Duncan and Magnuson (2011) found that the math achievement gap between bottom and top quintile socioeconomic groups was 1.34 standard deviation units in 1st grade and had increased only slightly, to 1.38 standard deviation units (3%), by 5th grade. Brooks-Gunn et al. (2006) found that the cognitive skill gaps between children raised by mothers with a college education versus those lacking a high school degree observed at age 18 were almost entirely formed by age 3.

2. Concluding that high-poverty schools enjoy better funding may go too far because high-poverty schools may have to direct a greater percentage of resources toward noninstructional purposes, but the larger point is that resource disparities are more modest than previously thought.

3. Author's calculations.

4. A comprehensive analysis would expand in at least two ways. First, we would explore inequality across other dimensions, such as race/ethnicity. At present the seasonal evidence for racial/ethnic patterns is mixed. For example, some seasonal scholars find evidence that schools are compensatory with respect to Black/White gaps (Heyns 1978), whereas others find more mixed patterns (Entwisle & Alexander, 1992). Our own work found indications that schools exacerbate the Black/White gap (Downey et. al., 2004). Surprisingly, more recent scholars find evidence that schools may not provide the best learning environment for Asians (Yood & Merry, 2015). Second, a more comprehensive analysis of the relationship between schooling and inequality would explore a broader range of outcomes, not just cognitive skills. It is possible that schools play a compensatory role with respect to math and reading skills, but a more pernicious one when it comes to promoting children's social/behavioral skills.

REFERENCES

Atteberry, A. (2011). *Defining school value-added: Do schools that appear strong on one measure appear strong on another?* Evanston, IL: Society for Research on Educational Effectiveness.

Brooks-Gunn, J., Cunha, F., Duncan, G., Heckman, J. J., & Sojourner, A. (2006). *A reanalysis of the IHDP Program. Infant health and development program.* Unpublished manuscript.

Corcoran, S. P., Evans, W. N., Godwin, J., Murray, S. E., & Schwab, R. M. (2004). The changing distribution of education finance, 1972–1997. In K. M. Neckerman (Ed.), *Social inequality.* New York, NY: Russell Sage Foundation.

Downey, D. B., von Hippel, P. T., & Broh, B. A. (2004). Are schools the great equalizer? Cognitive inequality during the summer months and the school year. *American Sociological Review, 69*(5): 613–635.

Downey, D. B., von Hippel, P. T., & Hughes, M. (2008). Are "failing" schools really failing? *Sociology of Education, 81*(July), 242–270.

Duffett, A., Farkas, S., & Loveless, T. (2008). *High-achieving students in the era of No Child Left Behind.* Washington, DC: Thomas B. Fordham Institute.

Duncan, G. J., & Magnuson, K. (2011). The nature and impact of early achievement skills, attention skills, and behavior problems. In G. J. Duncan & J. R. Murnane (Eds.), *Whither opportunity: Rising inequality, schools, and children's life chances* (pp. 47–69). New York, NY: Russell Sage Foundation.

Entwisle, D. R., & Alexander, K. L. (1992). Summer setback: Race, poverty, school composition, and mathematics achievement in the first two years of school. *American Sociological Review, 57*(1), 72–84.

Entwisle, D. R., Alexander, K. L., & Olson, L. S. (1997). *Children, schools & inequality.* Boulder, CO: Westview Press.

Fischer, C. S., Hout, M., Jankowski, M. S., Lucas, S. R., Swidler, A., & Voss, K. (1996). *Inequality by design: Cracking the bell curve myth.* Princeton, NJ: Princeton University Press.

Heyns, B. (1978). *Summer learning and the effects of schooling.* New York, NY: Academic Press.

Kozol, J. (1991). *Savage inequalities: Children in America's schools.* New York, NY: Harper Perennial.

Lubienski, C. A., & Lubienski, S. T. (2013). *The public school advantage: Why public schools outperform private schools.* Chicago, IL: University of Chicago Press.

Merry, J. (2013). Tracing the U.S. deficit in PISA reading skills to early childhood: Evidence from the United States and Canada. *Sociology of Education 86*(3), 234–252.

National Center for Education Statistics. (2012). *The condition of education, participation in education: Elementary/secondary enrollment, private school enrollment.* Indicator 5. Retrieved from http://nces.ed.gov/programs/coe/indicator_pri.asp

Piketty, T. (2014). *Capital in the twenty-first century.* Cambridge, MA: Belknap Press.

Reardon, S. F. (2011). The widening academic achievement gap between the rich and the poor: New evidence and possible explanations. In R. Murnane & G. Duncan (Eds.), *Whither opportunity? Rising inequality and the uncertain life changes of low-income children* (pp. 91–116). New York, NY: Russell Sage Foundation.

Reardon, S. F., & Raudenbush, S. W. (2009). Assumptions of value-added models for estimating school effects. *Education Finance and Policy, 4*(4), 492–519.

Seiler, M. F., Chilton, K., Nelson, D., Alexander, A., Landy, B., Olds, S., & Young, P. (2008). *Review of special education in Kentucky* (Report number 358). Frankfort, KY: Office of Education Accountability.

von Hippel, P. T. (2010). *Are schools the problem? The effects of school on learning and obesity* (Unpublished dissertation.) Ohio State University.

Yoon, A., & Merry, J. J. (2015). *Academic success despite discrimination? Asian Americans in US schools.* In Meetings of the American Sociological Association.

CHAPTER 2

Summer Setback in Baltimore

A Review and Update

Karl Alexander and Barbara F. Condliffe

A 20-year program of research on summer learning in Baltimore has helped to draw attention to the problem nationally, demonstrating that disadvantaged children fall behind their middle-class peers in reading comprehension and math during the long summer break and that these differences in summer learning account for much of the increase in the achievement gap across social lines over the elementary school years. In reading comprehension, the gap explodes from 0.5 grade equivalents in the fall of 1st grade to 3.0 grade equivalents at the end of 5th grade. Moreover, this huge disparity has consequences for children's later school success: In 9th grade, the first year of high school, two-thirds of the gap in reading comprehension (now 3.5 grade equivalents) originates in differential summer learning over the elementary school years. This paper will review the program's research and its implications for children's academic development. Using new, more current data, it also will assess whether summer learning loss remains a problem.

Baltimore, Maryland, arguably has been the epicenter for research on summer learning loss, a distinction warranted by the Beginning School Study (BSS) program of research on the topic.[1] This chapter provides background on the BSS and its insights regarding the seasonality of learning in the experience of Baltimore's schoolchildren. The BSS tracked the educational progress, social development, and later life successes of a representative random sample of city public school students from the time they began 1st grade in the fall of 1982 until well into their third decade, a quarter century in all.

Though this project has commanded considerable attention, its description of summer learning and of differences across social lines in school year and summer learning refer to a time 3 decades distant. To see whether the situation has changed over the ensuing years, our chapter also introduces new data on the seasonality of learning in Baltimore from 2011–2012. This updated account reveals that the city's low-income children are still losing ground academically over the long summer break.

THE FOUNDATIONAL STUDIES: HEYNS AND ECLS-K

BSS research did not "discover" summer learning loss, and it is local, not national in scope. Credit for the "discovery" goes to Barbara Heyns's seminal book *Summer Learning and the Lasting Effects of Schooling* (1978), which centered on Atlanta, Georgia.[2] The best-known studies to paint the picture of summer learning loss nationally use data from the Early Childhood Longitudinal Study-Kindergarten Cohort project (ECLS-K), which launched in the late 1990s (e.g., Burkam, Ready, Lee, & LoGerfo, 2004; Downey, von Hippel, & Broh, 2004).[3]

Heyns (1978) analyzed achievement gains by family income level and race/ethnicity (African American versus White) for a sample of nearly 3,000 Atlanta middle-school students over an 18-month period, bracketing two school years and the summer between. She found that children in lower-income households and African American children came close to keeping up academically during the school year. Indeed, all children, regardless of background, registered impressive school-year learning gains. But poor and minority children fell behind during the summer months, revealing the achievement gap across social lines to be substantially an opportunity gap originating in poor children's homes and their communities. This startlingly important insight helped launch the modern era of research on summer learning loss: Poor children suffer a deficit of out-of-school learning opportunities, one that presents itself in school in the form of depressed achievement test scores.

But circumstances vary from place to place, and one had to wonder whether the pattern Heyns observed for children in Atlanta also held in other localities. The ECLS-K project put that large concern to rest.

ECLS-K, initiated in 1998, tracked achievement gains fall to spring from the fall of kindergarten through the end of 1st grade for a large representative sample of school beginners—many thousands of children and roughly a thousand schools. Fall and spring testing is needed to separate school-year gains (fall to spring within the year) from summer gains (spring to fall across school years), so this design feature of the ECLS-K project was key.[4]

The ECLS-K studies are noteworthy for at least three reasons: they afford national coverage; they are more current than both the Atlanta and Baltimore studies; and ECLS-K administered its own achievement tests, so testing dates are known. The project also recorded school-year beginning and ending dates, which allow ECLS-K studies to adjust for the number of weeks of schooling *prior to* fall testing and *after* spring testing and so more accurately gauge school-year and summer achievement patterns. Without this capability, estimates from the Atlanta and Baltimore projects are less accurate, more akin to rough approximations. Nevertheless, the seasonality of children's learning in ECLS-K was broadly similar to that in Atlanta and Baltimore, especially for disparities along lines of family socioeconomic level:[5]

> Past seasonal researchers have argued that inequality in cognitive skills emerges primarily when school is not in session, and that it likely is a function of different family and neighborhood experiences. . . . With substantially better data than previous researchers, we provide the strongest support to date for this position. . . . With respect to socioeconomic status, the primary source of inequality lies in children's disparate non-school environments. (Downey et al., 2004, p. 632)

ECLS-K research thus confirms on a larger canvas the picture from Atlanta and Baltimore: Low-income children come close to keeping up academically during the school year but fall behind, and badly so, during the summer months owing to a dearth of out-of-school learning opportunities in their homes and communities.

The Baltimore-Based Beginning School Study

The original motivation for the BSS was to shed light on how children weather the transition from "home child" to "school child" at the start of their academic careers and then to trace whatever repercussions might follow from a successful 1st-grade experience against a less successful one. We were interested in supports and constraints in children's homes, schools, and local communities, conditions in the Baltimore area as a backdrop, and characteristic differences across social lines in children's developmental trajectories (by race/ethnicity, family socioeconomic background, and gender). To inform those issues, the BSS children, their parents, and their teachers were interviewed on many occasions over the years, and relevant data from school system records were compiled.

Two features of the BSS research design have been especially informative in extending the line of research initiated by Heyns: It is long-term longitudinal, and it is grounded in a scientifically strong sampling plan.[6]

On the second point, the project's sampling allows for secure generalization from the 790 study participants to conditions citywide at the time. In that respect, it is similar to the ECLS-K project, but at the local level. A single-site study obviously cannot speak with authority about conditions nationwide, but it can raise awareness of issues that might apply in like places. In this instance, the "like places" would be the other deindustrialized and deindustrializing cities of the eastern seaboard and Midwest rustbelt.

Every city has its particular history and distinctive current conditions, but classes of cities often share like challenges, and Baltimore epitomizes the challenges that accompany deindustrialization, population loss ("White flight" at first, followed by middle-class Black flight), and the attendant loss of wealth. And so we learn that when the children of the BSS were in elementary school, Baltimore already had become: "two cities—a city of developers, suburban professionals, and 'back-to-the-city' gentry . . . . and a city of impoverished blacks and displaced manufacturing workers, who continue to suffer from shrinking economic opportunities, declining public services, and neighborhood distress" (Levine, 1987, p. 103).

That account was from the 1980s, and the years since have been no kinder. According to a report by the Annie E. Casey Foundation (2010), for Baltimore the latter decades of the 20th century into the 21st were a time of:

> crippling trends and tragic events—the dramatic loss of manufacturing jobs and tax base, the ruinous riots of 1967 and 1968; the exodus of first white then African-American, middle class families; the sequential epidemics of heroin, crack cocaine, and HIV; the intensified crime and gang activity that fed and feasted off the drug trade; and the activities of slumlords, property flippers and predatory lenders. The end result has been an ever-deepening cycle of disinvestment and decline. (p. 2)

Baltimore's public school enrollment today is 84% low income and 83% African American (Baltimore City Public Schools, 2014); when the BSS began in 1982, the respective figures were 67% and 77%. Such a demographic profile poses obvious challenges: When there are large achievement gaps across social lines, it is mainly poor children in high poverty school systems who lag behind and suffer the consequences. The BSS indeed is a local study, but it is a local study of national import.[7]

The other consideration that is distinctive to the BSS is the project's 25-year span. The seasonal comparisons reported by both Heyns and ECLS-K examine one summer period bracketed by two school years. For Heyns, it is during the middle grades; in ECLS-K, the summer between kindergarten and 1st grade. The BSS, in contrast:

1. is anchored in 1st grade, the onset of formal schooling when the foundation for all later learning is being set;
2. affords seasonal comparisons that span the entirety of the elementary school years (1st grade through 5th)—5 school years and the 4 summers between; and
3. provides a long-term examination that can be used to trace the consequences of summer learning loss over the early years into high school and beyond.

Summer Learning Loss in the Beginning School Study

It is well known that over time and across grade levels, the academic achievement gap across social lines widens. This was first established in the *Equality of Educational Opportunity Report* (Coleman et al., 1966) and has been documented in many studies since (e.g., Jencks & Phillips, 1998). But the typical approach to assessment monitors achievement levels (and gains) spring to spring. This obscures the distinction between school-year and summer learning; it also conflates the family's and school's contributions as drivers of children's academic development.

A seasonality of learning perspective allows for their separation, much as in a natural experiment. Children are in their families and neighborhoods year-round but are in school intermittently. When achievement gains track differently over the summer months than during the school year, the most obvious difference in children's experience is that they are in school fall through spring and not in school during the summer.[8] Moreover, parental self-selection does not cloud the picture, as the school calendar applies to everyone. The long summer break thus affords leverage for isolating the contributions of home and school to children's learning.

When the BSS began, the Baltimore City Public Schools were conducting twice annual achievement testing, fall and spring, using the nationally normed California Achievement Test (CAT) battery. This stroke of good fortune is what allowed us to pose questions about summer learning as distinct from school-year learning in the panel's academic development. Our studies center on reading comprehension and math concepts/applications, foundational building blocks for all later learning.[9] Results are broadly similar in both areas; here we review those for reading comprehension as representative.

In comparisons across socioeconomic lines, lower-income children (shorthand for children of lower socioeconomic status)[10] scored, on average, a half grade level equivalent behind middle-income children in reading comprehension in the fall of 1st grade, their very first testing occasion. Hence in Baltimore, as nationally (e.g., Lee & Burkham, 2002), poor children started out already behind academically. And over time, they fell farther behind—in the BSS, three grade equivalents behind, on average, in reading comprehension by the end of 5th grade, the last year of elementary school in most Baltimore schools. That means the typical lower-income BSS child was reading at a 3rd or 4th grade level when preparing to move into middle school, a reading shortfall that most assuredly does not auger well.

The consequences we observed exposed some of those later challenges: In 9th grade, with the reading comprehension gap at 3.5 grade equivalents, lower-income children relative to their middle-class counterparts were much less likely to be in a college-bound high school program of study; then later, after 9th grade, they were much more likely to leave high school without a degree and much less likely to continue into college. Moreover, these differences of experience and accomplishment while in school foreshadowed depressed economic prospects later, in young adulthood (Alexander, Entwisle, & Olson, 2014).

The paths just described through school and over the years after are the fate experienced by too many of the urban disadvantaged. But there is an unexpected twist in the BSS account, or it would have been unexpected had it not been for Heyns's 1978 book: In our Baltimore studies, *the entire increase in the reading comprehension achievement gap from 1st grade through 5th grade* originated in differential learning over the summer months; additionally, two-thirds of the 3.5 grade equivalent disparity in 9th grade reading comprehension traced to those very same summer learning gaps.[11]

Four large conclusions follow from these patterns:

- Children learn more, and learn more efficiently, when they are in school.
- During the school year, lower-income children's skills improve at about the same rate as upper-income children's.
- During the summer, lower-income children's skills do not improve, while upper-income children's skills continue to improve.
- The summer learning shortfall over the elementary grades experienced by lower-income children has consequences that reverberate throughout their schooling, into high school and beyond.

These are important lessons, and the BSS studies (along with the others mentioned) have been impactful beyond academic circles. For example, Malcolm Gladwell, in his mega-hit book *Outliers* (2008), devotes several pages to the Baltimore picture specifically, concluding:

> Virtually all of the advantage that wealthy students have over poor students is the result of differences in the way privileged kids learn when they are *not* in school. . . . America doesn't have a school problem. It has a summer vacation problem. (pp. 258–260)

One could take issue with Gladwell's conclusion that all is well with American schooling, but his insight regarding America's summer learning problem is spot on. Studies of summer learning loss—ours and others'—have elevated the issue. They also have been used to help make the case for expanding disadvantaged children's access to high-quality summer programming. It would be pleasing indeed if this line of research has played a useful role in helping stem summer learning loss, but how can we know? A certain answer will require a new generation of studies: BSS research refers back to the decade of the 1980s, Heyns's *Summer Learning* was published in 1978, and even in the more recent ECLS-K studies, the focus is schooling in the 20th century, not the 21st.

This second wave of research is just getting under way. Chapter 3, by Atteberry and McEachin, presents one of the first such studies, which instructs us that the problem has not gone away: Summer learning loss remains prevalent throughout much of the country. Local studies are also needed, as these can drill down in ways not possible with broad-sweep national data. With that in mind, we turn again for guidance to the experience of Baltimore's children.

Summer Learning Loss in Baltimore Now

The issue of summer learning loss has received a great deal of practical attention in Baltimore City (in some measure owing to the research just reviewed). For example, innovative summer learning programs have been introduced that combine academic instruction and camp-like enrichment experiences for low-income students (National Summer Learning Association, 2012). With these initiatives in mind, we wondered whether the pattern of summer learning loss had changed in Baltimore City over the nearly 30 years since the children of the BSS were in elementary school. To address the question, the second author worked with the Baltimore Education Research Consortium (BERC) to analyze Baltimore City Public Schools seasonal testing data from 2011 to 2012.

In 2011, Baltimore City introduced a standardized formative literacy assessment system called the Dynamic Indicators of Basic Early Literacy Skills (DIBELS; Good & Kaminski, 2002), a well-validated measure of early literacy skills (Dynamic Measurement Group, 2008). Schools administered this assessment in the fall, winter, and spring to monitor student progress and, when called for, to guide instructional interventions. The beginning and end-of-year DIBELS assessments allow us to revisit the seasonality of learning in Baltimore.

DIBELS is a very different assessment system from the CAT battery,[12] and the sampling strategy for this new project was very different than that employed in the BSS. For those reasons, precise comparisons of achievement trajectories in Baltimore today to those observed in the BSS are not possible. Nevertheless, analysis of these new data can inform a key concern: whether the achievement gap across social lines still expands during the summer months.

The children included in our study (n=6,351) were general education students in 1st and 2nd grade during the 2011–2012 school year who were attending one of the 90 elementary schools using DIBELS as a formative assessment.[13] Though these schools were not selected to be representative of Baltimore City Public Schools (the strategy used in the BSS), coverage is quite broad as these 90 schools served approximately 87% of the district's kindergarten through 2nd-grade student population attending a noncharter public elementary school in 2011–2012.[14]

Reflecting the makeup of Baltimore City schools as a whole, the majority of children in the study qualified for free or reduced-price lunches (89.2%), most were African American (81%), and about half were male (48.8%). We call the 1st graders "Cohort 1" and the 2nd graders "Cohort 2." Both cohorts took the DIBELS assessments in the spring of 2011, fall of 2011, winter of 2012, and spring of 2012, allowing us to map learning trajectories from the summer of 2011 through the spring of the following school year.

Children in Cohort 1 were administered tests that measured their knowledge of basic letter sounds (phonological awareness), referred to as Nonsense Word Fluency (NWF). Testing was done in the spring of kindergarten and three times during their 1st-grade school year. Oral Reading Fluency (ORF) was assessed for Cohort 2 during the spring of 1st grade and three times during their 2nd-grade school year.

In comparing the learning trajectories of lower-income students to middle/higher-income students,[15] we followed the BSS (e.g., Alexander, Entwisle, & Olson, 2001) in using multilevel modeling to describe students' learning trajectories during the summer and academic year, as well as differences between their trajectories.[16] In both cohorts, there were statistically significant differences in the summer learning rates of the lower-income children and their middle/higher-income peers. Cohort 1 lower-income students on average dropped 2.98 points in their NWF score, whereas the typical middle/higher-income students dropped by only 0.25 points (gap of 2.73 points). In Cohort 2, lower-income students lost a full point on their ORF exam over the summer between 1st and 2nd grade, whereas their middle/higher-income counterparts on average gained 1.92 points over the same time period (gap of 2.92).

Although these differences are substantively small (in the vicinity of .09 –.13 sd), they are statistically significant. Furthermore, the fact that the pattern was consistent across two different cohorts transitioning between two different grades and taking two different literacy assessments echoes BSS results: Summer learning differences contribute to the achievement gap separating poor and nonpoor children.

The academic-year learning rates of the lower- and middle/higher-income students are informative in another respect. In both cohorts all students gained skills rapidly in the first half of the school year, with ORF and NWF scores increasing, on average, by more than 20 points between the fall and winter assessments. Progress continued in the spring as well, but at a slower rate.

These differences in the academic-year learning rates of lower-income and middle/higher-income students mostly mirror the findings of the BSS: In Cohort 1 the difference between their academic-year learning was not

CHAPTER 3

School's Out

Summer Learning Loss Across Grade Levels and School Contexts in the United States Today

Allison Atteberry and Andrew McEachin

Summer learning loss has been of interest for several decades, and over that time period researchers have contributed key pieces to what is becoming a larger understanding of the phenomenon. Existing projects have examined summer learning loss in a certain city, or in a specific grade, or in previous decades. Because there is reason to believe that summers play a central role in the production of achievement gaps, it is time for updated evidence about how this phenomenon operates in the modern era. In this chapter, we use a unique dataset that contains fall and spring test scores for all public school students in grades 2–9 from one Southern state between 2007–2008 to 2012–2013. We use a set of multilevel models to explore the differential patterns of student achievement growth trajectories in both the school year and summer period within students over time, as well as across school characteristics to produce a thorough overview of how different kinds of students gain and lose ground during the summer as they progress through school.

One of the most important questions in the field of education today is why some students seem to get more out of their schooling experiences than others. We are particularly concerned when these differences fall along social divides like race or socioeconomic status (SES), especially given the persistence of the Black–White achievement gap and the expansion of the income achievement gap since the 1960s (Neal, 2006; Reardon, 2011). However, one might also worry if the skills students acquire during their school years are just very unequal, even if those inequalities do not fall strictly along race and income dimensions.

As students begin formal schooling, they exhibit large differences in knowledge and preparation along race and class lines. Even in kindergarten these differences are about 0.50 student test score standard deviations, which some translate to about 6 months of learning (Halle et al., 2009; Reardon, 2014; Shonkoff & Phillips, 2000). The general consensus is that these differences grow as students progress through school (Phillips, Crouse, & Ralph, 1998). By the end of high school, students display a remarkable spread of outcomes: Some are ready to attend Ivy League colleges, while others struggle to pass exit exams of basic middle school math and reading skills. The conclusion, then, appears to be that schools exacerbate—or at least fail to ameliorate—these discrepancies.

Yet there is another possible story to be told, one that began to unfold with Heyns (1978) and continued with Alexander and Entwisle's Beginning School Study ("BSS"). Children experience vastly different home environments prior to formal schooling (Gilkerson & Richards, 2009; Kaushal, Magnuson, & Waldfogel, 2011; Kornrich & Furstenberg, 2013), and this preschool time leads to sizable achievement differences visible on day one of kindergarten (Lee & Burkam, 2002; Magnuson, Meyers, Ruhm, & Waldfogel, 2004). Often overlooked, however, is that children also spend much of their school-age years outside of school, particularly in the summer months—a time when schools play little or no direct role in the organization of children's activities. Instead, children return to the full-time care of families, who typically have vastly different options and preferences for how children spend this time. In fact, the variety of approaches to child time-use during the summer is likely far greater than the variety in how schools use time, even when looking across high- and low-quality schools. It follows that student achievement gaps may grow primarily during these summer months when child time-use is the most diverse.

This chapter summarizes the unique contributions of our work—based on Northwest Evaluation Association (NWEA) data—to the summer learning loss literature. To date, there is a common understanding among policymakers, researchers, and practitioners that student learning tends to stall out during the summer and that to some extent this phenomenon may be related to student demographics (Alexander, Entwisle, & Olson, 2001, 2007; Entwisle & Alexander, 1990, 1992). The findings from these studies have become the definitive word on summer setback, raising awareness of the phenomenon and the role it plays in growing educational inequalities. That said, it is unclear whether the results from those early studies generalize outside of their local contexts or to the vastly different educational landscape over 30 years later.

A handful of newer studies have moved to a national sample in a more recent time frame by using the 1999 Early Childhood Longitudinal Study-Kindergarten Cohort (ECLS-K) data (Benson & Borman, 2010; Downey, von Hippel, & Broh, 2004; Downey, von Hippel, & Hughes, 2008). However, this dataset only covers one summer between kindergarten and 1st grade for one-third of the ECLS-K sample. These studies cannot speak to summer learning loss in the mid- to late 2000s—a time with a significant amount of experimentation with teacher and school policies (e.g., high-stakes accountability); nor do they cover the later elementary and middle school grades.

The dataset used in this chapter contains both fall and spring test scores for students in grades 2 through 9 in 2008–2012. We applied a set of multilevel models to explore the differential patterns of student achievement growth trajectories in both the school year and summer period across student and school characteristics. Specifically, we explored the following four descriptive questions: (1) What is the average rate of learning during the school year versus the summer, and are those patterns of summer learning loss the same from early grades to later grades? (2) How much variability is there across students in terms of school year and summer learning rates? In other words, are the seasonal patterns around learning rates a shared experience for all students, or is there evidence that out-of-school time differentially affects students? (3) Do students of different race/ethnicities tend to systematically lose more ground during the summer, leading to widening race gaps in achievement? (4) Do certain kinds of schools (e.g., rural, urban, suburban) systematically serve students who experience greater summer learning loss?

EXISTING EVIDENCE ON SUMMER LEARNING LOSS

The summer learning loss literature was largely established by two foundational studies using data from the early 1970s and 1980s (see introductory chapter of this volume for more information on Heyns's Atlanta sample and Entwisle & Alexander's Baltimore BSS). Beyond simply documenting that, on average, learning slows during the summer, both sets of researchers also explored whether the magnitude of summer learning loss was associated with student characteristics, namely race and SES. In these early studies, both sets of characteristics were found to be predictive of summer learning loss differences.[1]

Findings on whether race/ethnicity predicts summer learning loss have been less consistent in recent work. Downey et al. (2004) used the ECLS-K to examine learning loss in the summer after kindergarten. While they found no differences in summer learning across race groups (after controlling for family SES), Burkam, Ready, Lee, and LoGerfo (2004) used the same data and found significant differences between Black and White students in summer growth in literacy, but not math.

The fact that researchers using the *same* data have come to different conclusions about predictors of summer learning loss highlights the importance of one's methodological approach on this topic. No author makes this point more clearly than Quinn (2014), who used the ECLS-K data to re-estimate the Black–White summer achievement gap using the full spectrum of methods that had been employed in previous work. Surprisingly, he showed that, depending on method used, one can basically find that Black students perform worse, the same, or better than their White counterparts during the summer. He went beyond this analytic exercise to talk through the idea that different models answer slightly different research questions and make different assumptions. Though some of the ambiguity about methods are moot when one has longitudinal, vertically scaled achievement data (as is the case in this chapter), Quinn pushed the field in an important direction by emphasizing the need to pay more attention to linking the model to the research question at hand.

To summarize, the extant research on summer learning loss took an important leap forward in the 1980s, and interest now seems to be resurging, particularly due to the availability of the ECLS-K data. This new research has sought to improve on the methods used in prior work (e.g., by taking into account the timing of tests), to update the time frame, and to cover a nationally representative sample (of kindergartners).

Our study seeks to contribute in a few additional, distinctive ways. First, vertically scaled tests of student math and reading achievement track student progress across a wide range of grades. As a result, some of the challenges documented by Quinn (2014) do not plague our analysis. Additionally, our data are from the post-accountability era, and it is certainly conceivable that the dynamics of access to quality schooling have changed since the 1980s. Finally, though we do not focus on the nuances of our estimation strategy in this chapter (for more technical detail, see Atteberry & McEachin, 2015), the results herein are based on a set of multilevel models that we think are more directly connected to the central research question in this domain: What is the average *rate* of learning during the school year vs. the summer? We also think that these models have heretofore been underutilized because one can use them to estimate not only mean learning rates, but importantly, the overall variance in summer learning rates across students or schools. This variability in learning rates is rarely reported but is of substantive interest.

DATA AND METHODS

Data for this study come from the NWEA Measures of Academic Progress (MAP) assessment. The MAP is a computer adaptive test given in math, reading, science, and social studies in select districts across all 50 states in the United States. It is scored using a vertical and interval scale, called the RIT (short for Rasch unit) scale. In theory, the vertical scale allows comparisons of student learning across grades and over time, while the interval scale ensures that a unit increase in a student's score represents the same learning gain for students across the entire distribution. The vertically scaled nature of this outcome data allowed us to examine differences in achievement disparities as students moved through grade levels. However, it is worth noting that vertical scaling is difficult to achieve and hard to verify (Briggs, 2013; Briggs & Weeks, 2009). Therefore, the findings regarding changes across grades rely on the assumption that NWEA's vertical scale is valid.

The data, which included basic demographic information, such as student race and gender,[2] came from a Southern state that administered the MAP assessment both fall and spring to students in grades 2 through 9 in all districts across 5 academic years: 2007–2008 through 2011–2012. This state used the MAP assessment as a supplementary tool to aid schools in improving instruction and meeting students' needs, not as a high-stakes test.

We made some adjustments to the observed RIT scores to address some of the methodological concerns that have arisen since the initial BSS publications.[3] Since schools typically do not give fall and spring tests on the first and last day of school, we combined information from NWEA test results in the fall and the spring, the date of those tests, and knowledge of the statewide school calendars to project scores to the first and last day of the school year. For more information on these adjustments, see Atteberry and McEachin (2015).

To estimate individual growth trajectories as students move across grades, we restricted the NWEA sample to the 89% of students who neither repeated nor skipped grades. Ultimately, we included 506,194 unique students in the analysis, with an average of 259,929 students per school year and 979 schools per year. Since each child typically possessed four test scores per school year (fall and spring tests in both math and reading), our final analytic sample consisted of 5,019,263 test score observations (1,068,858 observations if limiting the sample to students with no missing data).[4] This was a sizable dataset, especially relative the ECLS-K dataset, which contains information related to approximately 4,000 students that could be used to study summer learning loss.

We estimated the mean and variance of learning rates across students, as well as gaps in learning rates related to student and school characteristics. The models fit an individual learning trajectory for each student as they progressed through (up to) 5 sequential school years and summers.

We used two- and three-level random effects (hierarchical) models, where the outcome of interest was a test score for a given student in a given grade-semester (e.g., fall of 3rd grade). Each student possessed up to 10 test scores (fall and spring across 5 years), which were modeled as repeated observations (level one) nested within students (level two).[5] These models are similar to the hierarchical models used by Alexander et al. (2001); however, we adopted a slightly different dummy variable coding scheme that ensured that the level-one coefficients represent individual students' grade-specific school-year and summer learning rates (e.g., grade 2 school year learning rate, summer after grade 2 school year learning rate, etc.), rather than levels of achievement at the given point in time.[6] These student-level coefficients— i.e., the learning rates in each period—become the outcomes at level two.

We introduced time-invariant, student-level characteristics at level two to investigate whether the variation in summer learning rates was associated with these observable factors and how much of the variance remained unexplained after including them. In our final analysis, we explore how summer learning loss is distributed across schools, and we therefore introduce a third level to the multilevel model—students nested within schools.[7] We added time-invariant school-level predictors at level three to see if they predicted variability across schools in summer learning rates. We did so based on (a) the percentage of students in the school who are non-White; (b) the percentage of students who are eligible for the federal free or reduced-price lunch (FRPL) program; and (c) a set of indicator variables for the geographic type of each school—urban, rural, or town—with suburban the reference category.

RESULTS

Average Learning Rates in School Years versus Summers, across Grades

We expected to find—and indeed, we did find—that school-year learning rates were positive, as students acquired new knowledge during the school year. However, we were unsure *a priori* about the direction and magnitude of students' average *summer* learning rates. If, on average, students continued to learn at the same rate during the summer, then we would find no differences between school-year and summer slopes. If, on the other hand, students simply experienced a stagnation in their learning growth—that is, they exhibit no change in achievement between the last day of spring and the first day of the following fall—then the estimates of summer learning rates should have been statistically indistinguishable from zero (i.e., flat slopes). Finally, if the tendency was for students to actually lose ground during the summer, then these slopes should have been negative.

Figure 3.1 visually presents the findings from the multilevel model described above as predicted mean growth trajectories (grades 2 through 5 in the top panel, grades 6 through 9 in the bottom panel). The illustration consistently shows a zigzag pattern at every grade level, though the magnitude of the slopes decreases at higher grade levels. With respect to school-year learning rates, we found that students' gains were largest in the early grades and diminished over time. For instance, students gained on average 19.6 test score points in math and 20.3 test score points in reading during 2nd grade. The average school-year learning rate became less steep as students progressed through grade levels, to less than half that amount by grade 6. By grade 9, the average school-year learning rate slowed to 3.2 test score points in math and 2.7 points in reading. Throughout all grade levels and specifications, however, we observe positive learning rates in all school years in both subjects.

Figure 3.1. Projected School Year and Summer Learning Rates Across Grade Levels, by Subject

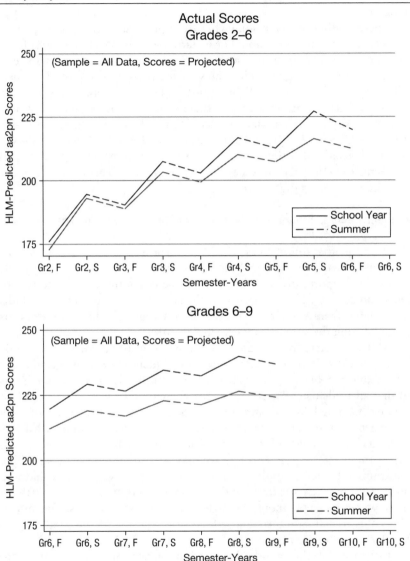

Interestingly, the patterns of summer learning rates were quite different from their school-year counterparts: The learning rates for all seven summers between grades 2 and grade 9 were *negative*, suggesting that students typically lost ground in math and reading during the summer months. During the summer, students lost between 25% and 30% of the growth they obtained during the preceding school year. This is particularly notable given that the school year is about three times longer than the summer.

These findings differed somewhat from previous work in the apparent magnitude of the phenomenon. For instance, Alexander et al. (2001) found a strong seasonal pattern to learning gains in their BSS sample. However, they found that average learning rates during the summer slowed dramatically but actually remained slightly positive. Downey et al. (2004) found in the ECLS-K data that, on average, students neither gained nor lost ground during the summer after kindergarten. While all three data sources—BSS (1980s), ECLS-K (1999), and this study's NWEA (2007–2012)—showed clear evidence that learning rates differ between summers and school years, ours is the only one that shows consistent evidence of learning *losses* during the summer at every grade level.

Variability across Students in the Extent of Summer Learning Loss

The random effects model described above allowed us not only to estimate the average learning rates in both the summer and school year (i.e., the slopes), but importantly to estimate the variances of these slopes across students and schools. If the variance of the summer learning rates was indistinguishable from zero, then we would conclude that *most* students lost ground during the summer at very similar rates.

In this scenario, one might view the problem of summer learning loss from a slightly different policy angle: Yes, students lose some ground during the summer, but perhaps this is just a natural side effect of taking time off that all students experienced equally. We would be less concerned about summer learning loss if all students were subject to it, because then it could not widen achievement gaps. If, however, the variance in summer learning rates was large, we would reach a very different conclusion: The mean summer learning rates documented above may *mask* the underlying variability in learning rates across students. In this case, the summer period would seem much more problematic because the summer could be a major contributor to the widening gaps among the highest and lowest achievers. Our models allowed us to estimate the standard deviations of the learning rates across students in each time period.

Estimates of the standard deviation of school-year learning rates across students were surprisingly consistent across grades, analytic samples, and subjects, ranging between 10 to 13 test score points. In 9th grade, when average growth was only 2.7 test score points during the school year, we estimate a 95% plausible value range across students of −24.4 to +29.9 points—a very large variance relative to the average gain. Plausible value ranges across grades and subjects were large and almost always contained zero in this analysis, suggesting that while the average student gained ground during the school year, many students lost ground as well. Another way to express this finding is to consider the ratio of each *mean* learning rate to the standard deviation of that learning rate across students. In 2nd grade that ratio was approximately 0.5 to 0.6. That ratio increases steadily through 9th grade when it reached 3.8 and the variability overshadowed the average. We compare these ratios to those of summers below.

While the variability in school-year patterns is interesting in and of itself, our main interest was whether the summer learning rates—a period already known for average learning losses—varied more than rates in the school year. This variability could have direct implications for our understanding of when discrepancies in student learning arise during the course of students' school-age years. We found that, in a relative sense, the estimated standard deviations of summer learning loss were much more profound relative to mean learning rates in the summer. The ratio of the mean to standard deviation of summer learning rates *after* 2nd grade was around 1.5 to 2.2, depending on sample and subject (compare to the 2nd-grade school-year ratio of about 0.5). This ratio increased at higher grades, and in the summer after 8th grade, the ratio was between 3.1 and 5.5 (compared to 1.5 to 2.5 for the 8th-grade school year). In other words, a student one standard deviation below the mean summer learning rate had an estimated growth rate 3 to 5 times *lower* than that of the average student. As a result, the range of plausible values for the learning rate in the summer after 8th grade was profound: Between –21.2 to +16.4 points lost/gained in math and –24.4 to +29.9 points lost/gained in reading, in only a matter of months.

This dramatic variability across students in their summer experiences supports the idea that the summer environment varied more than the school-year environment. Furthermore, we can infer that a great deal of the apparent variability in end-of-school outcomes actually arises during the summers rather than the school years. To illustrate this finding, Figure 3.2 (math) and Figure 3.3 (reading) depict the strong role of summer variability. The three lines in each panel represent three hypothetical students. All three students in this depiction began at the same level of achievement and experienced average school-year learning rates (note parallel slopes in school years). In other words, we assume temporarily that all discrepancies in pre-schooling achievement could be eliminated and that all students learn the same amount during the school year. The top line in each figure represents a student who gains one standard deviation above the average rate of summer learning each summer, the middle line represents a student who has the average summer learning rate, and the bottom line represents a student who experiences summer loss one standard deviation below the norm each summer. The results show how the differences in summer experiences by themselves can lead to sizable achievement gaps over time. This illustrates that even in

Figure 3.2. Math: Illustration of 3 Hypothtic Students (Average Summer, +/- 1 SD

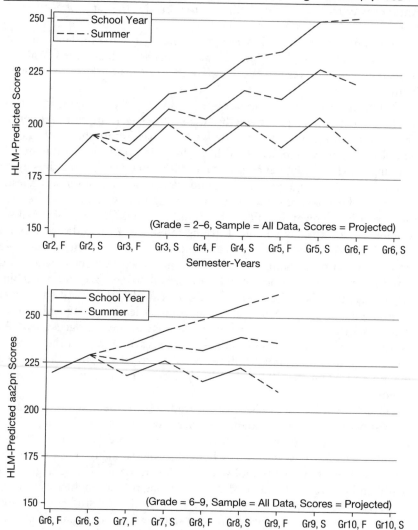

an ideal world where school inequities could be eliminated, achievement gaps would arise simply because of the summer break.

In sum, the typical finding that, on average, students' learning slows, stops, or even regresses during the summer obscures a more problematic pattern: For some as-yet unknown reason, certain students actually maintain their school-year growth rates throughout the summer, while other

Figure 3.3. Reading: Illustration of 3 Hypothetic Students (Average Summer, +/- 1 SD)

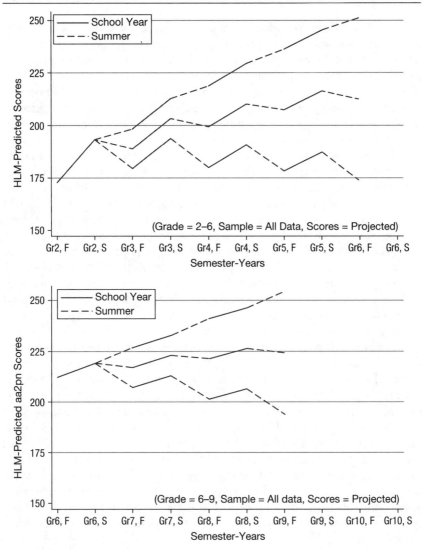

students lose almost as much ground during the summer as they gained during the previous school year. When this happens in systematic ways so that the same students tend to have higher or lower learning rates summer after summer, it leads to a dramatic "fanning out" of student outcomes as they progress through school. We would be particularly concerned if the students who exhibit the greatest summer losses also tend to be minority students.

The Association between Race/Ethnicity and Summer Learning Loss

As described above, we added to our model a set of student-level indicator variables at level two to predict school year and summer learning rates across students (Black, Latino, and other/unknown, with White students as the reference category).[8] The race patterns, estimated through multilevel models and depicted in Figure 3.4, were pervasive: Black and Latino students consistently *gained less* ground in school years and *lost more* ground in summers (only 3 of the 36 estimated coefficients capturing those differences were not statistically significant).

To summarize these findings, Table 3.1 presents the share of the annual achievement gaps between White and Black or Latino students that can be attributed to differential summer learning loss.[9] On average, the summer accounts for about 35% of the achievement gap that developed between grade 2 and grade 9. The results in Table 3.1 show that this percentage varies between 0 to 58% depending on grade, subject, sample, and gap group. Given that all but one proportion was greater than zero and most were greater than the portion of the year students spent in the summer (approximately 25%), the Table 3.1 results suggest that policymakers and educators interested in mitigating persistent achievement gaps would benefit from focusing on summer and/or interventions related to time spent out of school.

Given the immense variability across students in summer learning rates, the findings related to race/ethnicity beg the question: To what extent does race play a role in our understanding of the wide range of variability in school-year and summer outcomes across students? It turns out that including the three race indicator variables in the model at level two (across students) only explained between 2% and 11% of the variance in intercepts, school-year learning rates, or summer learning rates (across all permutations of grade, subject, and analytic sample). While non-White students experienced less growth in both school year and summer learning, it was clear that race was not the deciding explanation for which students experienced the greatest gains or losses. This implies that a great deal about what causes such differential summer experiences is not understood.

Differences in Summer Learning Rates by School Characteristics

Finally, we attempted to predict initial status, school-year learning rates, and summer learning rates with three time-invariant school-level predictors (percent FRPL-eligible, percent non-White, and geographic type). On one hand, one might hypothesize that characteristics of the school would have little to do with summer learning rates, since students are by definition not in school during this time period. However, it is possible that students are

Figure 3.4 Mean Growth Trajectories by Student Race Group

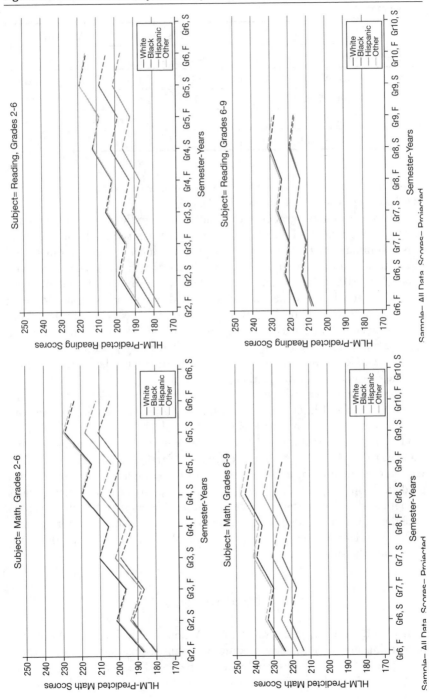

Table 3.1 Proportion of Annual Achievement Gap Growth Attributable to the Summer

		ANY DATA		ALL DATA	
Grades	Gap	Math	Reading	Math	Reading
2–5	Black–White	38%	38%	37%	34%
	Latino–White	0%	23%	59%	25%
6–9	Black–White	30%	31%	29%	51%
	Latino–White	58%	37%	43%	21%

sorted into schools in systematic ways that create differences in mean summer learning experiences across schools.

In the elementary grades, we found some significant relationships between summer learning losses and school characteristics. Table 3.2 presents a summary of these findings across grade levels, subjects, and school covariates (again, to see full set of empirical estimates, see Atteberry and McEachin, 2015). For instance, the school's percentage of students who were FRPL-eligible was negatively correlated with math summer learning rates, but not for reading. The average percentage of students in the school who were non-White was also negatively correlated with both math and reading summer learning rates during the elementary grades (top panel of Table 3.2). Geographic setting (urban, rural, or town relative to suburban contexts) was not a strong predictor of summer slopes.

Results were generally weaker in middle school grades, with virtually none of the school-level predictors exhibiting a predictive relationship with the average summer learning loss in the school (the one exception was the modest, negative relationship between "Percent FRPL" and reading summer learning rates). In results presented elsewhere (Atteberry & McEachin, 2015), we found that fully saturated models with the complete set of school-level predictors only accounted for 7–8% of variance in summer learning rates in math and 1–2% of the variance in reading. Taken together, this suggests that these traditional demographic school characteristics did not account for why students in some schools systematically lost more ground than others during the summer.

CONCLUSIONS

This chapter reviews our use of NWEA data to explore the seasonality of learning in one Southeastern state, with an emphasis on separating the school year from the nonschool summer period. The findings suggest that students do indeed lose ground during the summer period in both math and

Table 3.2 Summary of Direction and Strength of Results from L3 Model with School-Level Predictors, by Grade and Subject

Grades		MATH			READING		
		% FRPA	% Non-White	Urbanicity	% FRPA	% Non-White	Urbanicity
2–5	Initial Status (Fall, Gr 2)	—***	—***	—**	—***	—***	—**
	School-Year Learning Rates	—***	—***			—**	
	Summer Learning Rates	—***	—***			—***	
6–8	Initial Status (Fall, Gr 6)	—***	—***	—**	—***	—***	—*
	School-Year Learning Rates	—**	—***				
	Summer Learning Rates				—*		

Notes: Cell contents indicate the direction (− / +) and statistical significance (asterisk) of coefficients that related elements of the learning trajectories (i.e., initial starting point, school-year learning rates, or summer learning rates) to three sets of school-level covariates. School covariates include: percentage of students who are eligible for Free/Reduced-Price Lunch Program ("Percent FRPL"), percentage of students in the school who are non-White ("Percent Non-White"), and the school's "Urbanicity" (suburban relative to urban, rural, or town geographies). In the case of the set of three dummy variables capturing the four categories geography variables, we indicate the *average* statistical significance across the three dummy coefficients).

reading: The average student in the sample lost around 4 test score points in the summer (averaged across grade levels and model specifications), relative to an average school-year gain of around 13 points. We add to the existing research by estimating the variance across students in summer learning loss: In the summer after 2nd grade, the 95% plausible value range suggests that some students will *lose* as much as 23 math test score points during summer, while other students could *gain* up to 14 test score points.

Students also exhibited significant variance in school-year learning rates, though the 95% plausible value range during the school year did not consistently include zero (or zero was near the lower bound). This means that, while some students learned more than others during the school year, almost all students made learning *gains* while school was in session. On the other hand, during the summer, a little more than half of students exhibited summer learning losses, while the other half exhibited gains.

Clearly, the summer period is a particularly variable time for students. A student one standard deviation above the mean summer learning rate virtually maintained average school-year learning rates even in the absence of formal schooling. However, a student who was one standard deviation below the mean summer learning rate lost ground at a remarkable rate, in some cases virtually counteracting most of the gains made during the preceding school year. This noteworthy variability in summer learning rates may be a strong contributor to widening achievement gaps as students move through school.

In addition, race significantly predicted differential summer learning loss, with Latino and Black students starting school at different levels of achievement and falling steadily behind in both summers and school years. Roughly 35% of the growth in the Black–White achievement gap from 2nd to 9th grade (about 9 test score points) occurred during the summer which, it should be noted, only comprises about a quarter of students' time.

That said, student race accounted for at most 11% of the variance in summer learning rates. Though we had few other student-level measures to explore the variability across students in summer losses, future research should focus on how other aspects of the summer experience shape students' ability to maintain their learning during the long vacation.

Our results show that achievement disparities widen throughout both summers and school years. As such, we should continue to develop policies that change how students experience schools, particularly around issues of access to high-quality teachers and schools. However, even in an ideal scenario in which students all learn the same amount during the school year, achievement gaps will develop and accumulate during the summer. Since summer learning rates vary just as much as (if not more than) school-year learning rates, extending the school year might lessen the degree to which student learning rates diverge during the school year. Policies that consider extending the school year and/or other programs designed to bridge the gap between May and August (like summer school) may be a more direct way to address the wide spread of student skills acquired during the K–12 period.[10]

Finally, traditional school-level descriptors like percentage non-White, percentage FRPL-eligible, or urbanicity were not universally strong predictors of summer learning rate differences across schools. Taken together, this suggests that students are either sorted into schools in systematic ways relative to the summer learning experiences, or perhaps that schools have differential effects on summer learning loss. In either case, the school level variables at our disposal were not strong predictors of which schools had higher/lower average summer learning rates. If some schools serve students who are systematically more likely to lose ground during the summer, then these schools face a quite different challenge at the start of each school year to bring their students back to where they left off when school ended the previous spring. It remains an open but important question whether schools can (or should be expected to) influence students' summer learning experiences.

NOTES

1. Heyns (1978) found that socioeconomic indicators (family income, parental education, and household size) were predictive of achievement during the summers but not during the school year and that student race was associated with summer learning loss, even after controlling for SES. Entwisle and Alexander (1992) found differences by race/ethnicity, but those differences markedly decreased when controlling for SES.

2. The student-level file did not include indicators for whether the student was an English Language Learner, belonged to the federal FRPL program, or participated in special education.

3. There was some evidence that students tended to spend slightly less time on fall tests than spring tests. One would be concerned if this was a symptom that students did not put forward as much effort on their fall assessments, thus making summer learning losses appear larger than they actually were. The difference in time spent was not large (about 10 additional seconds per item, on average), and our results appeared robust to checks related to time spent on the test.

4. In the paper, we conducted all analyses on two subsamples in order to ensure that our results generalized to the larger population of students in the state. The first was a larger analytic sample that included any student with at least two observed test scores during the years of the panel. However, we were concerned that having an inconsistent sample of students across grade levels might bias our estimates of both summer and school-year learning rates. In other words, if the missing test score data occurred in a way that related to factors that affected learning rates, we could have over- or underestimated average test score changes from one time point to the next. We therefore conducted each analysis on a second, more restrictive subsample of students for whom we observed all available test scores during the panel. While we can be more certain that the patterns we observed in this subsample were not due to compositional changes from one time point to the next, only 21% of the students in the sample met this strict criteria. These two samples had different advantages in terms of internal and external validity, and we thought it important to demonstrate if and when results differed across these two groups.

5. At level one, students' growth trajectories were modeled using a set of dummy variables—Gr2_Fall, Gr2_Spr, Gr3_Fall, Gr3_Spr, etc.—for each grade-semester. These are coded as 1 if the observation occurred on or after the given grade-semester. Gr2_Spr, which captured the school-year learning rate for 2nd grade, took a 1 at the end of 2nd grade and stayed a 1 throughout the panel. This allowed each level-one

coefficient π_{qi} (where q simply indexed the coefficients) to vary randomly, assuming that level-two errors (r_{qj}) were normally distributed with a mean of 0 and a constant variance (τ_{qq}).

6. Instead of capturing the difference in means between a focal and reference group, as with dummy coding, this coding scheme captured the difference between the achievement in the current and the previous periods. These dummy variables turned on (=1) in a given period and remained on (=1); the sum of the coefficients up to time t captures the student's current achievement:

$$E \text{[Score}_{ti}] = \sum_{i=0}^{t}\beta_{i0}. \text{ Therefore, } E \text{[Score}_{ti}\text{- Score}_{(t-1)i}] = \sum_{i=0}^{t}\beta_{i0} - \sum_{i=0}^{t-1}\beta_{i0} = \beta_{t0} .$$

7. One challenge to this approach was that nearly all students *crossed* schools during the transition to middle school, and a smaller subset of students made other nonstructural school moves. The three-level model assumed a "clean" nesting structure in which students were assigned to only one school over time, and that school was attributed all of its students' test score history. To address this challenge, we ran two separate three-level models—one for the grades before the structural transition into middle school and one for the grades after. We also limited the sample to students who made no nonstructural moves and compared results to a model in which nonstructural movers were attributed to their modal elementary and middle schools.

8. Since this involved multiplying the number of estimated coefficients per model (17 coefficients—2 intercepts, 8 school-year learning rates, and 7 summer learning rates) by 3 (for Black, Latino, and students of other/unknown race), we simplified the piecewise growth model by estimating 1 average school-year learning rate and 1 average summer learning rate (collapsed across grades). We estimated whether students of different race groups had different *average* learning rates and explored what proportion of the variance in summer learning rates was explained by race. This helped provide some sense of how big of a role race (or other student-level factors) played in our understanding of why some students gained ground during the summer while others lost ground.

9. For these proportions, we divided the differential summer learning rates by the sum of the differential summer and school-year learning rates. This ratio captured the portion of each annual race achievement gap attributable to the summer.

10. There is growing evidence that summer interventions can help mitigate students' summer learning loss (Kim & Quinn, 2013; McCombs et al., 2012; McCombs et al., 2015). However, it is unclear that a year-round calendar mitigates summer learning loss more than a traditional 9-month calendar (Graves, 2011; McMullen & Rouse, 2012).

REFERENCES

Alexander, K. L., Entwisle, D. R., & Olson, L. S. (2001). Schools, achievement, and inequality: A seasonal perspective. *Educational Evaluation and Policy Analysis, 23*(2), 171.

Alexander, K. L., Entwisle, D. R., & Olson, L. S. (2007). Lasting consequences of the summer learning gap. *American Sociological Review, 72*(2), 167.

Atteberry, A., & McEachin, A. (2015). *School's out: The role of summers in understanding achievement disparities.* Under Review. Paper presented at the Society for Research on Educational Effectiveness (SREE) Conference in Washington, DC.

Benson, J., & Borman, G. (2010). Family, neighborhood, and school settings across seasons: When do socioeconomic context and racial composition matter for the reading achievement growth of young children? *Teachers College Record, 112*(5), 1338–1390.

Briggs, D. C. (2013). Measuring growth with vertical scales. *Journal of Educational Measurement, 50*(2), 204–226.

Briggs, D. C., & Weeks, J. P. (2009). The impact of vertical scaling decisions on growth interpretations. *Educational Measurement: Issues and Practice, 28*(4), 3–14.

Burkam, D. T., Ready, D. D., Lee, V. E., & LoGerfo, L. F. (2004). Social-class differences in summer learning between kindergarten and first grade: Model specification and estimation. *Sociology of Education, 77*(1), 1–31.

Downey, D. B., von Hippel, P. T., & Broh, B. A. (2004). Are schools the great equalizer? Cognitive inequality during the summer months and the school year. *American Sociological Review, 69*(5), 613.

Downey, D. B., von Hippel, P. T., & Hughes, M. (2008). Are "failing" schools really failing? Using seasonal comparison to evaluate school effectiveness. *Sociology of Education, 81*(3), 242–270.

Entwisle, D. R., & Alexander, K. (1990). Beginning school math competence: Minority and majority comparisons. *Child Development, 61*(2), 454–471.

Entwisle, D. R., & Alexander, K. L. (1992). Summer setback: Race, poverty, school composition, and mathematics achievement in the first two years of school. *American Sociological Review, 72*–84.

Gilkerson, J., & Richards, J. A. (2009). The power of talk. Impact of adult talk, conversational turns and TV during the critical 0–4 years of child development. Boulder, CO: LENA Foundation.

Graves, J. (2011). Effects of year-round schooling on disadvantaged students and the distribution of standardized test performance. *Economics of Education Review, 30*(6), 1281–1305.

Halle, T., Forry, N., Hair, E., Perper, K., Wandner, L., Wessel, J., & Vick, J. (2009). *Disparities in early learning and development: Lessons from the Early Childhood Longitudinal Study–Birth Cohort.* (ECLS-B). Washington, DC: Child Trends.

Heyns, B. (1978). *Summer learning and the effects of schooling.* New York, NY: Academic Press.

Kaushal, N., Magnuson, K., & Waldfogel, J. (2011). *How is family income related to investments in children's learning?* New York, NY: Russell Sage Foundation.

Kim, J. S., & Quinn, D. M. (2013). The effects of summer reading on low-income children's literacy achievement from kindergarten to grade 8: A meta-analysis of classroom and home interventions. *Review of Educational Research, 83*(3), 386–431.

Kornrich, S., & Furstenberg, F. (2013). Investing in children: Changes in parental spending on children, 1972–2007. *Demography, 50*(1), 1–23.

Lee, V. E., & Burkam, D. T. (2002). Inequality at the starting gate: Social background differences in achievement as children begin school. Washington, DC: Economic Policy Institute.

Magnuson, K. A., Meyers, M. K., Ruhm, C. J., & Waldfogel, J. (2004). Inequality in preschool education and school readiness. *American Educational Research Journal, 41*(1), 115–157.

McCombs, J. S., Augustine, C., Schwartz, H., Bodilly, S., McInnis, B., Lichter, D., & Cross, A. B. (2012). Making summer count: How summer programs can boost children's learning. *Education Digest: Essential Readings Condensed for Quick Review, 77*(6), 47–52.

McCombs, J. S., Pane, J. F., Augustine, C. H., Schwartz, H. L., Martorell, P., & Zakaras, L. (2015). *First outcomes from the National Summer Learning Study* (Brief No. RB-9819-WF). Santa Monica, CA: RAND Corporation. Retrieved from www.rand.org/pubs/research_briefs/RB9819.html

McMullen, S. C., & Rouse, K. E. (2012). The impact of year-round schooling on academic achievement: Evidence from mandatory school calendar conversions. *American Economic Journal: Economic Policy, 4*(4), 230–252.

Neal, D. (2006). Why has Black–White skill convergence stopped? In E. Hanushek & F. Welch (Eds.), *Handbook of the economics of education* (pp. 511–576). Amsterdam, Netherlands: ELSEVIER.

Phillips, M., Crouse, J., & Ralph, J. (1998). Does the Black–White test score gap widen after children enter school? In C. Jencks & M. Phillips (Eds.), *The Black–White test score gap* (pp. 229–272). Washington, DC: Brookings.

Quinn, D. M. (2014). Black–White summer learning gaps: Interpreting the variability of estimates across representations. *Educational Evaluation and Policy Analysis, 37*(1), 50–69.

Reardon, S. F. (2011). The widening academic achievement gap between the rich and the poor: New evidence and possible explanations. In G. Duncan & R. Murnane (Eds.), *Whither opportunity? Rising inequality, schools, and children's life chances* (pp. 91–116). New York, NY: Russell Sage Foundation.

Reardon, S. F. (2014). Education. In *State of the Union: The Poverty and Inequality Report 2014* (pp. 45–50). Stanford, CA: Stanford Center on Poverty & Inequality.

Shonkoff, J. P., & Phillips, D. A. (2000). *From neurons to neighborhoods: The science of early childhood development.* Washington, DC: National Academies Press.

CHAPTER 4

Contextualizing Summer Learning Inequality

The View from Canada

Scott Davies, Janice Aurini, and Emily Milne

This chapter will describe a Canadian summer learning project, noting its major motivations, the specifics of its national context, main findings to date, and their implications for summer learning research in general. Since 2010, we have evaluated public school summer learning programs in Ontario, an interesting context for the study of summer learning. Our research adds cross-national weight for the "summer setback" thesis: that nonschool time is a key generator of achievement gaps. We also find that summer programs have positive effects for their participants but do not necessarily benefit the poorest students the most.

International research in sociology of education has long highlighted the sheer consistency of the impact of children's socioeconomic background (SES) on their school achievement and attainment. While nations vary in their degree of educational stratification, cross-national research shows that school outcomes across all Western societies are subject to relatively powerful SES effects (Shavit, Arum, & Gamoran, 2007; Stefani, Pollak, Otte, & Gangl, 2007; United Nations, 2013).

Research on summer learning is a particular species of this broader sociological tradition of studying educational stratification. American studies find that children from lower-SES backgrounds are particularly susceptible to summer learning losses and that these losses can be potent sources of cumulative SES achievement gaps (e.g., Alexander, Entwisle, & Olson, 2007; Cooper, Nye, Charlton, Lindsay, & Greathouse, 1996; Cooper, Charlton, Valentine, Muhlenbruck, & Borman, 2000; Downey, von Hippel, & Hughes,

2008). Since virtually all nations have sizable SES gaps in school achievement, researchers might readily expect to find summer learning inequalities that roughly mirror those found in the United States in other nations.

This chapter examines patterns of summer learning just north of the U.S. border, in Ontario, Canada. Education in Canada falls under provincial jurisdiction; in Ontario, it is governed by the Ontario Ministry of Education, and schools are administered by district school boards, which are equivalent to school districts in the United States. Ontario is Canada's most populous province with 13.7 million people (Statistics Canada, 2015) and more than 2 million students attending almost 4,000 elementary and 1,000 secondary public schools, which are divided among 70 school boards. However, Ontario's public education system differs in two key ways from its American counterpart. First, the province fully funds Catholic schools (Canada has no legal separation of church and state). Roughly 30% of all students in the province attend publicly funded Catholic schools. Second, the province also fully funds French language schools, which are attended by roughly 5% of the province's students. In total, Ontario's public system consists of 31 English Public, 29 English Catholic, 4 French Public, and 8 French Catholic school boards (Ontario Ministry of Education, 2014). Our study reports on children from each of these four types of boards.

We begin by highlighting some key national similarities and differences between Canada and the United States that may have implications for summer learning disparities. We then describe major findings from our large-scale research project on summer learning and end by discussing implications of our Canadian study for summer learning research more broadly.

THE CANADIAN CONTEXT OF EDUCATION STRATIFICATION

Canada shares much with its southern neighbor. As in the United States, Canadian household income and wealth inequalities have grown in recent decades and are relatively high by international standards (Fortin, Green, Lemieux, Milligan, & Riddell, 2012; Lu, Morissette, & Schirle, 2011; Organization of Economic Co-operation and Development, 2011). Researchers have also documented rising levels of educational "homophily": Canadians increasingly marry, have children with, and live in neighborhoods with people who have similar levels of education and income (e.g., Cross & Mitchell, 2014; Hou & Myles, 2007; for U.S. research, see Reardon & Bischoff, 2011).

Importantly, Canadian researchers have long documented consistent achievement and attainment gaps along SES lines (Davies & Guppy, 2013). Despite having an almost entirely public higher education system with tuition fees that are relatively low compared to many U.S. institutions, Canadian students from high-income families are two to three times more likely to attend university than are those from low-income families (de Broucker,

2005) and are more likely to attend higher ranked and better resourced institutions than are young people from low-income families (Davies, Maldonado, & Zarifa, 2014; People for Education, 2013).

However, in some respects, Canada's education stratification may be weaker than that found in the United States. At a macro level, Canada has more upward social mobility, less income inequality, and less concentrated urban poverty than does the United States (Beller & Hout, 2006; Ley & Smith, 2000). Poverty in Canada is also less racially segregated than in the United States, in part because Canada lacks a comparable history of "white flight" from its cities. And, despite much de-industrialization over recent decades, formerly industrial Canadian cites have been far less marked by ongoing depopulation and neighborhood decay in comparison to formerly industrial U.S. cities (e.g., Cucchiara, 2013; Hwang & Sampson, 2014; Lichter, Parisi, & Taquino, 2015).

The provision of public schooling also differs somewhat between Canada and the United States. In the absence of comparable depopulation and urban blight, public education is fairly healthy north of the border. There are fewer warnings about looming crises of quality in Canadian schools and fewer calls to overhaul them by injecting more market mechanisms such as charter schools or voucher experiments. Canada's federal government plays only a very small role in K–12 education, leaving the vast bulk of policymaking and funding to provincial and territorial Ministries and Departments of Education, who tend to adopt fairly similar policies on school regulations, teacher training and hiring, and curricular foci. "Marketized" forms of education are limited to a relatively small private education sector that serves 6% to 8% of the student body (Davies & Aurini, 2011). The 12 charter schools that exist are located in the province of Alberta.

The length of the typical school year also differs. The summer vacation in Canada is typically 8 weeks, compared to the typical 12-week break in U.S. schools. In comparison, in Europe, the length of summer vacation varies from about 6 weeks in areas of Germany, the Netherlands, and the United Kingdom to about 13 weeks in Italy and Turkey (Eurydice, 2015).

Teaching in Canada remains a highly desirable occupation, attracting top university graduates, many of whom have postgraduate degrees or specializations and are comparably well paid. In Toronto, for example, a teacher with 10 years of experience can earn between $69,000 and $94,000 (CAD) depending on his/her qualifications, plus generous pension and other benefits (Elementary Teachers of Toronto, 2014–2015).

Canada's funding model may also generate fewer disparities among public schools. In the United States, nearly half of all school funding is generated through local taxes, creating large differences between wealthy and poor neighborhoods, while Ontario pools and then redistributes funds for elementary and secondary schooling according to a province-wide standard formula. Indeed, schools in economically and socially challenged neighborhoods receive additional support, including money, staff, and other resources. In 2015–2016, for example, Ontario gave an additional $500 million to support students "at greater risk of lower achievement," as well as a $193 million "geographic circumstance" grant to support schools in rural or small communities (Ontario Ministry of Education, 2015–2016). Perhaps as a result of these conditions, research suggests that compared to the United States, Canadian children have higher levels of school readiness (Merry, 2013), higher average achievement among high schoolers, and smaller SES disparities in achievement (Ministry of Industry, 2010; OECD, 2011).

Can these national social and schooling differences filter down and create dissimilar conditions for summer learning? On the one hand, there are reasons to believe that patterns of summer learning inequality may be muted north of the border. With less concentrated poverty in urban areas, and arguably strong welfare supports, fewer Canadian children may be exposed to the kinds of conditions that generate large summer learning losses.

On the other hand, there are reasons to expect to see sizable summer learning inequalities in Canada. As in other parts of the world, growing up in disadvantaged families in Canada is associated with lower educational achievement throughout regular schooling and fewer chances of university attendance (Caro, 2009; Dooley, Payne, & Robb, 2009; Phipps & Lethbridge, 2006). Crucially, achievement disparities emerge early, during preschool, before children have had very much exposure to formal schooling and then continue into the elementary grade levels (Hinton, 2014; Janus & Duku, 2007; Shulman, Hinton, Zhang, & Kozlow, 2014; Zhang, Shulman, & Kozlow, 2014).

Based on a 2013 report, one in four kindergarten students in Ontario were either not ready for school or deemed to be at risk at school entry (Calman & Crawford, 2013). Further, 18%–23% of Ontario students who were not on track in kindergarten did not meet provincial standards in grade 3, and 9%–14% were "newly at risk" since they did not meet grade 3 standards but were previously identified in kindergarten as on track.

Some small-scale Canadian research has documented summer learning losses among elementary school children (Canadian Council on Learning, 2008; Menard & Wilson, 2014). The implication of these studies is that early achievement disparities may signal the presence of unequal out-of-school learning opportunities, beginning in children's early years. Thus, despite having social and schooling conditions that might lessen educational stratification, there are strong reasons to believe that summer learning disparities are sizable north of the border.

Understanding how nonschool environments in Canada affect student achievement provides an important cross-national case for the broader summer learning framework. Next we describe our ongoing research study and then detail its major results.

THE ONTARIO SUMMER LEARNING PROJECT

Since 2010, we have evaluated public school summer learning programs in Ontario. Inspired by foundational work by Heyns (1978, 1987), Alexander et al. (2007), and Downey, von Hippel, and Broh (2004), in 2009 we advised the Ontario Ministry of Education (hereafter the Ministry) to try using summer interventions to narrow achievement gaps in the province. We described major research findings from the United States and hypothesized that summer learning inequalities may also exist in Ontario. The next year the Ministry launched a pilot program consisting of summer interventions in 28 of its 72 public school boards. Deeming that program to be successful, the Ministry has since increased the number of participating school boards and students every year. By 2016, almost every board was participating, reaching over 20,000 students.

Since they are offered across the province, these summer programs are set within many different kinds of settings, ranging from urban to suburban to rural communities, including remote northern jurisdictions. As a consequence, most children participating in our summer programs came from far less urbanized contexts than those reported in classic U.S.-based studies, such as those conducted in Baltimore by Karl Alexander and colleagues. While some of our programs are set in deindustrialized cities like Hamilton, St. Catharines, and Windsor, on the whole our locales are geographically diverse and rather different.

Based on our reading of the American summer learning literature, Ontario's summer programs are relatively "small-dose" and unstructured interventions. Unlike some U.S. programs, they provide intensive instruction in literacy or numeracy for only 2 or 3 weeks in July or August. Targeted at are relatively young students in grades 1, 2, and 3, they are free of charge and staffed by certified teachers. The Ministry dictates only some broad parameters: Programs must be taught by certified teachers along with an educational assistant; have 15–20 students per class; have a minimum duration of 2–3 weeks and total at least 45 hours of instruction; and have a daily recreational component. But within that broad template, school boards are granted the autonomy to tailor their program pedagogy, curricula, and timetables in ways that best suit their communities. Their programs are not, therefore, predesigned "interventions in a box," but instead vary across settings and have only broad parameters in common.

Another interesting comparative feature of the Ontario programs is that they target literacy in two languages—English and French—and also numeracy in both languages. Several boards designed English literacy programs with an embedded First Nation, Métis, and Inuit cultural theme, aimed at children with Indigenous heritage and developed and run in partnership with local Indigenous communities. Thus, the Ontario programs have linguistic and cultural components that differ somewhat from their American counterparts.

We have evaluated these programs using a quasi-experimental design. The findings presented here are based on five periods of data collection: June to September of 2010, 2011, 2012, 2013, and 2014. Since participants were chosen by educators, we could not randomly assign students to treatment groups, and so we designated control groups to be the school-year classmates of the summer participants, reasoning that they had been exposed to the same presummer teachers, schools, and neighborhoods as had the participants. We used various regression and matching techniques to estimate the "counterfactual—that is, the amount of summer learning gained by participants over and above what they would have likely gained without the benefit of the intervention.

Since our samples could not be generated through a systematic sampling frame, they do not necessarily reflect the provincial population but instead have disproportionate numbers of students with academic and social disadvantages. The Ministry mostly invited boards and schools in relatively needy areas; most participating schools had average test scores below the provincial average. Further, there was no explicit or systematic criterion for inviting students. While all students in grades 1–3 at participating schools were invited, educators at each school were asked to target students they believed would benefit from a literacy and/or numeracy intervention. Many but not all invited students accepted offers.

Available space was filled by students who were not necessarily deemed by educators as vulnerable to summer learning loss; the majority of programs had lengthy wait lists of interested families. But this nonrepresentativeness notwithstanding, these data are the best data ever collected on summer learning in Canada and are probably the largest outside of the United States.

Our data collection had three components. First, we tested students in June and again in September, tracking as many as possible who moved between schools within the same board. STAR testing was used for English language programs (https://www.renaissance.com/products/star-assessments). STAR is an online provider of literacy and numeracy computer-adaptive tests. French language programs used spring and fall Groupe Beauchemin (GB+) scores and Tâches diagnostiques en mathématiques to measure summer literacy and numeracy gains and losses. GB+ is a diagnostic reading assessment regularly administered in French language schools and Tâches diagnostiques en mathématiques is an assessment created specifically for this summer program evaluation.

Second, we collected report card measures, such as prior grades, to establish academic baselines. Third, we distributed a parent survey to collect many measures of family demographics and practices. The survey measured parents' educational attainment, income, race, country of birth, language used at home, number of children, and other demographics.

In addition, our study has a large qualitative component that focused on summer programs at four English school boards. We conducted semi-structured interviews with 70 educators and 158 parents and photo interviews with 35 children. Interviews were transcribed verbatim and ranged from 45 minutes to 3 hours in length. Over 3 summers, we also spent 18 weeks at the summer programs, observing classes, interacting with parents and teachers and participating in a variety of programs, including a daily parent engagement session. This field work gave us a deeper understanding of the programs, parent involvement in them, and parent-teacher interactions.

Main Findings: Quantitative Results

The Ontario study has uncovered several empirical patterns that have implications for understanding summer learning in cross-national context.

First, our control groups (students who did not have summer interventions) provide evidence that children's summer learning of literacy and numeracy is unequal in Ontario. In French and English literacy and in numeracy, most children kept pace over the summer months, with a median gain of 0 months, thus neither gaining nor losing an appreciable amount of literacy or numeracy (see Davies & Aurini, 2013). This average summer gain of 0 months differs a little from U.S. studies that estimate averages of about 1 month of learning loss (Borman & Boulay, 2004; Borman, Goetz, & Dowling, 2009; Burkam et al., 2004; Cooper et al., 1996; Cooper et al., 2000). Since our sample has a disproportionate number of children from challenged schools, we may be underestimating the true amount of summer gains in the province, and it may be likely that the average Ontario child loses a little less literacy and numeracy during the summer than does a U.S. counterpart. Nonetheless, we found summer learning gains and losses to be widely dispersed in Ontario. The distribution was normally shaped and centered on a large mode at zero, but many students suffered substantial gains and losses at either tail. The bottom quartile of students lost 3 or more months of literacy, while the top quartile gained about 3 months, learning at essentially school-year paces during the summer. Therefore, similar to U.S. studies, we found student fortunes to vary widely during the summertime.

Second, we found student SES to have sizable impacts on summer learning. In English literacy, for instance, one standard deviation increase in student SES was associated with a boost of 0.7 months in literacy over the summer. Breaking SES into quartiles, we found that summer learning differed little between the middle quartiles, but diverged dramatically between the bottom and top. Students in the bottom quartile lost almost 1 month of literacy, while students in the top quartile gained nearly 1 month. Controlling for a variety of demographics and family practices, we found SES literacy gaps between the top and bottom quartiles grew by nearly 2 months over the summer. In other words, one group learned at typical school-year rates and the other gained nothing. This pattern is reminiscent of those found in virtually all U.S. research on summer learning. Further, family practices like homework help, extracurricular activities, and various measures of family practices explained only about a third of those SES effects, leaving most of those effects unexplained. A similar inability to account for the bulk of SES effects has been encountered by Burkam and colleagues (2004).

These patterns of findings from Ontario add cross-national weight for the "summer setback" thesis, suggesting that nonschool time can be a key generator of achievement gaps not only in U.S. inner cities, but in other North American locales, including rural and suburban settings.

Third, and more encouraging, we also found that summer interventions, whether in English literacy, French literacy, or numeracy, brought positive and statistically significant boosts for their participants. For instance, we estimated treatment effect sizes (in standard deviation units) for French literacy programs to range from 0.3 to 0.5, which is quite sizable by the standards of elementary school interventions and summer programs (Davies, Aurini, Milne, & Jean-Pierre, 2015). For English literacy, treatment effect sizes tended to be smaller but consistent over several years, ranging between 0.15 and 0.20 (Aurini & Davies, 2015). Likewise, numeracy programs tended to narrow preexisting gaps by statistically significant amounts, with effect sizes ranging from 0.1 to 0.2 (Davies & McKerrow, 2015). Across all three types of summer programs, participants saw their preexisting gaps with their peers narrow between 10% and 30%. Our studies thus accord with other research showing that summer programs can not only reduce summer learning loss but also create literacy gains (Graham, McNamara, & Van Lankveld, 2011; Pagan & Senechal, 2014).

A fourth finding, one that is less encouraging, is that Ontario's summer programs appear to not necessarily benefit the poorest students. While specific patterns differ by English literacy, French literacy, or numeracy, children from higher-SES backgrounds tended to have the greatest learning gains from those programs (Davies & Aurini, 2015). That is, while children from all backgrounds tended to boost their learning scores after attending summer interventions, higher-SES children had significantly greater boosts than lower-SES children controlling for their previous academic records (grades, attendance) and other demographics (e.g., family size, region of the province).

Main Findings: Qualitative Results

Our qualitative study inquired about the impact of summer programs on home–school connections, parenting practices, and children's home reading practices. We found that these programs generated a variety of secondary benefits, beyond improving literacy or numeracy. Namely, the programs often enhanced the local school community and improved children's attitudes toward reading or math. As one parent told us, "What's great is the kids love to come, they're having fun. It shifts their perspective of school." Focusing on only reading or math allowed teachers to provide more intensive and constructive feedback to parents. As one teacher explained:

> Hosting a summer school program has extended a bridge to parents who have kids who are struggling at school. Many of the parents in our program are very interested in helping their children but didn't necessarily know how. Seeing parents come and pick up their child everyday allowed us an opportunity to discuss with them the ways they can help their kids become better readers.

Teachers also noted that the program kept children in the routine of school learning throughout the summer months, allowing them to be better prepared in September and "hit the ground running." Teachers also reported that some children started to redefine themselves as readers, and teachers witnessed a wholesale change in children's attitude about school more generally. As one student commented to his teacher, "I am beginning to enjoy this reading thing."

Further, we found some key differences by race and similarities by class. Comparing interviewees who self-identified as Indigenous (mainly Haudenosaunee, Anishinaabe, and Métis) to those who were non-Indigenous, we found crucial differences in orientations to school that were shaped by their historical collective memories. Over the 20th century ending in the 1980s, hundreds of thousands of Indigenous children throughout Canada were forced from their homes and local communities and placed in "residential schools," boarding schools that aimed to replace native languages and belief systems with English, French, and Christian religion. The declared aim of those schools was to "culturally modernize" those children and ready them for emerging job markets. The collective experience of residential schools, where physical and mental abuse was common, has been widely deemed to be a horrific event for Indigenous communities, prompting a formal apology from the federal government in 2008 (Milne, 2015). We found that this history seeped into parents' orientations to summer programs.

Specifically, Indigenous parents of participants in summer programs related to those programs in complex ways. The legacies of residential schools and other forms of discrimination against Indigenous peoples complicated parents' ability to form close relationships with summer educators (Milne, 2015, in press; see Lareau, 2011, for parallel findings based on Black and White families in the United States), with lingering feelings of distrust and doubt about the motives of these programs. However, we also found that the Indigenous-oriented programs, which provided literacy instruction based on Indigenous culture and heritage, helped facilitate relationships between Indigenous parents and local public schools, since Indigenous educators, parents, and community members participated in their development (Milne, 2015).

We found similar challenges among Indigenous and other parents based on social class. Despite enjoying high levels of support (e.g., waiting lists), many programs in disadvantaged areas, whether Indigenous-themed or not, had poor attendance. Parents had to register their children for the summer program, but attendance was entirely voluntary and parents were not legally obligated to send their children every day. In some cases, transportation issues and other distractions prevented some children from attending regularly. Not surprisingly, our interviewees noted that low attendance probably impacted learning outcomes for summer attendees. And summer teachers in disadvantaged areas, as they experienced in regular-year schooling, had to deal with behavioral issues, encountering students who seriously jeopardized not only the literacy goals of the program but also other students' morale and enjoyment. Likewise, we found that upper-SES parents, whether or not they self-identified as Indigenous, related more easily to summer educators. They tended to be knowledgeable about schooling and participated at higher levels than did other parents. Advantaged Indigenous parents were more guarded and wary to shield their children from any teacher or peer-based racism in the programs, yet tended to embrace these interventions nonetheless.

CONCLUSIONS

Our Canadian study provides cross-national support for the summer learning thesis while providing a context that offers some departures from U.S. settings. As in the United States, we find that many Canadian children suffer from "summer setback" and lose some literacy and numeracy skills over the summer months and that those losses are shaped by student SES. Those losses may be slightly smaller on average than those reported in U.S. studies but are noteworthy nevertheless. We also found that summer program participants raised their literacy and numeracy scores, though the poorest children did not gain most, as children from higher-SES origins tended to have the largest boosts.

Similar to U.S. research, our Canadian study provides justification for policies that aim to compensate for unequal learning opportunities during nonschool time (see Grahamn et al., 2011). But what should such policies look like? While some school reformers call for more school days or full-year schooling, our study points to another prescription. We suspect that the success of these programs can be partially attributed to three factors.

First, the programs we evaluated do not duplicate regular schooling. Rather than offering a comprehensive curriculum, the programs had an intensive literacy or numeracy focus. This focus allowed schools to target their interventions and rationalize their resources. Students were not only immersed together in the subject as a group but worked individually with highly trained literacy or numeracy coaches throughout the day (see Cooper, 2004).

Second, unlike regular school-year programs, the Ministry afforded boards a tremendous amount of autonomy in designing their summer programs. Rather than being a series of prepackaged programs, individual boards established their own timetables, resources, and activities, using this flexibility to meet to needs of their local populations. Teachers also had the flexibility to incorporate less conventional and more experiential teaching techniques. In several boards children blogged, wrote, directed, and acted out their own plays and "dove for numbers and words" at local community pools. Such activities promoted learning while engaging children. In fact, many children referred to these programs as simply "fun summer camps."

Third, summer programs created new opportunities for parent–teacher interactions. Since most did not provide transportation, parents had to enter schools and sign their children in and out, giving teachers opportunities to talk to them and exchange information. Several programs also encouraged parent participation in various classroom activities. One hosted "Family Math Fridays" that invited parents to "co-teach" a math lesson and work with their child. Another had parents participate for 30 minutes at the beginning *and* at the end of the day. In the morning, teachers modeled literacy strategies for parents, giving them opportunities to practice with their children. In the afternoon, parents and their children cocreated take-home activities related to that day's strategy. What is important is that these activities are not usually possible, nor welcomed, during the regular school year. While the literature on parent engagement has not found consistently strong and positive relationships between parent involvement and school achievement (Aurini, Milne, & Hillier, 2016), we believe these new connections had positive qualitative impacts on school communities.

In what directions should the next phase of summer learning research head? Our Ontario study is now examining the longitudinal benefits of summer programs. We are following students over consecutive summers in order to document their longer-term learning trajectories and determine whether summer gains/losses tend to compound over time. Specifically, we are investigating whether students benefit from attending summer programs over consecutive years—whether multiple "doses" improve participants' achievement—and whether summer program interventions have longer-term impacts into the following school year and summer.

REFERENCES

Alexander, K. L., Entwisle, D. R., & Olson, L. S. (2007). Lasting consequences of the summer learning gap. *American Sociological Review, 72*(2), 167–180.

Aurini, J., & Davies, S. (2015). *Summer learning report.* Submitted to the Ontario Ministry of Education.

Aurini, J., Milne, E., & Hillier, C. (2016). The two sides of vigilance: Parent engage-
ment and its relationship to school connections, responsibility, and agency. In
W. Lehmann (Ed.), *Education and society: Canadian perspectives*. Don Mills,
Ontario: Oxford University Press.

Beller, E., & Hout, M. (2006). Intergenerational social mobility: The United States in
comparative perspective. *The Future of Children, 16*(2), 19–36.

Borman, G. D., & Boulay, M. (Eds.). (2004). *Summer learning: Research, policies,
and programs*. Mahwah, NJ: Erlbaum.

Borman, G. D., Goetz, M. E., & Dowling, M. (2009). Halting the summer achievement slide: A randomized field trial of the kindergARTen summer camp. *Journal
of Education for Students Placed at Risk (JESPAR), 14*(2), 133–147.

Burkham, D. T., Ready, D. D., Lee, V. E., & LoGerfo, L .F. (2004). Social class differences in summer learning between kindergarten and first grade: Model specification and estimation. *Sociology of Education, 77*(1), 1–31.

Calman, R. C., & Crawford, P. J. (2013). *Starting early: Teaching learning and assessment*. Research Bulletin. Toronto, Ontario: Education Quality and Accountability Office.

Canadian Council on Learning. (2008). Summer learning loss: Lessons in learning.
Retrieved from http://enlighteninglearnersweblog.com/blogs/media/blogs/a/
Jun-12-08-Summer-Learning-L.pdf

Caro, D. H. (2009). Socio-economic status and academic achievement trajectories from childhood to adolescence. *Canadian Journal of Education, 32*(3),
558–590.

Cooper, H. (2004). Is the school calendar dated? Education, economics and the politics of time. In G. D. Borman & M. Boulay (Eds.), *Summer learning: Research,
policies, and programs* (pp. 3–25). Mahwah, NJ: Erlbaum.

Cooper, H., Charlton, K., Valentine, J. D., Muhlenbruck, L., & Borman, G. D. (2000).
Making the most of summer school: A meta-analytic and narrative review.
Monographs of the Society for Research in Child Development, 65(1), 1–127.

Cooper, H., Nye, B., Charlton, K., Lindsay, J., & Greathouse, S. (1996). The effects
of summer vacation on achievement test scores: A narrative and meta-analytic
review. *Review of Educational Research, 66*(3), 227–268.

Cross, P., & Mitchell, P. J. (2014). *The marriage gap between rich and poor Canadians: How Canadians are split into have and have-nots along marriage*. Institute of Marriage and Family Canada. Retrieved from www.imfcanada.org/
canadian-marriage-gap

Cucchiara, M. B. (2013). *Marketing schools, marketing cities*. Chicago, IL: University of Chicago Press.

Davies, S., & Aurini, J. (2011). Exploring school choice in Canada: Who chooses
what and why? *Canadian Public Policy, 37*(4), 459–477.

Davies, S., & Aurini, J. (2013). Summer learning inequality in Ontario. *Canadian
Public Policy, 39*(2), 287–307.

Davies, S., & Aurini, J. (2015). The impacts of discretionary spaces in schooling:
Do they reproduce inequality, equalize opportunity or partially compensate for
society? Presentation to the annual meetings of the American Sociological Association, Chicago, Illinois.

Davies, S., Aurini, J., Milne, E., & Jean-Pierre, J. (2015). Les effets des programmes
d'été de littératie: Les théories d'opportunités d'apprentissage et les élèves «

non-traditionnels » dans les écoles ontariennes francophones." (The effects of summer literacy programs: Learning opportunity theory and "non-traditional" students in Ontario French language schools). *Canadian Journal of Sociology, 40*(2), 189–222.

Davies, S., & Guppy, N. (2013). *The schooled society* (3rd ed.). Toronto, Ontario: Oxford University Press.

Davies, S., Maldonado, V., & Zarifa, D. (2014). Effectively maintained inequality in Toronto: Predicting student destinations in Ontario universities. *Canadian Review of Sociology, 51*(1), 22–53.

Davies, S., & McKerrow, M. (2015). Effects of summer programs on early numeracy: Findings from a large scale quasi-experiment using a counterfactual framework. Manuscript in preparation.

de Broucker, P. (2005). Getting there and staying there: Low-income students and post-secondary education. A synthesis of the research findings (Report Number W-27). Ottawa, Ontario: Canadian Policy Research Networks.

Dooley, M. D., Payne, A. A., & Robb, A. L. (2009). *University participation and income differences: An analysis of applications by Ontario secondary school students.* Toronto, Ontario: Higher Education Quality Council of Ontario.

Downey, D. B., von Hippel, P. T., & Broh, B. A. (2004). Are schools the great equalizer? Cognitive inequality during the summer months and the school year. *American Sociological Review, 69*, 613–635.

Downey, D. B., von Hippel, P. T., & Hughes, M. (2008). Are "failing" schools really failing? Using seasonal comparison to evaluate school effectiveness. *Sociology of Education, 81*(3), 242–270.

Elementary Teachers of Toronto. (2014–2015). *Salary grid for TDSB elementary teachers: 2014–2015.* Retrieved from www.ett.ca/salary-grid-for-tdsb-elementary-teachers-2014-2015/

Eurydice. (2015). *Organization of school time in Europe: Primary and secondary general education, 2014/15 school year.* Retrieved from http://eacea.ec.europa.eu/education/eurydice/documents/facts_and_figures/school_calendar_en.pdf

Fortin, N., Green, D. A., Lemieux, T., Milligan, K., & Riddell, W. C. (2012). Canadian inequality: Recent developments and policy options. *Canadian Public Policy, 38*(2), 121–146.

Grahamn, A., McNamara, J. K., & Van Lankveld, J. (2011). Closing the summer learning gap for vulnerable learners: An exploratory study of a summer literacy programme for kindergarten children at-risk for reading difficulties. *Early Child Development and Care, 181*(5), 575–585.

Heyns, B. (1978). *Summer learning and the effects of schooling.* Orlando, FL: Academic Press.

Heyns, B. (1987). Schooling and cognitive development: Is there a season for learning? *Child Development, 58*(5), 1151–1160.

Hinton, A. (2014). *Tracking student achievement in mathematics over time in English-language schools.* Research Bulletin. Toronto, Ontario: Education Quality and Accountability Office.

Hou, F., & Myles, J. (2007). *The changing role of education in the marriage market: Assortive marriage in Canada and the United States since the 1970s.* Retrieved from www.statcan.gc.ca/pub/11f0019m/11f0019m2007299-eng.htm

Hwang, J., & Sampson, R. J. (2014). Divergent pathways of gentrification: Racial inequality and the social order of renewal in Chicago neighborhoods. *American Sociological Review*, 79, 726–751.

Janus, M., & Duku, E. (2007). The school entry gap: Socioeconomic, family, and health factors associated with children's school readiness to learn. *Early Education and Development*, 18, 375–403.

Lareau, A. (2011). *Unequal childhoods: Race, class, and family life. Second Edition. A Decade Later.* Berkeley: University of California Press.

Ley, D., & Smith, H. (2000). Relations between deprivation and immigrant groups in large Canadian cities. *Urban Studies*, 37(1), 37–62.

Lichter, D. T., Parisi, D., & Taquino, M. C. (2015). Toward a new macro-segregation? Decomposing segregation within and between metropolitan cities and suburbs. *American Sociological Review*, 80(4), 843–873.

Lindahl, M. (2001). *Summer learning and the effect of schooling: Evidence from Sweden*. Bonn, Germany: IZA Discussion Paper Series, #262.

Lu, Y., Morissette, R., & Schirle, T. (2011). The growth of family earnings inequality in Canada, 1980–2005. *Review of Income and Wealth*, 57(1), 23–39.

Menard, J., & Wilson, A. M. (2014). Summer learning loss among elementary school children with reading disabilities. *Exceptionality Education International*, 23(1), 72–85.

Merry, J. J. (2013). Tracing the U.S. deficit in PISA reading skills to early childhood: Evidence from the United States and Canada. *Sociology of Education*, 86(3), 234–252.

Milne, E. (in press). "I have the worst fear of teachers": Moments of Inclusion and Exclusion in Family/School Relationships among Indigenous Families in Southern Ontario. *Canadian Review of Sociology*.

Milne, E. (2015). *Renegotiating family-school relationships among Indigenous Peoples in southern Ontario* (Doctoral dissertation). Waterloo, Ontario: University of Waterloo.

Ministry of Industry. (2010). *Measuring up: Canadian results of the OECD PISA study: The performance of Canada's youth in reading, mathematics and science.* Retrieved from www.cmec.ca/Publications/Lists/Publications/Attachments/254/PISA2009-can-report.pdf

Ontario Ministry of Education. (2014). *Education Facts, 2013–2014*. Retrieved from www.edu.gov.on.ca/eng/educationFacts.html

Ontario Ministry of Education 2015–2016. (2016). *A guide to grants for students' needs*. Retrieved from www.edu.gov.on.ca/eng/funding/1516/2015GSNguideEN.pdf

Organization of Economic Co-operation and Development. (2011). *Lessons from PISA for the United States, strong performers and successful reformers in education.* Paris, France: OECD Publishing.

Pagan, S., & Senechal, M. (2014). Involving parents in a summer book reading program to promote reading comprehension, fluency, and vocabulary in grade 3 and grade 5 children. *Canadian Journal of Education*, 37(2), 1–31.

People for Education. (2013). *Mind the gap: Inequality in Ontario's schools*. Retrieved from www.peopleforeducation.ca/wp-content/uploads/2013/05/annual-report-2013-WEB.pdf

Phipps, S., & Lethbridge, L. (2006). *Income and the outcomes of children* (Report No. 11F0019MIE-281). Ottawa, Ontario: Statistics Canada.

Reardon, S. F., & Bischoff, K. (2011). Income inequality and income segregation. *American Journal of Sociology, 116*(4), 1092–1153.

Shavit, Y., Arum, R., & Gamoran, A. (Eds.). (2007). *Stratification in higher education: A comparative study.* Palo Alto, CA: Stanford University Press.

Shulman, R., Hinton, A., Zhang, S., & Kozlow, M. (2014). *Longitudinal results of province-wide assessments in English-language schools.* Research Bulletin. Toronto, Ontario: Education Quality and Accountability Office.

Statistics Canada. (2015). *Population by year, by province and territory.* Retrieved from www.statcan.gc.ca/tables-tableaux/sum-som/l01/cst01/demo02a-eng.htm

Stefani, S., Pollak, R., Otte, G., & Gangl, M. (Eds.). (2007). *From origin to destination: Trends and mechanisms in social stratification research.* Chicago, IL: University of Chicago Press.

United Nations. (2013). *Report on the world social situation 2013.* Retrieved from www.un.org/esa/socdev/documents/reports/InequalityMatters.pdf

Zhang, S., Shulman, R., & Kozlow, M. (2014). *Tracking student achievement in literacy over time in English-language schools.* Research Bulletin. Toronto, Ontario: Education Quality and Accountability Office.

CHAPTER 5

Summer Learning and the Opportunity Gap

Sarah Pitcock

National polling data show that about one-third of households have a child enrolled in a summer learning program. More than half of those not enrolled report they would participate if an affordable program were available to them. Analyses of program availability from multiple cities underscore that the demand for free or affordable programs far outpaces supply. This chapter will explore what we know about the availability of programs, the resources that support them and the efforts underway to understand how long-held perceptions about summer school and the meaning of summer break influence participation by children and youth who need summer learning the most.

There has been a sustained, heightened focus on reforming our K–12 education system for the last 25 years. During this time, billions of public and private dollars have been invested in initiatives designed to strengthen academic achievement in our public schools, whether through stronger teaching, new technology, or improved curricula. Some racial achievement gaps have narrowed during this time, but income-based gaps persist and grow as the population of students classified as low income grows. Yet, research shows that growth does not happen during the school year. Public, compulsory education, whether in a well-off suburb or inner city, does a remarkably good job, on average, of moving young people forward at the same rate. Yes, far too many young people are missing critical benchmarks such as 3rd-grade reading proficiency. But data suggests that the achievement gap widens when young people are *out of school* in the summer, not in the classroom during the school year. Several researchers have posited that the achievement gaps we seek so fervently to narrow in public education are driven not by differences in the way young people learn when they are *in* school, but by a persistent opportunity gap that dictates how they learn when they are *out* of school.

WHAT IS THE OPPORTUNITY GAP?

The *opportunity gap* is the disparity in access to quality schools and other resources necessary for all children and youth to be academically successful. One way of understanding this gap is to look at Consumer Expenditure Surveys from the U.S. Bureau of Labor Statistics. Those statistics show that over the last 40 years, upper-income parents have increased the amount they spend on their children's enrichment activities, like tutoring, extracurricular activities, and summer camp, by $5,300 a year. Over the same time period, lower-income parents have only been able to increase their investment by $480, adjusted for inflation, meaning the most affluent parents' spending on enrichment activities for their children grew about two and a half times (250%) from 1972–1973 to 2005–2006, compared to an increase of only 57% for the least well-off parents, widening what was already a substantial gap (Duncan & Murnane, 2011). This data includes spending on private schools, which may go beyond what many consider enrichment. Nonetheless, the overall trend is clear. The opportunity gap as measured by spending on enrichment is growing rapidly.

Why do we have an opportunity gap? The composition and well-being of families and our workforce have both changed significantly since the 1960s. First, more children are living with single parents. The share of children born outside of marriage now stands at 41%, up from just 5% in 1960. In one of the largest shifts, 34% of children today are living with an unmarried parent, up from just 9% in 1960 and 19% in 1980. In most cases, these unmarried parents are single and therefore shouldering child care responsibilities on their own (Livingston, 2014).

In addition, since 1996, most recipients of public assistance must work in order to qualify for benefits, taking them out of the home year-round. At the same time, more people are working more jobs and longer hours for the same pay. The ranks of the working poor are growing because the value of the minimum wage has dropped, adjusted for inflation (Shierholz & Mishel, 2013). More than ever, parents are often left with a difficult decision of leaving children at home or in low-quality care settings or not working because of lack of summer care arrangements for their children (Schulman & Blank, 2014).

It follows, then, that in 2012, we crossed a disheartening threshold in the United States: More than half of public school children qualify for free or reduced-price meals at school, meaning that more than half of our students live in households with incomes up to 185% of the federal poverty line (Suitts, 2015).

Eighty-five percent of those students, for reasons ranging from lack of availability to stigma or lack of awareness, do not access the subsidized meals they qualify for in the summer months (Food Research and Action

Center, 2015). This is the best national indicator we have of how we are doing in caring for the basic needs of young people when the school doors are closed, and it raises serious concerns. Increased poverty and outdated notions of parental care have serious implications for the health and safety of children during the summer months.

National survey data enables us to zoom in on this opportunity gap to understand the summer story more clearly. The Afterschool Alliance, a policy and advocacy organization, conducts its America After 3PM (AA3PM) national survey every 5 years to document participation in and perceptions of after-school and summer programs among a representative sample of households. AA3PM data in 2013 showed that nationally, one-third of households reported having at least one child enrolled in a summer program, with higher than average participation among minority students. There is unmet demand: 51% of all nonparticipating families (roughly 20 million students) would likely enroll in a summer program if one was available to them. Participation is up 8% since 2008, and unmet demand is down 5%.

Why is there so much unmet demand? The national average reported cost for summer programs of $288 per week is nearly 30% of household income for a family of four whose children qualify for reduced-price meals and nearly 40% of household income for a family of four whose children qualify for free meals. State-to-state variance is enormous, with average per-week costs to families ranging from $115 (Idaho) to $639 per week (Nevada). Variations may be due to program intensity and length, local staffing and facilities costs, transportation, and other factors (Afterschool Alliance, 2015).

Accordingly, participation also varies by state. Washington, DC has the highest rate of reported participation at 61%, but also the highest demand at 73%, with an average cost of $488 per week. California has the highest participation in and demand for summer programs outside of the District of Columbia; 46% are enrolled versus the 33% national average. A variety of factors contribute to California's leading position, including a state funding stream and strong private investment in summer learning.

With high costs to families and little political opposition to summer programs, it is no surprise that public support for public funding of summer programs is high—85% in 2013, up from 83% in 2008.

PUBLIC FUNDING FOR SUMMER PROGRAMS

Fee-based summer programs are common, but even middle-income families will struggle to pay the average weekly costs, especially for multiple children. As such, public funding is an important supplement to parent fees and other types of private funding for summer programs. Before we begin to examine public funding for summer programs, it's helpful to look at school-year expenditures for context. Public school funding in the 2014–2015 school year totaled roughly $600 billion for 50 million students nationally, or roughly $12,000 per student per school year. Applying that formula to summer programs translates to spending $4,000 per student to keep those or similar systems going for an additional 3 months, which would total $200 billion for today's K–12 public school population (U.S. Department of Education, 2015).

We can use research on program costs to help narrow that estimate. In the report *Making Summer Count* (McCombs et al., 2012), researchers at RAND estimate a cost range of $7 to $14 per slot per hour in comprehensive, district-run summer programs. From this and a variety of school district and nonprofit program data the National Summer Learning Association (NSLA) has collected over the past decade, we believe that summer program costs range from $500 to $2,000 per youth, with programs at the higher end of the range typically having more experienced or credentialed instructors, lower adult-to-youth ratios, longer days, and/or wages or stipends for youth participants. If we are talking about an average 120-hour summer program for youth grades K–12, we would say the cost is less than $1,000 per youth.

Therefore, a more measured calculation that assumes public funding covers $1,000 per student for the half of the school-age population that qualifies for free or reduced-price meals would take our expectation of public funding for summer programs down to $25 billion.

Federal Funding

A cursory analysis of the major federal funding streams for summer programs reveals that the per-student funding logic does not carry into the summer, and neither does the tracking of attendance and participation in publicly funded programs. This section describes the data available and offers some opportunities for strengthening implementation and evaluation of these federal programs.

The main sources of federal funding for summer programs are administered through Nutrition, Child Care, Education and Workforce programs. Other federal programs include Temporary Assistance to Needy Families and Community Development Block Grants, which will not be discussed in this chapter because so little systematic data is collected on whether and how they are used to provide summer programs. Of those I will cover, only the Summer Food Service Program has a dedicated budget line item for summer programs; the other major federal programs include summer as an allowable but not required use of year-round funding and therefore do not currently require states to track expenditures or participation in summer separately from the school year. Table 5.1 provides an overall picture of the largest federal funding streams that allow spending on summer programs.

Table 5.1. Funding Level and Reach of Major Federal Summer Grant Programs

Federal Program	2015 Funding Level	Number of Students Served at Some Point During the Year	% of School Age Served
Nutrition Programs	$11.67 billion (Admin Request for full year National School Lunch Program) $493 million (Admin Request for Summer Food Service Program)	22 million on an average school day in 2014–2015; 3.2 million on an average summer day in 2014	44% (school year) 6.4% (summer)
21st Century Community Learning Centers	$1.1 billion	1.6 million total in school year and summer 2014	3.2% (full year)
Child Care Development Fund	$5.3 billion	1.4 million total in school year and summer 2014	2.8% (full year)
Migrant Education	$374 million	330,000 total in school year and summer 2014; 110,000 in the summer only, 2014	<.1% (full year)
Title I, Part A	$14.4 billion	56,000 + schools, more than 21 million children, 2009	42% (full year)

Nutrition. Two federal Summer Nutrition Programs—the National School Lunch Program (NSLP) Seamless Summer Option and the Summer Food Service Program (SFSP)—provide funding to schools and a variety of community-based organizations to serve meals. snacks to children over the summer. The U.S. Department of Agriculture (USDA) provides the funding for both programs through a state agency in each state, usually the state department of education. Sites must meet at least one eligibility criterion: at least 50% of the children in the geographic area must be eligible for free or reduced-price school meals or individually determined eligible for free or reduced-price school meals, or program sites must serve primarily migrant children. Once a meal site is determined eligible, all of the participating children can eat for free.

As previously noted, participation in the Summer Nutrition Program is significantly lower than in the school-year nutrition program. In July 2014, only one in six of the low-income children who rely on school lunch during the school year participated in the Summer Nutrition Programs (Fitzsimmons, Anderson, Hayes, & Burke, 2015). This disparity is caused by a number of factors affecting both supply and demand. First, participation in Summer Nutrition seems to be linked to funding for summer enrichment programming and child care. As many states experienced budget crises during the recession beginning in 2008, cuts to funding for summer school and other summer programs seemed to erode the platform for Summer Nutrition Programs, and participation in those programs began to fall as well. This trend began to reverse in 2012 with a slight increase in participation, followed by much larger increases in 2013 and 2014. In July 2014, on an average day, the Summer Nutrition Programs (SFSP and NSLP combined) served lunch to 3.2 million children. The total number of children participating in Summer Nutrition increased by more than 215,000, or 7.3%, from July 2013 to July 2014. Five states served at least 25% of their school-year totals in the summer of 2014: District of Columbia, New Mexico, New York, Connecticut, and Vermont.

Other barriers related to program administration keep the supply of summer meals programs significantly lower than the school year, including eligibility thresholds that differ from federal education programs and are challenging for rural areas to meet because of their low population density. Additionally, schools and CBOs must apply separately for eligibility for after-school and summer meals programs, requiring a great deal of paperwork and administrative expenditures, creating a disincentive to apply again for the summer.

On the demand side, providers and families report that transportation, particularly in rural areas, is a significant barrier to participation. It is also likely that lack of awareness and perceived stigma associated with meal sites limits participation in the summer. Particularly for older youth, the schedule and location of meal sites, as well as laws requiring meals to be consumed on site, can be barriers to participation.

Advocates are currently working to address these barriers through policy recommendations that align the eligibility threshold, allow year-round eligibility, fund transportation, serve three meals per day, and support partnerships to get meals and learning opportunities to where children are, including libraries, farmers markets, and WIC clinics.

Education. A number of education funding streams can be used to support summer learning programs, but none of them track those expenditures separately. I will examine programs in the Elementary and Secondary Education Act (recently reauthorized as the Every Student Succeeds Act) and the Individuals with Disabilities Education Act that have some data or relevance to summer.

Title IV, Part B, 21st Century Community Learning Centers. Formerly part of the Elementary and Secondary Education Act and now the Every Student Succeeds Act, 21st Century Community Learning Centers (21st CCLC) are administered as formula grants from the U.S. Department of Education (DOE) to states. State education agencies run competitive grant programs and sub-grant funding to local education agencies and nonprofit organizations to run before-school, after-school, and summer programs. According to the DOE, 21st CCLC "supports the creation of community learning centers that provide academic enrichment opportunities during nonschool hours for children, particularly students who attend high-poverty and low-performing schools" (2016).

It is difficult to tell how much of the total $1.1 billion federal appropriation for 21st CCLC is spent on summer learning programs. In the most recent national survey conducted by the DOE in 2016, half of all 21st CCLC grantees reported using a portion of their grant to offer summer programs. If we wanted to broadly and generously estimate based on that data that half of grantees use one-third of their funding to offer summer programs, we would say that a $183 million ceiling of funding spent on summer is likely, knowing that the full $1.1 billion appropriation does ot go to programming. To get a more current picture, the NSLA conducted email and phone surveys of 21st CCLC administrators in all 50 states and the District of Columbia. Findings include:

- Nine states require their 21st CCLC grantees to deliver summer programs (Arizona, Colorado, Maine, Michigan, Minnesota, Oklahoma, Pennsylvania, Rhode Island, and Washington).
- An additional eight states plus the District of Columbia place a priority on applications that include summer programming (Arkansas, Delaware, Georgia, Massachusetts, South Carolina, Vermont, West Virginia, and Wyoming).
- Thirty-one states do not require or prioritize summer programs in their 21st CCLC grant making.
- Of the 17 states and District of Columbia that require or prioritize summer programming, 15 reported tracking the reach of these funds. These 15 states track either the percentage of grantees that report delivering summer programs or actual counts of participants in summer programs.
- For states reporting the percentage of their sites offering summer learning, primarily the states that require it, the average percentage is above 75%.
- No state tracks the amount of funding spent on summer programs specifically.

Twenty-first CCLC is a critical program because of the requirement of school–community partnerships and the opportunity for year-round services. There are conversations underway in several additional states to begin to require grantees to offer summer programs. The data management system for 21st CCLC is currently offline while it is being built by a new DOE contractor. The NSLA is requesting improvements in how summer data is tracked and reported by states and by the DOE in the new system.

Title I, Part A, Education for the Disadvantaged. Designed to provide an equal education regardless of income level or local school funding, Title I, Part A is the largest source of federal education funding. In addition to the significant flexibility in current law surrounding the use of funds for Title I-receiving schools, the law specifically references summer learning as an allowable activity in several places, which means that there is an explicit authorization to use Title I funds for summer learning. The only way to assess the level of Title I funding being used in the summer is to go district by district, and even then, many districts may not track their expenditures for summer. Snapshot data from several districts in Table 5.2 provides a window into how major districts might use Title I in the summer and makes the case for future systematic research on the topic.

Title I, Part C, Migrant Education. The general purpose of the Migrant Education Program (MEP) is to ensure that migratory children fully benefit from the same free public education provided to other children. Federal funds are allocated by formula to SEAs based on each state's per pupil expenditure for education and counts of eligible migratory children, ages 3 through 21, residing within the state. Summer is one of many allowable uses of the funding, which includes before- and after-school, in-school, distance learning, and Saturday programming. MEP was appropriated $374 million in 2014–2015, and nearly 378,000 students were eligible for services that year.

There is wide flexibility in how MEP dollars are spent, with expenditures driven by a comprehensive needs assessment conducted in each state. From the most recent available state reports in 2012–2013, only one-third of eligible children received summer services through MEP. Although the services levels are low given the typically disadvantaged nature of the population, the fact that summer participation is tracked is at least helpful in understanding how the dollars are being used. There is an opportunity for states to use this data to set higher goals for summer participation.

Extended School Year. The Individuals with Disabilities Education Act (IDEA) provides for equal educational opportunity and individualized education plans for students with disabilities. As with many parts of IDEA, Extended School Year (ESY) services were added to the law following a series of court cases brought by the parents of children with a disability. In the cases precipitating ESY, parents claimed that their children would forget most of what they learned over the long summer break and take most of the next school year to relearn those skills, therefore making academic and developmental supports during the summer a necessity. ESY is delivered in a variety of settings, including home and school, and facilitated by teachers, community-based staff, or parents. Whether or not a child qualifies for ESY, including the number of weeks, days, and hours per day of service, is decided by his or her IEP committee. ESY is not found in the statute but was added to regulations in 2002. As such, it is largely an unfunded mandate (Bishop, 2013).

I discuss ESY here not because it is currently playing a significant role in keeping children healthy, safe, and learning over the summer, but because the case law on which it is based has so much relevance beyond children with disabilities. Because of its specific focus on summer, the criteria used to assess eligibility for ESY is quite compelling. Multiple criteria must be considered when determining whether a child qualifies for ESY (Cooperative Educational Service Agency, 1998). The criteria include:

- Regression/recoupment: likelihood of regression in academic or social skills.
- Emerging skills: also known in the case law as "breakthrough opportunities," or when a child is on the verge of a critical new competency, such as reading, and will be set far backward by a summer break.
- Ability of parents to provide an educational structure at home.

When considering the data on summer learning loss (average loss of 2 months in reading for low-income students and 2 months of math for all students), you might think that ESY would be a significant resource for children with disabilities and their families. However, steep eligibility requirements prevent most students from qualifying for the services. Regulations state that, to qualify, a child with a disability must lose two thirds of the skills learned during the school year and take between 6 and 9 weeks of the next school year to regain those skills. A number of students forget some of the skills they learn during the summer months; however, most do not lose as much as two-thirds, regardless of disability.

While I would argue that the regression bar is far too high, the most short-sighted feature of the eligibility determinants is that they ignore the fact that most students with disabilities are already behind. For context, in the reading portion of the 2015 NAEP test, 33% of 4th-graders with disabilities scored at or above a basic level, compared with 74% of students without disabilities. For the 8th-grade reading test, 37% of students with disabilities scored at or above basic, compared with 81% of students without disabilities. Differentials are similar for math (Samuels, 2015).

Moreover, with 80% of all minority students not reading proficiently by 4th grade, the notion that the summer break can disrupt a critical "breakthrough" in acquiring reading mastery makes this case law relevant for a much broader swath of students.

About 13% of the U.S. school age population in the 2012–2013 school year (most recent year available) was designated as qualifying for special education services (DOE, 2015).

Thirteen percent is not inconsequential, and expansion of eligibility for these services within the special education population is an opportunity. Consideration of the research and case law behind the criteria for these programs as a means to support a wider array of struggling students and families would be an appropriate recognition of the extra learning time that will be required to close the achievement gap between higher- and lower-income students.

Child Care: The Child Care Development Fund. The Child Care Development Fund (CCDF) is a federal program that assists low-income families in obtaining child care so that they can work or attend school. As with other federal programs, program administration, including income eligibility and reimbursement rates, varies widely by state. Unlike other federal programs discussed in this section, CCDF is administered as a subsidy or voucher to families instead of a grant to a service provider. Child care subsidies are available to children under age 13 whose families meet certain income eligibility requirements. CCDF was appropriated $5.6 billion in the 2015 budget, making it the largest source of federal funding dedicated to school-age care outside of public school funding. CCDF subsidies served 1.4 million children in an average month in 2014, based on preliminary estimates.

State-by-state data has not been collected to understand the percentage of subsidy dollars that go toward summer programs or care settings, so it is difficult to assess how widely it is used in the summer. One proxy we can use for comparison is Head Start, one of the largest federal child care/early learning programs. Similar to many child care programs, Head Start programs are required to operate a minimum of 30 weeks, or 180 days per year, but can use their funding to operate year round. A presentation from the Office of Child Care based on June 2015 survey data of Head Start sites reported that only 31% of Head Start students receive services for 180 or more days per year (Office of Head Start Administration for Children and Families, 2015).

Another way to look at the supply of child care vouchers is to examine state waiting lists. States may place eligible families on a waiting list or freeze intake (turn away eligible families without adding their names to a waiting list). Families on the waiting list may wait months before receiving child care assistance or may never receive it. Eighteen states had waiting lists or frozen intake in 2014 compared to 19 states in 2013 and 21 states in 2001. The average length of state waiting list, not weighted for overall population, is 10,300 children (Schulman & Blank, 2014).

CCDF was reauthorized in 2014, and a number of new regulations are being implemented to improve access, ease of use, and quality of programs. One new section of regulations aims to create more family-friendly eligibility policies by establishing a required 12-month eligibility redetermination period for CCDF families. This change should provide more seamless, year-round care for children and is a requirement for states' FY2016–2018 state plans. Establishing a 12-month eligibility period is one of the most significant areas of change made by Congress (U.S. Department of Health and Human Services, 2014).

Based on publicly available data, it appears that child care counts are collected monthly by states, although they are only reported as an annual monthly average. It seems there is an opportunity for the Office of Child Care to analyze and report whether and how rates and duration of services vary in the summer months to shed light on any seasonal disparities.

Workforce: Workforce Innovation and Opportunity Act. Changes in 2014 to the federal Workforce Innovation and Opportunity Act (WIOA) shift the emphasis to youth ages 16 to 24 who are not in school, but also require that at least 20% of the funds—about $830 million nationally—be spent on work experiences, which can include youth summer jobs. In practice, WIOA funds are not a significant source for summer youth employment programs.

State Funding

While most states do not allocate significant funds to summer programs specifically, state programs can be an important source of funding. State funding for summer is allocated through a variety of different types of programs, which may include noncompetitive grants targeted based on district or school poverty or achievement levels: enhancements of existing programs, such as STEM or professional development set asides, expansion of a proven model, or competitive grant programs to pilot a new program. Most state policies are not aligned with research on high-quality summer programs; however, some do require impact evaluation.

Several states have dedicated funding programs that are achieving some degree of scale and fidelity across the state.

New Mexico K-3 Plus. During the 2012 legislative session, K-3 Plus was converted from a 6-year pilot into a program of the Public Education Department. K-3 Plus provides funding for additional educational time for disadvantaged students in kindergarten through 3rd grade by extending the school year by at least 25 instructional days. The program is administered in schools with 80% or more of students eligible for free or reduced-price lunch or with a D or F grade the previous year.

A cost-benefit analysis of the program in 2014 showed that the benefits from reduced grade retention and remediation services offset all K-3 Plus costs, which were $1,366 per student in 2014, for a total of $15.9 million for 11,639 students. Since 2008, the Legislature has appropriated a total of approximately $81.9 million in General Fund revenue to fund the K-3 Plus Program, including $21.3 million in FY15 (Skandera, 2014).

California After School Education and Safety. California has more after-school programs than all other states combined, thanks to a unique dedicated state funding stream. The After School Education and Safety (ASES) Program is the result of the 2002 voter-approved initiative, Proposition 49. The ASES Program funds partnerships between schools and local community resources to provide "literacy, academic enrichment and safe constructive alternatives" for students in kindergarten through 9th grade. The current funding level for the ASES program is $550 million. For context, that is roughly half of the federal 21st Century Community Learning Center Funding for the entire United States. While the ASES program is by far the largest state-level commitment to after-school and summer programs, the relative proportion of funding dedicated for use in the summer (6%, or $32.6 million annually) falls far short of year-round parity, in which case 20%–25% of funding would be dedicated to the summer months.

California passed a law in 2010 that requires 15% of any future increase in federal 21st CCLC dollars flowing into the state be dedicated to summer programs, but because the 21st CCLC program has been flat-funded since that time, the new law has yet to yield any increased funding for summer programs. Advocates in the state are currently working in support of legislation that would create dedicated funding set aside for summer programs within the current federal appropriation to the state (California Department of Education, 2015).

Florida Supplemental Academic Instruction. The state of Florida has a pool of funding designated for "supplemental academic instruction" awarded to each district based on enrollment. The first priority of the funding is an extra hour of reading instruction per day in the 300 lowest-performing elementary schools in the state. After this requirement has been met, "supplemental instruction may be provided to a student in any manner and at any time during or beyond the regular 180-day term identified by the school as being the most effective and efficient way to best help that student progress from grade to grade and to graduate." Districts such as Duval County use this funding to offer comprehensive summer programs. Supplemental Academic Instruction was funded at $664,162,705 (2015–2016). There is no tracking of whether and how those dollars are spent in the summer, but it represents a significant resource for districts (Florida Legislature, 2016).

Wyoming Bridges. Whereas Florida's supplemental state funding stream has an initial priority on extending the school day, Wyoming's Bridges program requires districts to provide comprehensive summer programs *before* they can request or use any funds for extending the school day.

Since 2004, Wyoming Bridges has prioritized about $1,000 in supplemental per-student funding for summer learning programs for academically at-risk students. Forty-seven of 48 districts participate in the K–12 program and measure their effectiveness through standard assessments. The program has narrowed the achievement gap in math and reading in most grade levels since 2008 and serves about 10% of students in each district. The program was appropriated $16.5 million in funding in 2014 and 2015 (Sommers, 2011).

Local Funding

Local funding is an important piece of the summer program supply landscape. Unsurprisingly, there is no systematic collection of local data on the supply of summer programs. What we know comes from a series of small studies done by the NSLA dating back to 2008. In total, we have assessed the supply of publicly funded summer programs in about a dozen cities (including school districts) and five additional district-only surveys. The methodology varied somewhat across cities, and because data was collected over the course of 7 years spanning different political and economic contexts, I will not attempt to make strong comparisons across the cities; instead, I will use my expertise to make some summary statements.

Generally speaking, we can say that local data tends to mirror the national participation rate of 33%. Most cities we studied had slots for roughly 25% of their students, though participation ranges from 19% to 76% in the cities we studied.

Primary operators include schools, parks and recreation, libraries, summer youth employment programs, and a variety of large and small nonprofits. There is no difference in availability based on gender and little data on availability by race. Smaller cities seem to have better per-capita availability of programs, but more research is needed to understand why some cities achieve a degree of scale and others don't.

Schools. School districts are the largest providers/funders of summer programs, typically serving between 5% and 15% of their students in the summer. During the 2 years of the American Recovery and Reinvestment Act and the resulting infusion of federal funding, some districts served as many as 40% to 50% of their students in the summer. From NSLA's data, we can look at schools as a proportion of total slots in the city: In Newark, schools accounted for 76% of the slots in the city; in Austin, 31%; Baltimore, 39%; and Portland, Maine, 14%. Clearly, the source of summer programs varies widely from city to city.

Districts blend and braid federal, state, and local dollars to offer summer programs, which are typically targeted to students who are behind on credits or standardized tests and may be voluntary or mandatory. As mentioned previously, it is not possible to track the amount of Title I spent on the summer in any systematic way, but we can get a picture by going district by district, as seen in Table 5.2. Title I is a major source in some districts and not used at all in others, such as San Francisco. Of the districts NSLA profiled in 2014, Oakland has the most diverse funding. Some districts, such as New York City and Pittsburgh, have a heavy reliance on private funding, which is difficult to sustain without ultimately an increased public contribution. NSLA has seen 3-year pilot programs in both Baltimore City and New York City disappear or struggle after the initial private investment, despite promising results.

Parks and Recreation. Municipal departments of parks and recreation are providers of free or affordable summer programs. Many local departments operate on a self-sustaining model, charging fees to families based on a sliding scale that helps to cover the cost of programs for low-income families. Unlike school programs, recreation programs are more likely to be 1 week in length, but families can enroll in multiple weeks per summer. Parks and recreation programs seem to account for roughly 10% to 12% of the slots in a city, on average: Austin, TX, 11% (3,300), Baltimore, MD, 10% (2,100), and across five California jurisdictions (Fresno, Los Angeles, Oakland, Sacramento, and Watsonville), an average 13%.

Table 5.2. Summer Learning Budget Data from Selected School Districts (2013 and 2014)

District (Number of Youth Served)	Oakland (5,023)	Pittsburgh (2,800)	New York City (1,780)	San Francisco (7,500)	Seattle (1,000)
City Funds	$1.6M	0	$2M	$2.2M	$200,000
Title I	$500,000	$400,000		0	$1.8M
21st Century	$100,000	0	0	$2M	0
Migrant Ed	$ 25,000	0	0	0	0
Private Philanthropy	$430,000	$3.1M	$2.9M	0	0
Total	$2.7M	$3.5M	$4.9M	$4.2M	$2M

Mayors' Summer Youth Employment Programs. While there is some funding for summer youth employment in the Workforce Opportunities and
Investment Act, the primary federal funding stream for summer jobs was
eliminated in 2008, leaving cities to take up much of the responsibility. Loss
of federal funding has contributed to a nearly 40% decline in youth employment over last 12 years and a gap of 3.6 million teen summer jobs. Perhaps
unsurprisingly, this decline has affected low-income and minority youth the
most. In 2013, White male teens in high-income families were five times
more likely to be employed than Black male teens in low-income families
(JPMorgan Chase & Co., 2015).

Summer jobs programs have been shown to reduce rates of arrest, incarceration, and mortality among participants, in addition to raising earnings
in the short and long term (Heller, 2014). Many mayors believe the programs pay for themselves in savings in property and violent crime, adjudica-
tion, and incarceration, and we are beginning to see an increased focus of
limited city funds on these programs.

In 2015, Boston Mayor Martin Walsh allocated an additional $270,000
to the summer jobs program for 200 new slots, taking the city to over
10,000 total slots. Per capita, Boston has one of the most robust summer
jobs programs in the country, bolstered by strong support from the private sector. After the unrest in Baltimore in April 2015, Mayor Stephanie
Rawlings-Blake committed to finding a summer job for all interested teens
and raised funds to add 3,000 new slots, taking the total number to 8,000,
in a city slightly larger than Boston.

Washington, DC has been a leader in summer jobs programs, but has
faced criticism for cost overruns and quality lapses over the years. In 2015,
Mayor Muriel Bowser expanded the program to include 22- to 24-year-olds
and raised the hourly wage for youth ages 16–21. The program was expected to serve 15,000 and cost just over $12 million.

There is room for the private sector to increase its stake in summer
youth employment as part of efforts to create a skilled workforce pipeline,
and this is likely the only way we will see these programs grow and improve
in quality. However, many employers express concern over capacity to su-
pervise youth who are not job ready.

Libraries. Libraries are a significant provider of summer learning programs, typically by way of drop-in or at-home summer reading programs,
though there is a coordinated effort by libraries across the country to move
to a model of more intentional summer learning programming. NSLA and
the Urban Libraries Council conducted a survey of libraries in 2015 to begin
to assess the landscape. The roughly 75 libraries responding to the survey
reported a total of 1.5 million youth participated in summer reading and
summer learning, with the majority of those (63%) in traditional summer
reading programs as compared to summer learning programs. Individual

responses ranged from 40 to 128,430 youth served in a single library system during the summer. Large library systems such as Chicago and Brooklyn, New York, regularly reach more than 100,000 students in the summer, but the average size is much smaller. The average reported budget for summer programming was $91,900; the median was $42,500.

Nonprofits. There is very little, if any, systematic data on the scope and scale of nonprofit operators of summer learning programs, but they are worth noting as a significant provider. Nonprofits range from large operators like YMCAs and Boys and Girls Clubs to very small faith-based and single-site community-based programs. Nonprofit funding varies widely and includes both public and private sources.

Sustainability of Local Efforts. It bears noting that sustainability of summer learning is a struggle for communities. With little to no dedicated funding and virtually no long-term commitments to fund summer programs, communities experience wide swings in the access to and quality of opportunities. Because funding is episodic and treated as a last-minute "nice to have" or leftover strategy in many communities, providers struggle to engage and retain the same students and families for multiple summers, which research suggests is important to maintaining the benefits of program participation. NSLA recommends that cities take the long view and dedicate funds to summer programs. Two cities serve as models: Oakland and Seattle.

The Oakland Fund for Children and Youth was established in 1996 when Oakland voters passed the Kids First! Initiative, an amendment to the City Charter, to support direct services to youth under 21 years of age. The measure was reauthorized in 2009 for an additional 12 years (2010–2022). This measure sets aside 3% of the City's unrestricted General Fund and requires a 3-year strategic plan to guide the allocation of funds. The fund will disburse $13.5 million total in 2016–2017, of which a little less than one-third will go to summer programs.

The Families and Education Levy is a property tax levy approved by Seattle voters in 2011, with funding awarded from school year 2012–2013 through 2018–2019. It is administered by the City's Office for Education—distinct from, but in collaboration with, the Seattle School District—and accountable to a community Levy Oversight Committee and the Seattle City Council. The Levy funded 16 summer programs at 25 sites for a total of $1,694,354 in 2015.

Private Funding for Summer Programs: Philanthropy

Finally, private philanthropy is a significant source of funding for summer programs. Philanthropy may come from local or national foundations or businesses. These dollars primarily fund program slots but can also fund evaluation and professional development. In the best cases, these dollars should fund enhancements and things that public funding cannot. For many districts using Title I or local general funds, private dollars fund field trips and other kinds of enrichment. Looking across the seven districts NSLA profiled in 2014, on average, 40% of district budgets came from private funds. Similarly, when we examine the nonprofit and school district programs that were finalists for NSLA's Excellence in Summer Learning Awards, the percentage of overall budgets coming from corporate sponsorships and philanthropy ranges from 0 to 90%, with an average of 35%. Several large, national foundations have made significant investments in summer learning, meals, and jobs in recent years, including the Wallace, Walmart, David and Lucile Packard, New York Life, and JP Morgan Chase foundations.

CONCLUSIONS AND RECOMMENDATIONS

A growing income gap and outdated notions of parental care have led to an opportunity gap that is preventing low-income children and youth from realizing their academic and life potential. Low-income families can't afford the going rate for summer programs, leaving young people hungry and regressing or treading water in their academic and social development and holding constant a tragic achievement gap. Unmet demand is high, and accordingly, so is support for public funding of summer programs. There are a variety of federal, state, and local programs with promising results and infrastructure, but currently, public funding for summer programs is inadequate and poorly tracked.

While it's clear just by examining the broad strokes of public funding that we can do better for low-income families, there are many opportunities to go deeper and collect better data that helps us to understand what I hypothesize to be significant racial equity issues in the supply and quality of summer learning programs for low-income youth. Private funding is critical but cannot be the backbone of supporting children and families for 3 months out of the year. Instead, it will require a continued steady drumbeat of public awareness and advocacy efforts to create systemic policy change and disrupt the harmful misconception that low-income children and families have different needs in June, July, and August than during the rest of the year.

The good news is, there is great momentum at all levels—the Obama Administration is seeding the ground with expanded budget proposals for summer meals and jobs programs; it will be up to Congress and the next administration to legislate those commitments. The U.S. Department of Health and Human Services launched the National Center for Afterschool and Summer Enrichment in 2015, a 5-year, $10 million effort to strengthen and expand child care programs. At the state level, NSLA tracked 40 bills with a focus on summer learning that were signed into law in 2015. Additionally, legislative task forces formed by several states continue to study and recommend ways to improve access and quality to expanded learning opportunities, including summer. At the local level, mayors are taking strong leadership on summer learning, dedicating new budget dollars, expanding summer jobs programs, and beginning to focus on citywide coordination and pooled resources.

POLICY CONSIDERATIONS

I will close with five key recommendations for continuing to strengthen summer learning policies at the federal, state, and local levels.

Incentivize Partnerships and Improve Partner Alignment. Partnerships between summer providers serving similar groups of students ensure complete access to a broader range of services and less duplication of efforts. These partners may include summer meals sites and sponsors, schools, community-based and faith-based organizations, libraries, museums, parks and recreation centers, youth employment sponsors, and other agencies, service providers, and organizations that touch the lives of youth during the summer.

Improve and Promote Flexibility of Resources. Many existing funding streams are utilized by summer service providers. Greater local flexibility of education funding under the Every Student Succeeds Act will increase these opportunities. Local communities that choose to focus on summertime as a strategy for youth support and engagement should have clearly defined access to these multiple sources of funding already targeted to youth, especially those who are struggling academically or are considered at risk.

Invest in Structural Supports and Systems. Key to coordinating and sustaining summer learning initiatives are the structures and systems behind them. These systems promote coordination of summer services with each other and with school-year programs that serve the same students, leading to greater efficiency and better outcomes for youth. These structures also create mechanisms for monitoring and maintaining quality of programs through evaluation and professional development.

Promote Sustainability. Funding for summer learning is much more nuanced than a dedicated grant program. Many existing funding streams can be applied to support summer learning either as they currently stand or with more explicit expansion into the summer months. Smart use of existing pools of funding and greater collaboration between youth-serving sectors can greatly increase impact during the summer.

Expand the Knowledge Base. The research community continues to explore effective strategies and best practices for many aspects of summer learning opportunities, including summer school, youth employment, nutrition programs, enrichment programs, and more. The field continues to explore significant questions around program quality, access to programs, and program outcomes, determining *best fit* approaches for different kinds of students and communities. Better data on how youth spend their summer will help inform equity implications of summer investments. This expanding knowledge base is critical to ensuring smart investments in activities that make a real difference in the lives of youth.

REFERENCES

Afterschool Alliance. (2015). America After 3PM. Washington, DC: Author. Retrieved from http://www.afterschoolalliance.org/AA3PM/

Bishop, N. (2013, July 15). What are extended school year services and who qualifies? [Web log]. *Special Education Guide*. Retrieved from www.specialeducationguide.com/blog/what-are-extended-school-year-services-and-who-qualifies

California Department of Education. (2015). *Background information, program objectives, and requirements for the After School Education and Safety Program*. Sacramento, CA: Author.

Cooperative Educational Service Agency No. 7. (1998). Extended school year (ESY) standards. Memo. Bar-Lev, Nissan, Director of Special Education. Chilton, WI: Department of Special Education.

Duncan, G. J., & Magnuson, K. (2011). Introduction: The American dream: Then and now. In G. J. Duncan & J. R. Murnane (Eds.), *Whither opportunity: Rising inequality, schools, and children's life chances* (pp. 3–23). New York, NY: Russell Sage Foundation.

Fitzsimons, C., Anderson, S., Hayes, C., & Burke, M. (2015). *Hunger doesn't take a vacation*. Washington, DC: Food Research & Action Center. Retrieved from http://frac.org/pdf/2015_summer_nutrition_report.pdf

Florida Legislature. (2016). Bill No. ss. 1011.60.

Heller, S. (2014). Summer jobs reduce violence among disadvantaged youth. *Science, (346)*6214, 1219–1223.

JPMorgan Chase & Co. (2015). *Building skills through summer jobs, lessons from the field*. New York, NY: Author.

Livingston, G. (2014). *Fewer than half of U.S. kids today live in a 'traditional' family*. Washngton, DC: Pew Research Center Retrieved from www.pewresearch.org/fact-tank/2014/12/22/less-than-half-of-u-s-kids-today-live-in-a-traditional-family

McCombs, J. S., Augustine, C., Schwartz, H., Bodilly, S., McInnis, B., Lichter, D., & Cross, A. B. (2012). Making summer count: How summer programs can boost children's learning. *Education Digest: Essential Readings Condensed for Quick Review, 77*(6), 47–52.

Office of Head Start Administration for Children and Families. 2015.

Samuels, C. (2015). NAEP Scores for students with disabilities show wide achievement gap [Web log]. *Education Week*. Retrieved from http://blogs.edweek.org/edweek/speced/2015/10/naep_scores_for_students_with.html

Schulman, K., & Blank, H. (2014). *Turning the corner. State child care assistance policies 2014*. Washington, DC: National Women's Law Center.

Shierholz, H., & Mishel, L. (2013). *A decade of flat wages, the key barrier to shared prosperity and a rising middle class* (Report No. 365). Washington, DC: Economic Policy Institute.

Skandera, H. (2014). *K-3 Plus education annual report for school year 2013–2014*. Santa Fe, NM: New Mexico Public Education Department.

Sommers, R. (2011). *Wyoming Bridges, a legislative grant program. Funding summer school and extended-day learning opportunities for K–12 students in Wyoming*. Cheyenne, WY: Wyoming Department of Education.

Suitts, S. (2015). *A new majority research bulletin: Low income students now a majority in the nation's public schools*. Atlanta, GA: Southern Education Foundation.

U.S. Department of Education, National Center for Education Statistics. (2015). *The condition of education 2015 (NCES 2015-144), public school expenditures*. Washington, DC: Author.

U.S. Department of Education. (2016). *Office of academic improvement, program description*. Washington, DC: Author.

U.S. Department of Health & Human Services. (2014). *Child care and development block grant act (CCDBG) of 2014: Plain language summary of statutory changes*. Washington, DC: Administration for Children & Families, Office of Child Care.

CHAPTER 6

A National Review of Summer School Policies and the Evidence Supporting Them

Geoffrey D. Borman, Alex Schmidt, and Michelle Hosp

Despite recent growth of summer school programs across the nation, knowledge of their characteristics and effectiveness is sparse. This chapter begins by reviewing state legislation regarding summer school programs, describes the nature of summer school programs in general, and, given their increasing importance in connection with statewide literacy campaigns, describes programs that are supported by state policies to serve as an alternative to retention for students who do not meet grade-level literacy standards. In addition to this overview of state-legislated summer programs, we review quasi-experimental and experimental evidence of the impacts of these policies on student achievement and discuss a range of mediating programmatic factors that may impact effectiveness estimates in significant ways. Finally, we review prior research on summer school interventions and best practices and assess how it aligns with current national policies.

The primary data for this review are from 16 states with existing summer school legislation. The policies, in general, lack explicit guidance, and few states have conducted state or local evaluations of the policies' impacts on student achievement. The review also reveals that the types of policies and practices mandated by the 16 states are not generally aligned with the prior research evidence regarding summer school best practices. Using descriptive information from state legislation, we summarize the targeted goals of these policy mandates and, using the evidence derived from our review of best practices, we conclude by formulating guidance for developing practical, research-based policy to promote effective summer school programs designed to achieve these goals.

Over the past decade, numerous states have attempted to address early literacy gaps by legislating programs that require reading assessments, interventions, and grade retention if students are unable to meet specific literacy standards (Rose & Schimke, 2012). These programs aim to ensure students are reading at grade level by the time they enter 4th grade, at which point reading becomes a much more essential aspect of the learning process in schools. Research supports the importance of this juncture, suggesting that students not reading proficiently by 3rd grade are less likely to graduate from high school (Hernandez, 2011).

One state to recently adopt a literacy-based retention policy was Iowa, which in 2012 passed Senate File 2284. The act requires students who do not meet specified literacy levels by the end of 3rd grade to be retained in grade or, alternatively, to successfully complete an intensive summer reading program, after which they may be promoted to the 4th grade (Iowa Code § 279.68). It also mandates the creation of the Iowa Reading Research Center, which among other tasks, is responsible for setting standards for the summer school programs created under the new law (Iowa Code § 256.9). The Iowa Reading Research Center works under the auspices of the Iowa Department of Education and is part of Iowa's efforts to support early literacy. As a part of that process, the Iowa Reading Research Center worked collaboratively with researchers at the University of Wisconsin-Madison to develop a set of evidence-based best practices specific to intensive summer reading programs, which are planned to be enacted as Iowa law beginning summer 2017. The programs are to be implemented according to the best practice criteria that were developed and are designed to help struggling readers reach grade-level reading proficiency. In this chapter, we explain our process for creating these best practices in the hope of providing guidance both to other states and practitioners considering summer school programming and to policymakers and researchers interested in creating research-based best practices for similar educational interventions.

We begin by reviewing state summer school legislation across the United States, showing that the legislation is inconsistent in its inclusion of summer school best practices, with many states' statutes providing no guidance for implementation. We then describe the six summer school best practices we decided on together with the Iowa Reading Research Center, the process by which the best practice criteria were created, and the level of research evidence supporting each best practice. We end with a discussion of the implications of this work for future summer school legislation and for those who are attempting to create best practices for educational programs.

BEST PRACTICES IN SUMMER SCHOOL LEGISLATION

According to an Education Commission of the States (ECS) report, as of 2014, 18 states and the District of Columbia had statutory laws that either required or suggested the use of summer schools to remediate 3rd-grade students not meeting state reading standards (Workman, 2014). However, our reading of the statutes reveals vast discrepancies among states in terms of both the number and specificity of the laws regarding summer school programs. To provide a clearer picture of the remedial summer school policy landscape, we consulted the statutes of the 18 states and the District of Columbia to determine which types of best practices, if any, state legislatures require. We considered six broad categories of best practices that are discussed further below: (1) research-based practices/programs, (2) teacher qualifications/training, (3) program duration, (4) class/instructional group size, (5) attendance requirements, and (6) program evaluation.

Table 6.1 shows the extent to which each of the states with remedial summer school legislation includes statutory language concerning best practices across the six general categories. Of the 18 states and the District of Columbia, the legislation of 12 makes reference to at least one of the six best practice categories. The most frequently included are provisions that summer school programs or interventions be "research-based," which nine states include in their legislation. In practice, the number of states that regularly use research-based practices in their summer programs is likely even higher due to the frequent reference to "research-based instruction" made in many states' remedial literacy laws, even if such specific requirements are not made of their remedial summer school programs.

Noticeably, only the District of Columbia includes summer school attendance requirements, mandating that students will not be evaluated for promotion after summer school if they had more than three unexcused absences (Code of the District of Columbia § 38–781.05). The absence of attendance requirements is surprising given that states often allow students to be promoted to the next grade after attending and completing a remedial program like summer school (Rose & Schimke, 2012).

Overall, and with the exception of a few states like South Carolina, Connecticut, and Oklahoma, these descriptive results demonstrate that statutory language concerning best practices is relatively sparse in remedial summer school legislation. In considering the implications of these results, it is important to remember that although many state statutes did not make reference to best practices within the six general categories, it is possible that state boards of education create their own rules and regulations to govern summer schools. For instance, the statutes of Iowa, Oklahoma, and Virginia require boards of education to develop regulations for the legislated summer school programs. As such, remedial summer school programs created in states with broad legislation may still operate under a set of best practice requirements decided on by the boards of education.

However, the lack of guidance in state statutes means that those responsible for implementing these programs, including state boards of education and school districts, are often left to their own devices when determining

Table 6.1. Best Practices Found in Remedial Summer School Legislation by State

	Research-Based Practices	Teacher Qualifications / Training	Duration	Small Classes/ Instructional Groups	Attendance Requirements	Program Evaluation
Arizona						
California	✓					
Colorado	✓					✓
Connecticut	✓	✓		✓		
Delaware						
D.C.					✓	
Florida						
Iowa†						
Minnesota	✓					✓
Mississippi			✓			
Missouri	✓	✓	✓			
North Carolina	✓	✓				
Ohio	✓	✓				✓
Oklahoma	✓	✓	†			†
South Carolina	✓	✓	✓			✓
Texas				✓		
Utah	✓					
Virginia			†			†
Washington	✓					✓

† Indicates the statutes require the board of education to design regulations for this area, or in the case of Iowa, to design summer school requirements in general.

how summer school programs will be developed and managed. Therefore, to aid state lawmakers designing evidence-based summer school policy and practitioners tasked with carrying out policies that lack sufficient direction, we next present the six best practices for summer school implementation that we created in partnership with the Iowa Reading Research Center and the Iowa Department of Education.

DEVELOPING SUMMER SCHOOL BEST PRACTICES

To create a set of best practices when implementing an intensive summer reading program, we began by compiling nine recent summer school reviews from the academic literature (including meta-analyses) and from policy and advocacy groups. Our goal was to determine the practices that are associated with positive remedial reading outcomes and recommended by the authors of the reviews as summer school best practices. Few reviews specifically focused on remedial summer school reading programs, and we were forced to rely on a variety of reports, including those that evaluate general out-of-school-time programs (e.g., after-school programs). In the case where a report clearly indicated a certain practice was not related to students' remedial reading outcomes in summer school (e.g., a practice related to social development outcomes or outcomes in after-school programs), we did not include that practice in our final compilation of best practices.

After making note of the summer school best practices supported/recommended in each review, we combined similar practices into more general categories. For instance, some literature supports the importance of teaching quality to summer school outcomes, while other literature recommends training teachers in proper remediation techniques in order to increase teaching quality. We combined these two concepts into the criterion, "Hire skilled, experienced teachers and/or provide training." We removed practices that were not well defined in the reviewed reports and that would not fit within other categories (e.g., have a "clear mission"). The resulting list of summer intensive literacy program best practices and the supporting literature is shown in Table 6.2.

We examined more closely this set of best practices recommended by the academic and policy literature with a goal of deriving a more manageable core set of practices that is truly evidence based and that could be practically advanced at scale by statewide legislation and guidance. Some best practices suggested by the literature, such as "hire parents, community members, and/or college students as staff," may be desirable but are difficult or impossible to require of every public school and school system across the state.

In other cases, we found that several best practices supported or targeted a broader goal. For instance, encouraging parental involvement/meeting the needs of parents and offering enrichment activities and innovative teaching

Table 6.2. Best Practices for Intensive Summer Reading Programs as Suggested by the Academic and Policy Literature

	Academic Literature			Policy Literature					
	(1)	(2)	(3)	(4)	(5)	(6)	(7)	(8)	(9)
Begin planning early	✓			✓					✓
Hire skilled, experienced teachers and/or provide training				✓	✓	✓	✓	✓	✓
Hire parents, community members, and/or college students as staff						✓			✓
Promote enrollment and attendance				✓	✓				
Create safe and orderly environments	✓						✓		
Adopt research-based methods					✓			✓	
Limit class sizes and/or provide individualized or small-group instruction		✓	✓	✓		✓	✓	✓	✓
Coordinate with schools, including curriculum alignment				✓	✓	✓		✓	✓
Offer enrichment activities and innovative teaching				✓	✓	✓		✓	✓
Partner with CBOs, other school districts, and/or colleges				✓		✓		✓	✓
Foster strong student-teacher relationships			✓			✓	✓		✓
Encourage parental involvement and/or meet the needs of parents (e.g., meals, transportation)			✓	✓		✓		✓	✓
Set an appropriate duration*		✓	✓	✓	✓				
Allow for local program control			✓						
Evaluate the program			✓	✓	✓	✓	✓		

Notes: (1) McCombs et al. (2014); (2) Lauer et al. (2006); (3) Cooper, Charlton, Valentine, Muhlenbruck, & Borman (2000); (4) McCombs, Augustine, & Schwartz (2011); (5) Smink & Deich (2010); (6) Beckett et al. (2009); (7) Bodilly & Beckett (2005); (8) Terzian, Moore, & Hamilton (2009); (9) Wilmer & Gunther (2006). *Lauer et al. (2006) find the optimal duration to be between 44 and 84 hours, while Cooper et al. (2000) find the optimal duration to be between 50 and 120 hours.

target different aspects of summer programming, but both ultimately aim to more effectively keep students and parents engaged in the summer program and to maintain commitment to and attendance at the program. As such, both of these best practices might be suggested as practical guidance for achieving the ultimate goal suggested by the best practice, "promote enrollment and attendance." In situations such as this, we chose to advance the ultimate goal of promoting attendance as a best practice.

Based on the research literature, these various practical considerations, dozens of meetings and discussions with Iowa policymakers and practitioners, and our own expert opinion, we took the 15 best practices listed in Table 6.2 and developed a set of six program criteria for intensive summer literacy programs in Iowa. These six criteria were further refined through multiple meetings that included vetting of the recommendations by various stakeholders across the state, including parents; state, district, and school leaders; teachers; community partners; policymakers; and attorneys representing the Iowa Department of Education. Ultimately, Iowa developed eight criteria that included the six (i.e., criteria 1 through 6, below) we proposed, with the addition of criterion 7, which defines how a student demonstrates completion of the summer reading program, and criterion 8, which relates to administrative oversight of the program and contains specific language pertaining to Iowa state licensure requirements and an option for schools and parents to utilize private program providers. Below we provide a list of all eight criteria used by Iowa and acknowledge that states will have additional considerations beyond our original six recommendations.

Criterion 1. Each district shall adopt instructional practices or programs that have demonstrated success and that include explicit and systematic instruction in foundational reading skills based on student need. To meet this criterion, each district must (1) adopt an instructional program from the Department's review of evidence-based early literacy interventions or (2) adopt instructional practices or programs that have been empirically shown to increase student literacy achievement.

Criterion 2. Each district shall employ skilled, high-quality instructors or provide instructors with required training, or do both. To meet this criterion, a district must hire instructors whose qualifications and training meet the requirements of the evidence-based intervention chosen. In the absence of specifications from the intervention chosen, a district must hire instructors who, at a minimum, hold a current Iowa teaching license with an endorsement in elementary education or in reading (K–8) or as a reading specialist.

Criterion 3. Each district shall allow sufficient time for intensive reading instruction and student learning. To meet this criterion, a district must implement at a minimum the total number of hours of instructional time described by the evidenced-based intervention chosen. In the absence of specifications from the intervention chosen, a district must provide a minimum of 70 hours of intensive reading instruction.

Criterion 4. Each district shall provide intensive instruction in small classes and small groups. To meet this criterion, a district must employ the same instructional grouping formats described in the evidence-based intervention chosen. In the absence of specifications from the intervention chosen, a district must ensure it delivers whole-class instruction in class sizes of 15 or fewer students and it delivers targeted intervention based on student need in small groups of 5 or fewer students. A district may elect to provide class and group sizes smaller than specified in this criterion.

Criterion 5. Each district shall monitor and promote student attendance. To meet this criterion, each district must adhere to an attendance policy that requires 85% attendance by each student.

Criterion 6. Each district shall evaluate student outcomes and program implementation. Evaluation of student outcomes includes attendance data and student achievement data. On a weekly basis, each district shall use the Department-approved literacy assessments used during the school year to evaluate student progress toward end-of-3rd-grade proficiency. Evaluation of program implementation shall align with the district's plan to address reading proficiency in its comprehensive school improvement plan. Program evaluation shall also include a measure of fidelity in implementing, at a minimum, the following requirements: instructor qualifications, amount of instructional time, grouping size, attendance data, and progress monitoring data.

Criterion 7. Each district shall identify whether each student successfully completes the program. Each student who successfully completes the program is eligible for promotion to grade 4. Each district shall provide to the parents or legal guardians of each student written notice about whether the student successfully completed the program. The notice shall include information about attendance, academic performance, additional or continuing areas of need, and whether the child is eligible for promotion. Successful completion shall be defined as meeting either of the following standards:

1. Consistent attainment of an end-of-3rd grade proficiency standard, or
2. Attendance of no less than 85% of the program's sessions.

Criterion 8. Each program shall be under the leadership and supervision of at least one teacher, as described in criterion 2, and at least one appropriately licensed administrator. The two roles may be filled by the same individual. Either the teacher or the administrator shall hold a reading (K–8) endorsement or a reading specialist endorsement. Leadership and supervision under this paragraph shall include monitoring the program for compliance with the program criteria.

Additional Option to Use Private Providers. A district may enter into an agreement with a private provider to provide intensive summer literacy instruction at the election of a parent and in lieu of programming provided by the district. Any election under this paragraph shall be at the parent's sole cost. The private provider shall use evidence-based instructional strategies. If a child successfully completes a private program as defined in criterion 7, the child shall be eligible for promotion to 4th grade.

Evaluating the Evidence for the Best Practice Criteria

While we relied on both policy and academic literature to create our original compilation of 15 summer school best practices, discussions among experts (i.e., expert opinion) and practical and legal considerations raised by Iowa stakeholders and attorneys guided the creation of the final six criteria. As such, as a final step, we sought to provide policymakers with a more rigorous and comprehensive examination of the evidence supporting each of our original six criteria.

Methods. To do so, we conducted a search of five databases for journal articles published over the last 10 years, 2005–2015, that evaluated summer school programs. We limited the search to peer-reviewed academic journals and also included search terms to restrict results to studies using only the most methodologically rigorous research designs (i.e., experimental and quasi-experimental studies). We designed our main search terms to produce studies of summer school programs for primary- and secondary-school students. This search yielded 82 articles.

Of the 82 articles, only those meeting the following conditions were included in our review: (1) served elementary and/or middle school students; (2) was based in the United States; and (3) was organized by or conducted in partnership with a school or a school district. We then acquired copies of the nine studies that met these inclusion conditions.

After collecting the above-mentioned studies, we read each to determine the quality of the study using the What Works Clearinghouse (WWC) evidence standards (U.S. Department of Education, 2013). We assigned studies to the three WWC categories: meets standards; meets standards with reservations; and does not meet standards.

Of the nine studies that satisfied the preliminary inclusion conditions, seven studies of five distinct summer programs met the WWC evidence standards. The five summer programs are Teach Baltimore (Borman, Benson, & Overman, 2005; Borman & Dowling, 2006), the Stars Program (Berlin, Dunning, & Dodge, 2011), a summer reading day camp in Los Angeles (Schacter & Jo, 2005), KindergARTen (Borman, Goetz, & Dowling, 2009), and a summer literacy intervention in the Pacific Northwest (Zvoch & Stevens, 2011, 2013). Given the small number of recent summer school program evaluations our search returned, we also located two additional sources of evidence to strengthen our ability to draw conclusions: (1) meta-analyses of summer and out-of-school-time programs (Cooper, Charlton, Valentine, Muhlenbruck, & Borman, 2000; Kidron & Lindsay, 2014; Lauer et al., 2006) and (2) relevant studies from the regular-school-year literature (e.g., related to the effects of class size on student achievement or examining how teacher qualifications and training impact student achievement).[1] These additional studies were selected based on our knowledge of the literature.

Next, we used a strategy adapted from Beckett et al. (2009) to define the academic impacts found in the previously mentioned five summer school programs. A study was categorized as demonstrating: (1) *positive impacts* if it reported statistically significant, positive impacts on at least one academic outcome; (2) *mixed impacts* if it reported statistically significant, positive impacts on at least one academic outcome using methods with weaker causal interpretations, such as complier average causal effects; and (3) *no academic impacts* if all academic outcomes were statistically nonsignificant or negative.

Finally, we read each study to determine which of the best practice criteria the five evaluated summer programs satisfied. For instance, since one criterion is to set the duration of a summer program to at least 70 hours, we noted the length of each of the five summer school programs.

After completing the above steps, we assigned evidence levels to each of the original six summer school best practice criteria, again adapting the strategies used by Beckett et al. (2009). Each criterion was assigned to a *strong, moderate,* or *low* evidence level based on the number of recently evaluated summer school programs that satisfied the criterion, the academic impacts of these programs, the strength of evidence supporting the academic impacts of the programs, and the generalizability of the evidence. In doing so, we also took into account evidence from the previously mentioned meta-analyses and regular-school-year studies. The operationalization of the evidence levels is shown in Table 6.3.

RESULTS

Below, we provide the evidence level for each of the summer school best practice criteria and a brief description of the supporting evidence.

Criterion 1

Select an evidence-based summer school intervention, and adopt its requirements for teacher qualifications/training (criterion 2), duration (criterion 3), and class/instructional-group size (criterion 4).

Table 6.3. Benchmarks for Determining the Evidence Level of Summer School Criteria

Evidence Level	Benchmarks
High	Generally, programs that meet this standard yield positive academic impacts, while programs that do not meet the standard yield mixed or no academic impacts. The results are also widely generalizable due to the use of national samples or the presence of multiple smaller studies of diverse populations.
Moderate	Generally, programs that meet this standard yield positive or mixed academic impacts, while programs that do not meet this standard yield no academic impacts. Criteria supported by strong evidence are assigned a moderate evidence level if the supporting studies have low generalizability.
Low	Generally, evidence from the summer school program studies does not meet the benchmarks for *strong* or *moderate* evidence, but meta-analyses or evidence from related topics (e.g., findings from regular-school-year programs) support the criteria.

Evidence Level—High. By implementing literacy programs suggested by the Iowa Department of Education's prior review of evidence-based early literacy interventions and complying with these programs' teacher qualification, duration, and class size requirements, the highest evidence level is achieved. Because these interventions have been previously vetted and assigned the highest evidence rating by the Iowa Department of Education, they, by definition, also receive the highest evidence rating with respect to the implementation of these criteria.[2]

Criterion 2

In the absence of specifications from the intervention chosen, a district must hire instructors who, at a minimum, hold a current Iowa teaching license with an endorsement in elementary education or in reading (K–8) or as a reading specialist.

Evidence Level—Low. Of the five recently evaluated summer school programs found in our literature search, all five used certified and/or trained instructors to teach the program, and therefore no studies offer a comparison between the impacts of summer programs with and without credentialed teachers. However, one meta-analysis provides some evidence that teacher credentials are associated with improved learning outcomes.

The meta-analysis by Kidron and Lindsay (2014) examined 30 experimental or quasi-experimental studies of increased learning time programs (including summer school) in order to determine the relationship between various program characteristics and academic outcomes. Relying on the 16 studies that described teacher certification, the authors found that the 10 programs using certified teachers had, on average, a positive impact on student literacy achievement, while they found no effects for the programs that did not use certified teachers.

Criterion 3

In the absence of specifications from the intervention chosen, a district must provide a minimum of 70 hours of intensive reading instruction.

Evidence Level—Low. All five of the summer school programs found in our search provided around 70 hours of instruction. Again, the lack of variation among programs in their durations makes it impossible for us to draw conclusions about the appropriate summer program length. Fortunately, two meta-analyses of out-of-school-time programs provide stronger evidence that an instructional duration of around 70 hours is most suitable for a summer program. Cooper et al. (2000) found the largest effect sizes on academic outcomes for remedial summer school programs that were between 60 and 120 hours in length, while Lauer et al. (2006) found out-of-school-time reading programs of between 44 and 84 hours in length had the largest effects on reading outcomes. Together, these estimates suggest an appropriate program duration of between 44 and 120 hours. The 70-hour criterion falls within this range.

Criterion 4

In the absence of specifications from the intervention chosen, a district must ensure it delivers whole-class instruction in class sizes of 15 or fewer students and delivers targeted intervention based on student need in small groups of 5 or fewer students.

Evidence Level—Low. The class sizes for all five of the recently evaluated summer school programs were around 15 students, with the largest class size being 20 students. However, in the latter intervention, reading practice was conducted in groups of three to five students (Zvoch & Stevens, 2013, p. 26). Although the lack of variability across the programs in class sizes prevents us from drawing conclusions based on these program evaluations, Cooper et al.'s (2000) study of summer school programs indicates larger effects for those remedial summer school programs that had less than 20 students per class.

Criterion 5

Each district must adhere to an attendance policy that requires 85% attendance by each student.

Evidence Level—Low. Only three of the five programs found in the literature search provided average attendance data, and the only program with student attendance that reached the 85% threshold, the Stars Program, did not report statistically significant academic impacts (Berlin et al., 2011). The Teach Baltimore program evaluations provide some evidence that attendance is associated with student achievement in summer programs. Both evaluations of the program found no program effects in the main analyses, in part due to the low attendance rates. However, after taking attendance rates into account, the authors found that (1) short-term achievement gains were dependent on the number of weeks students attended the program (Borman et al., 2005) and (2) students who attended the program at an above-average rate for at least two summers experienced long-term reading gains (Borman & Dowling, 2006).

Criterion 6

Each district shall evaluate student outcomes and program implementation.

Evidence Level—Low. With the exception of the Los Angeles summer reading camp studied by Schacter and Jo (2005), the remaining four summer school programs each provided evidence that implementation data were collected. With little variation on this programmatic input, few legitimate comparisons can be made across programs that do and do not collect data and evaluate outcomes. Instead, evidence supporting this criterion is found in a meta-analysis of summer school programs that suggests larger academic impacts for those programs that report monitoring implementation fidelity (Cooper et al., 2000). Additionally, a recent large-scale randomized controlled trial, over the regular school year, across over 500 schools suggests that frequent evaluation of student outcomes, through the use of quarterly benchmark assessments, along with the training of teachers and school leaders in methods of data-driven instruction, had positive impacts on students' end-of-year state test scores (Carlson, Borman, & Robinson, 2011).

CONCLUSIONS

Though a growing number of states have recently legislated summer school as a remedial technique for improving student outcomes, there is little consistency in terms of including summer school best practices in their statutes, and when they do include best practice criteria, the criteria lack specificity. Initially, we considered modeling the Iowa legislation after legislation from other states with existing summer school policies. However, we found little existing legislation that would merit replication. To address this gap between the research on summer school best practices and legislated policy, we reviewed the literature on summer school implementation to create a set of six best practices for the implementation of remedial summer school programs in Iowa. Based on this work, Iowa can be viewed as a model for how to develop and provide criteria for an intensive summer program that will lead to positive outcomes for students. We hope that the suggested best practices will be useful to policymakers in other states aiming to craft legislation for effective summer schools, to departments of education that are creating rules and regulations for summer schools, and to school districts and private providers establishing their own summer school programs. Although our ultimate aim was to generate this set of best practices, we also believe that the process itself provided us with valuable insight that will be beneficial to others who hope to establish evidence-based best practices for implementing similar educational interventions.

IMPLICATIONS FOR DEVELOPING BEST PRACTICE LEGISLATION IN EDUCATION

As can be discerned from our process of developing summer school best practices, creating policy-relevant evidence-based criteria for the implementation of any program is not always straightforward. One issue we faced was the overabundance of possible best practices found within the academic literature and summer school policy area. In reading nine reviews from academic and policy sources, we found 15 possible best practices suggested by the literature. Some of these were quite specific (e.g., provide individualized or small-group instruction), while others were vague enough to raise questions as to their policy relevance (e.g., foster strong student-teacher relationships). Reducing the list was necessary to make it feasible for policymakers to craft a coherent set of criteria that provides sufficient guidance yet also allows for adjustment to local district contexts and needs.

The process we followed, therefore, and which we also suggest for others who seek to create a manageable set of evidence-based best practices, is to create a comprehensive list of best practices found in the policy and academic literature and then to narrow the list using various methods, such as discussions among policymakers and experts in related fields of research.

An alternative option is to consult the academic literature to determine the level of evidence supporting each practice. However, in doing so, policymakers, practitioners, and researchers are likely to face the same problem we confronted—namely, that there is a limited level of rigorous evidence to be found in the academic literature. The reasons for this are numerous. One is that experimental studies of summer school programs are rare. As such, experimental evaluations found in the literature typically involve basic testing of an intervention group against a control group. While these studies provide evidence of the effectiveness of a complete intervention package, they do not allow potentially important individual program components to be tested in context, such as class size or program duration. We found no experimental studies that systematically manipulated such program features as the size of instructional groups, the number of days or weeks of summer programming, or summer school teachers' credentials or training, to evaluate the efficacy of these discrete components. Given that the field has accumulated sound evidence that summer school programs, in general, do indeed appear to benefit students' academic outcomes, we must now begin to turn to more nuanced questions, including the particular summer school characteristics that are most important for producing success.

A more immediate solution to the lack of experimental evaluations of program characteristics is the method we adopted in this study. That is, comparing the characteristics and outcomes of numerous interventions in an attempt to locate patterns of positive association. However, as we show, it can be difficult to draw strong conclusions using this method, especially when there are a small number of program evaluations from which to choose and these programs are isomorphic in their characteristics.

However, using multiple sources of data makes it possible to draw conclusions through triangulation. In this study, we did so by consulting three different sources of evidence: (1) experimental evaluations of summer school programs, (2) meta-analyses and reviews of summer school impacts, and (3) studies from regular-school-year programs. Other forms of evidence that could be considered are interviews with practitioners or case studies. Although internal validity is a concern when using any of these types of studies independently, finding consistent evidence supporting a certain best practice or program characteristic across multiple studies of varying methodologies can provide stronger evidence than any one form of evidence could provide in isolation from the others.

An additional solution available to policymakers and practitioners when they determine that evidence supporting intervention best practices is weak or inconsistent is to simply mandate the use of specific replicable programs that have been found to be effective, as is reflected in the first best practice criterion. While the research may not show which individual program characteristics are most important for success, a rigorous experimental study can show whether an intervention, delivered as a complete package, is effective. Policymakers, therefore, do not need to concern themselves with defining the required length, class sizes, or teacher qualifications for an intervention. Instead, they can simply require districts to adopt an intervention (and the intervention's recommended duration, instructional group size, and teacher qualifications) from a set of programs that are supported by rigorous research as defined by, for instance, the What Works Clearinghouse or another trusted source. The Iowa Department of Education has made great strides in this area by reviewing primary studies of reading interventions and providing this information on their website for schools to use.

Another lesson for the creation of legislated best practices in education is that the best practices, and hence the legislation, cannot possibly account for every situation that may arise when implementing an educational intervention. As such, it may be helpful to create additional guidance and suggested solutions for effective implementation, which forecast and address possible contingencies. For instance, one concern we addressed in Iowa was a potential inability to hire enough summer school teachers who meet the qualification requirements specified by criterion 2. Reviewing the summer school literature reveals similar problems in past summer school programs, as well as potential solutions, like hiring early in the school year since teachers make summer plans in advance (McCombs et al., 2011, p. 61) and negotiating with teacher unions to ensure summer hiring decisions can be based on teacher characteristics apart from seniority (Augustine, McCombs, Schwartz, & Zakaras, 2013). By speaking to policy practitioners and soliciting feedback prior to the implementation of best practice regulations, policymakers can be better prepared to ensure that all possible concerns are sufficiently addressed and best practice compliance is high.

Readers should also remember that our process for developing the criteria for implementing intensive summer reading programs included a variety of stakeholders. Leadership from the Iowa Reading Research Center and the Iowa Department of Education provided other important perspectives, beyond our own, on the Iowa policy climate and the research on summer school both within and outside of the state. Educators, policymakers, parents, and community members also were involved in many hours of discussions concerning the development of the criteria and provided key voices in creating practical and actionable criteria. Finally, the attorneys working on behalf of the Iowa Department of Education took our original drafts of best practice recommendations and transformed them into clear legislative language, which left little ambiguity. At this stage, they also incorporated additional criteria necessary for the state of Iowa related to defining completion of the summer reading program and licensure requirements for staff.

The involvement of these multiple stakeholders and the representation of varying research-based, practical, and legal perspectives was essential to the development of the criteria for best practices referenced in this chapter. Through this inclusive and participatory process, we are hopeful that we have produced sound criteria for implementing effective summer school programs that meet the needs of struggling readers across the state and can act as a guide for other states crafting requirements for summer reading programs.

NOTES

1. Due to space limitations, in this summary we only reference one study from the regular-school-year literature (Carlson, Borman, & Robinson, 2011).

2. The methodology employed and the reviewed list of literacy interventions may be found at: www.educateiowa.gov/sites/files/ed/documents/Early%20Literacy%20Interventions%20Reviewed%20List.pdf

REFERENCES

Augustine, C. H., McCombs, J. S., Schwartz, H. L., & Zakaras, L. (2013). *Getting to work on summer learning: Recommended practices for success*. Santa Monica, CA: Rand.

Beckett, M., Borman, G., Capizzano, J., Parsley, D., Ross, S., Schirm, A., & Taylor, J. (2009). *Structuring out-of-school time to improve academic achievement: A practice guide (NCEE# 2009-012)*. Washington, DC: U.S. Department of Education, Institute of Education Sciences. National Center for Education Evaluation and Regional Assistance.

Berlin, L. J., Dunning, R. D., & Dodge, K. A. (2011). Enhancing the transition to kindergarten: A randomized trial to test the efficacy of the "Stars" summer kindergarten orientation program. *Early Childhood Research Quarterly, 26*(2), 247–254.

Borman, G. D., Benson, J., & Overman, L. T. (2005). Families, schools, and summer learning. *Elementary School Journal, 106*(2), 131–150.

Borman, G. D., & Dowling, N. M. (2006). Longitudinal achievement effects of multiyear summer school: Evidence from the teach Baltimore randomized field trial. *Educational Evaluation & Policy Analysis, 28*(1), 25–48.

Borman, G. D., Goetz, M. E., & Dowling, N. M. (2009). Halting the summer achievement slide: A randomized field trial of the KindergARTen Summer Camp. *Journal of Education for Students Placed at Risk, 14*(2), 133–147.

Carlson, D., Borman, G. D., & Robinson, M. (2011). A multistate district-level cluster randomized trial of the impact of data-driven reform on reading and mathematics achievement. *Educational Evaluation and Policy Analysis, 33*(3), 378–398.

Code of the District of Columbia § 38–781.05.

Cooper, H., Charlton, K., Valentine, J. C., Muhlenbruck, L., & Borman, G. D. (2000). Making the most of summer school: A meta-analytic and narrative review. *Monographs of the Society for Research in Child Development, 65*(1), i–127.

Hernandez, D. J. (2011). *Double jeopardy: How third-grade reading skills and poverty influence high school graduation*. Baltimore, MD: Annie E. Casey Foundation.

Iowa Code § 256.9.

Iowa Code § 279.68.

Kidron, Y., & Lindsay, J. (2014). The effects of increased learning time on student academic and nonacademic outcomes: Findings from a meta-analytic review (REL 2014–015). Washington, DC: U.S. Department of Education, Institute of

Education Sciences, National Center for Education Evaluation and Regional Assistance, Regional Educational Laboratory Appalachia.

Lauer, P. A., Akiba, M., Wilkerson, S. B., Apthorp, H. S., Snow, D., & Martin-Glenn, M. L. (2006). Out-of-school-time programs: A meta-analysis of effects for at-risk students. *Review of Educational Research, 76*(2), 275–313.

McCombs, J. S., Augustine, C. H., & Schwartz, H. L. (2011). *Making summer count: How summer programs can boost children's learning.* Santa Monica, CA: Rand.

Rose, S., & Schimke, K. (2012). *Third grade literacy policies: identification, intervention, retention.* Denver, CO: Education Commission of the States.

Schacter, J., & Jo, B. (2005). Learning when school is not in session: A reading summer day-camp intervention to improve the achievement of exiting first-grade students who are economically disadvantaged. *Journal of Research in Reading, 28*(2), 158–169.

U.S. Department of Education, Institute of Education Sciences. (2013). *What works clearinghouse: Procedures and standards handbook* (Version 3.0). Retrieved from http://whatworks.ed.gov

Workman, E. (2014). *Third grade reading policies.* Denver, CO: Education Commission of the States.

Zvoch, K., & Stevens, J. J. (2011). Summer school and summer learning: An examination of the short- and longer term changes in student literacy. *Early Education & Development, 22*(4), 649–675.

Zvoch, K., & Stevens, J. J. (2013). Summer school effects in a randomized field trial. *Early Childhood Research Quarterly, 28*(1), 24–32.

DRIVERS OF DIFFERENTIAL SUMMER LEARNING: FAMILY ADVANTAGE AND FAMILY DISADVANTAGE

CHAPTER 7

The Sunny Home Advantage

Class Differences in Resources to Support Summer Learning

Aaron M. Pallas

A substantial body of research has documented the role of summers in widening the academic achievement gap between economically disadvantaged children and their more-advantaged peers. This chapter takes a broad view of the advantages associated with social class position, treating it not only as a feature of the nuclear family but also as an indicator of the presence or absence of a broad array of neighborhood and school resources that might support children's learning and development. Understanding class advantages as both cultural and structural sharpens our understanding of how to design effective interventions.

Social class is one of the more vexing terms in the public vocabulary. Everyone has a social class position; Those who are at the top want to maintain their standing, and those who are lower wish to move up. The American ideology of meritocracy asserts that individuals wind up where they deserve to be: Regardless of where one starts, those who capitalize on their talents and work hard will move up (Hochschild & Scovronik, 2003; Johnson, 2006). Social mobility—usually conceived of as upward movement from a lower starting position to a higher destination, either within an individual's life course or across successive generations within a family—is viewed as the American dream.

Most people, if asked, will say they are middle class (Hout, 2008; Sosnaud, Brady, & Frenk, 2013). Perhaps Americans like thinking they are in the middle, neither too high nor too low. Politicians frequently appeal to the middle class, knowing that the ambiguities of social class position allow almost everyone to believe that "middle-class tax cuts" will apply to them, regardless of the details of a specific policy proposal. But beyond the ways in which people choose to identify their social class position, class has profound influences on the life chances of individuals, operating through a dense configuration of structural advantages and constraints.

In this chapter, I examine the basis of the social class positions held by the parents of school-age children. I suggest that a family's social class position is associated with access to resources that can support or hinder the learning and development of children. Although many of these resources are equally available during the school year and the summer, some things change when school is not in session. This phenomenon was labeled *faucet theory* by Entwisle, Alexander, and Olson (1997), a term intended to explain the well-known phenomenon of parallel gains in academic growth during the school year for middle-class and working-class children, coupled with continued, if slower, gains for the middle class and a plateauing or decline for working-class children, during the summer months.

During the school year, Entwisle, Alexander, and Olson (1997) contended, the flow of resources from the school faucet was very powerful, so much so that family background had surprisingly little consequence for fall-to-spring gains in measured academic achievement. In the summer, however, with the school resource faucet turned off, the resources associated with social class position become more salient. Middle-class families are able to draw on an array of compensatory resources that might support summer learning, whereas working-class and poor families have fewer resources to compensate for the loss of schooling. The fact that during the summer, relevant resources are more available to advantaged families than those who are not as well-off suggests a set of policy strategies to reduce inequalities of access in the hopes of minimizing the role of social class in producing and reproducing inequalities in summer learning.

CONCEPTUALIZING SOCIAL CLASS

Social class is at once an attribute of an individual (and, by extension, his or her family) and of a collectivity. For individuals, the key markers of social class position are educational attainment (i.e., the quantity and quality of one's schooling, typically indexed by educational credentials), occupational attainment (i.e., the job that one holds and its features, if one is in the labor force and working), income, and wealth. Each of these attributes varies across individuals, and they often "hang together," as those with more formal schooling hold more prestigious jobs that pay better than the jobs held by those with less schooling, and those with more prestigious jobs and higher salaries are able to accumulate wealth more rapidly than those with lower-status jobs, over and above the wealth that may be inherited from one's parents (Conley, 1999; Piketty & Tucman, 2015; Shapiro, 2005). Too, because individuals tend to marry others with similar levels of educational attainment (Schwartz & Mare, 2012), having attended the same or nearby schools (Nielsen & Svarer, 2009), there is a concentration of class advantages and disadvantages within families and households.

But class membership also identifies individuals as members of a group who have interests that may differ from those in other class categories. Wright (2008) argues that social classes are defined in relation to one another, in the sense that a capitalist class that employs others to produce surplus value for its members would not exist in the absence of a working class that sells its labor to those who hold the keys to the production of valuable goods and services. He refers to this dynamic as "the relationship of people to income-generating resources or assets of various sorts" (p. 331). Moreover, members of a class who are networked to one another may work together through organizations to maintain their advantages. This is the mechanism described by Tilly (1999) as *opportunity hoarding*, in which those with control over scarce and valuable resources create rules and policies that exclude those in other groups from access to those resources.

There is, for example, a great deal of residential segregation in American society. Those with economic means live in different neighborhoods and communities than those with less wealth, and the residences of people of color are segregated from those of the (increasingly dwindling) white majority. Cities differ from suburbs, and the basic public services and amenities in different neighborhoods also are distributed inequitably. This is especially true for the quality of local public schools; although federal programs such as Title I are intended to make school spending more equitable, the fact that approximately 90% of public school revenues are from state and local sources (Snyder, 2014) limits the capacity of the federal government to intervene. Moreover, the fact that many states continue to rely on local property tax revenues as a policy basis for school district funding, or allow wealthier districts to spend well beyond an "adequate" funding threshold set by the state (Rebell, 2012), perpetuates class-based inequalities through the mechanism of opportunity hoarding.

Neighborhoods and communities segregated by social class also differ in the quality of the public services they provide to their residents—the social and economic safety nets that enable people to feel secure about the quality and quantity of food, housing, medical care, and safety available to them. As I note later, some of these public services—or at least working-class and poor families' access to them—are less available in the summer than during the school year. In this sense, faucets of resources beyond exposure to the equalizing effects of formal schooling also may be switched off (or at least dwindle to a trickle) during the summer.

There are thoughtful yet contentious debates about whether classes exist independent of a broad socioeconomic gradient (e.g., Kingston, 2000), and if so, how many classes there are in a given society and how they should be labeled (Weeden & Grusky, 2012). Regardless of the details, it is understood that as an individual attribute that locates individuals in a social and economic structure, social class has pervasive effects on the experiences and life chances of individuals and their families, both direct and indirect. Here, I focus my attention on two claims: social class is associated with family child-rearing practices, and social class influences in which neighborhoods and communities families reside.

Social Class Differences in Child-Rearing

Why are there class differences in child-rearing orientations and practices? There is no definitive answer, but some analysts have pointed to the conditions of work as a central factor. Middle- and upper-class jobs differ from the jobs held by the working class and the poor in many ways beyond the economic rewards associated with each. The routines and statuses associated with jobs—which are a central part of adult life (Erikson & Vallas, 1990)—can have powerful socializing effects on their incumbents, shaping what they value and believe and how they act.

This is a central theme in the work of sociologist Melvin Kohn (1969/1977; 1983), who has argued that middle-class jobs, via their substantive complexity, lack of close supervision, and nonroutine activity, foster the value of self-direction, which in turn leads to middle-class parents valuing self-direction in their children. Conversely, working-class jobs, featuring the close regulation of routine activity, reward and reinforce the value of conformity to external authorities, propelling working-class parents to value conformity in their children. In sum, people come to value what is rewarded in their environments and to apply those values in their own households.

Writing in the same era, economists Samuel Bowles and Herbert Gintis (1975) offered a similar analysis of the material conditions of middle-class and working-class jobs. They too recognized that working-class jobs were marked by a clear hierarchy in which workers were under the direct authority of supervisors who closely regulated the work assigned to them and that the work itself was tedious, fragmented, often boring, and not intrinsically meaningful. Instead, those in working-class jobs were motivated by external rewards, in the form of wages, rather than the psychic gratification of engaging in interesting and challenging work performed at a realistic pace. Middle-class jobs, in contrast, offer more opportunities for self-supervision and control over the work process, complex and challenging nonroutine work tasks that are intrinsically rewarding and satisfying, and greater opportunity to assume positions that involve authority over other workers.

To be sure, these are patterns conditioned by technological change and workplace organization, and not absolute or essential. More problematic, perhaps, is the evidence that the intergenerational transmission of values may be weak or inconsistent. Parents often hold different values than their children, for reasons that are not due solely to the conflict of generations or societal trends towards different values (Gronhoj & Thogersen, 2009; Kohn, 1983; Min, Silverstein, & Lendon, 2012; Schonpflug, 2001). The weak linkage between parents' values and those of their children undermines some of the explanatory power of within-family cultural processes for social class effects on child outcomes.

Sociologist Annette Lareau has offered one of the most sophisticated accounts of the role that social class plays in how parents support their children's learning. In her earliest treatment of the topic, *Home Advantage* (2000), she contrasted the involvement of middle-class and working-class parents in their children's elementary school. It was clear that middle-class parents were more involved, and in different ways, than were working-class parents, but the explanation remained a mystery. Lareau contrasted three different explanations for the difference. First, she considered the possibility that middle-class parents were more involved in their children's schooling than working-class parents because they placed a higher value on getting a good education than did working-class parents. Second, she examined whether schools treated middle-class and working-class parents differently, expecting and demanding more involvement from middle-class parents than from working-class parents. Finally, she explored the hypothesis that the differing levels of involvement stemmed from the differing stocks of cultural capital available to middle-class and working-class parents.

Lareau rejected the values explanation, showing that in her sample of parents, the working-class parents felt that education was highly important to their children's futures. These parents wanted their children to succeed in school and were upset when they received low grades or were faced with the prospect of being retained in grade. Middle-class parents also wanted their children to succeed, and thus social class position was not associated with a different value placed on education. Critics of Lareau's argument pointed out that what counted as success varied substantially across social class categories: Whereas working-class parents often want their children to graduate from high school and to go further in school than they themselves did, middle-class parents set their sights higher. What counts as self-actualization is taking place on a different playing field for the middle class than for the working class (Pallas, 2008).

Lareau also rejected the second explanation, institutional discrimination against working-class parents, noting that the teachers at the middle-class school made similar requests of parents as did the teachers at the working-class school. They used similar modes of communication and were just as persistent in inviting working-class parents to attend school events as they were for middle-class parents. In fact, Lareau argued, the teachers at the working-class school were more zealous in seeking to engage parents in learning activities at home than were the teachers at the middle-class school. Of course, this is mainly because the middle-class parents were already reading to their children, monitoring their homework, and keeping tabs on what they were learning.

She also found that although the conversations with middle-class parents were more "at ease" than those with working-class parents, teachers did not typically form closer personal relationships with the middle-class parents than working-class parents, recognizing that their politeness and ease of conversation were reflections of their class advantage. Middle-class parents could turn on teachers if they felt that their children's interests were not being served, and casual social ties buffered the fallout.

What is perhaps missing from Lareau's account of the institutional discrimination hypothesis is the very real differences that exist across social class lines in the expectations that teachers and schools have for children's activities outside of the school day. Schools serving middle-class children clearly have different homework expectations than schools serving working-class children. It's difficult to say that teachers in working-class schools have the same expectations for parent involvement in learning at home as teachers in middle-class schools when the expectations for children's activities at home are so different.

The third hypothesis offered by Lareau to explain social class differences in parent involvement in their children's schooling is that class provides cultural resources that lead to a different quantity and quality of parent involvement. These cultural resources, which Lareau refers to as cultural capital, led to a fundamental opposition: Middle-class parents' relations with the school were characterized by interconnectedness, whereas working-class parents' relations reflected separation.

These class-based differences in family–school linkages are rooted in the cultural and material nature of social class. Middle-class parents, by virtue of their more successful educational careers, and comfort in traveling in social circles populated by professionals, feel a sense of competence and ease regarding the school and the teachers. They perceive teachers as equals and see the family and the school working together to advance the learning and development of their children. If they see something going wrong—an inappropriate special education placement or a teacher losing a student's homework—they have no compunctions about intervening at the school on their children's behalf. Middle-class parents also capitalize on their informal ties to other middle-class families and community members, socializing with educators and learning valuable information about the local schools and teachers.

In contrast, working-class and poor parents typically have had unhappy school careers, and the school may be a place to be shunned. Because they do not feel a sense of competence about education and the teaching of particular school subjects, they defer to the expertise of teachers and other professionals. They may, of course, challenge the school on matters of discipline—what mother doesn't think she knows her own child's moral character?—but rarely on matters pertaining to the learning of school subjects. There is a strong sense of separation between family and school within working-class families, with working-class parents viewing their job as getting their children to the school clothed and fed, after which it is the school's responsibility to do its part in teaching children the subjects that are the manifest curriculum of the school.

Material resources matter too, and it is for this reason that I prefer to refer to parental *behaviors* rather than parental *investments* in their children. Economists cast parent behaviors in a human capital framework, in which parents consider the costs and potential payoffs of various investments in their children, such as the purchase of a home that guarantees access to a high-quality school, or the purchase of after-school tutoring, or private lessons. Perhaps unintentionally, this perspective assumes that everyone recognizes what counts as a "good" investment and has the resources to choose among alternatives. But when poor families fail to purchase homes in expensive neighborhoods, a common strategy for having a child attend a "good" school, it is not that they choose not to do so in favor of some other alternative. Rather, the cost is prohibitive.

In her subsequent work, Lareau (2011) expanded her purview to consider not just parental involvement in schooling but rather a broader array of child-rearing practices that were associated with the social class position of parents. Lareau also sought to understand the implications of race for family life but concluded that among the families she studied, class differences within White families and Black families were substantial, whereas White and Black families on the same rung of the social class hierarchy had similar child-rearing practices. That is not to say that race didn't matter, nor that parents and children were not acutely aware of racial inequality in daily life. Lareau's argument was specifically about what she referred to as the cultural logic of child-rearing.

This cultural logic, she contended, was inscribed in two dominant patterns, one associated with families with economic and social advantages and the other with families with fewer economic and social resources. The former she termed *concerted cultivation*, and the latter *the accomplishment of natural growth*.

Concerted cultivation, typically observed among middle-class families, involves a purposive effort by parents to manage the development of children's talents and interests. The term *cultivation*, which we associate with agriculture, connotes conscious attention to growth—care and feeding of the growing organism and optimizing the environment by providing appropriate nutrients and removing threats. For children, concerted cultivation is observed in the ways that parents structure leisure activities, shuttling them to enrichment activities such as music lessons and sport competitions that teach technical and interpersonal skills that may pay off later as children move through school. The strategy results in middle-class children being exposed to more nonroutine or novel social environments than working-class and poor children (Phillips, 2011). Concerted cultivation also involves intervening on behalf of one's children when they interact with social institutions such as schools or the medical system and teaching children the skills to be able to act on their own behalf.

A crucial part of concerted cultivation consists of linguistic patterns in the home. Conversations between parents and children are characterized by reasoning and discussion, and it is common for children to challenge their parents and to resolve disagreements through negotiation. Words are more than weapons; they are tools for learning how to represent one's interests and achieve one's goals. The volume and variety of words used in family conversation is clearly linked to social class (Hart & Risley, 1995).

Children exposed to concerted cultivation develop a worldview in which they are active participants in the world, able to use the cultural and material resources available to them to overcome obstacles and get ahead. Lareau describes this way of thinking and being in the world as an emerging sense of entitlement that positions middle-class children to vault ahead of their peers by manipulating the social institutions that make up the modern world.

The contrasting logic of child-rearing, the accomplishment of natural growth, has very different features. This logic, observed mainly among working-class and poor families, does not involve the intensive management of children's lives associated with concerted cultivation. Rather, the accomplishment of natural growth is indeed "natural"—that is, an organic process of development not sullied by parental intervention. Working-class and poor parents care just as much about their children as do middle-class parents, Lareau argues, but they are happy to see them develop without activities organized and led by adults. If the child of concerted cultivation is being driven by his father to play in a league soccer match across town, the child of the accomplishment of natural growth is playing tag in the backyard with the children who live next door.

Discourse in households embracing the accomplishment of natural growth also is distinctive, as parents provide directives that children are expected to follow without questioning or negotiating. Whereas the negotiating that might take place in a concerted cultivation household places parents and children on the same plane and reduces the power and authority inequalities between parent and child, children in natural-growth households are denied the opportunity to challenge their parents when they see their interests at stake. Household discourse, rather than being a site for rehearsing how to negotiate with the social institutions encountered outside of the home, simply reinforces the view that children are the passive targets of the interests of those more powerful than them—well-meaning interests, in the case of household adults.

The social institutions of society, however—the education system, medical system, criminal justice and legal systems, the economy, and the government, to name but a few—are mainly staffed by and for the middle class and more advantaged members of society. The rituals and routines by which they operate work most smoothly for middle-class clients who know the rules of the game, and who have the cultural and economic resources that enable them to navigate these systems. Mismatches often do not end well. A child misses a deadline for applying for financial aid for college because no one in the extended family has ever gone to college and can advise on how to complete the forms. A parent is uncomfortable about talking to a doctor about her child, and the doctor fails to elicit information important to making a correct diagnosis. A job applicant feels ill at ease and doesn't make eye contact with or shake the hand of his interviewer and doesn't get the entry-level job, even though he is qualified (Rios, 2012).

An ongoing stream of unsatisfactory interactions further separates poor children and their families from middle-class institutions and instills a belief that those institutions aren't for people like them. There is an ongoing discomfort, to be contrasted with the ease with which the economically advantaged navigate these institutions. Whereas concerted cultivation generates an emerging sense of entitlement among middle-class children and youth, the child-rearing logic of the accomplishment of natural growth instills an emerging sense of constraint in working-class children. This world of middle-class institutions is uncomfortable and doesn't seem to be organized to help people like them to get ahead. It's one frustrating obstacle after another.

Part of what Lareau seeks to understand is the role of the family in the intergenerational transmission of inequality. Whether one views the glass as half-empty or half-full, a nontrivial fraction of individuals in the United States wind up in the same socioeconomic stratum as adults as did their parents, with the economically advantaged more likely to maintain their advantages and those born into poverty considerably more likely to remain on the lower rungs of the social hierarchy. Educational attainment helps to explain both this stability and departures from it, as how far one goes through school, and the quality of that schooling, both contribute to the kinds of jobs that individuals hold and the rewards associated with those jobs. On average, individuals who expect to go farther through school do so, but many more young people aspire and expect to graduate from college with a 4-year degree than actually will do so.

Where do these expectations come from? Lareau posits that the two cultural logics of child-rearing she describes—concerted cultivation, which is characteristic of middle-class and upper-class families, and the accomplishment of natural growth, found most frequently in working-class and poor families—instill an emerging sense of entitlement in middle-class and upperclass children and an emerging sense of constraint among working-class and poor children and youth. These ways of viewing the world—specifying which social roles and behaviors are appropriate for people like them, and which are inconceivable, and not meant for them—point individuals toward differing destinations.

French sociologist Pierre Bourdieu referred to such a worldview as a *habitus*, a set of habits and ways of seeing the world that are forged through experience and operate at a subconscious level to propel people to act across a range of social settings in ways that reproduce the logic of those formative experiences. As individuals experience new environments, their *habitus* may change in response, but minor tweaking is much more common than a fundamental reorganization of how one sees the world. Seeking to change the worldviews of working-class and poor children without addressing the material circumstances of their families and communities that shape those views seems like a fool's errand.

Social Class and Seasonal Differences in Child-Rearing

As I've suggested so far, social class has pervasive effects on family life and school achievement. But are class differences in values, orientations, and family practices a constant over the year, or do they vary by season? In particular, are there class-based differences in parenting practices that differ between the school year and the summer? Chin and Phillips (2004) raise this possibility in their study of child care and other activities during the summer vacation period between the end of one school year and the start of the next. The absence of the structure provided by mandatory schooling, they argue, allows for a clear-eyed examination of class differences in child-rearing values and practices.

Contrasting the summer activities of a sample of poor and working-class 4th graders and of middle-class 4th graders attending the same elementary school, they took account of family vacations, camp experiences, and lessons and other organized activities. There were indeed large differences in how working-class and middle-class children spent their summers, with evidence that children played an active role in constructing their summer experiences, articulating their preferences, and, at times, resisting those of their parents.

This "child capital"—variations among children in their talents and temperament—did not explain the class differences in summer activity patterns. Nor were these differences primarily due to class-linked differences in parents' commitments to supporting their children's development of their talents and interests. Rather, Chin and Phillips (2004) argued, the key class difference accounting for the ways in which middle-class children's summers diverged from those of working-class and poor children was economic advantage. Middle-class families had more dollars to devote to stimulating summer activities and had more discretionary time available for parents and children to spend time together. They also had greater knowledge of which activities might enrich their children's learning and how to subsidize these activities via scholarships and discounts.

Chin and Phillips concluded that class differences in the cultural logic of child-rearing were probably smaller than those reported by Lareau (and also probably larger than they observed in their study). Rather, according to them most of the action lay in the material and cultural advantages associated with class position, a theme certainly not ignored by Lareau but often positioned behind class cultures as an explanatory mechanism.

More recently, Boulay (2015) explicitly contrasted child-rearing practices during the summer and the school year for a sample of middle-class and working-class parents of 2nd-grade students. Drawing on the work of Lareau and Chin and Phillips, he sought to understand if parenting practices changed with the seasons, and if so, why.

They did, in both expected and unexpected ways. Middle-class and working-class families alike experienced the summers as a discontinuity, with some easily adjusting to the change and others struggling to manage the shift in schedules and activities. For some poor and working-class families, the summer evoked a heightened sense of stress for parents and children. Often, the closing of school was accompanied by the closing of school-based programs that provided structure and supervision of children, especially those with special needs. Parents with limited economic resources were challenged to manage their children without the supports of programs staffed by adults. This was particularly acute if the household lived in a neighborhood lacking a safe place for children to play outside (cf. Rhodes & DeLuca, 2014).

In contrast, some middle-class families saw the summer as a welcome respite from the structure of the school year, affording families the opportunity to take a break from the highly pressurized schedule of organized activities in which their children participated. Few middle-class families actually took the summer "off," however; rather, they shifted the organized activities to more leisurely paced family vacations and summer camps. And, in contrast to the neighborhoods inhabited by the working-class and poor families, the more affluent families lived in newer or renovated neighborhoods that were "child-friendly," with sidewalks, playgrounds, and lower speed limits. These neighborhoods posed fewer threats to the well-being of children, and middle-class parents were comfortable allowing their children to play outside.

Other forms of discontinuity that Boulay observed involved bedtime and screen time. The school year provides a regular routine, with predictable bedtimes (and, in turn, predictable times to wake up and get ready for school). Across both working-class and middle-class families, the enforcement of bedtime routines and timetables was relaxed in the summer months, with less monitoring of bedtimes and a reduction in routines associated with student learning, such as bedtime reading with the child's parent or on one's own. The maintenance of bedtime and waking routines was most common when it was dictated by a parent's work schedule.

Screen time was a frequent source of conflict in both middle-class and working-class households, with children almost invariably seeking to expand the amount of exposure to television, PlayStations, computers, cellphones, and other electronic devices with screens. Some devices have educational programming that can enable children to practice skills or learn new ones, but those applications typically hold little interest for children. And in a zero-sum world, time spent absorbed with an electronic device is time not spent reading or interacting directly with others in the household and neighborhood. As was true for bedtime routines, children's use of electronic devices was less regulated in the summer than during the school year, both with regard to the quantity of screen time and the content appearing on the screen.

There were continuities as well as discontinuities, though, including what Boulay labeled "carry-over effects." For example, parents may take their cues about expectations for homework during the summer from teachers' homework assignments during the school year. Summer "homework" here does not mean teacher-assigned tasks that students perform at home to reinforce or advance what a child has learned in school during that day or week but rather a broader approach by parents to have their children practice school-based skills, such as reading or math skills, during the summer. Whereas middle-class and working-class parents alike were less likely to engage their children in math practice than literacy practice during the summer, middle-class parents did expect their children to participate in academically oriented learning activities much more so than did working-class and poor parents. This paralleled the social class difference in homework assignments during the school year, as the teachers in middle-class schools assigned substantially more homework than did those in the schools attended by working-class and poor children.

In a sense, then, the shift from the school year to the summer Boulay (2015) described amplified the consequences of the child-rearing logics of concerted cultivation and the accomplishment of natural growth. Along with the faucet for school resources, the faucets for neighborhood and school resources flowed at a different rate during the summer, in ways that middle-class families could adjust to much more easily than those families of lesser economic means. Although many features of children's lives were less regulated during the summer, middle-class families continued to provide customized—and costly—experiences for their children, many of which could yield academic benefits. Conversely, working-class and poor children frequently were left even more to their own devices—especially devices with screens.

Social Class and Neighborhood Residence

Neighborhoods, for their part, vary in a number of ways that are relevant to children's learning and development, and a family's social class position is strongly linked to the features of the neighborhood in which it resides. More affluent families can choose where to live, and few choose to live amidst the poor. Conversely, families of limited economic means often have few choices and thus are rarely found in middle-class neighborhoods with expensive housing markets.

Urban scholars have paid particular attention to neighborhoods that have a cluster of structural attributes representing potential barriers to academic and social success. The term *concentrated disadvantage*, for example, typically refers to neighborhoods with high rates of poverty, welfare receipt, and unemployment, a high rate of female-headed households, and a high density of children (Sampson, Sharkey, & Raudenbush, 2008). As these neighborhood features tend to cluster together, the neighborhood poverty rate may serve as a proxy for this more complex pattern, and by definition, most of the residents in such neighborhoods are in the lower social class strata.

The Chicago School of Urban Sociology theorized that the structural features of neighborhoods, including the attributes described above, are associated with their social features, contrasting what they referred to as social organization and social disorganization. The level of community social organization, represented by the density and strength of the social ties among the members of that community, shapes the ability of the community to govern itself and ward off threats to its well-being. The presence of such social ties propels individuals in the community to conform to agreed-upon standards of conduct and goals, a process known as *social control*. Sampson (2012) offers the example of neighborhood residents who know one another collaborating to keep an eye on a stranger who might potentially victimize a neighborhood member.

Social control and victimization are central themes here, as neighborhoods with concentrated disadvantage and limited social organization also have high rates of criminal behavior, and especially high rates of violence. Direct or indirect exposure to violence is a nonroutine breach of daily life that may disrupt normal psychological, and even physical, functioning, compromising healthy personal relationships, the expression of positive emotions, and basic cognitive processes. Because not everyone who is exposed to violence suffers these consequences, exposure to violence is best characterized as a potentially traumatic event (Bonanno & Mancini, 2008).

Exposure to concentrated disadvantage may reduce academic achievement, although there is not as strong an evidence base for this claim as we might wish to have and the mechanisms by which this occurs are not yet understood. Sampson et al. (2008) argue that there is a lagged effect of concentrated disadvantage on the standardized test performance of African American children in Chicago neighborhoods, suggesting that in violent neighborhoods, parents "turn inward" to protect their families, reducing their exposure to social support networks and organizations and restricting children's exposure to a rich vocabulary of public expression.

More direct evidence of the effect of exposure to violence on children's school performance is found in the work of Patrick Sharkey and Julia

Burdick-Will, both of whom have studied Chicago schoolchildren, and Jondou Chase Chen, who has conducted similar analyses in New York City. Sharkey (2010) showed that there is a brief window during which exposure to a homicide in a child's neighborhood depresses scores on standardized tests of reading performance. The longer the time elapsed between exposure and the testing date, the weaker the effect, which is observed for African American children but not for those of Hispanic origin. Sharkey is unable to assess the longer-term consequences of this measure of reduced cognitive functioning, and if performance "bounces back" relatively quickly, it may not be that consequential in the long run. Conversely, he argues that for some African American children living in the most violent of Chicago's neighborhoods, the rate of exposure to homicides may impair cognitive functioning for about one-quarter of the school year.

Whereas concentrated disadvantage and high rates of violence are observed primarily in central cities, it would be worrisome if the entire evidence base hinged on the city of Chicago, as extrapolating to other locales would hinge on many untested or untestable assumptions. It is thus reassuring, though perhaps disappointing, that the linkage between exposure to violence and student achievement is also observed in Chen's (2013) study of elementary and middle school students enrolled in New York City public schools between 2006 and 2010. Net of neighborhood poverty and a host of student attributes, both prior police-reported felony violence rates surrounding a school and felony violence in the current school year affect students' performance on standardized state assessments in English Language Arts and mathematics. Performance drops were larger for mathematics than English and larger too for middle school students than elementary school students.

Although school choice plans have the capacity to weaken the extent to which children attend neighborhood schools, most children in the United States do attend schools in their neighborhoods. For children in neighborhoods displaying concentrated disadvantage, this typically entails attending a school that is "failing" on any number of metrics: student achievement, retention of qualified teachers and principals, and school disorder. How much of the neighborhood effect on student outcomes is mediated by school features remains an active area of research.

Burdick-Will (2013), for example, examined violent crime within Chicago public high schools, showing that the incidence of violent crimes within a school was associated with lower scores on standardized tests, but was not correlated significantly with students' grades. Violent crimes, she concluded, were more stressful and disruptive to the classroom as a learning environment than were nonviolent crimes, and the presence of either type of crime in a given school year had little bearing on overall assessments of a school's safety or climate. Because the incidence of violent crimes within a school is not highly correlated with the crime level in the neighborhood surrounding the school, these associations are not easily interpreted as neighborhood effects on student test performance.

Social Class and Seasonal Differences in Neighborhood Effects

Even if we heed Entwisle's (2007) admonition to avoid "trickle-down" theories of how neighborhoods affect their passive residents, the dangers posed by neighborhoods characterized by concentrated disadvantage are consequential. These dangers, and the opportunities to accumulate resources to support children's learning and development, may differ by season. Neighborhood rhythms—the patterns of threats and organizational and social supports embedded within neighborhoods—are seasonal, with summers offering greater dangers and fewer supports than the remainder of the year.

An overly individualistic account of how parents and children respond to neighborhood stressors such as exposure to violence might describe some of them as "resilient"—that is, able to maintain an even psychological keel in the face of such stressors due to individual temperament (American Psychological Association, 2014). Most people *are* resilient, in the sense that they return to a state of equilibrium relatively soon after exposure to a potentially traumatic event (Bonanno & Mancini, 2008). But this pattern may hinge as much on the organizational and social supports in the community as on intra-individual differences.

This point is made forcefully by Small (2009), who studied the ways in which child-care centers in New York City could serve as unexpected sources of social capital that could pay off for mothers and their children. Small suggests that organizations can serve as brokers that connect individuals to other individuals, or to other organizations, thereby connecting them to the resources at the disposal of those other individuals and organizations. A new tie between two individuals can yield all of the customary features of social capital: access to new and useful information, someone who can be trusted to act on an individual's behalf, and a sense of reciprocal obligation.

Organizations can serve as brokers of social capital either by design or unintentionally. But some organizational rituals and routines are more likely to create opportunities for garnering social capital than others. Small points especially to organizational routines that place individuals in regular and sustained interactions with one another, with a minimum of competition and a shared set of goals or objectives, especially those that pertain to organizational survival. When people routinely work together on tasks that are intended to promote a common good, the stage is set for the creation of both strong and weak social ties that can yield benefits in the form of new information and social support.

In the context of the child-care center, fund-raisers, field trips, and holiday celebrations are examples of organizational events that bring parents together to cooperate to get things done that benefit the organization overall, and not just their individual children. These settings go beyond the more episodic daily opportunities to run into other parents while dropping off or picking up one's child. Some child-care centers also rely on rules and expectations regarding "checking in," which routinizes engagement with the center and other parents and facilitates trust among parents and a repertoire of shared obligations that support parents as they pursue multiple agendas, some far-removed from the daycare center itself.

Not all parents send their children to child-care centers, of course, and not all communities provide ready access. One of the most important implications of Small's research is that the configuration of a web of nonprofit service providers in a community conditions the availability of social capital generated by organizational brokers and that communities differ dramatically in the density of these organizations. Even though there may be a higher density of nonprofit organizations in neighborhoods of concentrated disadvantage than in more affluent neighborhoods, the residents of high-poverty neighborhoods need these services much more so than do families residing in more-advantaged neighborhoods. For economic reasons, working-class and poor families may be tied to their local neighborhoods, and the specific mix of organizations located in or near those neighborhoods. Middle-class families, on the other hand, may be able to travel further distances to access organizations and in any event are less dependent on public or nonprofit services.

There are two ways in which seasonal differences figure into this story. One is the possibility that the availability of nonprofit service providers in high-poverty neighborhoods might vary by season. This is especially likely for services that are in some way keyed to the school year, such as after-school and other extended-time programs. Turning off the faucet of such services during the summer will be much more consequential for the learning and development of poor children than middle-class children, who are less reliant on such services; the market for private services is arguably is not tethered to the school-year calendar.

Second, within neighborhoods with concentrated disadvantage and especially those with high levels of violence, parents may wish to keep their children off the streets during the summer, holding them close to home and regulating their behavior more vigorously than is necessary during the structure of the school year. This may have the unplanned consequence of limiting parents' and children's exposure to community-based social support networks that might buffer children from the adverse effects of exposure to violence. This is *not* a matter of individual temperament; rather, it reflects how a family engages with community resources that can offer support after exposure to a potentially traumatic event.

Much of what we know about urban poverty, Small suggests, is based on sociological studies of the south side of Chicago, which suffered from generations of political neglect and thus lacks many of the social service organizations and community "amenities" found in other poverty-stricken communities around the country. For historical reasons, the nonprofit sector in Harlem and other parts of New York City is much stronger, providing many more opportunities for poor families to accumulate resources that can advance children's educational opportunities, even in the face of neighborhoods marred by high rates of unemployment, crime, and physical neglect. I have offered some hypotheses about seasonal differences in the availability and utilization of these resources in high-poverty communities, but there is a need to document whether these differences exist across high-poverty neighborhoods in different cities.

CONCLUSION

In this chapter, I have suggested that social class has powerful effects on the academic achievement of children, operating through families and communities that vary in their stock of cultural and material resources to support learning. For the most part, these influences are not seasonal, though we have learned that parenting logics may vary between the school year and the summer and that the institutions and organizations that can help support children's learning and development may be more or less available during the summer months. In light of these findings, what can social policy do?

First and foremost, effective policies and programs depend on an accurate diagnosis of the social problem they are intended to address and on a compelling theory of action specifying how the elements of the program or policy will change the behavior of the targets of the program. An important part of this is incorporating the voices and interests of those who are the targets of these program—often, poor parents and children and the street-level service providers who interact with them.

An example is Shedd's (2015) study of low-income adolescents in Chicago. She observed that school choice—the decoupling of dangerous or "bad" neighborhoods from schools—can have the unintended consequence of forcing youth to cross segregated and unequal neighborhoods that vary according to social class, racial/ethnic makeup, and gang affiliations. The youth she observed and interviewed explained how traveling to school through such neighborhoods honed their sense of justice and injustice and shaped the futures they envisioned and sought for themselves. Urban policies that criminalize the behavior of adolescents may be especially problematic when policing, surveillance, and punishment differ across neighborhoods. Thus, engaging stakeholders about proposed policies and programs before these policies and programs are implemented may yield insights into whether these strategies are likely to have the desired consequences.

More generally, however, it seems likely that the best policy strategy is capacity-building: Helping families and communities to enhance their capacity to thrive via the expansion of public and private sector social welfare organizations that can assist families and neighborhoods to support the learning and development of children during the summer. Shutting off some faucets during the summer can be offset by the presence of others that operate year-round.

REFERENCES

American Psychological Association. (2014). *The road to resilience.* Washington, DC: Author.

Bonanno, G., & Mancini, A. (2008). The human capacity to thrive in the face of potential trauma. *Pediatrics, 121*(2), 369–375.

Boulay, M. (2015). *Parental attitudes, expectations and practices during the school year and summer* (Unpublished doctoral dissertation). Columbia University.

Bowles, S., & Gintis, H. (1975). *Schooling in capitalist America: Educational reform and the contradictions of economic life.* New York, NY: Basic Books.

Burdick-Will, J. (2013). School, violent crime, and academic achievement in Chicago. *Sociology of Education, 86*(4), 343–361.

Chen, J. C. (2013). *No crime left behind: Exposure to neighborhood violence and school performance in New York City* (Unpublished doctoral dissertation). Columbia University.

Chin, T., & Phillips, M. (2004). Social reproduction and child-rearing practices: Social class, children's agency and the summer activity gap. *Sociology of Education, 77*(3), 185–210.

Conley, D. (1999). *Being black, living in the red: Race, wealth, and social policy in America.* Berkeley: University of California Press.

Entwisle, B. J. (2007). Putting people into place. *Demography, 44*(4), 687–703.

Entwisle, D. R., Alexander, K. L., & Olson, L. (1997). *Children, schools, and inequality.* Boulder, CO: Westview Press.

Erikson, K., & Vallas, S. (Eds.). (1990). *The nature of work: Sociological perspectives.* New Haven, CT: Yale University Press.

Gronhoj, A., & Thogersen, J. (2009). Like father, like son? Intergenerational transmission of values, attitudes and behaviours in the environmental domain. *Journal of Environmental Psychology, 29*(4), 414–421.

Hart, B., & Risley, T. R. (1995). *Meaningful differences in the everyday experiences of young American children.* Baltimore, MD: Brookes.

Hochschild, J., & Scovronick, N. B. (2003). *The American dream and the public schools.* New York, NY: Oxford University Press.

Hout, M. (2008). How class works: Objective and subjective aspects of class since the 1970s. In A. Lareau & D. Conley (Eds.), *Social class: How does it work?* (pp. 25–64). New York, NY: Russell Sage Foundation.

Johnson, H. B. (2006). *The American dream and the power of wealth: Choosing schools and inheriting inequality in the land of opportunity.* New York, NY: Routledge.

Kingston, P. W. (2000). *The classless society.* Stanford, CA: Stanford University Press.

Kohn, M. L. (1969/1977). *Class and conformity: A study in values—with a reassessment.* Chicago, IL: University of Chicago Press.

Kohn, M. L. (1983). On the transmission of values in the family: A preliminary formulation. In A. C. Kerckhoff (Ed.), *Research in sociology of education and socialization* (vol. 4, pp. 3–12). Greenwich, CT: JAI.

Lareau, A. (2000). *Home advantage: Social class and parental intervention in elementary education.* New York, NY: Rowman & Littlefield.

Lareau, A. (2011). *Unequal childhoods: Class, race, and family life* (2nd ed.). Los Angeles: University of California Press.

Min, J., Silverstein, M., & Lendon, J. P. (2012). Intergenerational transmission of values over the family life course. *Advances in Life Course Research, 17*(3), 112–120.

Nielsen, H. S., & Svarer, M. (2009). Educational homogamy: How much is opportunities? *Journal of Human Resources, 44*(4), 1066–1086.

Pallas, A. M. (2008). The American dream and the power of wealth [Review of the book *The American dream and the power of wealth: Choosing schools and inheriting inequality in the land of opportunity,* by H. B. Johnson]. *Sociological Forum, 23*(3), 633–639.

Phillips, M. (2011). Parenting, time use, and disparities in academic outcomes. In G. J. Duncan & R. J. Murnane (Eds.), *Whither opportunity? Rising inequality, schools, and children's life chances* (pp. 207–228). New York, NY: Russell Sage Foundation.

Piketty, T., & Tucman, G. (2015). Wealth and inheritance in the long run. In A. Atkinson & F. Bourguignon (Eds.), *Handbook of income distribution* (vol. 2B, pp. 1304–1368). Amsterdam, The Netherlands: North-Holland.

Rebell, M. (2012). The right to comprehensive educational opportunity. *Harvard Civil Rights-Civil Liberties Law Review, 47*(1), 47–117.

Rhodes, A., & DeLuca, S. (2014). Residential mobility and school choice among poor families. In A. Lareau & K. Goyette (Eds.), *Choosing homes, choosing schools* (pp. 137–166). New York, NY: Russell Sage Foundation.

Rios, V. M. (2012). Stealing a bag of potato chips and other crimes of resistance. *Contexts, 11*(2), 48–53.

Sampson, R. J. (2012). Neighborhood inequality, violence, and the social infrastructure of the American city. In W. F. Tate, IV (Ed.), *Research on schools, neighborhoods, and communities: Toward civic responsibility* (pp. 11–28). Lanham, MD: Rowman & Littlefield.

Sampson, R. J., Sharkey, P., & Raudenbush, S. (2008). Durable effects of concentrated disadvantage on verbal ability among African-American children. *Proceedings of the National Academy of Sciences, 105*(3), 845–852.

Schonpflug, U. (2001). Intergenerational transmission of values: The role of transmission belts. *Journal of Cross-Cultural Psychology, 32*(2), 174–185.

Schwartz, C. R., & Mare, R. D. (2012). The proximate determinants of educational homogamy: The effects of first marriage, marital dissolution, remarriage, and educational upgrading. *Demography, 49*(2), 629–650.

Shapiro, T. M. (2005). *The hidden cost of being African American: How wealth perpetuates inequality.* New York, NY: Oxford University Press.

Sharkey, P. (2010). The acute effect of local homicides on children's cognitive performance. *Proceedings of the National Academy of Sciences, 107*(26), 11733–11738.

Shedd, C. (2015). *Unequal city: Race, schools, and perceptions of injustice.* New York, NY: Russell Sage Foundation.

Small, M. L. (2009). *Unanticipated gains: Origins of network inequality in everyday life*. New York, NY: Oxford University Press.

Snyder, T. (2014). *Digest of education statistics, 2014*. Washington, DC: National Center for Education Statistics, Institute of Educational Sciences, U.S. Department of Education.

Sosnaud, B., Brady, D., & Frenk, S. M. (2013). Class in name only: Subjective class identity, objective class position, and vote choice in American presidential elections. *Social Problems, 60*(1), 81–99.

Tilly, C. (1999). *Durable inequality*. Berkeley: University of California Press.

Weeden, K. A., & Grusky, D. B. (2012). The three worlds of inequality. *American Journal of Sociology, 117*(6), 1723–1785.

Wright, E. O. (2008). Logic of class analysis. In A. Lareau & D. Conley (Eds.), *Social class: How does it work?* (pp. 329–349). New York, NY: Russell Sage Foundation.

CHAPTER 8

Learning Outside of School

The Implications of Shadow Education for Seasonal Learning Patterns

Joseph J. Merry, Claudia Buchmann, and Dennis J. Condron

Private tutoring, after-school programs, cram schools, test prep, and commercial learning centers are becoming more common across diverse nations. These varying practices, commonly referred to as "shadow education" or "supplemental education," represent a largely uncoordinated and hidden sector of national education systems. Services range in their scope, mission, target audience, funding, setting, and intensity, but they all constitute academic-oriented lessons that occur outside of formal schooling. In light of the summer learning research suggesting that socioeconomic inequalities grow faster when school is out of session versus in session, the question becomes, how might the increasing prevalence of shadow education affect this pattern?

In this chapter, we first define the characteristics of shadow education and then survey its expansion, paying particular attention to the U.S. context. We then develop an argument for the ways in which the growth of supplemental education services may promote unequal learning opportunities across social lines. In particular, we stress the relevance of this trend for seasonal learning disparities along the lines of socioeconomic status. On one hand, targeted and subsidized supplemental programs may combat "summer setback" for disadvantaged students. On the other hand, however, the availability of such services, especially those for profit, may exacerbate socioeconomic learning inequalities by providing a greater range of market-based resources for advantaged families.

In this chapter we offer insight on the intersection of two growing bodies of literature. First, we consider the importance of research on *shadow education,* a term generally understood as referring to structured, academic instruction taking place outside of regular school hours. To do so, we draw on international evidence to situate patterns of shadow education participation in a broader context before then directing our discussion to focus primarily on these patterns in the United States. Second, we propose a framework for integrating shadow education research into the ongoing dialogue about summer learning and summer learning loss. We summarize the implications of shadow education practices for seasonal learning disparities and discuss the role that such educational services might play in either exacerbating or ameliorating socioeconomic achievement gaps. Our discussion brings to light important implications for policy, practice, and future research.

SHADOW EDUCATION

The definition of shadow education has evolved as researchers continue to understand more comprehensively the variety of educational services offered beyond the boundaries of formal schooling. One of the earliest definitions of the term describes shadow education as "learning activities for the clientele of the formal school which take place outside the regular school instruction program for a fee or as a community service" (Marimuthu et al., 1991, p. 5). Since this time, various researchers have conceptualized shadow education (or particular elements thereof) specifically as "private supplementary tutoring"[1] (Bray & Kobakhidze, 2014, p. 590), "educational activities that occur outside formal schooling and are designed to enhance the student's formal school career" (Stevenson & Baker, 1992, p. 1639), and "academic-oriented instruction that does not lead to formally recognized educational credits or credentials" (Aurini, Davies, & Dierkes, 2013, p. xv).

In these views, researchers agree that this type of learning occurs beyond, outside, or in addition to formal schooling. The fact that shadow education is supplementary, therefore, is the most consistent element across a broad range of research. In fact, the supplementary nature explains the use of the word "shadow"—these practices effectively shadow the learning that occurs during formal school hours, and in many cases these practices (especially private tutoring services) operate "in the shadows," hidden from scrutiny. Beyond this point of consensus lies substantial variation in the arrangement of shadow education practices. For instance, shadow education can vary by setting (school, home, commercial learning center, cram school), instruction style (group or individual), intensity (hours), purpose (remedial vs. enrichment), and curriculum.

In a broad review of the literature, Park, Buchmann, Choi, and Merry (in press) include shadow education and other conceptualizations of supplementary education practices under the common theme of "student participation in *academically-oriented* learning activities outside of formal schools."

The authors argue that these activities constitute a "third institution" for student learning (the two more familiar and more often researched institutions being family and formal schooling). In this chapter, we adopt this broad conceptualization of shadow education as an array of supplemental learning activities constituting a third institution for student learning.

Cross-national research reveals substantial variation in how shadow education is practiced in different settings. Indeed, Bray et al. (2013) note that the demand and character of these educational activities are "historically situated" phenomena, often shaped by local patterns, political transitions, and forces of globalization. For example, cram schools (typically for-profit institutions meant to boost student performance for high-stakes examinations) are most highly attended in East Asian countries such as Japan (where these settings are referred to as *juku*) and South Korea (*hagwon*) (Park et al., in press). Meanwhile, Buchmann, Condron, and Roscigno (2010) argue that SAT prep courses in the United States constitute "American style" shadow education. With this array of definitions and cross-national variation comes the need to specify the different forms and variations of shadow education.

For our purposes, as we connect the literature on shadow education to the empirical evidence on seasonal learning disparities, we focus primarily on two related, and often overlapping, distinctions—whether the educational services are offered for a fee or at a reduced or wholly subsidized cost and whether the purpose of the lesson is for academic enrichment or for remediation.[2] We also note that forms of shadow education may vary considerably by age and grade level, with test prep in particular being more common in secondary school. Much of our discussion can be applied to the effects of shadow education throughout students' educational careers, but because the existing research concentrates on practices in later grade levels, we refer most directly to these circumstances. In the following sections we describe shadow education patterns and research in the United States and offer some insights into the expansion of these services in recent years.

WHAT DOES SHADOW EDUCATION LOOK LIKE IN THE UNITED STATES?

Compared to other nations, the level of participation in shadow education in the United States is rather modest. The best estimates suggest that roughly 20% of U.S. secondary school students utilize private tutoring or participate in lessons at learning centers (Southgate, 2013). Buchmann et al. (2010) report similar proportions of students participating in private courses or working with private tutors to prepare for college entrance exams such as the SAT and ACT. In comparison, nations such as Japan, South Korea, Greece, and Turkey all report student participation rates above 40%. Of course, these comparisons rely on cross-national data and may not capture the full extent of these practices and the idiosyncrasies of different national contexts (Bray & Kobakhidze, 2014). In the United States, it is important to differentiate between private tutoring for which students pay a fee and subsidized services offered specifically as a result of the No Child Left Behind Act (NCLB).

Private forms of shadow education in the United States represent one side of supplementary education services—private tutoring, for-profit learning centers such as Sylvan, and private SAT preparatory courses. These services typically cater to economically advantaged student populations and are designed specifically to improve learning and test scores, often for the purposes of academic enrichment or to secure satisfactory results on college-entrance exams. Parents of financial means often seek out these supplementary opportunities as a way to enrich their children's academic experiences. Using data from the National Education Longitudinal Study, Buchmann et al. (2010) document significant socioeconomic inequalities in SAT test prep courses and private tutoring among high school students. Specifically, high-income students are more likely to use this type of shadow education compared to low-income and middle-income students.

More broadly, research shows that parents of financial means use their resources (economic, social, and cultural capital) to advance and customize the type of events, activities, and enrichment opportunities their children experience after regular school hours (Bennett, Lutz, & Jayaram, 2012) and during the summer months (Chin & Phillips, 2004). As it stands, however, the amount of U.S. research specifically addressing forms of private supplementary tutoring is rather modest, perhaps due to the lower overall participation rates by international standards. In contrast, a substantial body of research exists on private tutoring in East Asian countries, where shadow education is much more common and institutionalized (Dang, 2007; Kim & Chang, 2010; Stevenson & Baker, 1992).

Remedial and subsidized forms of shadow education have garnered more attention in the U.S. context, especially in the past decade. In particular, these services are included under NCLB legislation as "Supplemental Education Services." The passage of NCLB introduced required markets for Supplemental Education Services in underperforming districts. In essence, the federal government requires school districts to inform families of these education/tutoring services and pay for the expense; 20% of a district's Title 1 funds are designated for this purpose[4] (Lubienski & Lee, 2013; Mori, 2013).

While participation rates in NCLB-sponsored Supplemental Education Services programs have fluctuated since the mandate's creation in 2002, overall participation has been much lower than expected, at around 20% of those eligible (Lubienksi & Lee, 2013). Reporting findings from a large, urban district in Wisconsin, Heinrich, Meyer, and Whitten (2010) document stagnant registration rates and declining attendance among registered children as they progress through school. Low rates of participation notwithstanding, the NCLB Supplemental Education Services mandate has institutionalized tutoring services in the United States in an important way (Mori, 2013).

Researchers consistently find that low-income students in underperforming schools are the most likely to sign up for Supplemental Education Services provisions, but they are also significantly less likely to attend after registering.[5] In terms of effectiveness, the benefits of Supplemental Education Services programs on academic performance are modest. Many studies on the efficacy of Supplemental Education Services programs find no significant gains in student's math and reading achievement (Heinrich et al., 2010; Mori, 2013; Ross et al., 2008). However, some evidence suggests that significant gains are visible after sustained commitment of 2 years or more in tutoring programs (U.S. Department of Education, 2007).

Beyond evaluations of the NCLB related services, researchers find that out-of-school-time programs can improve achievement levels of disadvantaged or poorly performing students. In a meta-analysis of 35 studies, Lauer and colleagues (2006) find small but significant positive effects of programs taking place outside of regular school time on students' reading and math achievement. In many cases however, researchers note the considerable difficulties in evaluating such programs (Heinrich et al., 2010; Burch, Steinberg, & Donovan, 2007).

The provision of Supplementary Education Services through NCLB has contributed to a unique framework concerning the nature and use of shadow education practices in the United States. For instance, Lubienski and Lee (2013) offer a U.S./South Korea comparison that illuminates the distinctive form of U.S. shadow education. As a low-intensity shadow education nation, the United States attempts to deploy subsidized supplemental education as a way to address the negative consequences associated with unequal public schooling. On the other hand, as a high-intensity nation, South Korea promotes school-based services to help mediate private market inequalities in tutoring programs. In both cases, education authorities are promoting some form of learning opportunities that occur beyond the regular school day.

There is good reason to believe that these commitments to shadow education or supplementary education will continue to expand (Bray, 2009) and that these developments will continue to reflect the historical and political contexts of the nations in which they occur (Bray, Mazawi, & Sultana, 2013). In particular, shadow education in the United States takes on a unique mix of private forms (paid tutoring or extra classes, often in the form of test prep or for the purpose of academic enrichment) and NCLB subsidized forms (remedial tutoring). These services reflect a number of deeply entrenched American ideals, including a preference for private markets, an emphasis on individual student achievement, and a strong reliance on educational systems as the principal mechanism in addressing social inequalities (McCall, 2013).

Explaining the Growth of Shadow Education

The use of shadow education is on the rise across the globe, and the United States is no exception. In terms of remedial and subsidized approaches, Supplementary Education Services have become institutionalized and recognized as a path to address learning inequalities. In addition, there is a notable trend for public schools and local communities to increase exposure to additional learning environments in hopes of reducing achievement disparities. For instance, 21st Century Community Learning Centers strive to provide "academic enrichment opportunities during nonschool hours for children, particularly students who attend high-poverty and low-performing schools" (U.S. Department of Education, 2015).

It also appears that U.S. students are relying more on private tutors and/or organized classes outside of formal schooling than they have in the past. Repeated cross-sectional evidence from different waves of the Programme for International Student Assessment (PISA, 2003, 2012) reveals that U.S. students spent more time with tutors during an average week in 2012 (.43 hours) than in 2003 (.30 hours).[6] In addition, the share of students using shadow education, defined by private tutoring or organized outside classes, has increased from 17% in 2003 (Southgate, 2013) to 19.5% in 2012 (authors' calculations using PISA 2012). While this increase is modest and still places the United States in the category of "low-intensity" nations, the upward trend in this participation is notable. But why is this happening? Why are more families relying on educational services outside the school walls?

A principal consensus in the literature is that increasing rates of shadow education participation are taking place in accordance with a rise in educational intensity. This pattern has a number of related facets. First, education specialists and policymakers are placing more and more emphasis on measurement of student outcomes and performance benchmarking (Kamens & McNeely, 2010; Schneider & Keesler, 2007). Next, researchers have documented an especially pernicious trend associated with rising inequality: Returns to educational credentials are increasing, inequality in parents' economic resources is widening (Reardon, 2011), and those parents who have sufficient financial resources are choosing to invest that capital in their children's education (Kaushal, Magnuson, & Waldfogel, 2011), more so than in previous decades (Duncan & Magnuson, 2011; Kornrich & Furstenburg, 2013). For instance, Duncan and Murnane (2011) report that high-income families spent about $2,700 more per year on child enrichment than did low-income families in the early 1970s; by 2005–2006, that figure had jumped to $7,500 in constant dollars.

This divide in educational investment is also apparent when it comes to parents' time allocation. Since the 1990s, maternal time spent with children has increased overall, but the increase is twice as large among college-educated mothers (Gershenson, 2013; Ramey & Ramey, 2010).

Inequalities in parental education levels also contribute to the specific services that families use in order to secure educational advantages for their children. Southgate (2013) notes that those students who participate in shadow education are more likely to have highly educated parents who emphasize and believe in the efficacy of such practices. "It is not necessarily the case that parents who can pay for extra-schooling do so, but that families decide to purchase supplementary education when they see such extracurricular education as the path to educational success. Those who buy into this ideology are generally those who have themselves benefitted from education" (Southgate, 2013, p. 254).

A final trend that is likely related to the increasing use of shadow education pertains to Americans' growing dissatisfaction with the public education system. One of the most consistent findings in cross-national research on shadow education is that participation increases in settings where families deem the formal education system to be lacking in some regard (Baker & LeTendre, 2005; Dang, 2007; Kim & Chang, 2010). In a similar fashion, Davies (2004) links the rise of private tutoring in Canada to the increasing demand for school choice. Those parents who hire tutors are generally less satisfied with public education than other parents, and they tend to be more involved in their children's education. Historical results from Gallup polls show that the percentage of Americans expressing a "great deal" of confidence in public schools has declined from 30% in 1973 to only 12% in 2014. Similarly, the percentage of those indicating "very little" confidence has tied the all-time high of 28% (this figure was reported in both 2012 and 2014 Gallup results). Given these recent and ongoing patterns, it is likely that shadow education practices will continue to expand in the coming years.

SHADOW EDUCATION AND SEASONAL LEARNING PATTERNS

Thus far, we have established that shadow education may be of either an enrichment variety or a remedial variety, may cost money or be free/subsidized, and appears in all of these forms in relatively low intensity in the United States. The use of shadow education has been expanding in recent years due in part to increases in educational intensity, economic inequality, rising resources that high-SES parents devote to their children, and dissatisfaction with public schooling. But how does the expansion of shadow education relate to the central focus of this volume—summer learning and summer learning loss? Specifically, what implications do shadow education and its expansion have for socioeconomic learning disparities that emerge during the summer months or when school is not in session?

Socioeconomic Disparities in Learning

Numerous studies have established that, on average socioeconomically disadvantaged children do not do as well in school as their advantaged counterparts (Bowles & Gintis, 1976; Coleman et al., 1966; Gamoran, 2001). One of the most intriguing findings to emerge from research attempting to understand the sources of socioeconomic achievement gaps pertains not to questions of why or how such disparities emerge but rather to the question of *when* they emerge. Indeed, studies by Heyns (1978), Entwisle and Alexander (1992), and Downey, von Hippel, and Broh (2004), and others reveal the same general pattern in different data from different decades: Socioeconomic learning disparities grow faster during the summer than they do during the school year. While few would argue that the U.S. education system provides high- and low-SES students with equal opportunities, and while schools do not eliminate socioeconomic achievement gaps but rather temper their growth while in session, the seasonal comparisons research does shift the spotlight to nonschool contexts as key sources of such gaps.

Many studies have examined the role of extracurricular activities in promoting educational disparities between high- and low-SES children (Bennett et al., 2012; Chin & Phillips, 2004; Covay & Carbonaro, 2010; Freeman & Condron, 2011), but shadow education constitutes curricular, academically oriented activities. To understand the role that shadow education plays in learning over the summer compared to during the school year and how it affects socioeconomic learning disparities in both seasons, we must set aside extracurricular activities and instead focus on the impact of educational activities/programs on high- and low-SES students. When we do so, we find that this is an area in need of more research, especially when it comes to understanding the experiences of secondary school students.

Summertime Shadow Education

The first issue to confront when considering what we call "summertime shadow education" is the lack of data allowing for comparisons of shadow education activities during the summer versus during the school year. Data sources that allow for seasonal comparisons are scarce. The current state of data limitations and lack of research justifies the agenda-setting tone in the following section, which begins by raising questions about shadow education in the seasonal comparisons context before turning to what is known and what we still need to know about those questions.

In Which Season Is Shadow Education More Prevalent? To the extent that students engage in shadow education activities, do they do so primarily when school is in session or during summers? As noted previously, we are concerned here not with extracurricular activities or time use across socioeconomic lines (Chin & Phillips, 2004; Gershenson, 2013) but rather curricular, academically oriented activities.

Studies drawing on large-scale international datasets such as the Trends in International Mathematics and Science Study (TIMSS) and PISA have provided fewer clues than one might expect. These comparative data collection efforts have recognized the concept of shadow education and have attempted to gauge it, but in limited ways. While TIMSS and PISA have surveyed respondents about supplemental lessons for both remedial and enrichment purposes inside and outside of schools, the questions have not asked about how such courses and lessons are funded or whether they occur in summers versus school years (Bray & Kobakhidze, 2014). Some single-country research does find evidence for seasonal variations in the use of shadow education. One recent study of shadow education and stress among Hong Kong students finds that students spend more time in private tutoring "during examination time" and less time in private tutoring "during holiday time" compared to "during ordinary time" (Bray, 2013, p. 22).

In the U.S. context, no large-scale/national datasets at the secondary level allow for seasonal comparisons, and we have very limited evidence at the primary level from the Early Childhood Longitudinal Study-Kindergarten Cohort of 1998–1999 (ECLS-K). In Burkam et al.'s (2004) analysis of socioeconomic learning disparities during the summer between kindergarten and 1st grade using the ECLS-K data, "the magnitudes of the SES effects on summer learning remain nearly constant even when out-of-school educational activities are taken into account" (p. 22). Variables measuring summer literacy activities, educational use of computers, and summer school attendance had very limited impacts, while a measure of mathematics activities had no effect at all and thus was not even included in the final models. In considering the question "Why are these findings so modest?" the authors rightfully point primarily to the crudeness with which many of the summertime educational activities were measured, and they call for greater depth in the measurement of the "content, structure, and duration" of summertime educational activities in future research (Burkam et al., 2004, p. 22).

Bray's (2013) findings from Hong Kong reveal seasonal variations in shadow education that make intuitive sense and suggest the need for seasonal comparisons of shadow education in the United States. Do U.S. students engage in shadow education to a greater extent around the time of examinations? Although "examinations" might have different implications in Hong Kong and the United States, U.S. testing has increased in the past couple of decades, and it seems reasonable to suspect that students might be more engaged in shadow education when, for instance, annual state proficiency tests or exams required for graduation are on the horizon. In order to make such seasonal comparisons of shadow education use, however, we need the improved measures of shadow education activities called for by Burkam et al. (2004) and Bray and Kobakhidze (2014). We need to know why students are engaged in a given activity (i.e., for remedial or enrichment purposes), how much the activity costs, where it occurs, and what its structure, content, frequency, and duration are. Such information will enable researchers to address important questions about shadow education and seasonal learning patterns, including the following:

Are Particular Varieties of Shadow Education Season-Specific? Once we have a complete picture of all the shadow education activities with which students are involved—including *when* such activities take place—we can begin to understand potential distinctions between summer and school-year shadow education. One possibility is that remedial forms of shadow education dominate during the summer to prevent summer setback, while enrichment forms dominate during the school year when advantaged students are ready to learn even more than what they are learning in school. A second possibility is that remedial varieties are more common during the school year when disadvantaged students need extra help to keep up with their advantaged counterparts, while enrichment varieties prevail during the summer when advantaged families use such activities to fill their children's free time. A third possibility is that each type of shadow education is used consistently throughout the year. In addition, these patterns are likely influenced by the age of the student. Preparation for college admission tests surely affects the type and frequency of shadow education participation in secondary school.

The fact that high-SES children do indeed learn more than low-SES children during the summer appears consistent with the second possibility above. This, however, is pure speculation based on an assumption that high- and low-SES families differ in their summertime shadow education activities in the same way that they differ in their summertime extracurricular activities (e.g., Chin & Phillips, 2004). The faster summer learning of high-SES students could be entirely family-driven and unrelated to any potential shadow education activities. Such possibilities need to be examined carefully and considered within the broader context of socioeconomic inequalities in learning. The preceding discussion leads to this critical question:

How Does Summertime Shadow Education Shape Socioeconomic Achievement Disparities? Unfortunately, the lack of concrete evidence at this point precludes a definitive answer. On the one hand, summertime shadow education of the remedial variety may combat "summer setback," with free/ subsidized programs helping low-SES students in particular. On the other hand, summertime shadow education of the costly enrichment variety may contribute to the growth of socioeconomic learning disparities to the extent that advantaged families utilize such services.

A comprehensive understanding of the relationship between shadow education and inequalities in educational achievement will require tending to the related questions raised here. First, we need to know when shadow education use is more prevalent (summer or school year) and whether the different types of shadow education are season-specific so that we can sort out who is doing what and when. Only then can we gain leverage to determine the role that summertime shadow education plays in socioeconomic achievement gaps. For example, if high-SES children are benefiting from enrichment shadow education during the summer, whether that contributes to the socioeconomic achievement gap depends on what is occurring with low-SES children. If low-SES children are benefitting from shadow education themselves, then shadow education may not play a role in summer setback at all. If, however, high-SES children participate in and benefit from summertime shadow education at higher rates than low-SES children, one of the mechanisms through which the summer break contributes to the socioeconomic achievement gap will be identified.

DISCUSSION AND CONCLUSION

The best evidence suggests that the use of shadow education will become more widespread and institutionalized in the United States. Moving forward, researchers and policymakers must consider carefully the consequences of a growing reliance on this "third institution" for learning. As we have shown, a particular set of considerations has to do with children's seasonal learning patterns. Private forms of shadow education may advantage high-SES students throughout the calendar year but may contribute to especially unequal growth during the summer months when children's environments and resources are more disparate.

Our review suggests that high-quality summertime shadow education for disadvantaged students may help prevent summer setback, but the development of further policy and practice in this regard must be informed by careful evaluation of such programs, a greater effort to inform families of available options, and a growing understanding of which students participate in shadow education and the details and goals of their participation. A final point is the importance of early intervention: The necessary resources and staff in our schools must be present in order to allocate the best services/lessons to those students who will benefit the most from them. Trying to reverse accumulated learning disadvantages, totaled up over many years, is not reasonable over a single summer. Subsidized forms of shadow education may prevent learning loss for disadvantaged students to some degree over a particular summer, but these services must be part of a more comprehensive reform agenda that confronts the early formation of learning inequalities.

We have outlined a broad agenda for future research that addresses, for the first time, the intersection of shadow education and seasonal learning. A crucial missing piece of this puzzle is a descriptive understanding of the broad range of academic activities offered beyond the scope of formal schooling in the United States. As we have discussed, these activities vary in their format, purpose, setting, and timing. In order for researchers to build an empirical foundation on this topic, we need more data, more specific measures of shadow education activity, and a greater awareness of how these practices vary between summer and school periods.

NOTES

1. The authors explain that this concise description itself is in need of specification. Each term comes with an array of implications. For instance, researchers must define what they mean by "private." Does this mean that a fee is required? Or does "private" refer to a private setting or one-on-one instruction?

2. Globally, researchers find that the vast majority of shadow education is used for remedial purposes (Baker & LeTendre, 2005; Southgate, 2013). But, as Bray and Kobakhidze (2014) note, there are certain limitations with the distinction of remedial versus enrichment in the first place. Depending on students' reference groups, remedial and enrichment forms of tutoring become highly subjective in terms of their ultimate purpose.

3. Typically, districts rely heavily on private sector tutoring services to fulfill SES requirements. In this way, the intention is to present parents with adequate choice and introduce competition among private sector providers. State and local education bodies are also required to assess the effectiveness of private providers and distribute performance information to parents (Heinrich et al., 2010).

4. Recent changes in the Supplemental Education Services mandate may alter the context of subsidized academic services offered beyond normal school hours. Currently, a majority of states have voted not to uphold the original mandate, thereby providing greater flexibility in how underperforming schools choose to address their students' learning outcomes. Now, instead of setting aside funds strictly for Supplemental Education Services programs, schools may opt to utilize funds for different forms of school improvement and after-school offerings (Mori, 2013).

5. Steinberg (2011) also shows that Chicago Public School students with lower noncognitive outcomes (e.g., motivation, school engagement) and a greater number of school-year absences are less likely to enroll in Supplemental Education Services, suggesting that the services are not supporting some of the students most in need.

6. Source: PISA student questionnaire compendiums for 2003 and 2012. See http://pisa2003.acer.edu.au/downloads.php and http://pisa2012.acer.edu.au/downloads.php

REFERENCES

Aurini, J., Davies, S., & Dierkes, J. B. (2013). *Out of the shadows: The global intensification of supplementary education*. Bingley, UK: Emerald Group.

Baker, D., & LeTendre, G. (2005). *National differences, global similarities: World culture and the future of schooling*. Stanford, CA: Stanford University Press.

Bennett, P. R., Lutz, A. C., & Jayaram, L. (2012). Beyond the schoolyard: The role of parenting logics, financial resources, and social institutions in the social class gap in structured activity participation. *Sociology of Education, 85*(2), 131–157.

Bowles, S., & Gintis, H. (1976). *Schooling in capitalist America: Educational reform and the contradictions of economic life*. New York, NY: Basic Books.

Bray, M. (2009). *Confronting the shadow education system: What government policies for what private tutoring?* Paris, France: United Nations Educational, Scientific and Cultural Organization, International Institute for Educational Planning.

Bray, M. (2013). Benefits and tensions of shadow education: Comparative perspectives on the roles and impact of private supplementary tutoring in the lives of Hong Kong students. *Journal of International and Comparative Education, 2*(1), 18–30.

Bray, M., & Kobakhidze, M. N. (2014). Measurement issues in research on shadow education: Challenges and pitfalls encountered in TIMSS and PISA. *Comparative Education Review, 58*(4), 590–620.

Bray, M., Mazawi, A. E., & Sultana, R. G. (2013). *Private tutoring across the Mediterranean: Power dynamics and implications for learning and equity*. Rotterdam, Netherlands: Sense.

Buchmann, C., Condron, D. J., & Roscigno, V. J. (2010). Shadow education, American style: Test preparation, the SAT and college enrollment. *Social Forces, 89*(2), 435–461.

Burch, P., Steinberg, M., & Donovan, J. (2007). Supplemental educational services and NCLB: Policy assumptions, market practices, emerging issues. *Educational Evaluation and Policy Analysis, 29*(2), 115–133.

Burkam, D. T., Ready, D. D., Lee, V. E., & LoGerfo, L. F. (2004). Social-class differences in summer learning between kindergarten and first grade: Model specification and estimation. *Sociology of Education, 77*(1), 1–31.

Chin, T., & Phillips, M. (2004). Social reproduction and child-rearing practices: Social class, children's agency, and the summer activity gap. *Sociology of Education, 77*(3), 185–210.

Coleman, J. S., Campbell, E. Q., Hobson, C. J., McPartland, J., Mood, A. M., Weinfield, F. D., & York, R. L. (1966). *Equality of educational opportunity*. Washington, DC: U.S. Government Printing Office.

Covay, E., & Carbonaro, W. (2010). After the bell: Participation in extracurricular activities, classroom behavior, and academic achievement. *Sociology of Education, 83*(1), 20–45.

Dang, H.-A. (2007). The determinants and impact of private tutoring classes in Vietnam. *Economics of Education Review, 26*(6), 683–698.

Davies, S. (2004). School choice by default? Understanding the demand for private tutoring in Canada. *American Journal of Education, 110*(3), 233–255.

Downey, D. B., von Hippel, P. T., & Broh, B. (2004). Are schools the great equalizer? Cognitive inequality during the summer months and the school year. *American Sociological Review, 69*(5), 613–635.

Duncan, G. J., & Magnuson, K. A. (2011). The nature and impact of early achievement skills, attention skills, and behavior problems. In G. J. Duncan & J. R. Murnane (Eds.), *Whither opportunity: Rising inequality, schools, and children's life chances* (pp. 47–70). New York, NY: Russell Sage Foundation.

Duncan, G. J., & Murnane, R. J. (2011). Introduction: The American dream, then and now. In G. J. Duncan & J. R. Murnane (Eds.), *Whither opportunity: Rising inequality, schools, and children's life chances* (pp. 3–26). New York, NY: Russell Sage Foundation.

Entwisle, D. R., & Alexander, K. L. (1992). Summer setback: Race, poverty, school composition, and mathematics achievement in the first two years of school. *American Sociological Review, 57*(1), 72–84.

Freeman, K. J., & Condron, D. J. (2011). Schmoozing in elementary school: The importance of social capital to first graders. *Sociological Perspectives, 54*(4), 521–546.

Gamoran, A. (2001). American schooling and educational inequality: A forecast for the 21st century. *Sociology of Education, 74*(Extra Issue), 135–153.

Gershenson, S. (2013). Do summer time-use gaps vary by socioeconomic status? *American Educational Research Journal, 50*(6), 1219–1248.

Heinrich, C. J., Meyer, R. H., & Whitten, G. (2010). Supplemental education services under No Child Left Behind: Who signs up, and what do they gain? *Educational Evaluation and Policy Analysis, 32*(2), 273–298.

Heyns, B. L. (1978). *Summer learning and the effects of schooling.* New York, NY: Academic Press.

Kamens, D. H., & McNeely, C. L. (2010). Globalization and the growth of international educational testing and national assessment. *Comparative Education Review, 54*(1), 5–25.

Kaushal, N., Magnuson, K. A., & Waldfogel, J. (2011). How is family income related to investments in children's learning? In G. J. Duncan & J. R. Murnane (Eds.), *Whither opportunity: Rising inequality, schools, and children's life chances* (pp. 187–206). New York, NY: Russell Sage Foundation.

Kim, J., & Chang, J. (2010). Do governmental regulations for cram schools decrease the number of hours students spend on private tutoring? *Journal of Educational Policy, 7*(1), 3–21.

Kornrich, S., & Furstenberg, F. (2013). Investing in children: Changes in parental spending on children, 1972–2007. *Demography, 50*(1), 1–23.

Lauer, P. A., Akiba, M., Wilkerson, S. B., Apthorp, H. S., Snow, D., & Martin-Glenn, M. L. (2006). Out-of-school-time programs: A meta-analysis of effects for at-risk students. *Review of Educational Research, 76*(2), 275–313.

Lubienski, C., & Lee, J. (2013). Making markets: Policy construction of supplementary education in the United States and Korea. In J. Aurini, S. Davies, & J. Dierkes (Eds.), *Out of the shadows: The global intensification of supplementary education* (pp. 223–244). Bingley, UK: Emerald Group.

Marimuthu, T., Singh, J. S., Ahmad, K., Lim, H. K., Mukherjee, H., Osman, S., . . . & Jamaluddin, W. (1991). Extra-school instruction, social equity and educational quality. [In Malaysian.] Singapore: International Development Research Centre.

McCall, P. L. (2013). *The undeserving rich: American beliefs about inequality, opportunity, and redistribution.* Cambridge, MA: Cambridge University Press.

Mori, I. (2013). Supplementary education in the United States: Policy context, characteristics, and challenges. In J. Aurini, S. Davies, & J. Dierkes (Eds.), *Out of the shadows: The global intensification of supplementary education* (pp. 191–208). Bingley, UK: Emerald Group.

Park, H., Buchmann, C., Choi, J. & Merry, J. J. (in press). Learning beyond the school walls: Trends and implications. *Annual Review of Sociology*, 42.

Ramey, G., & Ramey, V. (2010). The rug rat race. *Brookings Papers on Economic Activity*, *2010*(1), 129–200.

Reardon, S. F. (2011). The widening academic achievement gap between the rich and the poor: New evidence and possible explanations. In G. J. Duncan & J. R. Murnane (Eds.), *Whither opportunity: Rising inequality, schools, and children's life chances* (pp. 91–116). New York, NY: Russell Sage Foundation.

Ross, S. M., Potter, A., Paek, J., McKay, D., Sanders, W., & Ashton, J. (2008). Implementation and outcomes of supplemental educational services: The Tennessee state-wide evaluation study. *Journal of Education for Students Placed at Risk (JESPAR)*, *13*(1), 26–58.

Schneider, B. L., & Keesler, V. A. (2007). School reform 2007: Transforming education into a scientific enterprise. *Annual Review of Sociology*, *33*(1), 197–217.

Southgate, D. (2013). Family capital: A determinant of supplementary education in 17 nations. In J. Aurini, S. Davies, & J. Dierkes (Eds.), *Out of the shadows: The global intensification of supplementary education* (pp. 245–258). Bingley, UK: Emerald Group.

Steinberg, M. P. (2011). Educational choice and student participation: The case of the supplemental educational services provision in Chicago public schools. *Educational Evaluation and Policy Analysis*, *33*(2), 159–182.

Stevenson, D. L., & Baker, D. P. (1992). Shadow education and allocation in formal schooling: Transition to university in Japan. *American Journal of Sociology*, *97*(6), 1639–1657.

U.S. Department of Education. (2007). *State and local implementation of the No Child Left Behind Act: Vol. 1—title 1 school choice, supplemental educational services (SES) in the No Child Left Behind Act*. Washington, DC: Author.

U.S. Department of Education. (2015). *21st century community learning centers: Program description*. Washington, DC: Author. Retrieved from www2.ed.gov/programs/21stcclc/index.html

CHAPTER 9

Selecting Summer

How Elementary School Parents Make Choices About Summer Programs

Barbara F. Condliffe

Many urban districts have sought to curb summer learning loss among low-income elementary school students by offering free or reduced- cost summer learning programs. We know very little about how low-income families navigate their summer learning program choices. This qualitative study investigates the processes through which low-income African American families made decisions about whether to enroll their 1st-grade students in summer learning programs.

Research has demonstrated that high-quality summer learning programs can improve the academic achievement of low-income students (e.g., Borman, Goetz, & Dowling, 2009; Kim & Quinn, 2013; McCombs et al., 2014). However, analysis of national data has shown that disadvantaged children participate in fewer extracurricular activities (including structured summer activities) than their more advantaged peers (Covay & Carbonaro, 2010). For voluntary summer learning programs to help narrow achievement gaps, the most disadvantaged children need to have access, and their families must choose to participate. Therefore, understanding the factors that facilitate and those that inhibit the enrollment of low-income children into summer learning programs is critical. This chapter investigates how low-income parents[1] of 1st-grade students attending elementary school in a high-poverty Baltimore City neighborhood decided whether to enroll their children in a summer learning program.

Qualitative research (Bennett, Lutz, & Jayaram, 2012; Chin & Phillips, 2004) seeking to explain social class gaps in children's out-of-school-time (OST) learning activities has found that across social classes most parents want to enrich their children's OST learning experiences. However, the high cost of many programs and the limited supply of high-quality opportunities in poor neighborhoods constrain the choices of working class and poor families (Bennett et al., 2012; Chin & Phillips, 2004).

Clearly the limited supply of affordable high-quality programs in low-income neighborhoods helps to explain some of the disparities in children's participation. However, the qualitative research (e.g., Bell, 2009; Condliffe, Boyd, & DeLuca, 2015; DeLuca & Rosenblatt, 2010; Mavrogordato & Stein, 2014) on how disadvantaged families make school choice decisions suggests that additional factors might influence the choices low-income families make about summer programs. This body of research has demonstrated that access to information about high-quality school choice opportunities is a critical resource often in short supply in underprivileged communities and that sometimes disadvantaged families facing a choice about where their children attend school need to maximize nonacademic factors like safety over academic quality.

The aim of the study summarized in this chapter was to investigate the summer program choice decision-making process of a group of low-income families in order to identify factors that facilitate the enrollment of some children and those that inhibit the participation of others. Because the city offered free and reduced-cost opportunities for elementary schoolchildren that either included free transportation or were located in the neighborhood of study participants, this study is able to consider whether and how factors beyond affordability and accessibility influenced parents' decision making.

The next section describes the research design and the sample of participants. Then an overview of the summer learning opportunities available to the families in the study is provided. The fourth section describes the summer learning choice processes parents described in interviews. Finally, I discuss the implications of the findings for the research literature and for policymakers and practitioners interested in increasing low-income families' participation in voluntary summer learning programs.

RESEARCH DESIGN

The parents recruited for this study had a child enrolled in 1st grade during the 2012–2013 school year in one of two Baltimore City Public Schools— Springfield and Cedar Elementary.[2] Springfield and Cedar both fit predetermined selection criteria regarding the socio-demographic characteristics of the school. Both schools had a student population that was predominantly low income and African American, and they were located in the same high-poverty neighborhood.[3]

Any parent of a 1st-grade student attending Springfield and Cedar Elementary Schools during the 2012–2013 school year was eligible to participate in the study. With the help of the Baltimore Education Research Consortium (BERC) and the permission of Baltimore City Public Schools, I recruited parents through a flier sent home in 1st-grade student backpacks as well as in-person canvassing at the schools during student drop-off. Parents also were recruited at a bus stop in the neighborhood where children were being picked up to travel to summer programs and at a neighborhood association meeting.

The study procedures involved in-depth semi-structured interviews during July and August 2013 with 24 parents.[4] With two exceptions, all interviews were conducted in family homes. Recordings of structured field notes with observations of the home and neighborhood environment followed each interview. All interviews touched on a core set of topics, with the order of questions developing naturally and differently in the course of conversation. The topics included each parent's personal history and current situation (e.g., educational background, employment status, family structure, and residential mobility) as well as their thoughts on the quality of the neighborhood and elementary school. All parents were asked about their 1st-grade students' summer and school-year activities and academic and social experiences. Interviews also addressed the decision-making process regarding children's summer activities.

CONTEXT: SUMMER LEARNING OPPORTUNITIES IN BALTIMORE CITY

Starting in the summer of 2012, a number of Baltimore City public agencies, including the Mayor's office and Baltimore City Public Schools, joined local nonprofits to develop "The Baltimore City Super Summer Initiative." The partnership aims to ensure that all families have information about and access to summer learning activities and services (e.g., free meals).

Table 9.1 describes the three most accessible summer learning programs for the families in this study—Read to Succeed, Super Kids Camp, and a variety of camps run by the Department of Recreations and Parks. All three were either free or offered at a reduced cost and were publicized by the school system and/or the Baltimore City Super Summer initiative's online guide to summer learning programs. Additionally, the three programs either provided free transportation or had at least one site that was less than 2 miles from the participating schools.

The three programs varied in their structure and duration. However, according to their informational materials, all featured a blend of academic and nonacademic programming. As described by parents and discussed in the findings, it is important to recognize that parents of students reading below grade-level had more free options than those with students reading on grade-level since Read to Succeed was intended for students in need of additional literacy support.

HOW DO LOW-INCOME FAMILIES MAKE CHOICES ABOUT SUMMER LEARNING PROGRAMS?

Ten of the 24 parents who participated in the study experienced a "successful" summer program choice process. They had information about summer

Table 9.1. Summer Learning Programs Most Accessible to Cedar and Springfield Families

	Program Description	Cost	Location/ Transportation
Read to Succeed	Full-day 5-week program of academic and enrichment activities. K–3 students identified as reading below grade level were targeted for enrollment.	Free	Hosted at elementary schools across the city. Students provided with free transportation if they did not live within walking distance.
SuperKids	Full-day 6-week program of academic and enrichment activities managed by a local nonprofit organization. Open to all children in grades 1–3.	$60 fee, waived if parent could demonstrate financial hardship	Hosted at sites across the city. All students provided with free transportation.
Parks and Recreation Centers	Some recreation centers offered their own camp programs. Many included an academic component and were open to all students (NSLA, 2012).	Camp fees ranged depending on duration and offerings	Hosted at Parks and Recreation Centers across the city, including one site less than 2 miles from the participating schools.

learning programs and enrolled their children in one. The interviews with these parents were analyzed to understand how parents accessed information and made the decision to enroll. Fourteen parents did not enroll their children in a program. Their interviews were analyzed to understand their preferences for summer learning programs, the information they had about summer learning opportunities, and any obstacles they faced in acting on information and preferences.

Parent of Enrolled Children: Independent and Brokered Choices

Among the 10 parents who enrolled their children in a summer learning program, 2 parents, Rita (mother of a 1st grader at Springfield, Laura) and Marissa (mother of a 1st grader at Cedar, Denise), indicated that their choice process was executed independently. These mothers described efforts to seek out information instead of indicating that they acted on information given to them. Rita explained:

> I just went on the website and just looked for my own program for her [Laura] from the website. . . . They had different programs for different activities in different time frames and things like that. So I picked the one that . . . I felt like would best fit her.

It is important to note that both of these mothers also described independent efforts to avail their children of other OST enrichment opportunities, including after-school activities, music classes, and dance lessons. Rita was also participating in school choice; she was dissatisfied with her daughter's elementary school and was researching charter school options for the future.

The other eight parents who enrolled their children in a program described a "brokered" enrollment process. *Brokerage* refers to the bringing together of unconnected individuals or institutions in order to enhance the resources of one or both parties (Small, 2006; Stovel & Shaw, 2012). Stovel and Shaw explain that brokers "bridge a gap in social structure" by helping "goods, information, opportunities, or knowledge flow across that gap" (2012, p. 141).

The city's Super Summer Initiative and the school district made efforts to engage in brokerage by providing schools and families with information about summer learning opportunities through the creation and distribution of digital and hard-copy promotional materials. Recognizing that this form of brokerage might not be enough for all parents, the district sent a personalized letter home about the Read to Succeed program (signed by the school principal) with students identified as most in need of additional support in the development of their literacy skills. There were also less formal forms of brokerage. Several parents spoke of individuals, most often school staff, reaching out to inform them of summer learning opportunities. Only two of the eight parents who described a brokered process indicated that informational materials sent by the school (e.g., letter from the principal) were enough. The rest noted at least one individual as the source of their information, suggesting that this more personalized and intensive outreach was important to their children's enrollment.

Cynthia is a mother of four children, the oldest of which, Anita, was a 1st grader at Cedar Elementary. Cynthia, who enrolled Anita in Read to Succeed, referenced multiple forms of brokerage:

> I'm like, "I need to jump on it [signing her up for Read to Succeed] because that can help her." The school, family, all of them is recommending it and it [the letter from the school] got her name literally printed on the paper for it. So I'm like "She going to do that. She occupied for the summer."

Cynthia was flooded with information about summer programming from multiple sources. The volume of personalized information seems to have been important to her daughter's participation.

Danielle found out about Read to Succeed from her child's principal, but in an informal way. Danielle's daughter Aisha, a 1st grader at Springfield, attended Read to Succeed in summer 2012 and returned in 2013. Danielle said Springfield's principal saw her in church one day in 2012 and asked her what Aisha would be doing over the summer. When Danielle said she had no plans, the principal responded, according to Danielle, "Okay, just bring her up there [to Springfield] on Monday and we can enroll her." Danielle did not see re-enrollment in 2013 as a choice: "I guess because she was already in it last year, they [the school] just went ahead and put her back in it." Although Danielle had, in fact, exercised choice by enrolling her daughter in the voluntary 2012 and 2013 programs, in her eyes, the principal and the school facilitated the entire process.

Six other interviews, in addition to Cynthia's and Danielle's, indicate the importance of brokerage. With the exception of two parents who named other brokers (a case worker and a personal friend), all these remaining parents cited the school system or an individual at the school as their primary source of information about the opportunity.

The interviews with parents who experienced brokerage suggest that in the absence of brokerage, their children may not have attended any summer learning program. Most did not know of other opportunities available to children over the summer, few had enrolled their 1st grader in a program during the previous summer, and no one had plans to enroll their children in another formal summer learning activity after the summer learning program was over in the first week of August.

Parents of Children Not Enrolled: Constrained Choice and Failed Brokerage

Fourteen of the 24 parents in the study did not enroll their child in a summer learning program. I asked 12 of these parents what their children would be doing over the summer if money were no object. All 12 indicated that they wanted their children to participate in a program that included learning and fun activities. The blending of academic and enrichment activities (e.g., recreation, music, and art) was a cornerstone of most of the available programs. Tonea, whose two school-age daughters were not enrolled in a summer learning program, described her ideal program: "It will always be between work and fun. . . . You know, 3 hours working your brain then there's lunch time, let's go have a little fun to show off the good work you did."

Read to Succeed and SuperKids satisfied Tonea's criteria for a strong summer experience. Indeed, most of the parents who did not enroll their children were concerned about children's academic development over the summer and wanted to find a summer learning program for their child.

The question then becomes why were these parents not able to act on those preferences?

Of the 14 parents who did not enroll their children in a summer learning program, 9 said they wanted to and had accurate information about at least one available opportunity. However, significant constraints precluded enrolling their children.

Some of these constraints align with what prior research on inequalities in children's OST activity participation has noted—limited material resources and a limited supply of affordable programming (Bennett et al., 2012; Chin & Phillips, 2004). For example, some parents cited the limited supply of free options for children not in need of remediation and not invited to Read to Succeed. Clearly, supply and cost are important factors. However, noncost factors that are often associated with life in high-poverty contexts such as concerns about neighborhood safety, residential mobility, complicated child-care arrangements, and rigid job schedules also impeded parents' summer program choice process.

These noncost factors directly or indirectly constrained the choice process of six of the nine parents who valued summer learning opportunities and had access to accurate information but did not enroll their children in a program. The complexity of these issues and how they constrained the choice process are illustrated through the stories of Tia, Gabriella, and Lauren.

Tia is the mother of four children whose youngest son, Michael, was a 1st grader at Cedar Elementary. Tia was well informed about summer learning opportunities in the city. She had enrolled her middle-school-aged son in a summer enrichment camp at a local university and knew about summer learning opportunities for Michael. She said he was not enrolled in Read to Succeed due to the limited spaces available to students who read on grade level. Tia said she would have sent him to another day camp since she thought summer learning programs were very important and Michael "wanted to do the whole summer camp thing," but she hadn't sought information about other alternatives because of an impending family and residential change.

Tia was in the process of separating from Michael's father and planning a move with her children. Tia said these impending changes made her schedule very busy, and she did not want to complicate things even more by enrolling Michael in activities over the summer. She said it was "kind of good" that Michael did not get a spot in the Read to Succeed program, given these constraints: "I'm going through a change anyway so I kind of didn't want to commit to too many things. . . . Yeah so that's the only reason why I didn't try to push him and get him into something [a summer program]." Her older son was old enough to get himself up in the morning and out of the door to camp without her help, but making time for getting Michael to a program each day would pose too much of a problem given how busy Tia was.

Gabriella is the mother of three young children, including Jordan who was a 1st grader at Springfield. Gabriella had accurate information about summer learning opportunities in 2013. In fact, for the summer of 2012 she had found and enrolled Jordan in a summer camp run by a community organization that involved academics and sports. However, housing instability and unemployment had blocked the process in 2013.

Gabriella described the row home where she lived with her family as "hell on earth." Half of the houses on her block were vacant, and all of the homes on a block adjacent to hers were boarded up. Her home had holes in the walls that she had covered with masking tape to deter the rats from entering. The tiles were coming apart all over the kitchen and cockroaches were a significant issue. Gabriella noted a hole in the stove that prevented her from cooking. She also said that testing had revealed lead paint.

When we spoke, Gabriella was actively trying to secure the resources to find another place for her family to live. She was collecting Temporary Cash Assistance (TCA), participating in its workforce program, and attending college full-time so that she might someday secure employment. She was incredibly busy. A subsidized daycare program could accommodate all three of her children; getting Jordan to the Read to Succeed site while bringing her other two young children to daycare would have made it impossible to get to her appointments at 9 A.M. She expressed regret at having to make this trade-off since she felt that the daycare was not meeting Jordan's needs. "They play and things like that, but it's just like being watched at home 'cause it's a home daycare." Gabriella felt as strongly as any of the parents whose children attended a summer learning program that it would benefit her child, but she could not make it happen.

Lauren also thought a summer reading program would benefit her 1st grader, Alice. Lauren was well aware that children can lose ground academically over the summer and thought it was important for parents to prevent it. Alice had attended a summer learning program at a local university in the summer of 2012 that Alice enjoyed and Lauren thought was very enriching academically. However, Alice was not attending any program in summer 2013, and Lauren was very distraught about this.

While Gabriella and Tia were planning to move, Lauren's family had recently moved. She and Alice had been living in the neighborhood of Springfield Elementary, where she had attended 1st grade, but Lauren decided to move across town because she was concerned about the violence in the neighborhood and wanted to be closer to her ailing mother. This was clearly a stressful time for Lauren, who did not have full-time employment and was using a wheelchair at the time of the interview: "I've been dealing with a lot of stuff far as my mother, and I have been putting stuff on hold because I'm dealing with it by myself."

Lauren had not had time to search for a summer program for Alice before the school year ended, and she said all the free programs in the city were full. During the first few weeks of the summer vacation, she tried to find an affordable program for Alice. She had asked at Springfield and at Alice's new school in her new neighborhood, as well as online and through word of mouth. Lauren was still looking when we spoke in early July, but she said that her only option left was to go to the local community organization "and beg."

Parents like Tia, Gabrielle, and Lauren were concerned about summer learning and adept at accessing information about summer learning opportunities. However, their choices were constrained by a number of factors associated with having limited economic means and living in high-poverty contexts, including a limited supply of affordable programs in high-poverty neighborhoods and unexpected family, housing, and financial instability.

Five of the fourteen parents who did not enroll their 1st grader described inaccurate or incomplete information that they received from the school about summer learning programs. I refer to these examples as "failed brokerage" because in each case the parent had interactions with the school system about summer learning experiences, but the school system's information was either delivered inaccurately or the parent misinterpreted it. The parents' perspective on how and why this happened are instructive to designers of summer learning recruitment efforts, as they suggest ways to improve brokerage and reasons why well-intentioned brokerage can fail.

Michelle is a mother of two children, including a 1st grader at Cedar, Derik, whom she wanted to attend a summer learning program. When asked to describe what Derik would be doing over the summer if money were no object, Michelle said, "Something where you're going to learn something; it's going to be fun but you're going to learn something. . . . Just something to keep him from being sitting outside doing nothing with trouble lurking around him."

Michelle was aware of some camps and summer programs at the school that focused on reading, but said Derik's teacher told her that he didn't need to go to a camp because he wasn't behind on his reading: "She told me that if he was behind on something or whatever issues that she noticed, she would recommend for them to go to one of those camps." While it is true that Derik was not below-grade level and therefore not technically eligible for Read to Succeed, SuperKids camps featured exactly what Michelle was looking for in that they offered children of any skill level the opportunity to engage in an academic program and have a traditional camp experience. Perhaps most importantly for Michelle who wanted her son to do something that would prevent him from being outside in her neighborhood with "trouble lurking around him," SuperKids camps took children out of their neighborhoods for the day and exposed them to a variety of enrichment activities across the city.

Dana's son Frank was also a 1st grader at Cedar, but he had struggled with reading and behavior problems in 1st grade, and the school recommended he repeat the grade. Dana said her son was spending most of the summer outside playing basketball with his friends. When asked if the school had recommended any summer programming, Dana said the teacher had originally given her papers for the "summer school program" [Read to Succeed], but she had never followed up after she had agreed to the school's proposal that Frank be retained in 1st grade. In Dana's eyes, the decision to retain Frank in 1st grade meant that he didn't "need" to go to the summer program:

> They was saying that they wanted him to go to summer school, so I filled it out, took it back to the teacher and she said that she had it, but, after that, that's when I got called in for another meeting to come to discuss about him repeating the 1st grade again, so I guess they never sent [it].

When I asked if Dana heard anything more about the program, Dana said she hadn't. It appears that the school initiated a process of brokering Frank's participation, but no one followed up with Dana. Since Dana thought that the school's summer program was credit-bearing and therefore unnecessary if her son was being retained, she seems to have interpreted the school's silence on the issue of the summer program to mean that her son didn't need to attend.

Since interviews with teachers were not a part of this study, it is not clear whether the misunderstanding about Frank's eligibility was the result of the teacher's or Dana's confusion. What is clear, however, is that Frank would likely have benefited from more intensive or directed brokerage; his mother was open to the program but misunderstood or was misinformed about its purpose and his eligibility, which grade retention did not negate.

Lisa is another example of brokerage misfiring. Lisa's daughter Taylor, a 1st grader at Cedar, was recommended for Read to Succeed. Lisa rejected the invitation for a number of reasons, including concerns about safety and a desire to give her daughter a real break over the summer. In regard to safety, Lisa was worried that the program was not hosted at Cedar; she was suspicious of the types of children who would be attending and the staff who would be running the program. This distrust of people around her was a theme throughout her interview and seemingly related to a long history of living in a violent neighborhood.

She also said she rejected the invitation because it was important for her daughter to have more opportunities for play over the summer, saying that she does not "think kids should go to school all year long." However, many of the "fun" activities she said she wanted her daughter to engage in over the summer, such as field trips and swimming, were featured in Read to Succeed.

It seems the program was aligned with what Lisa wanted, and efforts were made to broker her daughter's connection to the program, but the school did not customize their message sufficiently to meet Lisa's stated preferences. Lisa might have benefited from more intensive brokerage efforts, such as a meeting with a trusted staff member at the school about summer learning programs. This type of meeting could have informed Lisa of the program activities and helped to identify and allay concerns she had about safety.

Leah and Ashley also declined their children's invitation to Read to Succeed. Similar to Lisa who was distrusting of the neighborhood, mistrust toward the school seems to have played a role in Leah and Ashley's decisions.

Leah's daughter, Kate, was a 1st grader at Cedar. In the summer of 2013, Kate and Leah were living with Leah's elderly father, who was financially supporting them because Leah did not have full-time employment. Leah did not complete high school and was very down about not being able to find a job. When I spoke to her, Leah was also very angry at Cedar's teachers and administration because they had recommended Kate for retention. She was concerned her daughter was going to be upset and embarrassed by this.

Leah also expressed frustration because she felt Kate's 1st-grade teacher had called Leah too often to report on concerns about Kate's skills. Leah felt the teacher needed to do more to address these issues and interpreted the calls as the teacher trying to shirk her responsibilities. When the school recommended to Leah that Kate attend Read to Succeed, Leah turned down the invitation:

> I guess it was like some little summer program, school . . . I didn't even want to deal with them [the school]. I didn't even feel like dealing with them no more. I don't feel like dealing with them. August, maybe I'll deal with them, but not right now.

Leah's rejection of the invitation for Kate to attend Read to Succeed seems to be directly connected to her fraught relationship with the school and her desire not to have to "deal with them" over the summer.

Like Leah, Ashley rejected the invitation for her daughter, Renee, who had been a 1st grader at Springfield Elementary. Ashley described Renee as an excellent reader and mentioned that she encouraged Renee to read each day. The school told Ashley that Renee was behind on her reading and suggested that she attend the summer program, which Ashley interpreted as a "summer school." Ashley was upset by the letter recommending Renee to Read to Succeed since she blamed the school for whatever difficulties Renee was having in reading. She told me that her daughter had a substitute teacher for much of the school year and that the classroom was chaotic during that time. Ashley felt it was unfair that the school was now suggesting that her daughter attend summer school, since she thought it was their fault if her daughter was behind:

How do you let that happen? [a chaotic classroom with a substitute]
And then now you're sending me a letter telling me that my child is
below in reading and she's going to need to go to summer school.

Read to Succeed was intended to help children, not punish them for
falling behind. However, Leah and Ashley interpreted the invitation to the
program as an unfair judgment and punishment. In both cases the school
reached out about the opportunity that the two children may have benefited
from, but a fractured parent–school relationship made it difficult for the
school to broker effectively.

CONCLUSION

This chapter investigated the process through which low-income families
made decisions about whether to enroll their children in summer learning
programs. While 2 of the 10 parents who enrolled their children in a program described a relatively independent, smooth process, the interviews with
the other 8 parents of enrolled children indicated that their process was brokered in some way. Often an individual at the school served as the broker by
informing parents of the opportunity and facilitating their children's enrollment. It is possible that some of these children would have enrolled without
brokerage, but interviews suggest that in most cases a broker was vital.

Fourteen of the parents I spoke with did not enroll their children in a
summer learning opportunity. Nine of these parents were concerned about
summer learning loss and were equipped with information about a variety
of opportunities (sometimes from a broker), but faced constraints that prevented them from acting on their preferences. A limited supply of affordable
programs for students on grade level was a significant obstacle for some.
However, most of these nine parents also spoke of noncost factors, including
residential mobility, that directly or indirectly made it difficult for them to
engage in the summer program marketplace.

The other five parents described failed brokerage. In some cases, an
individual at the school seems to have supplied inaccurate or incomplete
information about summer learning opportunities. In other cases, the parent
misinterpreted and/or rejected the messaging from the school. Importantly,
all but one of these children were invited to Read to Succeed and thus identified as below reading level in 1st grade; participation in the summer reading
program may have helped them to catch up to their peers.

IMPLICATIONS FOR RESEARCH AND POLICY

Prior research on the opportunity gap in out-of-school-time learning (Bennett et al., 2012; Chin & Phillips, 2004) found that parents of all social

classes want their children to engage in high-quality out-of-school-time learning activities, but working class and poor parents are often unable to access these opportunities due to a limited supply of high-quality, affordable OST learning programs in their high-poverty neighborhoods. The findings described in this chapter align with this research. Even with the significant investment of public and private money into summer learning programs, supply of affordable summer programs was a significant obstacle for some families. Clearly, increasing the supply of affordable opportunities and providing free transportation to those programs will help to narrow opportunity gaps for some.

Because this study was conducted in a context where some free and low-cost programs were available to families, I was able to explore factors beyond access and cost that facilitated the enrollment of some and inhibited the enrollment of others.

The families who enrolled their children in a program most often described the school or school staff as their primary source of information. This finding is consistent with the research on school choice. Middle- and upper-income families often report that they rely on their social networks for information about their school choice options (e.g., Bell, 2009; Holme, 2002; Kimelberg & Billingham, 2012). Families with limited resources do the same, but their social networks often do not include individuals with information about high-quality educational opportunities (e.g., Bell, 2009; DeLuca & Rosenblatt, 2010; Mavrogordato & Stein, 2014). The successful brokerage process experienced by most of the parents of enrolled students suggests that one way to narrow educational opportunity gaps (during the summer and school year) is to formalize the role of school staff members as educational opportunity brokers for their students.

For school staff to be effective summer learning brokers requires they be aware of issues of summer learning loss, motivated to address the problem, and informed about all the summer learning opportunities available to children in the community, including activities outside of school. School staff will also need to be supported with the time and resources to engage in intensive and personalized brokerage efforts for those families that need it.

The accounts shared in this chapter also highlight the importance of teachers and other school staff being aware of constraints like housing and financial instability that might interfere with the enrollment of their students in summer learning programs. Providing school staff with this awareness and with information about community resources to address these issues is likely to be important to the development of effective summer learning brokerage.

While training school staff in these regards may help connect more low-income children to summer learning opportunities, it will not work for all, as the school's attempts to broker children's enrollment into summer learning opportunities sometimes backfired. This highlights the important role of an individual's attitude toward and trust in the summer learning broker. If schools institutionalize the process of summer learning brokerage, a parent's engagement in and relationship to the school will surely influence the effectiveness of the school's attempts. Future research should consider when and why acts of brokerage fail so that policymakers and practitioners can identify families that will require a different approach.

Finally, it is important to recognize that even though increasing the supply of high-quality summer learning programs for low-income students and institutionalizing school staff's roles as summer learning brokers will likely help to narrow summer learning opportunity gaps, these efforts will not work for all. The unanticipated instabilities that some of the families in this study faced created complexities that forced parents to make difficult trade-offs when making decisions about summer activities. The stories of these families demonstrate that fully addressing inequality in children's summer learning experiences and achievements will require much broader and holistic approaches to improving conditions and increasing economic opportunities in high-poverty neighborhoods.

NOTES

1. I use the term *parents* throughout this chapter. However, the study participants also included two caregivers that were not biological parents: one stepfather and one great-grandmother.

2. Names of schools, parents, and children have been changed.

3. Although the catchment areas of the two schools span two different community statistical areas, study participants and other residents I spoke with considered the catchment areas of both schools as part of the same neighborhood.

4. Thirty-four caregivers agreed to be interviewed after in-person recruitment efforts. I was unable to interview 10 of the 34 because they could not be found after recruitment despite numerous attempts at follow-up.

REFERENCES

Bell, C. A. (2009). All choices created equal? The role of choice sets in the selection of schools. *Peabody Journal of Education, 84*(2), 191–208.

Bennett, P. R., Lutz, A., & Jayaram, L. (2012). Beyond the schoolyard: The contributions of parenting logics, financial resources, and social institutions in the social class gap in structured activity participation. *Sociology of Education, 85*(2), 131–157.

Borman, G. D., Goetz, M. E., & Dowling, N. M. (2009). Halting the summer achievement slide: A randomized field trial of the KindergARTen Summer Camp. *Journal of Education for Students Placed at Risk, 14*(2), 133–147.

Chin, T., & Phillips, M. (2004). Social reproduction and child-rearing practices: Social class, children's agency, and the summer activity gap. *Sociology of Education, 77*(3), 185–210.

Condliffe, B. F., Boyd, M. L., & DeLuca, S. (2015). Stuck in school: How social context shapes school choice for inner-city students. *Teachers College Record, 117*(3).

Covay, E., & Carbonaro, W. (2010). After the bell participation in extracurricular activities, classroom behavior, and academic achievement. *Sociology of Education, 83*(1), 20–45.

DeLuca, S., & Rosenblatt, P. (2010). Does moving to better neighborhoods lead to better schooling opportunities? Parental school choice in an experimental housing voucher program. *The Teachers College Record, 112*(5), 1443–1491.

Holme, J. J. (2002). Buying homes, buying schools: School choice and the social construction of school quality. *Harvard Educational Review, 72*(2), 177–206.

Kim, J. S., & Quinn, D. M. (2013). The effects of summer reading on low-income children's literacy achievement from kindergarten to grade 8: A meta-analysis of classroom and home interventions. *Review of Educational Research, 83*(3), 386–431.

Kimelberg, S. M., & Billingham, C. M. (2012). Attitudes toward diversity and the school choice process: Middle-class parents in a segregated urban public school district. *Urban Education, 48*(2), 198–231.

Mavrogordato, M., & Stein, M. (2014). Accessing choice: A mixed-methods examination of how Latino parents engage in the educational marketplace. *Urban Education*, DOI: 0042085914553674.

McCombs, J. S., Pane, J. F., Augustine, C. H., Schwartz, H. L., Martorell, P., & Zakaras, L. (2014). *Ready for fall? Near-term effects of voluntary summer learning programs on low-income students' learning opportunities and outcomes.* Santa Monica, CA: RAND Corporation.

National Summer Learning Association (NSLA). (2012). *A scan of summer learning opportunities in Baltimore.* Baltimore, MD: Author. Retrieved from http://c.ymcdn.com/sites/www.abagrantmakers.org/resource/resmgr/glr/nsla_summer_learning_opportu.pdf

Small, M. L. (2006). Neighborhood institutions as resource brokers: Childcare centers, interorganizational ties, and resource access among the poor. *Social Problems. 53*(2), 274–292.

Stovel, K., & Shaw, L. (2012). Brokerage. *Annual Review of Sociology, 38*, 139–158.

CHAPTER 10

The Roles of Summertime in Child Obesity

Risks and Opportunities

Amy Bohnert, Nicole Zarrett, and Amy Heard

This chapter discusses how the summer months can contribute to child obesity. Depending on how summertime is spent, it can represent either a season of high risk for obesity or one of extended health promotion. We begin by describing the child obesity epidemic as an emerging global phenomenon and then outline major factors implicated in the historic rise of obesity in the United States. Costs and consequences of child obesity, as well as populations of young people at particular risk for becoming obese, will be summarized. Next, we review evidence on seasonal differences in the risk for obesity by discussing the most relevant factors to summertime weight gain. Obesity risk appears to be high for those with limited access to health-promoting activities and affordable, nutritious foods. However, parenting practices, sleep patterns, and unhealthy habits may also contribute to summer weight gain. From a positive youth development perspective, we review evidence on the link between how young people spend their out-of-school time and the development of obesity. This body of research suggests that different out-of-school contexts may pose differential risk for developing obesity during childhood. We conclude with examples of policy initiatives at the local, state, and federal levels that effectively incorporate summertime in efforts to reduce obesity and promote the healthy development of young people. We also identify gaps between existing science and policies and suggest areas where additional research is needed (e.g., modified school calendars, the content of activities during expanded learning time, quantity and quality of summer activities and programs).

The prevalence of obesity among children has tripled in the last 40 years (Ogden et al., 2006), and current estimates show that approximately one-third of children ages 2 to 19 are overweight or obese (Ogden, Carroll, Kit, & Flegal, 2014). The health implications of obesity are striking. Among children, obesity is associated with poorer levels of insulin, lipids, and blood pressure (Freedman, Mei, Srinivasan, Berenson, & Dietz, 2007). Obesity and related diseases (e.g., Type 2 Diabetes, cardiovascular disease) persist throughout the life span, with approximately 80% of overweight children becoming overweight adolescents (Nader et al., 2006), and overweight adolescents more likely to become overweight adults (Guo, Wu, Chumlea, & Roche, 2002). Accounting for weight gain throughout adulthood, it is estimated that the fact: lifetime incremental cost of childhood obesity ranges from approximately $12,000 to almost $20,000 (Finkelstein, Graham, & Malhotra, 2014), and annual hospital costs related to obesity in children 6 to 17 years old are close to $127 million per year (Goran, Ball, & Cruz, 2003). In addition to increased health costs, childhood obesity may be associated with compromised academic performance and cognitive functioning, such as impaired planning, inhibition, and problem-solving skills (Davis et al., 2007; Hillman, 2014).

Although the obesity epidemic is a public health concern affecting all demographics, low-income youth are disproportionately affected. Latino and black children are also more likely to be obese than their white counterparts (Drewnowski & Specter, 2004; Ogden et al., 2014). The problem of race and income are often confounded, making it difficult to disentangle the role of one factor versus another on obesity.

Schools, a focus of recent intervention efforts, have sought to provide healthier environments for their students. Although school intervention has been critical, evidence suggests that how youth spend their time when they are out of school, particularly during the summer months, may make a more significant contribution to obesity rates and BMI. Representing a quarter of the calendar year for average youth, summertime waking hours nearly equal the number of hours spent in school over the entire academic year (Mahoney, 2011), but rates of weight gain appear to be greater during these months.

Initial evidence of disproportionate weight gain during the summer months was reported in a study by von Hippel and colleagues (2007). Using nationally representative longitudinal data (N = 5380), results indicated that youths' average Body Mass Index (BMI: weight in kilograms divided by height in meters squared) growth was twice as fast during the summer months as compared to either the kindergarten or 1st-grade school years. Youth who were initially overweight exhibited a more pronounced decline in BMI during the school year as compared to normal-weight children. Ethnic differences in BMI increases were only evident[1] during the summer months. Black and Hispanic children exhibited greater BMI gains during the summertime as compared with White children.

Two other large-scale longitudinal studies drawing on data collected from a diverse sample of elementary school-age children in southeastern

Texas reported similar findings. The first study (N = 3734) published in 2013 by Moreno, Johnston, and Woehler, compared changes in zBMI (i.e., transformation and standardization of BMI, which indicates how many units a child's BMI is above or below average BMI based on sex and age) and BMI percentiles[3] during the school year as compared with the summer months, Moreno et al. found that children's BMI percentiles decreased by 1.5 percentile points during the school year, only to increase by 5.2 percentile points over the summer months. Although all youth gained weight during the summer months, only overweight and obese youth decreased their zBMI during the school year. Unlike von Hippel, Powell, Downey, and Rowland (2007), these patterns did not differ based on race or ethnicity.

In a second large-scale longitudinal study (N = 7599) by Moreno and colleagues (2015) relying on data from the same school district, consistent year-by-year fluctuations in zBMI started in 1st grade and prevailed through the start of 5th grade with zBMI increases during the summer months and zBMI decreases during the school year. This pattern emerged earlier (i.e., starting in kindergarten) among overweight and obese as well as Hispanic youth. The magnitude of the increases in zBMI diminished across the elementary school years. Collectively, these three studies use the largest and most representative data sets, but other noteworthy studies have reported summertime weight gain with more restricted samples.

Notably, Smith, Bartee, Dorozynski, and Carr (2009) conducted a longitudinal study using a convenience sample of American Indian elementary and middle school-age children (3rd through 8th grade; N = 141) and found that BMI during the summer months increased significantly among either boys or girls in all but 7th grade. Further, this study provided additional evidence that weight status is a risk factor for summertime weight gain with overweight and obese children evidencing significant increases in BMI that were not found among normal-weight children. These same effects were not replicated when zBMI was used. Another short-term, small-scale longitudinal study of similarly aged children (N = 30 4th and 5th graders) in rural Minnesota reported significant increases in BMI and BMI percentiles over the course of one summer (McCue, Marlatt, Sirard, & Dengel, 2013).

In contrast, a longitudinal, large-scale study of 454 younger American Indian children (Zhang et al., 2011) did not find evidence of summertime weight gain. Findings suggested lower zBMI growth during the summer months between kindergarten and 1st grade as compared to the kindergarten school year, and no variations in summertime weight gain based on weight status. Researchers speculated that the use of zBMI (rather than BMI or BMI percentile) as well as differences associated with American Indian reservation life may have contributed to the lack of findings. Although not mentioned by the authors, the age of the sample may have also contributed to the null findings given the less consistent findings regarding weight gain during the summer following kindergarten (see von Hippel et al., 2007, for an exception).

All of these studies, with the exception of Moreno et al. (2015), are included in two recent narrative reviews of summertime weight gain (see Baranowski et al., 2014; Franckle, Adler, & Davidson, 2014). Both reviews conclude that there is ample support of accelerated weight gain during the summer months for at least a portion of the study populations in both U.S. and international samples. Franckle and colleagues (2014) also highlight disparities in weight gain suggesting most robust increases among Black, Hispanic, and overweight children and adolescents. Both reviews also included studies of school-year weight-control interventions; in all instances, improvements in body weight, composition, and fitness made during the school year were lost during the summer months (Carrel, Clark, Peterson, Eickhoff, & Allen, 2007; Gillis, McDowell, & Bar-Or, 2005; Gutin, Yin, Johnson, & Barbeau, 2008; Yin, Moore, Johnson, Vernon, & Gutin, 2012). In addition to critically examining and summarizing the existing literature on summertime weight gain, both reviews also suggest potential mechanisms that may explain this effect.

CONTRIBUTING FACTORS TO SUMMERTIME WEIGHT GAIN

To date, no study has formally tested mechanisms or contributing factors to summertime weight gain using appropriate statistical modeling techniques (e.g., mediation). The two previously mentioned narrative reviews, however, propose several potential mechanisms. Baranowski and colleagues (2014) include a model of weight gain resulting from an energy imbalance that is attributed to child behaviors (i.e., physical activity, screen use, sleep, and diet), which are differentially affected by home and school environments during summer months (versus school year) as well as child weight status. Franckle and colleagues (2014) review the various obesogenic behaviors that have been *proposed* to contribute to summertime weight gain, including dietary intake (e.g., increases in unhealthy snacking, less access to healthier meals provided via school), physical activity (PA), sedentary behaviors, and irregular sleep patterns. Although no studies have empirically tested these mechanisms, a few studies have examined changes in these obesogenic behaviors during the summer months, but these results are far from being conclusive given study limitations in terms of methods and design.

One study of 30 elementary school-age children in rural Minnesota reported no differences in kilocalories (kcal) or macronutrients (e.g., protein, total fat, carbohydrates) consumed during the summertime versus the school year as assessed via a self-report food frequency questionnaire (McCue et al., 2013). Physical activity was also assessed in this study via accelerometers worn for a week. Increases in sedentary time and decreases in light and moderate activity during the summer as compared with the school year were noted, but there were no changes in MPVA or vigorous PA from school year to summertime.

Other studies of summertime physical activity and energy expenditure are inconclusive. One cross-sectional study of overweight and obese youth (N = 162) assessed during the summer compared with similar youth during the school year used doubly labeled water (i.e., a measure of elimination of various isotopes in bodily fluids that are consumed via dose of isotope-laden water) to measure total energy expenditure (TEE). Results suggested no differences in TEE between the school year and summer months (Zinkel et al., 2013). A recent review of seasonal differences in PA and sedentary time assessed via accelerometers suggests there is evidence that children engaged in more PA during the summer months as compared to the winter with more pronounced seasonal variations among younger children. Findings on sedentary behaviors were less conclusive (Rich, Griffiths, & Dezateux, 2012), but the authors state that further inquiry is needed. It is also important to highlight that summertime differences in PA and sedentary behaviors could vary based on weight status or race/ethnicity as is the case with BMI, but to date no study has examined this possibility.

One final obesogenic behavior that may vary from summertime relative to school year is sleep. Studies suggest that shorter sleep duration is associated with concurrent and future obesity risk (Hirshkowitz et al., 2015; Snell, Adam, & Duncan, 2007). Despite the relevance of sleep and the fact that children may go to sleep later in the summertime due to increased hours of daylight (Bénéfice, Garnier, & Ndiaye, 2004), only one study has considered summertime sleep patterns. Relying on a sample of school-age children (N = 591), Nixon and colleagues (2008) reported that during the summer, as compared to other seasons, children experience significant decreases in sleep duration and later bedtimes as assessed objectively using actigraphy.

EFFECTS OF STRUCTURED SUMMERTIME PROGRAMS ON BMI AND OBESOGENIC BEHAVIORS

Given the escalating individual and societal costs of obesity and the fact that summertime is a risk period for increased BMI and related obesogenic behaviors, it is imperative to identify solutions that may ameliorate summertime weight gain. Several studies have investigated the health benefits of structured summertime care and programs among community samples. Findings suggest that providing youth with structured programming during the summer months may be the most compelling solution to address weight gain.

Two recent studies relied on a nationally representative sample of youth ages 10–18 to consider the role of a variety of regular summertime arrangements on BMI. Arrangements included both structured and unstructured care. Approximately one-third of youth participated in organized activities as part of regular summer care. Controlling for youths' prior BMI as well as demographic factors associated with obesity, youth (N = 1766) who were involved routinely in structured care during the summertime were significantly less likely to be obese than youth whose summer care arrangements consisted solely of parent care without organized activities and care by other adults (Mahoney, 2011). This effect was most pronounced during early adolescence. A second study by this research team using the same data set suggested that after controlling for youths' prior BMI as well as demographic factors, those with regular involvement in structured summertime care arrangements had lower BMIs the following school year (Parente, Sheppard, & Mahoney, 2012). In addition, youth in self-care who also engaged in structured activities had lower BMIs than those in self-care alone. This effect was not found for youth in parent care or other adult care.

Another recent study of urban elementary school-age children (N = 57) examined whether obesogenic behaviors (physical activity and dietary intake) varied based on summer care arrangements (Tovar et al., 2010). Levels of sedentary behavior were highest when in the care of others (46%) and parents (41%) as opposed to camp (32%). Children with a greater percentage of time spent in structured programming were also significantly more active. In addition, after accounting for differences in maternal education, children who attended less than 5 weeks of camp were 4.5 times more likely to eat meals in a room with the TV turned on often/almost all the time.

Further evidence of the relevance of structured summertime programming comes from a recent study that considered the effects of a specific form of structured summertime programming (i.e., summer school) on weight and fitness among a group of low-income Hispanic adolescents. In this quasi-natural experiment, summertime weight gain was assessed among high school freshman who enrolled in a 5-week full-day mandatory summer school program (with academic enrichment as well as a daily 1-hour physical activity period) and compared with sophomores at the same high school who were not required to participate in any summer programming (Park & Lee, 2015). Results showed no significant weight gain for those enrolled in summer school, while students who did not attend summer school demonstrated significant increases in body weight and percent body fat as well as decreased aerobic fitness as measured at the beginning and end of the summer break. Furthermore, poorer self-esteem and body image were associated with greater fitness declines and more weight gain only among the students who did not attend summer school.

Rather than examining effects across different camps and care arrangements, Bohnert and colleagues (2014) investigated the effects of a 4-week summer program among 46 urban, low-income, predominately African American and Latina girls 10 to 14 years of age. The program provided physical activity as well as age-appropriate health and nutrition education. Participants were assessed prior to the start and during the final week of programming. Significant increases in MVPA and decreases in sedentary time of almost 2 hours/day were found, and these improvements did not vary by weight status or age. Despite the improvements in activity, girls experienced significant increases in zBMI (though not BMI percentile) over the course of programming.

FUTURE RESEARCH DIRECTIONS

To date, studies provide compelling evidence that summertime weight gain is prevalent among youth and that involvement in structured programming during the summer months may result in improved weight outcomes and reductions in obesogenic behaviors. However, several methodological limitations of the current studies need to be addressed in future work. First, very few studies have considered variations in obesogenic behaviors during summertime versus the school year to determine if there are true differences (see Nixon et al., 2008, for an exception). Second, and similarly, there is a need for a prospective, longitudinal study with shorter assessment intervals to better measure/capture BMI shortly before, during, and immediately after the summer (Mahoney, 2011). Third, the timing of the summer break from school in the United States does not allow for separation of what is a "no-school effect" from a seasonal effect (Baranowski et al., 2014; Franckle et al., 2014; Zhang et al., 2011). International data or schools in the United States with nontraditional calendars could help disentangle these effects. Fourth, closer attention needs to be paid to the use of BMI, zBMI, and BMI percentiles. In some instances, results vary based on which indices were used. zBMI is not thought to be as sensitive to change as BMI or BMI percentile (see Franckle et al., 2014). In addition, BMI norms used to calculate zBMI scores and percentiles were collected almost two decades ago and may not reflect secular changes in the population related to BMI (Zhang et al., 2011).

Finally, none of the studies of structured programs were randomized controlled trials, making it difficult to discern whether weight gain differences were a function of involvement in programming versus normal development. Further, a prospective study with randomized groups would also allow for full consideration of selection effects that are likely to play a substantial role in terms of determining whether children are enrolled in summer programs (e.g., Mahoney, 2011).

Related to selection effects, future research should consider that youth who are enrolled in structured summertime programming are likely to reside in families who have more rules and routines and engage in parenting practices that would promote signing up for such programming. These summertime experiences may also operate synergistically to facilitate the implementation of family rules and routines, particularly around mealtimes and bedtimes, due to demands from programming. Indeed, summer is likely to be accompanied by changes in household routines, such as mealtimes, snacking, and sleep, all of which are typically facilitated by the degree of structure offered during the school year (Moreno et al., 2015). One study interviewed parents about summertime care and found that families reported relaxing rules during these months (Tovar et al., 2010), despite their health-promoting benefits.

ADDRESSING OBESOGENIC BEHAVIORS IN PROGRAMS

Recognizing that the modification of contexts where youth spend their time may be a primary obesity prevention and intervention strategy, the Healthy Out-of-School Time Coalition was formed in 2009 to send a clear message about best health promotion practices in out-of-school-time (OST) programs. A collaborative effort between the National Institute on Out-of-School Time (NIOST), the University of Massachusetts Boston, and the YMCA of the USA led to the development of a comprehensive set of standards for promoting healthy eating and physical activity (HEPA) for youth attending OST programs, including summertime programs. Adopted by the National AfterSchool Association (NAA) in 2011, the HEPA standards provide guidelines and implementation strategies for meeting the USDHHS (2008) national recommendations for youth to accrue 60 minutes of daily physical activity and to meet nutritional standards of serving youth ample fruits and vegetables, beverages without added sugars (with water accessible at all times), and minimally processed foods made with whole grains, heart-healthy oils/fats, and without added sugar or trans-fat (Wiecha, Hall, Gannett, & Roth, 2011). A comprehensive list of HEPA standards can be found at www.niost.org.

Although research on the implementation of HEPA standards within organized summer programming is limited, initial studies suggest that youth are not accruing the recommended amounts of physical activity during program hours (Beets, Tilley, Weaver, Turner-McGrievy, & Moore, 2013; Hickerson & Henderson, 2013; Zarrett, Skiles, & Sorenson, 2012; Zarrett, Sorenson, & Skiles, 2013). In addition, studies using systematic observation found that while staff were consistently present, they were seldom observed demonstrating or participating in the physical activity with youth, or providing verbal praise or encouragement to initiate or increase physical activity (Weaver, Beets, Saunders, & Beighle, 2014; Weaver, Beets, Webster et al, 2014; Zarrett et al., 2012; Zarrett et al., 2013). Other studies have suggested that servings of water, fresh fruits and vegetables, and higher-fiber grains are too low, and snacks containing trans-fat and servings of fruit juice are too high, with staff not providing adequate nutrition promotion (e.g., discuss, emphasize, value HE, model their own HE), mentoring, or education as recommended by the HEPA guidelines (Tilley, Beets, Jones, & Turner-McGrievy, 2015; Weaver et al., 2014).

Reflective of these findings, local program leaders consistently report challenges in implementing HEPA-based standards (Hastmann, Bopp, Fallon, Rosenkranz, & Dzewaltowski, 2013; Mozaffarian, Andry, Lee, Gortmaker, & Wiecha, 2012; Zarrett, Abraczinskas, Cook, Wilson, & Ragaban, in press). For example, healthful foods are often perceived to be more expensive than less healthful snacks, with one study demonstrating that healthful snacks were 50% more expensive than the less healthful counterpart (Mozaffarian et al., 2012). Because OST programs operate on limited budgets and in some cases must follow federal menu guidelines (e.g., USDA's Summer Meals Program), program staff need guidance on identifying healthful snacks that are affordable and meet reimbursement guidelines.

Some programs provide little to no food or beverages to attending children, leaving parents responsible for the provision of snacks and lunch and making the challenge of meeting program standards for healthy eating that much more difficult (Beets et al., 2014). Similarly, barriers to implementation of PA within summer programming have been identified, including structural challenges such as access to ample recreational indoor and outdoor spaces (Zarrett et al., 2012) and social-contextual challenges such as appealing to all children's interests, competing with non-PA interests (e.g., smartphones, video games), managing peer cliques, and addressing children's self-consciousness, poor PA self-efficacy, and misbehaviors/discipline. Staff need guidance and training to develop effective strategies for engaging all program youth in PA (Weaver, Beets, Saunders, & Beighle, 2014; Zarrett et al., 2013).

Researchers have begun to develop several strategies to address HEPA implementation challenges. For example, YMCA sites in South Carolina, in collaboration with the University of South Carolina, have implemented a competency-based training procedure based on the 5Ms (Mission, Model, Manage, Monitor, Maximize) and LET US Play principles (lines, elimination, team size, uninvolved staff/kids, space, equipment, and rules) (Weaver, Beets, Webster, Beighle, & Huberty, 2012), to align program staff behaviors with those specified by the HEPA standards. The Harvard School of Public Health's Out of School Nutrition and Physical Activity (OSNAP) Initiative provides several summer programs online tools and training that guide them through a series of steps to assess the program's HEPA environment, identify areas of improvement, provide adequate staff training, build communication across all stakeholders, set goals for change, and re-evaluate the program environment (Lee et al., 2014).

For program sites that do not provide meals and/or snacks, the "Healthy Lunchbox Challenge" addresses how to regulate the nutritional value of the foods and beverages children bring to the program (Beets, Tilley, Weaver, Turner-McGrievy, & Moore, 2014). This program provides parents a guide to what constitutes a healthy lunchbox, tips on making healthy purchases at lower cost, and group-based competitions for youth that provide weekly incentives (e.g., extra swim time, movie tickets) to bring fruit, vegetables, and water for lunch/snack to the program daily.

Given all these implementation challenges, it is clear that under-resourced and/or short-duration programs, typically led by volunteers, would face additional struggles when implementing the HEPA standards. To address the specific needs of these programs, Silwa and colleagues (2014) used an advanced mixed-methods approach to derive the three evidence-based guidelines that are most feasible for short duration programming: "1) Drink right (choose water instead of sugar-sweetened beverages); 2) Move more (boost movement and physical activity during program time); 3) Snack smart (fuel up on fruits and vegetables)." To disseminate and provide resources to support the adoption of these guidelines, the ChildObesity180 group at Tufts University developed the Healthy Kids Out-of-School (HKOS) initiative and website tool kit (ChildObesity180, n.d.). The initiative was launched in 11 partner youth programming organizations, including the Boy Scouts of America, the Girl Scouts of America, and the National Council on Youth Sports. The efforts of HKOS and similar initiatives (e.g., Jago et al., 2006; Rosenkranz, Behrens, & Dzewaltowski, 2010; Thompson et al., 2009) provide an accessible and feasible solution to promoting HEPA practices and behavioral norms in short-duration programming that nicely complement the NAA-derived HEPA efforts adopted in other longer-duration youth OST settings.

One final issue that needs to be addressed given the challenges of implementing healthier practices is the motivation and incentive that programs have for making changes. The American Camp Association's national survey of summer programs in 2011 reported that "healthy eating and physical activity of attending youth" was a primary issue/concern facing summer camps (American Camp Association, 2011). However, even if programs may understand and wish to make changes, they may need to be incentivized to take on implementing HEPA standards, similar to the way school food quality has been quantified and incentivized in U.S. schools.

POLICY IMPLICATIONS

Summertime needs to be prioritized as a key context in which declines in academics *and* health can and must be addressed. Children at greatest risk for obesity during the summer months are the same children who experience high degrees of learning loss over the summer. Indeed, a common set of social-environmental factors affect both health and academics, putting the same subpopulations of American youth at greater risk during the summer (McLaughlin, 2012). Research suggests that getting youth engaged in structured summertime experiences over the summer is paramount to keeping both academic declines and weight gain at bay during the summer months.

In addition, summertime experiences among youth not only illustrate stark contrasts of resources, but also magnify existing inequalities in health and school performance.

The American Recovery and Reinvestment Act of 2009 provided a $10 billion increase in Title I funds that included the development of new summer activities. However, there are far too many children who are not able to access summertime programming. Although city mayors, such as Bill deBlasio in New York City, have expanded summer enrichment programs substantially, further efforts have fallen short, and calls for targeted education taxes to support summer programming are unpopular (Mead, 2015). Academic skills-based programs are more likely to get funded, allowing them to reach students who would not otherwise be able to attend an organized, academic program during the summer. Thus, another route to addressing summertime weight gain may be to leverage community connections to enhance health and reduce obesogenic behaviors at summer programs that address academics as a primary focus.

West Virginia's Energy Express program is one innovative example of a dual achievement/health program (West Virginia University, 2015) that focuses on enhancing literacy skills for a wide variety of both special and regular education children. Federally funded AmeriCorps service members staff the program, keeping the costs low. Almost three-fourths of Energy Express participants qualify for free or reduced-price lunch, and thus the secondary focus of Energy Express is providing nutritious, family-style meals to participants through the USDA Summer Food Service Program (SFSP). Other programs, like the YMCA Summer Learning Program, also focus on addressing academic skills using certified teachers for instruction while providing meals to participants through either federally funded programs like the SFSP or through support from private organizations (YMCA, 2012, 2015). The Y programs are also able to provide opportunities for physical activity for youth using their existing facilitates and other resources. In both of these programs, children receive high-quality instruction at a low cost and often receive one or two free meals in addition to opportunities to engage in physical activity. These programs have a unique opportunity to impact both the academic and physical health of their participants, and by combining nutrition and academics, the door may be open for additional funding opportunities that would not be available to academic-only programs.

In order to address obesity, it is essential that researchers and policymakers begin to consider summertime influences on obesity. To date, evidence suggests that summertime programming may be a more cost-effective strategy for addressing the disproportionate rates of obesity among youth. Encouraging legislators and policymakers to prioritize initiatives aimed at influencing youths' out-of-school time, particularly during the summer months, will best position our country to reverse summertime slide and address the obesity epidemic.

NOTES

1. These differences were evident as compared with the school year.

2. Standardized score of BMI, which indicates how many units a child's BMI is above or below average BMI based on sex and age.

3. Using sex and age normative data from the Centers for Disease Control and Prevention (Kuczmarski et al., 2000).

REFERENCES

American Camp Association. (2011). *2011 Camp emerging issues survey.* Martinsville, IN: Author. Retrieved from www.acacamps.org/research/improve/emerging-issues

American Recovery and Reinvestment Act of 2009, 111 U.S.C. (2009). Retrieved from www.gpo.gov/fdsys/pkg/PLAW-111publ5/html/PLAW-111publ5.htm

Baranowski, T., O'Connor, T., Johnston, C., Hughes, S., Moreno, J., Chen, T. A., Baranowski, J. (2014). School year versus summer differences in child weight gain: A narrative review. *Childhood Obesity, 10*(1), 18–24.

Beets, M. W., Tilley, F., Weaver, R. G., Turner-McGrievy, G. M., & Moore, J. B. (2014). Increasing fruit, vegetable and water consumption in summer day camps-3-year findings of the healthy lunchbox challenge. *Health Education Research, 29*(5), 812–821.

Beets, M. W., Weaver, R. G., Beighle, A., Webster, C., & Pate, R. R., (2013). How physically active are children attending summer day camps? *Journal of Physical Activity and Health, 10*(6), 850–855.

Bénéfice, E., Garnier, D., & Ndiaye, G. (2004). Nutritional status, growth and sleep habits among Senegalese adolescent girls. *European Journal of Clinical Nutrition, 58*(2), 292–301.

Bohnert, A. M., Ward, A. K., Burdette, K. A., Silton, R. L., & Dugas, L. R. (2014). Active summers matter: Evaluation of a community-based summertime program targeting obesogenic behaviors of low-income, ethnic minority girls. *New Directions for Youth Development, 2014*(13), 133–150.

Carrel, A. L., Clark, R. R., Peterson, S., Eickhoff, J., & Allen, D. B. (2007). School-based fitness changes are lost during the summer vacation. *Archives of Pediatrics and Adolescent Medicine, 161*(6), 561–564.

ChildObesity180. (n.d.). *Healthy kids, bright futures.* Retrieved from http://healthykidshub.org

Davis, C. L., Tomporowski, P. D., Boyle, C. A., Waller, J. L., Miller, P. H., Naglieri, J. A., & Gregoski, M. (2007). Effects of aerobic exercise on overweight children's cognitive functioning: A randomized controlled trial. *Research Quarterly for Exercise and Sport, 78*(5), 510–519.

Drewnowski, A., & Specter, S. E. (2004). Poverty and obesity: The role of energy density and energy costs. *American Journal of Clinical Nutrition, 79*(1), 6–16.

Finkelstein, E. A., Graham, W. C. K., & Malhotra, R. (2014). Lifetime direct medical costs of childhood obesity. *Pediatrics, 133*(5), 854–862.

Franckle, R., Adler, R., & Davison, K. (2014). Accelerated weight gain among children during summer versus school year and related racial/ethnic disparities: A systematic review. *Preventing Chronic Disease, 11,* E101.

Freedman, D. S., Mei, Z., Srinivasan, S. R., Berenson, G. S., & Dietz, W. H. (2007). Cardiovascular risk factors and excess adiposity among overweight children and adolescents: The Bogalusa Heart Study. *Journal of Pediatrics, 150*(1), 12–17.e2.

Gillis, L., McDowell, M., & Bar-Or, O. (2005). Relationship between summer vacation weight gain and lack of success in a pediatric weight control program. *Eating Behaviors, 6*(2), 137–143.

Goran, M. I., Ball, G. D. C., & Cruz, M. L. (2003). Obesity and risk of type 2 diabetes and cardiovascular disease in children and adolescents. *Journal of Clinical Endocrinology and Metabolism, 88*(4), 1417–1427.

Guo, S. S., Wu, W., Chumlea, W. C., & Roche, A. F. (2002). Predicting overweight and obesity in adulthood from body mass index values in childhood and adolescence. *American Journal of Clinical Nutrition, 76*(3), 653–658.

Gutin, B., Yin, Z., Johnson, M., & Barbeau, P. (2008). Preliminary findings of the effect of a 3-year after-school physical activity intervention on fitness and body fat: The Medical College of Georgia Fitkid Project. *International Journal of Pediatric Obesity, 3*(sup.1), 3–9.

Hastmann, T. J., Bopp, M., Fallon, E. A., Rosenkranz, R. R., & Dzewaltowski, D. A. (2013). Factors influencing the implementation of organized physical activity and fruit and vegetable snacks in the HOP'N After-School Obesity Prevention Program. *Journal of Nutrition Education and Behavior, 45*(1), 60–68.

Hickerson, B. D., & Henderson, K. A. (2013). Opportunities for promoting youth physical activity: An examination of youth summer camps. *Journal of Physical Activity and Health, 11*(1), 199–205.

Hillman, C. H. (2014). An introduction to the relation of physical activity to cognitive and brain health, and scholastic achievement. *Monographs of the Society for Research in Child Development, 79*(4), 1–6.

Hirshkowitz, M., Whiton, K., Albert, S. M., Alessi, C., Bruni, O., DonCarlos, L., & Hillard, P. J. A. (2015). National Sleep Foundation's sleep time duration recommendations: methodology and results summary. *Sleep Health, 1*(1), 40–43.

Jago, R., Baranowski, T., Baranowski, J. C., Thompson, D., Cullen, K. W., Watson, K., & Liu, Y. (2006). Fit for Life Boy Scout badge: Outcome evaluation of a troop and internet intervention. *Preventive Medicine, 42*(3), 181–187.

Kuczmarski, R. J., Ogden, C. L., Grummer-Strawn, L. M., Flegal, K. M., Guo, S. S., Wei, R., Johnson, C. L. (2000). CDC growth charts: United States. *Advance Data, 314,* 1–27.

Lee, R. M., Emmons, K. M., Okechukwu, C. A., Barrett, J. L., Kenney, E. L., Cradock, A. L., . . . Gortmaker, S. L. (2014). Validity of a practitioner-administered observational tool to measure physical activity, nutrition, and screen time in school-age programs. *International Journal of Behavioral Nutrition and Physical Activity, 11*(1), 145.

Mahoney, J. L. (2011). Adolescent summer care arrangements and risk for obesity the following school year. *Journal of Adolescence, 34*(4), 737–749.

McCue, M., Marlatt, K., Sirard, J., & Dengel, D. (2013). Examination of changes in youth diet and physical activity over the summer vacation period. *Internet Journal of Allied Health Science and Practice, 11*(1), 1–6.

McLaughlin, B. (2012). *Healthy summers for kids: Turning risk into opportunity.* Retrieved from https://c.ymcdn.com/sites/www.summerlearning.org/resource/resmgr/Healthy_Summers_/NSLA_Healthy_Summers_for_Kid.pdf

Mead, R. (2015, May 29). The cost of New York's summer slide. *New Yorker.* Retrieved from www.newyorker.com/news/daily-comment/the-cost-of-new-yorks-summer-slide

Moreno, J. P., Johnston, C. A., Chen, T. A., O'Connor, T. A., Hughes, S. O., Baranowski, J., & Baranowski, T. (2015). Seasonal variability in weight change during elementary school. *Obesity, 23*(2), 422–428.

Moreno, J. P., Johnston, C. A., & Woehler, D. (2013). Changes in weight over the school year and summer vacation: Results of a 5-year longitudinal study. *Journal of School Health, 83*(7), 473–477.

Mozaffarian, R. S., Andry, A., Lee, R. M., Gortmaker, S. L., & Wiecha, J. L. (2012). Price and healthfulness of snacks in 32 YMCA afterschool programs in 4 U.S. metropolitan areas, 2006–2008. *Preventing Chronic Disease, 9,* E38.

Nader, P. R., O'Brien, M., Houts, R., Bradley, R., Belsky, J., Crosnoe, R., Susman, E. J. (2006). Identifying risk for obesity in early childhood. *Pediatrics, 118*(3), e594–e601.

National AfterSchool Association. (2011). *National AfterSchool Association standards for healthy eating and physical activity.* Retrieved from www.naaweb.org/downloads/resources/HEPAStandards8-4-11final.pdf

Nixon, G. M., Thompson, J. M., Han, D. Y., Becroft, D. M., Clark, P. M., Robinson, E., & Mitchell, E. A. (2008). Short sleep duration in middle childhood: Risk factors and consequences. *Sleep, 31*(1), 71–78.

Ogden, C. L., Carroll, M. D., Curtin, L. R., McDowell, M. A., Tabak, C. J., & Flegal, K. M. (2006). Prevalence of overweight and obesity in the United States, 1999–2004. *JAMA, 295*(13), 1549–1555.

Ogden, C. L., Carroll, M. D., Kit, B. K., & Flegal, K. M. (2014). Prevalence of childhood and adult obesity in the United States, 2011–2012. *JAMA, 311*(8), 806–814.

Parente, M. E., Sheppard, A., & Mahoney, J. L. (2012). Parental knowledge as a mediator of the relation between adolescent summer care arrangement configurations and adjustment the following school year. *Applied Developmental Science, 16*(2), 84–97.

Park, K. S., & Lee, M. G. (2015). Effects of summer school participation and psychosocial outcomes on changes in body composition and physical fitness during summer break. *Journal of Exercise Nutrition and Biochemistry, 19*(2), 81–90.

Rich, C., Griffiths, L. J., & Dezateux, C. (2012). Seasonal variation in accelerometer-determined sedentary behaviour and physical activity in children: A review. *International Journal of Behavioral Nutrition and Physical Activity, 9*(1), 49.

Rosenkranz, R. R., Behrens, T. K., & Dzewaltowski, D. A. (2010). A group randomized controlled trial for health promotion in Girl Scouts: Healthier troops in a SNAP (Scouting Nutrition & Activity Program). *BMC Public Health, 10*(81), 1–13.

Sliwa, S. A., Sharma, S., Dietz, W. H., Dolan, P. R., Nelson, M. E., Newman, M. B., & Economos, C. D. (2014). Peer reviewed: Healthy kids out of school: Using mixed methods to develop principles for promoting healthy eating and physical activity in out-of-school settings in the United States. *Preventing Chronic Disease, 11,* E227.

Smith, D. T., Bartee, R. T., Dorozynski, C. M., & Carr, L. J. (2009). Peer reviewed: Prevalence of overweight and influence of out-of-school seasonal periods on body mass index among American Indian schoolchildren. *Preventing Chronic Disease, 6*(1), A20.

Snell, E. K., Adam, E. K., & Duncan, G. J. (2007). Sleep and the body mass index and overweight status of children and adolescents. *Child Development, 78*(1), 309–323.

Thompson, D., Baranowski, T., Baranowski, J., Cullen, K., Jago, R., Watson, K., & Liu, Y. (2009). Boy Scout 5-a-Day Badge: Outcome results of a troop and internet intervention. *Preventive Medicine, 49*(6), 518–526.

Tilley, F., Beets, M. W., Jones, S., & Turner-McGrievy, G. (2015). Evaluation of compliance to national nutrition policies in summer day camps. *Public Health Nutrition, 18*(9), 1620–1625.

Tovar, A., Lividini, K., Economos, C. D., Folta, S., Goldberg, J., & Must, A. (2010). School's out: What are urban children doing? The summer activity study of Somerville youth (SASSY). *BMC Pediatrics, 10,* 16–27.

von Hippel, P. T., Powell, B., Downey, D. B., & Rowland, N. J. (2007). The effect of school on overweight in childhood: Gain in body mass index during the school year and during summer vacation. *American Journal of Public Health, 97*(4), 696–702.

Weaver, R., Beets, M., Saunders, R. P., & Beighle, A. (2014). A coordinated comprehensive professional development training's effect on summer day camp staff healthy eating and physical activity promotion behaviors. *Journal of Physical Activity and Health, 11*(6), 1170–1178.

Weaver, R., Beets, M. W., Webster, C., Beighle, A., & Huberty, J. (2012). A conceptual model for training after-school program staffers to promote physical activity and nutrition. *Journal of School Health, 82*(4), 186–195.

Weaver, R., Beets, M., Webster, C., & Huberty, J. (2014). System for observing staff promotion of activity and nutrition (SOSPAN). *Journal of Physical Activity and Health, 11,* 173–185.

West Virginia University. (2015, June 11). *What is Energy Express?* Retrieved from http://energyexpress.ext.wvu.edu

Wiecha, J. L., Hall, G., Gannett, E., & Roth, B. (2011). *National after school association standards for healthy eating and physical activity.* Retrieved from www.niost.org/Standards-andGuidelines/national-afterschool-association-standards-for-healthy-eating-andphysical-activity-in-out-of-school-time-programs

Yin, Z., Moore, J. B., Johnson, M. H., Vernon, M. M., & Gutin, B. (2012). The impact of a 3-year after-school obesity prevention program in elementary school children. *Childhood Obesity, 8*(1), 60–70.

YMCA of the USA. (2012). *The Y is 'serving up summer' with Walmart Foundation to fight child hunger* [Press release]. Retrieved from www.ymca.net/news-releases/20120620-summer-food.html

YMCA of the USA. (2015). *Achievement gap*. Retrieved from www.ymca.net/achievement-gap

Zarrett, N., Abraczinskas, M., Cook, B., Wilson, D.K. & Ragaban, F. (in press). Promoting physical activity within under-resourced afterschool programs: A qualitative investigation of staff experiences and motivational strategies for engaging youth. *Applied Developmental Science*.

Zarrett, N., Sorensen, C., & Skiles, B. (2013). Environmental and social-motivational contextual factors related to youth physical activity: Systematic observations of summer day camps. *International Journal of Behavioral Nutrition and Physical Activity, 10*, 63–76.

Zhang, J., Himes, J. H., Hannan, P. J., Arcan, C., Smyth, M., Rock, B. H., & Story, M. (2011). Summer effects on body mass index (BMI) gain and growth patterns of American Indian children from kindergarten to first grade: A prospective study. *BMC Public Health, 11*(1), 951.

Zinkel, S. R. J., Moe, M., Stern, E. A., Hubbard, V. S., Yanovski, S. Z., Yanovski, J. A., & Schoeller, D. A. (2013). Comparison of total energy expenditure between school and summer months. *Pediatric Obesity, 8*(5), 404–410.

CHAPTER 11

Summertime and Youth's Psychosocial Well-Being

Amy Bohnert, Dorothy McLeod, Heather Marshall,
and Kathryn Grant

This chapter examines the implications of summertime for youth's psychosocial well-being, reviewing the existing literature on seasonal variations in psychological well-being. Particular attention is paid to the unique challenges associated with different environments (urban vs. suburban vs. rural) during the summer months. For instance, urban low-income youth often experience higher rates of crime during the summer months, which has implications for well-being. In reviewing the existing literature, we highlight the role of different care situations during the summer months and the potential influence of these situations on promoting better psychosocial outcomes. Finally, several examples of programs and/or citywide initiatives that have demonstrated success in promoting psychological well-being among youth are explored to offer a primer on best practices that can be used by agencies to improve summertime offerings for youth.

For most American youth, the 3-month summertime period is characterized by a lack of formal schooling as well as seasonal differences compared with the other 9 months of the year. The implication of these changes is that youth's daily experiences and activities are quite different than when they are enrolled in school. These differences are likely to be more pronounced among youth who have limited access to summer programming because of cost or availability. In addition, for children living in urban communities, summertime with its warmer weather also brings increases in crime and greater risk for exposure to violence (Anderson, Bushman, & Groom, 1997; Bushman, Wang, & Anderson, 2005; Kenrick & MacFarlane, 1986;

Reifman, Larrick, & Fein, 1991). They may also experience higher levels of alienation, which occur predominately in the context of unstructured activities, such as television viewing (Larson & Kleiber, 1993), which characterizes many urban youths' summers (Gershenson, 2013).

Despite the fact that summertime represents a significant portion of children's time and is characterized by notable differences in their daily lives, there is limited information about youths' summertime experiences and the impact of these experiences on psychological well-being. In this chapter, we seek to (1) describe summertime experiences for youth, with particular attention paid to the unique challenges associated with low-income status and living in an urban environment; (2) highlight the role of different care arrangements, including various types of structured programming, during the summer months and their potential to promote better psychological outcomes; and (3) describe limitations and future directions for research on summertime programs as well as policy implications of the work conducted to date.

Summertime care arrangements vary considerably across families and on a daily basis among youth residing in the United States. A report by the U.S. Census Bureau found that during the summer, less than half of school-age children were in a regular child-care arrangement. Employed mothers were more likely to have regular summertime care arrangements than unemployed mothers, though both employed and unemployed mothers showed an increase in overall hours of care from the spring to the summer (Laughlin, 2010). Similarly, one report (Wimer et al., 2006) indicates that only 36% of American youth ages 6 to 11 participate in any type of structured or organized activities during summertime. The rates are even lower among low-income youth (4%).

Further evidence of the disparities in how youth spend their time during the summer months was found in a recent time use study. Compared to children from more affluent households, children from low-income households watch significantly more television, spend significantly less time conversing with adults, and experience significantly less parental involvement in their day-to-day-life over the summer (Gershenson, 2013). Researchers have coined the term "faucet theory" to describe how children in low-income households are not as able to compensate as their high-SES counterparts when the flow of resources from the school tap are shut off during the summer months (Entwisle, Alexander, & Olson, 2001). Not only do low-income youth have less access to valuable resources during the summer, they may also experience greater challenges to their psychological well-being, most notably in the form of increased risk of exposure to violence.

Children and adolescents living in low-income communities are at highest risk for exposure to violence and the many psychological problems associated with it. Many studies of low-income urban adolescents have demonstrated that remarkably high percentages of these youth have witnessed or heard shootings themselves or heard about someone they know being a victim of gun violence (Pastore, Fisher, & Friedman, 1996; Fowler, Tompsett, Braciszewski, Jacques-Tiura, & Baltes, 2009). Research suggests that rates of exposure rise during the summer months, when violence peaks (e.g., Anderson, Bushman, & Groom, 1997; Bushman, Wang, & Anderson, 2005; Kenrick & MacFarlane, 1986; Reifman, Larrick, & Fein, 1991). To illustrate, Chicago has made the national news with skyrocketing shootings— over 200 per month in 2014, with the highest incidence of gun violence during the summer months (Chicago Tribune, n.d.).

Some of the very characteristics that make summertime unique (e.g., reduced structure, more time with peers, warm weather, more hours of sunlight) also increase the likelihood that youth will be exposed to violence. The heat hypothesis, or the idea that aggression is heightened when temperatures reach uncomfortably hot levels, has received some research support (Anderson et. al., 1997; Larrick, Timmerman, Carton, & Abrevaya, 2011; Preti, Miotto, De Coppi, Petretto, & Carmelo, 2002), but others have suggested that the relation between heat and violence is likely to be curvilinear, such that individuals are more likely to be violent when the temperature is most comfortable for being outside (Rotton & Cohn, 2000). With more pleasant temperatures and longer days, more people spend time out of doors for extended hours, providing increased opportunities for all types of behavior, including violence (Cohn & Rotton, 1997). The trend for escalated alcohol consumption during summer has also been implicated in increased rates of violence during summertime (Bushman & Cooper, 1990).

Even more established than the link between summertime and violence exposure are the associations between violence exposure and psychological well-being in children and adolescents. Numerous studies have demonstrated that exposure to community violence not only poses physical risks for young people but also leads to a range of psychological problems. These include post-traumatic stress disorder (PTSD), depression, alcohol and drug abuse, conduct problems, sleeplessness, emotion regulation problems, and suicide (Boxer et al., 2008; Buka, Stichick, Birdthistle, & Earls, 2001; Fowler et al., 2009; Kliewer & Lepore, 2015).

Although it has been established that rates of violence increase in the summertime, no study to date has directly addressed whether youth are disproportionately exposed to community violence during this season. However, it is highly probable that their exposure risk increases over the summer months given the lack of availability of and involvement in structured settings, in the form of school or other care arrangements. Supporting this notion is a daily diary study that found African American youth in Chicago were exposed to, on average, one form of community violence per day. These rates were higher in the afternoons, and even though youth spent about 20% of their time outside of school and home, about half of the incidents of exposure occurred in a public (nonschool) setting (Richards et al., 2015). Further support comes from a study conducted with low-income, urban Latino youth that found spending unstructured time with peers during after-school hours increased the likelihood of being a victim of violence or witnessing violence (Kennedy & Ceballo, 2013). These findings suggest a need for further research on how violence in summer months affects the amount of violence exposure or victimization experienced among urban youth populations.

There is less information about exposure to violence for rural and suburban youth, but existing evidence suggests that children who live in suburban and rural areas also experience relatively high exposure to community violence (Johnson et al., 2008) and face additional risk when there is a lack of parental supervision (Slovak & Singer, 2001). Youth in rural and suburban areas also experience psychological symptoms in response to gun violence (Fowler et al., 2009; Slovak & Singer, 2001), yet the problem is less recognized and there are even fewer mental health services available to families in rural communities (Merwin, Hinton, Dembling, & Stern, 2003).

In addition to increased violence risks, boredom and alienation are negative emotional states that may characterize summertime, particularly for youth who are not involved in any structured care. Studies of time use indicate that adolescents experience higher levels of intrinsic motivation, challenge, positive affect, and attention/concentration as well as low levels of alienation during structured after-school activities, such as sports, arts, and organizations, as compared with unstructured activities (Bohnert, Richards, Kolmodin, & Lakin, 2008; Csikszentmihalyi & Larson, 1984; Larson & Kleiber, 1993; Shernoff & Vandell, 2007; Vandell et al., 2005). In contrast, watching television and other unstructured, passive activities are associated with higher levels of alienation and lower levels of challenge, positive affect, and attention/concentration (as compared with structured activities) among adolescents (Larson & Kleiber, 1993).

The experience of alienation and boredom may be particularly prevalent among low-income youth during the summer months given that they watch significantly more television, spend significantly less time conversing with adults, and experience significantly less parental involvement in their day-to-day-life over the summer than peers from high-SES households (Gershenson, 2013), as reviewed above.

Alienation is associated with elevated levels of delinquent behaviors (O'Donnell, Schwab-Stone, & Ruchkin, 2006), as well as psychological distress, including depressive symptoms (O'Donnell et al., 2006; Segrin & Abramson, 1994; Shevlin, Murphy, & Murphy, 2014; Stader & Hokanson, 1998). Additionally, with less attention from parents and therefore likely greater unsupervised time with friends, low-income adolescents may be more likely to use drugs and alcohol (Lee & Vandell, 2015).

In sum, children and adolescents residing in low-income households are potentially at greatest risk for summertime violence exposure. Combined with the lack of structured care, high levels of violence may mean that youth are spending many hours indoors watching television, an experience that is likely to lead to feelings of boredom, alienation, and loneliness. Collectively, this suggests that there is a need for summertime experiences and settings that can contribute positively to youth's development.

Various theoretical frameworks offer unique perspectives on how care arrangements during the summer months contribute to youth's psychological well-being. Positive youth development is a strengths-based conception of development holding that change is a consequence of mutually influential relationships between the developing person and his/her biology, psychological characteristics, family, community, and culture (Lerner, Almerigi, Theokas, & Lerner, 2005). The Five Cs of competence, confidence, connection, character, and caring are a common conceptualization of the key tenets of positive youth development (Lerner et al., 2005).

Another theoretical framework, the bio-ecological perspective (Bronfenbrenner & Morris, 2006) identifies contextual influences, particularly at the microsystem level (i.e., characterized by activities and/or in-person interactions at school or in the neighborhood) as especially important to the developing individual. Involvement in structured settings, such as programming or camps, may both help youth avoid adverse outcomes and promote positive development in spite of challenges (e.g., Bialeschki, Henderson, & James, 2007). An implication of this theory is that the consequences of involvement vary depending on what other resources and supports are available to youth (Mahoney, Vandell, Simpkins, & Zarrett, 2009). Thus, the impact of structured settings may be greater during the summer months due to the lack of school as a developmental context, particularly for those who experience increased risks to their psychological well-being.

To date, the most comprehensive study of the influence of summertime care arrangements was conducted by Parente, Sheppard, and Mahoney (2012). Using a large, nationally representative sample (PSID-CDS, with 1766 participants ages 10–19; 49% male; 62% White), researchers sought to identify common summertime arrangements and establish associations with both positive and negative psychological well-being, including emotional well-being, externalizing behavior, and internalizing behavior. Parents were asked to report on care arrangements that were used on a regular basis by their child during the summer. Responses were grouped into three categories (dichotomously coded): (1) parent care, (2) self-care, (3) care from other adults. These categories were then subdivided into whether the child had regular participation in organized activities (OA), resulting in six mutually exclusive categories. Finally, a seventh group comprised children who reported OA as their primary summer care arrangement.

Findings suggested that the majority of youth's summer arrangements did not involve OA participation. However, involvement in organized activities during the summer months was associated with significantly better emotional well-being and fewer externalizing behaviors in the following academic year, even after accounting for demographic variables and baseline levels of functioning. These effects of summertime on outcomes were replicated in both younger and older samples, but were most pronounced for adolescents who were regularly unsupervised during the summer months (i.e., self-care).

Parente and colleagues (2012) also considered whether the benefit of being involved in structured OA settings during the summertime provided an advantage to psychological well-being because parents knew where their children were during the daytime hours. Youth were asked to report on parents' knowledge of youth's free time activities and friends, as well as how the youth spent their money. As expected, parental knowledge mediated the relation between OA and emotional well-being, as well as the relationship between OA and externalizing behaviors, especially for youth regularly involved in self-care. Collectively, these findings suggest that involvement in structured care settings over the summer months is advantageous when considering multiple aspects of psychological well-being, and this may be due in part to the fact that parents know where their children are when they are involved in structured settings during the summer months.

Another notable effort to evaluate summertime care arrangements and psychological well-being is the review conducted by Bialeschki and colleagues (2007) as part of an effort by the American Camp Association (ACA). These authors compiled studies on camp settings, a majority of which occur during the summer, and developmental outcomes for youth, finding positive effects within four categories: self-constructs, social relationship outcomes, skill-building outcomes, and spiritual outcomes. Results of the review revealed that children experience some positive outcomes in each of these categories as a result of participation, thus making an argument that camp contributes to positive youth development.

In addition to this review of the research, another important contribution arose from the ACA's evaluation of its own camp programming. In the first longitudinal study of the value of camp programming for child development, Henderson and colleagues (2006) developed the Camper Growth Index (CGI). This survey measures growth in four domains: positive identity (e.g., self-esteem), social skills (e.g., friendship skills), physical and thinking skills (e.g., environmental awareness), and positive values/spirituality (e.g., values/decisions). The CGI was then administered to a large, representative sample of ACA-accredited camps serving youth between the ages of 8 to 14 years, pre- and post-programming (Thurber, Scanlin, Scheuler, & Henderson, 2006).

Findings from this study indicated that children reported significant improvements predominately in the positive identity domain, including self-esteem, independence, and leadership skills, as well as in the domain of social skills (e.g., friendship skills). In addition, parents also completed an adapted version of the CGI pre- and post-programming. Similar to youth reports, parents reported significant improvements in all four domains assessed (Thurber et al., 2006). The researchers created a nonrandomized comparison group from the sample itself by using the youth's pre-programming scores to calculate derived scores for post-programming outcome variables, using an expected age function to model maturation processes. By comparing actual measured change in outcomes to the modeled effects, they concluded that the improvements among camp participants were significantly greater than would be predicted due to maturation. This major study is yet another compelling piece of evidence that summer programming enhances well-being outcomes among youth.

Beyond the realm of literature reviews and large-scale, national studies, other programmatic evaluations have indicated that summertime programming can have a variety of positive effects on youth's well-being. These effects fall into three broad categories: self-perceptions, delinquency, and psychological distress.

SELF-PERCEPTIONS

Summertime programming research has widely used self-report measures to study outcomes, and therefore a majority of findings in the area have used self-perception variables. Self-constructs, which include self-esteem, self-confidence, self-identity, self-efficacy, and self-determination, all deal with perceptions of the individual (Bialeschki et al., 2007), and, in a reflection of findings from the large-scale study by Thurber et al. (2006), these constructs have been found to improve with participation in summer programming. For example, at-risk urban youth, ages 6 to 12 years of age, who participated in a residential, "sleep-away" camp program exhibited increases in self-esteem following programming (Readdick & Schaller, 2005).

The related constructs of self-worth and hope for the future also deal with positive thoughts directed towards the self and have also been associated with participation in summer programming. In particular, research suggests that low-income youth (ages 8–13) who were long-term (i.e., multiple-year) participants of a 4-week summer program focused on teaching various sports and physical activities reported increases in self-worth and hopefulness at the completion of programming. Notably, multi-year participants demonstrated higher increases in self-worth than those youth who participated in programming for only one summer (Ullrich-French & McDonough, 2013). This suggests that there may be some additive effect of structured summertime programming, such that participating across multiple years increases its positive effects. Additionally, Kirschman, Roberts, Shadlow, and Pelley (2010) found that there was an increase in hopeful thinking following participation in a dance-based 6-week summer day camp for 11- to 14-year-old, at-risk urban youth.

Although all of these aforementioned studies involved the use of youth self-report measures, parents of youth participating in summer programming have corroborated improvements in self-perceptions. One qualitative study interviewed parents of 10- to 12-year-olds who were involved in summer sport-based youth development programs. These interviews, conducted during the course of programming, revealed that parents perceived their children were experiencing significant improvements in beliefs about the self as a result of programming (Riley & Anderson-Butcher, 2012).

DELINQUENCY

Summertime programming may also serve to prevent future criminal involvement among youth who are at high risk. Research examining a summertime youth program for at-risk 16- to 21-year-olds, which included employment and volunteering opportunities, reported that the more hours youth spent engaged in employment and volunteering, the less likely they were to be rearrested (Naccarato, Brophy, & Courtney, 2010). Heller (2014) also found that summertime employment programs for 14- to 21-year-old at-risk youth reduced future violent arrests, regardless of whether youth received additional programming in socio-emotional learning. This suggests that the structure provided by the summertime programming may have been more influential than its specific content.

PSYCHOLOGICAL DISTRESS

One final way in which summertime programming may enhance well-being is to prevent psychological distress. Ehrenreich-May and Bilek (2011) detail the implementation of an anxiety- and depression-prevention program within the context of a 15-session recreational sports summer camp for 7- to 10-year-olds. There were significant decreases in anxiety symptoms from pre- to post-programming, but no significant changes for depressive symptoms and emotion regulation.

FUTURE DIRECTIONS

Although this is a comprehensive review of all the known research on summer programming and well-being, many questions remain unanswered. None of studies of programming effects used a randomized, controlled design, meaning that it is not possible to know if the documented changes in well-being are due to maturation or program participation. Furthermore, without the use of randomized designs, the possibility of selection effects cannot be eliminated. That is, youth who enroll and participate in summer programming are likely to be different than those who do not enroll. Future work should seek to understand from adolescents' and parents' perspectives why they choose certain summertime arrangements and not others (Parente et al., 2012). In addition, it will be important for more studies to consider summer care arrangements from a bioecological perspective, including more attention to how the effects of participating in specific programs may be enhanced based on other ecological factors at the individual, familial, and neighborhood levels (Parente et al., 2012). One final point to consider is publication bias and how the desire to disseminate only studies showing positive effects may exaggerate the effectiveness of summertime programming to improve psychological well-being. Nevertheless, this is an exciting area of study and one that merits more attention.

POLICY IMPLICATIONS

Although there is reason to believe that summer programming, particularly if it is high quality and follows principles of positive youth development, is likely to be a protective setting for youth, there are not enough opportunities for youth to engage in such programs. Families most in need may not only lack the resources to access summer programming, but also lack knowledge about their existence, as well as the important benefits that may be follow from participation.

Chin and Phillips (2004) argue that the evidenced social class differences in children's summertime engagement stem almost entirely from parents' differential access to resources, including money and the human, cultural, and social capital necessary to know (1) how to assess children's skills, (2) which methods would be helpful for improving these skills, and (3) how to locate programs to accomplish these goals. Programming should therefore aim to be easily accessed by a diverse group of families by providing financial aid and transportation options whenever possible. In particular, research suggests that programming will be especially valuable to youth who are likely to be unsupervised during the summer months (Parente et al., 2012). Schools may be the ideal setting in which information about high-quality summer programs could be easily disseminated via summertime fairs or parent workshops.

Increasingly, cities are developing initiatives that attempt to increase participation in after-school programs, including ensuring that families have equitable access to and information about after-school opportunities (Little, Wimer, & Weiss, 2008). Cities like Chicago have also recognized the same need during summertime. To address this need, in 2013, Chicago's Summer Learning Initiative began as the "first coordinated and dedicated approach of its kind to provide youth in every Chicago neighborhood access to high-quality programs that will help them continue to learn throughout the summer months" (Chicago Public Schools, 2013). This evolved in 2014 into part of the Cities of Learning (COL) Initiative. In this initiative, students can earn virtual badges for logging in and reporting activities, which are offered online or through a network of libraries, museums, parks, or other institutions. Although this program is well intended, research suggests that the youth most in need of programming during the summer (those of lower socioeconomic status) are those who are least likely to have access to phones or Internet connections (Madden, 2013). In addition, studies have shown that the best out-of-school-time programming to reach all youth, particularly those most in need, provides youth with clear structure and supervision, provides a setting for connections to staff, and develops close relationships with families (Little et al., 2008).

In summary, although there is limited research on the relevance of summertime for well-being, there is a wealth of knowledge that can be drawn on to inform practice based on studies of after-school programming. Substantial research suggests that how youth spend their out-of-school time has significant short-term and long-term benefits for well-being (i.e., Mahoney, Vandell, Simpkins, & Zarrett, 2009). Unfortunately, for many reasons, including the lack of access to youth as study participants over the summer months, very little is known about the benefits and consequences of time use over the summer months. This knowledge gap needs to be filled, especially as we seek to address inequalities among America's youth. In the meantime, policymakers should focus efforts on enhancing summertime care options, including high-quality programs, particularly for those from low-income and urban households who are obliged to find their own care arrangements in under-resourced communities when the school faucet turns off, the time when they arguably most need those critical child supports.

REFERENCES

Anderson, C. A., Bushman, B. J., & Groom, R. W. (1997). Hot years and serious and deadly assault: Empirical tests of the heat hypothesis. *Journal of Personality and Social Psychology, 73*, 1213–1223.

Bialeschki, M. D., Henderson, K. A., & James, P. A. (2007). Camp experiences and developmental outcomes for youth. *Child and Adolescent Psychiatric Clinics of North America, 16*(4), 769–788.

Bohnert, A. M., Richards, M. H., Kolmodin, K. E., & Lakin, B. L. (2008). Young urban African American adolescents' experiences of discretionary time activities. *Journal of Research on Adolescence, 18*(3), 517–539.

Boxer, P., Sheffield Morris, A., Terranova, A. M., Kithakye, M., Savoy, S. C., & McFaul, A. F. (2008). Coping with exposure to violence: Relations to emotional symptoms and aggression in three urban samples. *Journal of Child and Family Studies, 17*, 881–893.

Bronfenbrenner, U., & Morris, P. A. (2006). The bioecological model of human development. In W. Damon & R. M. Lerner (Eds.), *Handbook of child psychology, Vol. 1: Theoretical models of human development* (6th ed., pp. 793–828). New York, NY: John Wiley.

Buka, S. L., Stichick, T. L., Birdthistle, I., & Earles, F. J. (2001). Youth exposure to violence: Prevalence, risk, and consequences. *American Journal of Orthopsychiatry, 71*, 298–310.

Bushman, B. J., & Cooper, H. M. (1990). Effects of alcohol on human aggression: An integrative research review. *Psychological Bulletin, 107*, 341–354.

Bushman, B. J., Wang, M. C., & Anderson, C. A. (2005). Is the curve relating temperature to aggression linear or curvilinear? A response to Bell (2005) and to Cohn and Rotton (2005). *Journal of Personality and Social Psychology, 88*, 74–78.

Chicago Tribune. (n.d.). Chicago shooting victims [Graphic illustrating monthly totals and locations of shootings]. Retrieved from http://crime.chicagotribune.com/chicago/shootings

Chicago Public Schools. (2013). *Mayor Emanuel, city officials and more than 140 leading community and civic organizations launch first-ever citywide summer learning initiative* [Press release]. Retrieved from http://cps.edu/News/Press_releases/Pages/03_12_2013_PR1.aspx)

Chin, T., & Phillips, M. (2004). Social reproduction and child-rearing practices: Social class, children's agency, and the summer activity gap. *Sociology of Education, 77*(3), 185–210.

Cohn, E. G., & Rotton, J. (1997). Assault as a function of time and temperature: A moderator-variable time-series analysis. *Journal of Personality and Social Psychology, 72*, 1322–1334.

Csikszentmihalyi, M., & Larson, R. W. (1984). *Being adolescent: Conflict and growth in the teenage years.* New York, NY: Basic Books.

Ehrenreich-May, J., & Bilek, E. L. (2011). Universal prevention of anxiety and depression in a recreational camp setting: An initial open trial. *Child & Youth Care Forum, 40*(6), 435–455.

Entwisle, D. R., Alexander, K. L., & Olson, L. S. (2001). Keep the faucet flowing: Summer learning and home environment. *American Educator, 25*(3), 10–15, 47.

Fowler, P. J., Tompsett, C. J., Braciszewski, J. M., Jacques-Tiura, A. J., & Baltes, B. B. (2009). Community violence: A meta-analysis on the effect of exposure and mental health outcomes of children and adolescents. *Development and Psychopathology, 21*, 227–259.

Gershenson, S. (2013). Do summer time-use gaps vary by socioeconomic status? *American Educational Research Journal, 50*(6), 1219–1248.

Heller, S. B. (2014). Summer jobs reduce violence among disadvantaged youth. *Science, 346*(6214), 1219–1223.

Henderson, K. A., Thurber, C. A., Whitaker, L. S., Bialeschki, M. D., & Scanlin, M. M. (2006). Development and application of a Camper Growth Index for Youth. *Journal of Experiential Education, 29*(1), 1–17.

Johnson, A. O., Mink, M. D., Harun, N., Moore, C. G., Martin, A. B., & Bennett, K. J. (2008). Violence and drug use in rural teens: National prevalence estimates from the 2003 youth risk behavior survey. *Journal of School Health, 78*, 554–561.

Kennedy, T. M., & Ceballo, R. (2013). Latino adolescents' community violence exposure: After-school activities and familismo as risk and protective factors. *Social Development, 22*(4), 663–682.

Kenrick, D. T., & MacFarlane, S. W. (1986). Ambient temperature and horn honking: A field study of the heat/aggression relationship. *Environment and Behavior, 18*, 179–191.

Kirschman, K. J. B., Roberts, M. C., Shadlow, J. O., & Pelley, T. J. (2010). An evaluation of hope following a summer camp for inner-city youth. *Child and Youth Care Forum, 39*(6), 385–396.

Kliewer, W., & Lepore, S. J. (2015). Exposure to violence, social cognitive processing, and sleep problems in urban adolescents. *Journal of Youth and Adolescence, 44,* 507–517.

Larrick, R. P., Timmerman, T. A., Carton, A. M., & Abrevaya, J. (2011). Temper, temperature, and temptation: Heat-related retaliation in baseball. *Psychological Science, 22*(4), 423–428.

Larson, R. W., & Kleiber, D. (1993). Daily experiences of adolescents. In P. H. Tolan & B. J. Cohler (Eds.), *Handbook of clinical research and practice with adolescents: Wiley series on personality processes* (pp. 125–145). Oxford, England: Wiley.

Laughlin, L. (2010). *Who's minding the kids? Child care arrangements: spring 2005 and summer 2006.* Washington, DC: U.S. Census Bureau.

Lee, K. T. H., & Vandell, D. L. (2015). Out-of-school time and adolescent substance use. *Journal of Adolescent Health, 57*(5), 523–529.

Lerner, R. M., Almerigi, J. B., Theokas, C., & Lerner, J. V. (2005). Positive youth development a view of the issues. *The Journal of Early Adolescence, 25*(1), 10–16.

Little, P. M. D., Wimer, C., & Weiss, H. (2008). After school programs in the 21st century: Their potential and what it takes to achieve it. Harvard Family Research Project Brief Series: Issues and Opportunities in Out-of-School Time Evaluation, No. 10.

Madden, M. (2013). Technology use by different income groups [Lecture Slides]. Washington, DC: Pew Research Center.

Mahoney, J. L., Vandell, D. L., Simpkins, S., & Zarrett, N. (2009). Adolescent out-of-school activities. In R. M. Lerner & L. Steinberg (Eds.), *Handbook of adolescent psychology* (3rd ed., pp. 228–269). New York, NY: Wiley.

Merwin, E., Hinton, I., Dembling, B., & Stern, S. (2003). Shortages of rural mental health professionals. *Archives of Psychiatric Nursing, 17,* 42–51.

Naccarato, T., Brophy, M., & Courtney, M. E. (2010). Employment outcomes of foster youth: The results from the Midwest Evaluation of the Adult Functioning of Foster Youth. *Children and Youth Services Review, 32*(4), 551–559.

O'Donnell, D. A., Schwab-Stone, M. E., & Ruchkin, V. (2006). The mediating role of alienation in the development of maladjustment in youth exposed to community violence. *Development and Psychopathology, 18,* 215–232.

Parente, M. E., Sheppard, A., & Mahoney, J. L. (2012). Parental knowledge as a mediator of the relation between adolescent summer care arrangement configurations and adjustment the following school year. *Applied Developmental Science, 16*(2), 84–97.

Pastore, D. R., Fisher, M., & Friedman, S. B. (1996). Violence and mental health problems among urban high school students. *Journal of Adolescent Health, 18,* 320–324.

Pretti, A., Miotto, P., De Coppi, M., Petretto, D., & Carmelo, M. (2002). Psychiatric chrono-epidemiology: Its relevance for the study of aggression. *Aggressive Behavior, 28,* 477–490.

Readdick, C. A., & Schaller, G. R. (2005). Summer camp and self-esteem of school-age inner-city children. *Perceptual and Motor Skills, 101*(1), 121–130.

Reifman, A. S., Larrick, R. P., & Fein, S. (1991). Temper and temperature on the diamond: The heat-aggression relationship in major league baseball. *Personality and Social Psychology Bulletin, 17,* 580–585.

Richards, M. H., Romero, E., Zakaryan, A., Carey, D., Deane, K., Quimby, D., Patel, N., & Burns, M. (2015). Assessing urban African American youths' exposure to community violence through a daily sampling method. *Psychology of Violence, 5*(3), 275–284.

Riley, A., & Anderson-Butcher, D. (2012). Participation in a summer sport-based youth development program for disadvantaged youth: Getting the parent perspective. *Children and Youth Services Review, 34*(7), 1367–1377.

Rotton, J., & Cohn, E. G. (2000). Violence is a curvilinear function of temperature in Dallas: A replication. *Journal of Personality and Social Psychology, 78,* 1074–1081.

Segrin, C., & Abramson, L. Y. (1994). Negative reactions to depressive behaviors: A communication theories analysis. *Journal of Abnormal Psychology, 103*(4), 655–668.

Shernoff, D. J., & Vandell, D. L. (2007). Engagement in after-school program activities: Quality of experience from the perspective of participants. *Journal of Youth and Adolescence, 36*(7), 891–903.

Shevlin, M., Murphy, S., & Murphy, J. (2014). Adolescent loneliness and psychiatric morbidity in the general population: Identifying "at risk" groups using latent class analysis. *Journal of Psychiatry, 68*(8), 633–639.

Slovak, K., & Singer, M. (2001). Gun violence exposure and trauma among rural youth. *Violence and Victims, 16*(4), 389–400.

Stader, S. R., & Hokanson, J. E. (1998). Psychosocial antecedents of depressive symptoms: An evaluation using daily experiences methodology. *Journal of Abnormal Psychology, 107*(1), 17–26.

Thurber, C. A., Scanlin, M. M., Scheuler, L., & Henderson, K. A. (2006). Youth development outcomes of the camp experience: Evidence for multidimensional growth. *Journal of Youth and Adolescence, 36*(3), 241–254.

Ullrich-French, S., & McDonough, M. H. (2013). Correlates of long-term participation in a physical activity-based positive youth development program for low-income youth: Sustained involvement and psychosocial outcomes. *Journal of Adolescence, 36*(2), 279–288.

Vandell, D. L., Shernoff, D. J., Pierce, K. M., Bolt, D. M., Dadisman, K., & Brown, B. B. (2005). Activities, engagement, and emotion in after-school programs (and elsewhere). In H. B. Weiss, P. M. D. Little, & S. M. Bouffard (Eds.), *New directions for youth development: No. 105. Participation in youth programs: Enrollment, attendance, and engagement* (pp. 121–129). San Francisco, CA: Jossey-Bass.

Wimer, C., Bouffard, S. M., Caronongan, P., Dearing, E., Simpkins, S., Little, P. M. D., & Weiss, H. (2006). *What are kids getting into these days? Demographic differences in youth out-of-school time participation.* Cambridge, MA: Harvard Family Research Project.

Part III

STEMMING SUMMER LEARNING LOSS: LESSONS FROM AND ABOUT RESEARCH

CHAPTER 12

Best Practices in Summer Programming

Andrew McEachin, Catherine Augustine, and Jennifer McCombs

This chapter presents new data on the impact of participating in a large, voluntary, urban school district summer learning program on outcomes in the early fall. More than 5,000 students across the country participated in a randomized controlled trial examining the impacts of five different summer learning programs. We show how these students performed on standardized, general assessments of mathematics and reading in the first 3 to 5 weeks of school. In addition to discussing these outcomes, we investigate the features of the summer learning programs that were related to student outcomes. Examined features include student attendance, hours of relevant academic instruction, teacher qualifications, quality of instruction, site climate, class size, and the appropriateness of the curriculum, as reported by teachers.

Educators and policymakers have struggled for decades to close persistent racial, economic, and linguistic achievement gaps. The summer is a key time in students' social and cognitive development and plays an important role in the development of achievement gaps. Summer interventions have the potential to not only mitigate summer learning loss but also reduce persistent achievement gaps.

Cooper et al.'s (2000) foundational meta-analysis covers the early attempts to use summer interventions to reduce summer learning loss in order to shrink achievement gaps. They found that, on average, these interventions had moderate positive effects on students learning, approximately equivalent to a few months of extra learning, and were at least equal to, if not larger than, estimates of students' summer learning loss. However, in the past 15 years there have been a number of new evaluations of summer programming. In addition to adding rigorous evidence about program effectiveness, this literature is also beginning to answer a key question that can drive policy and practice: *What student characteristics and programmatic features influence summer program effectiveness?*

In this chapter, we review the existing literature on the effectiveness of summer learning programs. We start with a brief review of the meta-analysis conducted by Cooper, et al. (2000) and add evidence from 25 experimental or quasi-experimental studies since 2000. The programs covered in our review include voluntary at-home summer reading programs, voluntary classroom-based summer programs, and mandatory summer programs that students must attend to avoid in-grade retention.

We start with a description of the overall effects of summer learning programs on students' academic and nonacademic outcomes, including how these effects vary over time and how subject, student demographics, grade level, and attendance mediate them. We then discuss the characteristics of effective summer learning programs and conclude with implications for future summer learning programming.

EFFECTIVENESS OF SUMMER LEARNING PROGRAMS

Cooper et al.'s (2000) meta-analysis was the first synthesis of the effectiveness of summer learning programs. The authors reviewed more than 300 studies between 1966 and 1998 and found that students in summer learning programs experienced moderate positive gains in math and reading achievement. Furthermore, the effects remained when the authors restricted their analysis to the small number of random assignment studies.

However, only 11 of the 300 studies included in the meta-analysis used experimental or quasi-experimental methods. As such, the results of the meta-analysis should be seen as an excellent first step in developing our understanding of the potential impact of summer learning programs on students' outcomes, but there is still much to learn from more recent studies that used more rigorous research methods.

In building on Cooper et al.'s (2000) meta-analysis, we identified 25 studies of summer learning programs published since 2000 that used either experimental or quasi-experimental methods. We include only studies that used rigorous research methods to limit the possibility that the effects reported were driven by students' backgrounds and prior achievement rather than the summer programs. The results of these studies expand our understanding of summer program effectiveness and of the characteristics of effective programs.

In general, we find that these programs have small-to-moderate effects, similar to the random-assigned studies reviewed by Cooper et al. (2000); however, some studies found no positive effects. The programs included in our review cover a wide range of delivery methods, including classroom-based remedial programs, voluntary (but academic) summer programs, and at-home interventions that provide students and families tools to continue academic activities over the summer.

We reviewed four studies of remedial education summer learning programs that met our research design criteria. Two studies, Jacob and Lefgren (2004) and Matsudaira (2008), studied a remedial education policy in an urban school district. Elementary students who did not attain a high enough test score were recommended for summer school, while students above the score did not have to attend. Both studies found that students who just qualified for summer school had small positive increases in math and reading achievement the next spring compared to students who scored just high enough not to attend summer school. McCombs, Kirby, and Mariano (2009) evaluated the effects of a similar retention policy in New York City, and Mariano and Martorell (2013) used the same data to evaluate the sensitivity of the earlier findings to measurement issues. McCombs et al. (2009) found students who attended the remedial summer school program scored 0.1 to 0.15 SD higher in math and reading at the end of both 6th and 7th grade compared students who just did not qualify for summer school. Mariano and Martorell (2013) test sensitivity of the earlier results to a number of model specifications and find that only the positive reading effects maintain.

We also reviewed a number of voluntary summer learning programs that invited students to attend in-person interventions but did not require attendance for grade promotion (Borman, Benson, & Overman, 2005; Borman, Goetz, & Dowling, 2009; Chaplin & Capizzano, 2006; Herrera, Linden, Arbreton, & Grossman, 2011; Herrera, Linden, & Grossman, 2013; Linden, Herrara, & Grossman, 2013; MacIver & MacIver, 2014; Mariano & Martorell, 2013; McCombs et al., 2014; Schacter & Jo, 2005; Snipes, Huang, Jaquet, & Finkelstein, 2015; Somers, Welbeck, Grossman, & Gooden, 2015; Zvoch & Stevens, 2011, 2013, in press). *Across these studies, authors tend to find small-to-moderate (0.05 to 0.15 SD) positive effects in math and reading, although the findings are less consistent in reading than in math.*

In one of the largest evaluations of voluntary summer learning programs, McCombs et al. (2014) conducted randomized controlled trials in five urban school districts that served approximately 5,000 rising 4th-grade students in their voluntary summer programs. Districts targeted low-performing students to attend the program, but attendance was voluntary and some higher-performing students attended as well. Students randomized to the treatment condition saw small positive gains in math achievement the fall after the summer intervention, compared to students who expressed an interest in attending the summer program but were randomized to a control condition. Students in the treatment condition did not perform any better in reading the following fall compared to the control students.

Similarly, Herrera, Grossman, and Linden (2013) evaluated the impact of a summer learning program, Higher Achievement (HA), targeted toward motivated low-income rising 5th and 6th graders. The HA program provides students summer learning and after-school programming to enhance academic achievement, promote positive social and emotional skills, and support matriculation to a high-quality high school. The authors found that the HA program had positive effects in mathematics problem-solving, which lasted 4 years after the end of the intervention, but no reading comprehension effects beyond the 2nd year.

Other programs, however, do not achieve significant impacts on students' achievement. In a large evaluation of Building Educated Leaders for Life (BELL), a summer learning program geared for rising 5th and 6th graders who are achieving a few years below grade-level, Sommers et al. (2015) did not find significant effects on students' math or reading achievement.

Recent studies of at-home reading programs using random assignment designs have found promising or significant short-term effects (Allington et al., 2010; Guryan, Kim, & Park, 2015; Kim, 2006; Kim & White, 2008) and cumulative effects over time (Allington et al., 2010). However, other studies found no overall reading effects among students who were part of the treatment group (Kim, 2004; Borman et al., 2009; Kim & Guryan, 2010).

Nonacademic Outcomes. Some summer programs also have a secondary goal of improving students' nonacademic outcomes, including social and emotional competencies such as self-regulation and motivation. Linden, Herrara, and Grossman (2013) found an increase in the likelihood of attending a selective private high school and a decrease in the likelihood of attending a lower-performing public school for middle school students. However, the authors did not find any lasting effects on students' social and emotional outcomes. Furthermore, McCombs et al. (2014) and Sommers et al. (2015) also found no effect on social and emotional competencies.

Snipes et al. (2015) found that while a short summer algebra readiness program improved students' achievement, it did not have a significant effect on students' interest or sense of competence in math. An earlier evaluation of Building Educated Leaders for Life (BELL) found positive effects on the degree to which parents encouraged their children to read, but it found no influence on students' academic self-perceptions or social behaviors (Chaplin & Capizzano, 2006). McCombs et al. (2014) note that while program leaders might desire to affect social and emotional competencies, the programs are not always designed to do so, which may help explain the lack of findings in this area.

Long-Term Effects. Neither our literature search nor the search by Cooper et al. (2000) found a study that evaluated the long-term benefit of attending summer learning programs. However, a handful of studies have examined whether effectiveness persists for at most 2 years after participation, including the four studies of mandatory summer programs for students at risk of being retained in grade. Each of these studies examined the effect of summer programming on state assessment outcomes and found gains for participants relative to comparison students, though none of the studies tracked whether the summer program resulted in eventual proficiency.

Kim and Quinn (2013) analyzed seven studies that included multiple posttreatment assessments and found students' reading achievement was higher when measured immediately after the end of the intervention compared to their achievement measured a few months later. The positive effects in these seven studies decayed by roughly one third within a 3-month period, but remained positive and statistically significant. Similarly, Schacter and Jo (2005) randomly assigned students to a 7-week summer reading intervention and a control condition and measured students' decoding and reading comprehension immediately after the end of the intervention, 3 months after the end, and 9 months after the end. They too found evidence of decay. Although the authors found initial positive effects in decoding and reading comprehension, effects on decoding were not statistically significant 9 months later, and the reading compression effects, although still statistically significant, decreased by 65%.

Summary. Taken together, the evidence from the variety of summer programs implemented since 2000, along with Cooper et al.'s (2000) meta-analysis, suggest that many types of summer learning programs have the potential to reduce summer learning losses and perhaps create learning gains. However, implementing a summer program does not guarantee positive effects on students' learning. The variation in the results of these studies raises a key question: What factors make a summer learning program effective?

In what follows, we focus explore the variation in program effectiveness by mediating variables. These include subject (i.e., math versus reading), student demographics, grade level, and attendance. We conclude by highlighting key programmatic characteristics that are more likely to lead to positive student experiences and outcomes. These include the size of the program, program alignment, teacher qualifications, differentiated and high-quality instruction, site culture, maximized student participation, and program duration.

VARIATION IN EFFECTIVENESS OF SUMMER LEARNING PROGRAMS

Cooper et al. (2000) found that summer programs led to more favorable outcomes on mathematics assessments than on reading assessments, similar to our review of mandatory summer programs (Jacob & Lefgren, 2004; Matsudaira, 2008; McCombs et al., 2009). However, in other cases the positive effects show up in math only (McCombs et al., 2014) or reading only (Mariano & Martorell, 2013).

Demographic Groups. The early summer learning research suggests that learning during the school year is not substantively influenced by demographic group (c.f. Alexander, Entwisle, & Olson, 2001). This indicates that summer learning programs should have consistent benefits across different demographic groups. However, the research on differential impacts by student demographics, including race and income, does not tell a consistent story. Kim and Quinn's (2013) meta-analysis found that summer literacy programs with majority low-income samples had moderate positive effects on students' reading outcomes while programs with mixed-income samples often had no statistically significant effects.

However, McCombs et al.'s 2014 and Linden et al.'s 2013 randomized controlled trials across a handful of school districts did not find differential impacts by student characteristics, including race, English language learner status, and eligibility for free or reduced-price lunch.

At-home reading interventions have found differences by demographic group. An early randomized controlled trial of an at-home reading program found larger treatment effects for Black students than other students in the experiment (Kim, 2006). Similarly, Allington et al. (2010) found the largest effects for economically disadvantaged students. Furthermore, White et al. (2013) found that an at-home reading intervention had small positive effects for high-poverty schools (at least 75% FRPL), compared to negative effects for moderate-poverty schools (45%–74% FRPL). It is likely that the marginal benefit of receiving extra books for these students was significantly greater than for other students who might already have many books at home.

However, at-home programs also have important limitations. For example, these programs require time, energy, and intellectual capital from parents and students. If the parents are unable to help because they are either working long hours or English is not their first language, then simply providing books to students and limited training to parents will likely not produce significant learning gains. In this vein, Kim and Guryan (2010) found that a reading-at-home program was not effective in a district populated predominately by English language learners, which may imply the need for alternative strategies for reaching and advancing the summer learning of English language learners and for involving their families in this effort.

Grade. In their meta-analysis, Cooper et al. (2000) found that summer programs had larger effects for early primary and secondary grades compared to late primary grades, consistent with the finding that treatment effects are often smaller in later grade levels (Hill, Bloom, Black, & Lipsey, 2008). It is important to bear in mind, however, that students' learning progression slows down as children move through later grades. When comparing effect sizes across grades, it is important to compare the size of the effect to the norms of the specific context (i.e., grade-level learning patterns). For example, an effect size of 0.05 SD in 8th grade would be considered more meaningful than an effect size of 0.05 SD in kindergarten. Students' learning gains (as measured by standardized assessments) are, on average, larger in kindergarten than in 8th grade.

A nice way to study the effect of grade levels on program effectiveness is to study the same program implemented in different grades. In his examination of the effects of a mandatory summer school program in an urban district, Matsudaira (2008) found that students in higher grades benefited more from summer school than did students in 3rd grade. However, studies of mandatory summer programming in Chicago (Jacob & Lefgren, 2004; Roderick, Engel, & Nagaoka, 2003) and New York City (McCombs et al., 2009) included multiple grades but did not find significant differences between grades.

Attendance. Unsurprisingly, studies that have examined the link between outcomes and attendance have found that increased attendance improves outcomes. In their study, McCombs et al. (2014) found that the stronger the attendance, the better students performed on a fall mathematics test. They also found that increased hours of instruction were associated with higher mathematics scores. While the estimates in reading trended upward with increased attendance and hours of instruction, they did not find statistically significant relationships between attendance and reading achievement across their five study districts.

In a study of New York City's 5th-grade mandatory remediation program, the authors found a threshold effect for mathematics under which students who had attended 7 to 14 sessions outperformed their peers who had attended fewer than 7 sessions (McCombs et al., 2009).

Further evidence regarding the influence of attendance on outcomes comes from a randomized controlled trial of a voluntary summer program offered over three summers to randomly selected kindergarten and 1st-grade students in 10 Baltimore schools. Borman, Benson, and Overman (2005) found that simply offering students a voluntary summer learning program had no effect on reading achievement. However, each additional week of attendance in the program was associated with a 0.05 standard deviation increase in fall test scores. Analyzing the same data, Borman and Dowling (2006) reported positive effects only for those children who participated for at least two summers with attendance rates of greater than 39% (only 46% of the students assigned to the treatment condition met this attendance requirement). Students who participated less frequently did not outperform their peers who were not assigned to the treatment group. The results of this experiment highlight a key challenge facing voluntary programs—incentivizing attendance so that students will benefit from programming. Programs that seek to engage students for consecutive years face the additional challenge of incentivizing attendance across multiple years.

Attendance (or participation) is further complicated in at-home summer interventions. These interventions, which often require students to complete assignments under little to no supervision from the school, place more of the learning responsibility on students and their families, compared to in-school programs, which center the learning responsibility on teachers. At-home programs have tried to increase student participation using a number of methods, including phone calls from teachers (White et al., 2013) and attaching incentives to the number of books read over the summer (Guryan, Kim, & Park, 2015). Reaching out to students over the summer and/or attaching incentives to the quantity and quality of summer work sounds good in theory, but in practice studies using random assignment found no differences between treatment groups that did and did not receive incentives to complete assignments or phone calls from teachers. In fact, in the study by Guryan et al. (2015), the authors found that only motivated students, as measured by a pretreatment survey, responded to performance-based incentives. The biggest effects from summer reading came for students who were motivated and provided with books matched to their reading levels.

COMPONENTS OF QUALITY SUMMER LEARNING PROGRAMS

We now turn to whether the structural components of the programs, such as the duration, nature of the curricula, and teacher characteristics, contribute to the variation in program effectiveness. In this section, we explore the program characteristics in the 25 studies in our literature review as well as in Cooper et al. (2000).

Small Class Sizes. Small class sizes might provide teachers with more time to work individually with students and to create greater opportunities to differentiate instruction based on student needs. Small class size may be particularly beneficial during the summer when teachers have much less time to get to know the students in their classroom. Research has found that small class size is associated with summer program effectiveness; Cooper et al. (2000) found that summer programs in which class size was capped at 20 students were more effective than others in producing achievement gains. Although Kim and Quinn (2013) found no statistically significant relationship between class size and program quality, they did see effects from combining class size with dosage. They analyzed 12 studies with enough detail to investigate whether program resources mediated students' learning, defined by class sizes no more than 13, at least 4 hours of participation per day, and at least 70 hours of total participation. The five studies that met these criteria had large statistically significant, positive effects on students' learning, and the seven studies that did not meet the criteria had no statistically significant effect on students' learning.

McCombs et al. (2014) similarly combined instructional hours with class size to test whether more individual attention offered due to smaller classes might improve results. Although they found that the number of hours of instructional time was related to mathematics treatment effects, they did not find a relationship when further combined with class size. This may be because prevailing class sizes across the five studied districts were all small, ranging from an average of 8 to 14 students per teacher. Furthermore, Zvoch and Stevens (2013) found large positive effects of an intense summer literacy program on students' reading outcomes. The program used daily small-group (3 to 5 children), research-based instruction.

Aligned to Student Needs. Learning science recommends that in order to maximize the benefit of academic experiences, especially in literacy, students' assignments should be well aligned to their interests and needs (c.f. Wright & Stone, 2004). Summer learning programs should therefore align instruction to school-year activities, and instruction should be tightly focused on addressing students' needs with high-quality instruction (c.f. Zvoch & Stevens, 2013, 2015). The findings from the many replications of Project READS (Guryan et al., 2015; Kim, 2004, 2006; Kim & Guryan, 2010; Kim & White, 2008), an at-home summer literacy intervention, clearly show that students are not only more likely to read over the summer when books are aligned to their interests and matched to their reading levels, but they are also more likely to comprehend what they are reading, and these comprehension effects persist into the following school year.

The results from Project READS also suggest that sending students books matched to their reading levels and interests over the summer with the expectation that they will read them is not enough. In the absence of a structured school setting, struggling students also need continued support during the summer. For example, Kim and White (2008) tested whether students in the treatment group who were given at-home proxies for instruction outperformed students in the treatment group who were just given basic prompts to read books over the summer. They found that students responded to nudges from the research team to read aloud to their parents and/or practice their reading comprehension skills.

Finally, the Project READs work also suggests that student-oriented incentives, as opposed to nudges to read with parents and/or use good literary practices, are less effective in changing students' reading habits and improving literacy and reading comprehension. Guryan et al. (2015) provided incentives for reading books over the summer to half of the treatment group. The intervention was effective only for motivated students (as measured by baseline surveys), and the use of incentives actually widened the achievement gap between motivated and unmotivated students. It is not only important to align student work with their interests and ability levels, but also to build in structures to support student learning during the summer, especially for at-home programs.

Qualified Teachers. McCombs et al. (2014) found a positive, statistically significant association between prior teaching experience and reading outcomes. Specifically, they found that students who had summer teachers who had just taught either their sending or receiving grade performed better than other students on a fall reading assessment. In order to recruit and hire the right teachers, Augustine, McCombs, Schwartz, and Zakaras (2013) recommend developing rigorous selection processes to recruit motivated teachers and, to the extent possible, taking teachers' school-year performance into consideration. They also stress the importance of hiring teachers with not only grade-level but also subject matter experience and, if possible, familiarity with the students. In addition, they recommend negotiating with teachers' unions, if necessary, to establish a competitive selection process.

High-Quality Instruction. In addition to the importance of recruiting qualified teachers, their instruction of the curriculum is important. McCombs et al. (2014) observed and evaluated instructional quality for each classroom in their study. Their analysis found a positive association between quality of instruction and better student performance in reading. They did not find a relationship between quality of instruction and student performance in mathematics. Furthermore, Kim and Quinn (2013) examined voluntary and at-home literacy programs that used research-based instruction (as operationalized by the National Reading Panel, 2000), such as guided repeated oral reading, relating readings to students' prior experiences, and explicitly modeling strategies for students. Programs that included these practices had significantly larger positive effect on students' reading outcomes than programs that did not use such instructional practices.

In efforts to ensure high-quality instruction, researchers recommend anchoring the program in a commercially available and evidence-based curriculum (Augustine et al., 2013); providing professional development to teachers (Bell & Carrillo, 2007; Boss & Railsback, 2002; Denton, 2002; McLaughlin & Pitcock, 2009); tying small-group instruction explicitly to learning goals (Zvoch & Stevens, 2013); and providing teachers with instructional support such as coaching during the summer program (Augustine et al., 2013).

Site Culture. McCombs et al. (2014) expected that students in more orderly sites would have better outcomes because they and their teachers would be less likely to be distracted by misbehavior. To evaluate student discipline and order in the district programs they studied, they created a scale for each site within each district based on teacher survey data. On the survey, teachers were asked for their observations of student bullying, physical fighting, and other indicators of orderliness. They found that students who attended more orderly sites outperformed other students on the fall reading assessment.

Policies to Maximize Participation and Attendance. As discussed earlier, consistent attendance is not only crucial for school-year learning but for summer learning as well (Borman et al., 2005; Borman & Dowling, 2006; McCombs et al., 2009; McCombs et al., 2014). Cooper et al. (2000) did not find differences in program effectiveness between summer programs that did and did not monitor attendance, so tracking attendance, while a good policy, is likely insufficient to increase attendance. To promote consistent attendance, Augustine et al. (2013) recommend setting enrollment deadlines, establishing a clear attendance policy, and providing field trips and other incentives for students who attend. They also found that it is not necessary to disguise academics to boost attendance: The district with the highest attendance rate in the study ran the most "school-like" program, with the most explicit academic instruction.

Sufficient Duration. Researchers generally distinguish between allocated time (the time on the school calendar for a given content area) and academic learning time (the amount of time students spend working on rigorous tasks at the appropriate level of difficulty). Academic learning time is more predictive of student achievement (Fisher et al., 1980; Harnischfeger & Wiley, 1976; Hawley, Rosenholtz, Goodstein, & Hasselbring, 1984; Karweit, 1985; Karweit & Slavin, 1982). Furthermore, research also suggests that spaced practice (once a day for several days) as opposed to one long, concentrated lesson (all day long for just one day) appears to be more effective in facilitating learning (Rohrer & Pashler, 2010; Rohrer & Taylor, 2006; Walberg, 1988). When focusing on boosting students' literacy skills, Zvoch and Stevens (2013) recommend that students receive at least 2 hours of teacher-directed daily instruction blended between whole-group and small-group (three to five students) lessons and that the program meets regularly during the week (four to five times) for at least 5 weeks.

Similarly, McCombs et al. (2014) recommend that school districts plan for programs to run at least 5 weeks and schedule 60–90 minutes of mathematics per day to maximize effectiveness. Because instructional time on task is reduced due to student absences and inefficient use of time inside the day, McCombs et al. suggest special efforts to promote consistent attendance, maintain daily schedules, and ensure teachers maximize instructional time inside the classroom.

CONCLUSIONS

In the past 2 decades, a number of exciting developments have taken in place in the research and delivery of summer learning programs. The 25 experimental and quasi-experimental studies covered in this review shed new light on the overall effectiveness of summer learning programs and on mediating factors and important program components. These studies highlight that summer programs can have a positive effect on student achievement and that the effectiveness of the program is positively mediated by students' attendance. We also find that the effectiveness of the summer learning programs is inconsistently mediated by students' backgrounds and the grade level of the intervention. This implies that there is no "best" target population for summer programming. Furthermore, simply offering a program does not guarantee it will benefit students. There are a number of important factors to considering when implementing summer learning programs.

Research indicates that in order for summer programs to be effective, programs need to be of sufficient duration (i.e., of at least 5 weeks in length or 70 hours of academic programming) and achieve consistent student attendance. Students also benefit from individualized and aligned instruction and class sizes smaller than 20 students. In addition, high-quality instruction (promoted through careful hiring and professional development) by teachers who have recently taught the sending or receiving grade contribute to positive student outcomes, as does providing that instruction in orderly summer sites with low levels of physical fighting or bullying. In order to enact quality components, districts and providers must identify a target population and carefully plan for summer programming to ensure effectiveness.

REFERENCES

Alexander, K. L., Entwisle, D. R., & Olson, L. S. (2001). Schools, achievement, and inequality: A seasonal perspective. *Educational Evaluation and Policy Analysis, 23*, 171–191.

Allington, R. L., McGill-Franzen, A. M., Camilli, G., Williams, L., Graff, J., Zeig, J., Zmach, C., & Nowak, R. (2010). Addressing summer reading setback among economically disadvantaged elementary students. *Reading Psychology, 31*(5), 411–427.

Augustine, C. H., McCombs, J. S., Schwartz, H. L., & Zakaras, L. (2013). *Getting to work on summer learning: Recommended practices for success.* Santa Monica, CA: RAND.

Bell, S. R., & Carrillo, N. (2007). Characteristics of effective summer learning programs in practice. *New Directions for Youth Development, 2007*(114), 45–63.

Borman, G. D., Benson, J., & Overman, L. T. (2005). Families, schools, and summer learning. *The Elementary School Journal, 106*(2), 131–150.

Borman, G. D., & Dowling, N. M. (2006). Longitudinal achievement effects of multiyear summer school: Evidence from the Teach Baltimore randomized field trial. *Educational Evaluation and Policy Analysis, 28*(1), 25–48.

Borman, G. D., Goetz, M. E., & Dowling, N. M. (2009). Halting the summer achievement slide: A randomized field trial of the KindergARTen summer camp. *Journal of Education for Students Place at Risk, 14*, 133–147.

Boss, S., & Railsback, J. (2002). *Summer school programs: A look at the research, implications for practice and program sampler.* Portland, OR: Northwest Regional Educational Laboratory.

Chaplin, D., & Capizzano, J. (2006). *Impacts of a summer learning program: A random assignment study of Building Educated Learners for Life (BELL).* Washington, DC: Urban Institute.

Cooper, H., Charlton, K., Valentines, J. C., & Muhlenbruck, L. (with G. D. Borman). (2000). Making the most of summer school: A meta-analytic and narrative review. *Monographs of the Society for Research in Child Development, 65*(1), 1–118.

Denton, D. R. (2002). *Summer school: Unfulfilled promise.* Atlanta, GA: Southern Regional Education Board.

Fisher, C. W., Berliner, D. C., Filby, N. N., Marliave, R., Cahen, L. S., & Dishaw, M. M. (1980). Teaching behaviors, academic learning time, and student achievement: An overview. In C. Denham & A. Lieberman (Eds.), *Time to learn: A review of the Beginning Teacher Evaluation Study* (pp. 7–32). Sacramento, CA: California State Commission for Teacher Preparation and Licensing.

Guryan, J., Kim, J. S., & Park, K. (2015) *Motivation and incentives in education: Evidence from a summer reading experiment.* NBER Working Paper No. 20918. Cambridge, MA: National Bureau of Economic Research.

Harnischfeger, A., & Wiley, D. E. (1976). The teaching-learning process in elementary schools: A synoptic view. *Curriculum Inquiry, 6*(1), 5–43.

Hawley, W. D., Rosenholtz, S., Goodstein, H. J., & Hasselbring, T. (1984). Good schools: What research says about improving student achievement. *Peabody Journal of Education, 61*(4), iii–178.

Herrera, C., Grossman, J. B., & Linden, L. L. (2013). *Staying on track: Testing higher achievement's long-term impact on academic outcomes and high school choice.* New York, NY: MDRC.

Herrera, C., Linden, L. L., Arbreton, A., & Grossman, J. B. (2011). *Testing the impact of higher achievement's year-round out-of-school-time program on academic outcomes.* Philadelphia, PA: Public/Private Ventures.

Hill, C. J., Bloom, H. S., Black, A. R., & Lipsey, M. W. (2008). Empirical benchmarks for interpreting effect sizes in research. *Child Development Perspectives, 2*(3), 172–177.

Jacob, B. A., & Lefgren, L. (2004). Remedial education and student achievement: A regression-discontinuity analysis. *The Review of Economics and Statistics, 86*(1), 226–244.

Karweit, N. (1985). Should we lengthen the school year? *Educational Researcher, 14*(6), 9–15.

Karweit, N., & Slavin, R. E. (1982). Time-on-task: Issues of timing, sampling, and definition. *Journal of Education Psychology, 74*(6), 844–851.

Kim, J. S. (2004). Summer reading and the ethnic achievement gap. *Journal of Education for Students Placed at Risk, 9*(2), 169–188.

Kim, J. S. (2006). The effects of a voluntary summer reading intervention on reading achievement results from a randomized field trial. *Educational Evaluation and Policy Analysis, 28*(4), 335–355.

Kim, J. S., & Guryan, J. (2010). The efficacy of a voluntary summer book reading intervention for low income Latino children from language minority families. *Journal of Educational Psychology, 99*(3), 505–515.

Kim, J. S., & Quinn, D. M. (2013). The effects of summer reading on low-income children's literacy achievement from kindergarten to grade 8: A meta-analysis of classroom and home interventions. *Review of Educational Research, 83*(3), 386–431.

Kim, J. S., & White, T. G. (2008). Scaffolding voluntary summary reading for children in grades 3 to 5: An experimental study. *Scientific Studies of Reading, 12*(1), 1–23.

Linden, L. L., Herrara, C., & Grossman, J. B. (2013). Achieving academic success after school: A randomized evaluation of the higher achievement program. Working paper. Austin, TX: University of Austin.

MacIver, M. A., & MacIver, D. J. (2014). "STEMming" the swell of absenteeism in urban middle grades schools: Impacts of a summer robotics program. Paper presented at the Society for Research on Educational Effectiveness, Washington, DC.

Mariano, L. T., & Martorell, P. (2013). The academic effects of summer instruction and retention in New York City. Educational Evaluation and Policy Analysis, 35(1), 96–117.

Matsudaira, J. D. (2008). Mandatory summer school and student achievement. Journal of Econometrics, 142(2), 829–850.

McCombs, J. S., Kirby, S. N., & Mariano, L. T. (2009). Ending social promotion without leaving children behind: The case of New York City. Santa Monica, CA: RAND.

McCombs, J. S., Pane, J. F., Augustine, C. H., Schwartz, H. L., Martorell, P., & Zakaras, L. (2014). Ready for fall? Near-term effects of voluntary summer learning programs on low-income students' learning opportunities and outcomes. Santa Monica, CA: RAND.

McLaughlin, B., & Pitcock, S. (2009). Building quality in summer learning programs: Approaches and recommendations. New York, NY: Wallace Foundation.

National Reading Panel. (2000). Teaching children to read: An evidence-based assessment of the scientific research literature on reading and its implications for reading instruction. Washington, DC: National Institute of Child Health and Human Development.

Paris, S. G. (2005). Reinterpreting the development of reading skills. Reading Research Quarterly, 40(2), 184–202.

Roderick, M., Engel, M., & Nagaoka, J. (2003). Ending social promotion: Results from Summer Bridge. Chicago, IL: Consortium on Chicago School Research, University of Chicago.

Rohrer, D., & Pashler, H. (2010). Recent research on human learning challenges conventional instructional strategies. Educational Researcher, 39(5), 406–412.

Rohrer, D., & Taylor, K. (2006). The effects of overlearning and distributed practice on the retention of mathematics knowledge. Applied Cognitive Psychology, 20(2), 1209–1224.

Schacter, J., & Jo, B. (2005). Learning when school is not in session: A reading summer day-camp intervention to improve the achievement of exiting first-grade students who are economically disadvantaged. Journal of Research in Reading, 28(2), 158–169.

Snipes, J., Huang, C.-W., Jaquet, K., & Finkelstein, N. (2015). The effects of the Elevate Math summer program on math achievement and algebra readiness. REL 2015–096. Washington, DC: U.S. Department of Education.

Somers, M. A., Welbeck, R., Grossman, J. B., & Gooden, S. (2015). An analysis of the effects of an academic summer program for middle school students. New York, NY: MDRC.

Walberg, H. J. (1988). Synthesis of research on time and learning. Educational Leadership, 45(6), 76–85.

White, T. G., Kim, J. S., Kingston, H. C., & Foster, L. (2013). Replicating the effects of a teacher-scaffolded voluntary summer reading program: The role of poverty. *Reading Research Quarterly*, 49(1), 5–30.

Wright, B. D., & Stone, M. H. (2004). *Making measures*. Chicago: Phaneron Press.

Zvoch, K., & Stevens, J. J. (2011). Summer school and summer learning: An examination of the short and longer term changes in student literacy. *Early Education and Development*, 22(4), 649–675.

Zvoch, K., & Stevens, J. J. (2013). Summer school effects in a randomized field trial. *Early Childhood Research Quarterly*, 28(1), 24–32.

Zvoch, K., & Stevens, J. J. (in press). Identification of summer school effects by comparing the in- and out-of-school growth rates of struggling early readers. *Elementary School Journal*.

CHAPTER 13

Year-Round School Calendars

Effects on Summer Learning, Achievement, Parents, Teachers, and Property Values

Paul von Hippel

About 3,700 U.S. schools follow a "year-round" school calendar in which the summer vacation is shortened and the usual 175–180 instruction days are distributed more evenly across all four seasons of the year. What effect does the year-round calendar have on children's learning? What interest groups promote and resist the year-round calendar, and what are their motives? What kinds of states, districts, and schools adopt year-round calendars, and what kinds of children attend them? Do families and teachers prefer year-round or 9-month calendars, and how do their preferences affect property values and teacher recruitment and retention?

Over the past 3 decades, the number of schools using year-round calendars has increased nine-fold, from 410 in 1985 to 3,700 in 2011–2012 (Skinner, 2014). More than 2 million children now attend year-round schools—as many as attend charter schools—yet year-round schools have attracted relatively little attention from researchers and the public.

In this chapter, I define year-round schools, describe their characteristics, and discuss the educational, political, and financial reasons why schools do or do not adopt year-round calendars. I then review the evidence for the effects of year-round calendars on test scores. Once thought to be positive, these effects now appear to be neutral at best. Although year-round calendars do increase summer learning, they reduce learning at other times of year, so that the total amount learned over a 12-month period is no greater under a year-round calendar than under a 9-month calendar. I also review evidence that year-round calendars make it harder to recruit and retain experienced teachers, make it harder for mothers to work outside the home, and reduce property values. I conclude by discussing the remaining uses for year-round calendars and posing questions for future policy and research.

WHAT IS A YEAR-ROUND CALENDAR?

Unlike the much rarer "extended-year" calendar, which can have more than 200 days of instruction, a year-round calendar does not increase instruction time. Instead, a year-round calendar takes the usual 175–180 instruction days and redistributes them, replacing the usual schedule—9 months on, 3 months off—with a more "balanced" schedule of short instruction periods alternating with shorter breaks across all four seasons of the year. There are several year-round calendars in use; the most popular alternate 9- or 12-week instruction periods with 3- or 4-week breaks. Year-round calendars include a summer break that is longer than other breaks during the year, but still shorter than the summer break on a traditional 9-month calendar.

Table 13.1a compares the calendars of 30 year-round and 595 9-month public elementary schools in the nationally representative Early Childhood Longitudinal Study–Kindergarten Cohort of 1998–1999 (ECLS-K).[1] On average, the year-round schools offer 2–3 fewer instruction days, but the year-round schools start more than a month earlier and end 2–3 weeks later than the 9-month schools, so that on average 11 months elapse between the first and last day of the year-round school year. Because the year-round calendar spreads the same amount of instruction over 11 months rather than 9, the pace of instruction is more leisurely in year-round schools than in 9-month schools. Between the first and last days of the school year, year-round students attend school 1 day out of 2, while 9-month students attend school 3 days out of 5 (Table 13.1a). Later we will see that the leisurely pace of the year-round calendar may have implications for the pace of learning.

WHY DO SCHOOLS ADOPT YEAR-ROUND CALENDARS?

Crowding

Schools adopt year-round calendars for two different reasons. One is to reduce crowding. About 40% of year-round schools are so crowded that they would find it hard to serve all of their students simultaneously on a 9-month calendar (Cooper, Valentine, Charlton, & Melson, 2003). These schools handle crowding with a "multi-track" year-round calendar that splits students into 3–5 groups who attend school on a staggered schedule.

Table 13.1. Characteristics of Year-Round and 9-Month Schools

A. Calendars

	Year-Round	9-Month	Difference National	Difference Within Strata
Kindergarten first day	Jul 18, 1998	Aug 25, 1998	−38 *** (3)	−40 *** (3)
last day	Jun 25, 1999	Jun 5, 1999	21 *** (3)	19 *** (3)
First grade first day	Jul 19, 1999	Aug 24, 1999	−36 *** (3)	−38 *** (3)
last day	Jun 20, 2000	Jun 3, 2000	17 *** (3)	15 *** (3)
Calendar days (first to last): kindergarten	343	284	59 *** (3)	59 *** (3)
first grade	337	284	54 *** (3)	54 *** (3)
Instruction days kindergarten	175	178	−3 *** (0.8)	−3 *** (.8)
first grade	177	179	−2 ** (0.6)	−2 *** (.6)
Instruction days kindergarten	.51	.63	−.12 *** (.005)	−.12 *** (.006)
first grade	.53	.63	−.10 *** (.005)	−.11 *** (.005)

B. School Characteristics

	Year-Round	9-Month	Difference National	Difference Within Strata
Kindergarten enrollment	124	68	56 *** (8)	45 *** (9)
Crowded (principal's 5-point scale)	3.2	2.6	0.6 * (.3)	0.5 † (.3)
Central city	43%	34%	9% (10%)	−7% (10%)
Urban fringe and large town	46%	35%	11% (10%)	−2% (10%)
Small town and rural	11%	31%	−20% ** (7%)	9% (7%)
West	80%	19%	61% *** (9%)	0%
South	13%	33%	−20% * (8%)	0%
Northeast	0%	20%	−20% *** (2%)	0%
Midwest	6%	28%	−21% *** (6%)	0%

C. Teacher and Classroom Characteristics

	Year-Round	9-Month	Difference National	Within Strata
Class size kindergarten	21	20	1 (0.9)	0 (0.7)
first grade	20	20	0 (0.5)	1 † (0.3)
Half-day kindergarten	78%	38%	41% *** (9%)	5% † (3%)
Teacher experience kindergarten	11	14	−3 ** (1)	−4 *** (1)
first grade	11	14	−2 * (1)	−4 *** (1)

D. Student Characteristics

	Year-Round	9-Month	Difference National	Within Strata
Hispanic	50%	17%	33% *** (7%)	13% (8%)
White	34%	59%	−25% *** (6%)	−6% (7%)
Black	8%	17%	−9% ** (3%)	−5% (4%)
Asian	5%	3%	2% (1%)	0% (2%)
Hawaiian/ Pacific islander	1%	0%	1% (1%)	−1% (1%)
Native American	0%	2%	−2% *** (.5%)	−2% ** (.5%)
Multiracial	−31%	−56%	25% *** (6%)	6% (7%)
Qualifies for free lunch kindergarten	58%	38%	21% ** (6%)	12% † (7%)
first grade	54%	37%	17% ** (6%)	8% (7%)
Qualifies for reduced lunch kindergarten	7%	11%	−3% (2%)	−3% (2%)
first grade	8%	10%	−3% (2%)	−3% (2%)
Household income (thousands)	$39	$46	−$6 ($5)	−$2 ($6)
Siblings in household	1.5	1.5	.06 (.07)	−.01 (.08)
Parents in household	1.8	1.7	.05 (.03)	.04 (.04)

Mother has no high school diploma/ GED	28%	15%	13% ** (4%)	7% (5%)
has no bachelor's degree	87%	80%	7% (4%)	3% (5%)
Mother employed kindergarten	49%	56%	−7% * (3%)	−2% (4%)
first grade	50%	59%	−9% ** (3%)	−5% (3%)
Birth date	Mar 13, 1993	Feb 7, 1993	34 ** (11)	14 (12)

*$p<.05$, **$p<.01$, ***$p<.001$. Standard errors in parentheses. *Note.* Means and percentages use survey weights, and standard errors account for the clustering of students and teachers in schools. Missing values were multiply imputed at the school, classroom, and student level.

When one group is on break, the other groups are in session, so that only a fraction of students (2/3, 3/4, or 4/5) is in the building on any given day.

Multi-track year-round calendars are especially popular when the demand for classrooms increases quickly or unexpectedly. For example, between 1995 and 2007, school enrollments increased by two-thirds in Wake County, North Carolina (greater Raleigh), and nearly doubled in Clark County, Nevada (greater Las Vegas). By 2007, one-third of Wake County and one-half of Clark County elementary schools had adopted a multi-track year-round calendar, which saved Clark County half a billion dollars in new school construction (Year Round Calendar Study Group, 2007). Clark County returned to a 9-month calendar when Las Vegas's population fell after the 2007–2009 recession, but now that Las Vegas is growing again, 24 Clark County elementary schools have switched back to multi-track year-round calendars (McCabe, 2015).

A multi-track calendar is not just suited to handle a surge in enrollment; it can also handle a surge in teachers. In California, for example, a 1996 class-size reduction law forced elementary schools to hire 25,000 new K–3 teachers in 2 years (Jepsen & Rivkin, 2009). Lacking classrooms for the new teachers, one quarter of California elementary schools used multi-track calendars (Graves, 2010). Later, as new buildings and portable classrooms became available, some of California's multi-track schools switched back to single-track year-round or 9-month calendars. Yet even a decade after class-size reduction, California still had half of the nation's year-round schools, enrolling more than 1 million students (Graves, 2010; National Association for Year Round Education, 2007).

Table 13.1b confirms, using ECLS-K data, that year-round schools are often crowded. Average kindergarten enrollment is twice as high in year-round schools as in 9-month schools. On a 1-to-5 scale of crowding, year-round principals rate their schools as significantly more crowded than do 9-month principals. Eighty percent of year-round schools are in the western census region, which has long been the fastest-growing part of the United States; most of the rest are in the south, which is also growing faster than other regions. In fact, the four states with the most year-round schools are all in the west (California, Hawaii, Arizona, and Nevada), and several southern states (Georgia, North Carolina, Texas) are close behind (National Association for Year Round Education, 2007), although Texas's use of a year-round calendar declined after a 2006 law forbade schools from starting before the last Monday in August (Texas Association of School Boards, 2012). Only 11% of year-round schools are in small town and rural areas, where crowding is less common.

Table 13.1c shows that, despite high enrollments, average class sizes are no larger in year-round schools than they are in 9-month schools. Evidently the year-round calendar helps to control class size by increasing capacity for extra classes—just as it was intended to do in California.

Table 13.1c also shows that year-round schools tend to favor half-day kindergarten; half-day kindergarten is twice as common in year-round schools as in 9-month schools. Half-day kindergarten may be another way to handle crowding. Like the year-round calendar, half-day kindergarten staggers children's schedules—half attend in the morning, half in the afternoon—so that twice as many kindergartners can be served by the same number of teachers and classrooms.

Some characteristics of year-round schools are truly associated with the year-round calendar, while other characteristics are merely associated with the geographic areas where year-round calendars are used. To clarify the geographic issue, it is helpful to compare year-round schools with 9-month schools that are in the same area. The last two columns of Table 13.1 do this by comparing year-round schools to 9-month schools that are in same ECLS-K survey stratum, where a stratum is defined as a single large county or a group of similar and contiguous small counties (Tourangeau, Le, Nord, Sorongon, & Chapman, 2009). Because year-round schools are geographically concentrated, all 30 of the year-round schools in the ECLS-K are in just 15 strata, which contain only one-fifth of the 9-month schools. The last two columns of Table 13.1 are limited to these 15 strata and use stratum fixed effects to compare each year-round school to 9-month schools that are in the same stratum.

Within the same strata, some but not all of the differences between year-round and 9-month schools become much smaller. For example, within strata, year-round schools are only 5 percentage points more likely than 9-month schools to offer half-day kindergarten. Yet even within strata, year-round schools remain more crowded than 9-month schools; kindergarten enrollments at year-round schools are more than 50% higher in year-round schools than in 9-month schools in the same stratum.

Achievement

Another goal of the year-round calendar is to raise achievement. Achievement gains may or may not be expected when schools use a multi-track calendar for crowding, but gains are invariably promised when a district adopts a single-track year-round calendar as an educational reform. In 2010, when the Indianapolis and Oklahoma City Public Schools started using single-track year-round calendars in some schools, the Oklahoma City superintendent predicted that the new calendar would have "a positive effect on student growth and achievement" (Adcock, 2010), and the Indianapolis Public Schools announced that the calendar would "provide additional opportunities for our children to be academically successful" (Indianapolis Public Schools, 2010).

It is debatable whether a year-round calendar, by itself, can increase achievement. For skeptics, the bottom line is clear: Since year-round calendars do not increase instruction time or change instruction practices, they cannot be expected to increase achievement.

Advocates, on the other hand, make several arguments for the year-round calendar's potential to raise achievement. One argument, especially salient to readers of this book, is that shortening the summer vacation should increase summer learning, especially for the socioeconomically disadvantaged students who are most vulnerable to summer learning loss (Ballinger, 2000; Stenvall, 1999). The argument is not just that the year-round calendar increases summer learning, but that year-round teachers can spend less of the fall reviewing what students have forgotten over the summer.

A weakness of this argument is that, in many year-round schools, the summer vacation remains surprisingly long. In Oklahoma City and Indianapolis, conversion to a year-round calendar has only shortened the summer vacation from 3 months to 2 months, and even on the "balanced" calendar recommended by the National Association for Year-Round Education, the summer vacation is still 6 weeks long. Over a 2-month or even 6-week summer vacation, it seems likely that a fair amount of summer stagnation or setback will occur. Further stagnation and setback may take place in the 3- to 4-week breaks that year-round calendars intersperse through the fall, winter, and spring.

Another argument in favor of year-round calendars is that learning is more effective if it is broken into short periods with frequent breaks. This argument relies on the psychological evidence for "spaced" rather than "massed" practice (Dempster, 1988). Unfortunately, the evidence for spaced practice is inconsistent—"now you see it, now you don't," according to one review (Donovan & Radosevich, 1999)—and experiments on spaced practice have used breaks of a few minutes, hours, or days, which are far shorter than the 3–6 week breaks in year-round school calendars.

The achievement argument for year-round calendars is most compelling when a year-round calendar includes supplemental instruction in the "intersessions" between instruction periods. For example, when Indianapolis adopted a year-round calendar in some schools, it announced that students who were below grade level would be required to attend 20 days of remedial instruction during intersessions (Indianapolis Public Schools, 2010). Unfortunately, due to tight budgets, the district was never able to fund more than 10 days of intersession instruction, and today, according to a district administrator, the decision to offer intersession instruction is left to individual schools (Deborah Leser, personal communication, October 22, 2015).

Of course, the possibility of supplemental instruction is not limited to the year-round calendar. On a 9-month calendar, children can also receive supplemental instruction outside of regular school hours—after school, on weekends, or during the summer. While many types of out-of-school-time instruction can be effective (Lauer et al., 2006), it is unclear whether out-of-school-time instruction would be more convenient or effective on a year-round calendar. The proper comparison for a year-round school with intersession instruction is a 9-month school with a summer learning program.

EFFECTS OF YEAR-ROUND CALENDARS

Effects on Test Scores

Over the past 5 years, the weight of evidence has shifted against the idea that year-round calendars increase test scores. A 2003 meta-analysis estimated that year-round calendars improved student test scores by an amount that, though small on average (0.05 standard deviations [SD]), was larger for socioeconomically disadvantaged children (0.2 SD) (Cooper et al., 2003). However, more recent research estimates that year-round calendars have not improved test scores on average and that any effects on disadvantaged children's scores are small (0.05 SD) and as likely to be negative as positive (Graves, 2010, 2011; McMullen & Rouse, 2012b).

Why are recent studies of year-round schools more negative than older studies? One reason is that recent studies use more rigorous research designs. Before 2003, most year-round studies did not control for confounding differences between year-round and 9-month schools (Cooper et al., 2003). These differences are considerable, as Tables 13.1c–d show. Although the differences between year-round and 9-month students vary from place to place, on a national level year-round students are much more likely than 9-month students to be Hispanic and to qualify for free lunch. The mothers of year-round students are less likely to have a high-school diploma and less likely to work outside the home. Year-round students are on average a month younger than 9-month students. Most student-level differences shrink when we limit comparisons to the same strata, but even within strata there are some significant differences. For example, year-round teachers are on average 4 years less experienced than 9-month teachers in the same stratum.

Most studies before 2003 failed to control for observed differences between year-round and 9-month schools (Cooper et al., 2003). Hardly any studies were designed to control for unobserved differences that might have biased the results after observed differences were taken into account.

But not all studies before 2003 were poorly designed. The best was a study that compared the 67 year-round and 1,364 9-month elementary and middle schools in North Carolina (McMillen, 2001). Two features made this study more compelling than previous studies of year-round schools. First, in addition to controlling for student demographics, the North Carolina study controlled for prior test scores. Controlling for prior test scores is a simple but effective technique that can remove 80%–100% of the bias from estimated effects. As a result, studies that control for prior test scores sometimes predict the results of randomized experiments with remarkable accuracy (Cook, Shadish, & Wong, 2008; Kane & Staiger, 2008; Steiner, Cook, Shadish, & Clark, 2010).

Another strength of the North Carolina study was that, in addition to comparing schools that used the same calendar schoolwide, the North Carolina study also examined 39 "schools-within-a-school" where some children followed a year-round calendar and others followed a 9-month calendar. It is revealing to compare year-round students to 9-month students at the same school, because the comparison holds constant all school-level variables—such as the neighborhood, the administrators, the library, and the computers. In addition, year-round and 9-month students who attended the same school were more demographically similar than students who attended different schools (McMillen, 2001).

The North Carolina study concluded that year-round calendars did not improve test scores on average. More recent rigorous studies have reached similar conclusions. The most impressive recent studies follow schools over time as they convert between 9-month and year-round calendars. Like a study of schools-within-a-school, a study of calendar conversion is compelling because it makes comparisons within the same school, holding many student and school characteristics constant, while little but the calendar changes from year to year.

Calendar conversion studies have focused on both Wake County, North Carolina, which converted 22 elementary schools to a multi-track year-round calendar in 2007 (McMullen & Rouse, 2012b), and California where, between

1998 and 2005, 936 elementary schools switched between multi-track year-round, single-track year-round, and 9-month calendars (Graves, 2010).

The Wake County study found that year-round calendars had no significant effect on average test scores (McMullen & Rouse, 2012b), while the California studies found that year-round calendars, especially the multi-track variety, actually *reduced* average test scores by 1–2 percentile points, or 0.05–0.11 SD (Graves, 2010).

Conversion to year-round schools may be one of the reasons that California's class-size reduction did so little to raise test scores. To reduce class sizes, California hired to 25,000 novice teachers, many of whom were uncertified, and it has been shown that the low effectiveness of these teachers offset the benefits of reduced class sizes in the early years of the class size reform (Jepsen & Rivkin, 2009). But that may not be the whole story. To accommodate the new teachers, many California schools switched to multi-track year-round calendars (Graves, 2010), and these may have also have reduced test scores, offsetting the class-size effect even more.

Although year-round calendars have not raised achievement on average, we might hope that they raised achievement among disadvantaged or underachieving children. After all, these are the children who are most vulnerable to summer learning loss (Alexander, Entwisle, & Olson, 2001; Downey, von Hippel, & Broh, 2004). Unfortunately, the effects of year-round calendars on disadvantaged children have been disappointing as well. In Wake County and the rest of North Carolina, year-round calendars have not raised the achievement of non-White, Black, or Hispanic students (McMillen, 2001; McMullen & Rouse, 2012b). In California, year-round calendars have actually reduced the achievement of Black, Hispanic, and socioeconomically disadvantaged students more than they have reduced the achievement of White students (Graves, 2011).

The effects of year-round calendar on other low-achieving students have been more mixed. In California year-round calendars have had a more negative effect on the bottom of the achievement distribution than on the top (Graves, 2011). But in North Carolina, year-round calendars appear to have raised the scores of students who were near the bottom of the achievement distribution (McMillen, 2001; McMullen, Rouse, & Haan, 2015). One suggested reason for this effect is that more than half of North Carolina's year-round schools require intersession instruction for low-achieving students (McMillen, 2001). But the lowest-achieving students also appear to benefit from the year-round calendar in Wake County (McMullen et al., 2015), where intersession instruction is not required (Katy Rouse, personal communication, November 2015). Whatever the cause, the effect of year-round calendars on North Carolina's low-achieving students is quite small in schools that use the calendar schoolwide (0.05 SD) (McMillen, 2001; McMullen et al., 2015), and no effect is evident in the state's schools-within-a-school (McMillen, 2001).

Effects on Summer and School-Year Learning

The disappointing effects of year-round calendars on achievement may puzzle some readers. Don't year-round calendars increase summer learning? And if they do, why don't they increase achievement overall? Past studies could not address these questions because they used data that only tested students once a year.

To address the question of summer learning in year-round schools, we use data from the ECLS-K. The ECLS-K tested students twice a year for the first 2 years of elementary school, giving math and reading tests in the fall and spring of kindergarten and 1st grade, which were scored using an ability scale (or theta scale) that was constructed using item response theory (IRT).[2] The ECLS-K's twice-yearly tests permit us to estimate learning rates during summer and during the 9 months of the traditional school years. We can also estimate learning rates over the months before kindergarten, by estimating the association between test scores and age at the start of kindergarten.

Given the number of potentially confounding differences between the year-round and 9-month schools in Table 13.1, it may seem daunting to try and estimate the effects of the year-round calendar. Using the ECLS-K we cannot observe the same schools under both a year-round and a 9-month calendar, as we could if there were calendar conversions or schools-within-a-school. Fortunately, we can take several steps to increase the comparability of year-round and 9-month schools.

First, we do not have to compare year-round and 9-month schools nationwide. Instead, we limit our analysis to public schools in the 15 ECLS-K survey strata that contain year-round schools. Within those strata, year-round and 9-month schools are much more similar, as the last two columns of Table 13.1 show. Results from these 15 strata are limited in generality, but this limitation is unavoidable because year-round schools are so geographically concentrated. No analysis of the ECLS-K could tell us anything about the effects of year-round calendar in, say, the Northeast, because there aren't any year-round schools in the northeastern strata of the ECLS-K (Table 13.1b).

In addition to limiting our analysis to strata with year-round schools, we use stratum fixed effects to control for unobserved differences between strata. Stratum fixed effects ensure that each year-round school is compared to 9-month schools that are in the same stratum. To control for differences between schools in the same stratum, we include as covariates all of the potentially confounding variables in Table 13.1. Estimates are obtained using a multilevel growth model that we describe in the Appendix (Singer & Willett, 2002).

Are these steps adequate to control for preexisting differences between year-round and 9-month students? We can check, because children in the ECLS-K were tested near the beginning of kindergarten. If our covariates and fixed effects are adequate, we should find that, net of those controls, the test scores of year-round and 9-month children do not differ significantly when kindergarten starts.

And, that is exactly what we find. In Table 13.2 we estimate children's average reading and math scores on July 18, 1998, which is the average start date for year-round kindergarten. Within strata, holding all of the variables in Table 13.1 constant at their means, we find no significant differences between the reading and math scores of children who are about to enter year-round or 9-month schools.

According to Table 13.2, year-round students do learn faster than 9-month students during the summer, but 9-month students learn faster during the rest of the year. More specifically, year-round students learn significantly faster when 9-month students are on summer vacation (June 6–August 23), but 9-month students learn significantly faster than year-round students during 9-month kindergarten (August 25–June 5) and during 9-month 1st grade (August 24–June 3). This pattern is consistent with the idea that learning increases with school exposure. During the summer, year-round students are in school, while 9-month students are not. During the 9-month school year, all students are in school 1 day out of 2, but 9-month students are in school more often, 3 days out of 5 (Table 13.1a).

In effect, the year-round calendar redistributes learning, just as it redistributes days of instruction. As a result, the year-round calendar does not yield a net increase in average learning. The increase in summer learning on a year-round calendar is almost perfectly offset by the decrease in learning during the rest of the year. Over a 12-month period—e.g., August to August, or June to June—the total amount learned on a year-round calendar is not significantly different from the total amount learned on a 9-month calendar, according to Table 13.2.

Figure 13.1 summarizes the results graphically, showing that year-round students pull ahead during the summer, but 9-month students catch up and pull ahead during the rest of the year. Year-round students make slow, steady progress all year long, while 9-month students surge during their school year but slow down or stall out during the summer. Over a full calendar year, the gains of year-round and 9-month students are equal.

Effects on Teachers, Mothers, and Property Values

Research has evaluated the effects of year-round calendars not just on students, but also on teachers and parents. Here, too, the weight of evidence has recently shifted against year-round schools. Although research reviewed in 2003 suggested that parent and staff attitudes toward year-round calendars were "overwhelmingly" positive (Cooper et al., 2003), research since 2012 has found that both parents and teachers are more likely to respond negatively than positively to year-round calendars.

Year-round calendars reduce mothers' employment rates by about 4 percentage points, especially in predominantly White communities where

Table 13.2. Learning Rates in Year-Round and 9-month Schools

	Dates	READING			MATH		
		Year-Round schools	9-month schools	Differences	Year-Round schools	9-month schools	Differences
Ability at baseline	Jul 18, 1998	-1.603*** (0.035)	-1.637*** (0.022)	0.034 (0.036)	-1.468*** (0.027)	-1.438*** (0.017)	-0.030 (0.028)
Monthly learning rates	Jul 18–Aug 25, 1998	0.086*** (0.003)	0.017*** (0.002)	0.069*** (0.004)	0.075*** (0.002)	0.018*** (0.002)	0.056*** (0.003)
	Aug 25, 1998–Jun 5, 1999	0.086*** (0.003)	0.105*** (0.001)	-0.019*** (0.003)	0.075*** (0.002)	0.086*** (0.001)	-0.011*** (0.002)
	Jun 6–Aug 23, 1999	0.089*** (0.014)	0.018* (0.009)	0.070*** (0.015)	0.079*** (0.012)	0.041*** (0.008)	0.038** (0.012)
	Aug 24, 1999–Jun 3, 2000	0.061*** (0.005)	0.085*** (0.003)	-0.023*** (0.005)	0.052*** (0.004)	0.063*** (0.003)	-0.011** (0.004)
12-month gains	Aug 25, 1998–Aug 23, 1999	1.038*** (0.041)	1.030*** (0.027)	0.009 (0.046)	0.908*** (0.036)	0.914*** (0.023)	-0.005 (0.036)
	Jun 5, 1999–Jun 3, 2000	0.810*** (0.025)	0.841*** (0.013)	-0.031 (0.027)	0.700*** (0.021)	0.702*** (0.011)	-0.003 (0.022)

Note. These estimates come from a multilevel growth model (Singer & Willett, 2002) fit to multiply imputed test scores from which imputed test scores were deleted (von Hippel, 2007).

Figure 13.1. Learning in Year-Round and 9-month Schools from the Start of Kindergarten to the End of First Grade

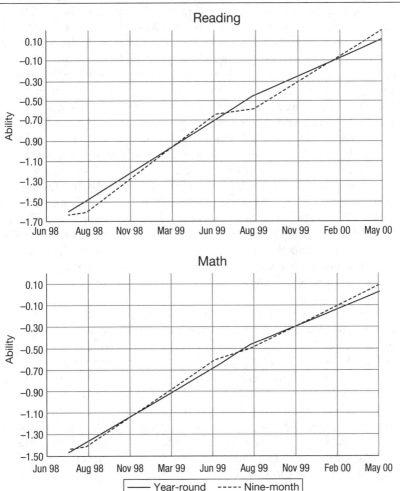

mothers are more likely to rely on formal child-care arrangements rather than informal kin networks (Graves, 2013). The finding that year-round calendars reduce maternal employment is consistent with news reports that year-round calendars complicate family schedules, especially in families where one sibling attends a year-round school and the other attends a 9-month calendar, or in families where children attend year-round schools on different tracks (e.g., CBS News Chicago, 2013; Haug, 2010).

Some families are willing to pay a premium to avoid year-round schools, and as a result living in the attendance area of a year-round school reduces property values by 1%–2% (Depro & Rouse, 2015).

Schools using year-round calendars find it harder to recruit and retain effective and experienced teachers, at least in California schools serving predominantly poor and minority populations (Graves, McMullen, & Rouse, 2015). The effects of the year-round calendar on teacher turnover, experience, and quality may be part of the reason why year-round calendars have reduced test scores in California, especially in high-poverty, high-minority schools where teachers are already hard to attract and retain (Graves et al., 2015). Teachers' distaste for the year-round calendar was evident when the Chicago Teachers Union, as one of the conditions for ending its 2012 strike, demanded that the Chicago Public Schools discontinue use of the year-round calendar (CBS News Chicago, 2013). Perhaps teachers, like parents, experience scheduling conflicts when working under a year-round calendar. For example, it could be difficult if the calendar at the school where a teacher works does not line up with the calendar at the schools their children attend.

Why weren't the negative externalities of the year-round calendar evident at the time of the 2003 meta-analysis? Again, many studies conducted before 2003 were poorly designed. When older studies measured attitudes, they used surveys, and they did not employ a control group. They asked whether attitudes at year-round schools were positive on average (Cooper et al., 2003), but they did not ask whether attitudes were more positive at year-round schools than at 9-month schools.

Recent studies are better designed, using longitudinal designs to track changes in outcomes when schools convert to or from a year-round calendar (Depro & Rouse, 2015; Graves, 2013; Graves et al., 2015). In addition, recent studies do not measure attitudes using surveys, but instead use concrete behaviors such as teachers' decisions to take or leave jobs at year-round or 9-month schools (Graves et al., 2015); mothers' decisions to work or stay home while their children are enrolled in year-round or 9-month schools (Graves, 2013); and the prices that families are willing to pay for homes near year-round or 9-month schools (Depro & Rouse, 2015). Although surveys can be informative, behaviors show teachers and parents voting with their feet. Actions speak louder than words.

POLITICS OF YEAR-ROUND CALENDARS

It would be comforting to imagine that policy regarding year-round calendars is determined by an impartial review of evidence regarding what is best for parents and children. Unfortunately, this is not always how policy is set. Both proponents and opponents of year-round calendars often have ulterior motives.

As discussed earlier, the year-round calendar is often adopted for financial reasons. The multi-track year-round calendar saves money when schools face a shortage of classrooms. The single-track year-round calendar does not save money, but it costs very little, and that increases its appeal when little funding is available for high-poverty districts under pressure to do *something* about chronically low achievement. The low cost of the year-round calendar may explain why two large, high-poverty districts—Indianapolis and Oklahoma City—adopted it during the recent recession.

In some districts, the year-round calendar can also be a way to game high-stakes state tests by increasing the amount of instruction that children receive before the test date. In Indianapolis, for example, a district administrator told me that the year-round calendar became attractive when state-required "testing was in the fall, because [the year-round calendar] allowed the district more time with students before they took high stakes tests. This has since changed when Indiana moved testing back to the spring" (Deborah Leser, personal communication, October 22, 2015). When used to increase pretest instruction, the year-round calendar, along with other calendars that have early start dates, can be one of the "nonacademic strategies" (Koretz, 2009) that districts adopt to improve test scores without actually increasing educational effectiveness. States should adjust their testing schedules to discourage such calendar games, as both California and North Carolina have already done (Graves, 2010; Katy Rouse, personal communication, November 2015).

Opponents of the year-round calendar often have nonacademic motivations as well. Trade groups representing summer camps, amusement parks, and tourist destinations oppose year-round calendars because year-round calendars reduce summer visits from families with children and make it harder to hire students as summer employees (Peercy & McCleary, 2011). I found it hard to believe that tourism interests could shape education policy—until an Ohio legislator contacted me about year-round calendars, explaining that he got my name from an executive at Cedar Point, the state's largest amusement park. The legislator asked me to testify in favor of a bill forbidding schools to open before Labor Day (Ohio 129th General Assembly, 2011). I declined, but similar calendar laws have passed in 11 states (Education Commission of the States, 2011), although the laws in North Carolina and Texas explicitly exempt year-round districts (North Carolina State Legislature, 2013; Texas Association of School Boards, 2012).

In various states, groups opposed to year-round calendars have formed under names such as Save Tennessee Summers, Save Alabama Summers, Save Pennsylvania Summers, etc. (a current list of state groups is available on the website of the San Antonio-based Coalition for a Traditional School Calendar, www.schoolyear.info/stcoalition.html). In newspaper interviews, opposition leaders often appear to be middle-class parents; the leader of a Florida group, for example, is described as "a nonpracticing lawyer and mother of two" (Janofsky, 2005). Given the effects of year-round calendars on vacation plans, property values, and maternal employment, it is plausible that these groups represent concerned families. However, in newspaper stories several state and national groups have acknowledged receiving funding from trade groups representing summer camps and amusement parks

(Chaker, 2005; Cumming, 1993; MacFarquhar, 1995). A contribution to the Coalition for a Traditional School Calendar is disclosed on the tax return of one summer camp group (Association of Independent Camps, Inc., 2008).

This does not necessarily mean that parent opposition groups are mere puppets of business interests. They could simply be allies, political bed-fellows brought together by shared goals. Future research should seek to better understand the connections and motivations of groups opposed to year-round calendars.

CONCLUSION

Given the current state of evidence, it is hard to argue for year-round cal-endars as a way to increase achievement. On average, year-round calen-dars have not improved achievement, and in California they have slightly reduced achievement, especially in disadvantaged populations, in part by making it harder to attract and retain experienced teachers. In addition, year-round calendars are somewhat unpopular with parents and teachers, and very unpopular with business interests that depend on summer vacation to bring them customers and employees.

Although year-round calendars do not increase average achievement by themselves, they might have benefits, at least for low-achieving students, if combined with substantial amounts of remedial instruction during intersessions. Some results from North Carolina suggest that year-round calendars help the lowest achievers (McMillen, 2001; McMullen et al., 2015), and it is plausible that this is in part due to intersession remediation (McMillen, 2001). Yet results from California suggest that year-round calendars are worst for low achievers (Graves, 2011). It is hard to sort out these discrepant results because data on year-round schools rarely indicate which schools offer intersession instruction. This gap in data needs to be filled so that we can fully understand the potential of intersession instruction under a year-round calendar. Districts that are using or considering a year-round calendar should offer intersession instruction, at least for students who are behind. The effects of the district's intersession program should be rigorously evaluated.

Whatever their effects on achievement, year-round calendars are likely to persist because they offer an inexpensive way to handle crowding. Crowded schools have to find some way to serve all students, and the achievement effects of year-round calendars are no worse than other approaches to crowd-ing, such as portable classrooms (McMullen & Rouse, 2012a). Another way to handle crowding is to bus children from more crowded to less crowded schools, and busing can also be used to promote integration of school choice.

Crowding can negatively affect achievement, however it is handled (McMullen & Rouse, 2012a), so portable classrooms and year-round calendars should be treated as temporary measures to be used only until new buildings are completed. If a district chooses to save money by using year-round calendars instead of building new schools, the district should invest some of its savings in other programs with greater potential to raise achievement and help working parents to manage the complexities of the year-round calendar.

METHODOLOGICAL APPENDIX

This Appendix describes the statistical model that Chapter 13 used to estimate the learning rates of year-round and 9-month students in the Early Childhood Longitudinal Study, Kindergarten class of 1998–99 (ECLS-K). Estimates from this model are displayed in Table 2 and Figure 1.

Statistical Model

The ECLS-K tested children's reading and math skills on four occasions in the first two years of elementary school: the fall and spring of kindergarten and the fall and spring of first grade. The tests in the fall of first grade were limited to a random 30 percent subsample of schools. Test dates varied both between and within schools; on each occasion, the test date had a between-school SD of 15–16 days and a within-school SD of 4–6 days.

Average test dates are given in Table A1. The dates are similar for year-round and 9-month schools, except in the fall of kindergarten, when year-round students took the tests 22 days before 9-month students (or 20 days earlier, if we restrict the comparison to schools in the same strata). Our model controls for the fact that different students have different amounts of school exposure on each test occasion.

On each test occasion, we calculate the number of months that each child has been exposed to periods that we define as *9-month kindergarten* (Aug 25, 1998–Jun 5, 1999), *9-month summer* (Jun 6–Aug 23, 1999), and *9-month first grade* (Aug 24, 1999–Jun 3, 2000). We define these periods using the average dates for the start and end of the 9-month school year. Note that year-round students start school before the beginning of 9-month

Table A1. Average test dates in year-round and 9-month schools

	TEST DATE		DIFFERENCE, IN DAYS					
Test occasion	Year-round	9-month	National			Within strata		
Kindergarten, fall	Oct 8, 1998	Oct 31, 1998	-22	***	(3)	-20	***	(3)
Spring	May 6, 1999	May 2, 1999	4		(3)	2		(4)
First grade, fall	Oct 8, 1999	Oct 10, 1999	-2		(7)	-2		(7)
Spring	May 4, 2000	Apr 29, 2000	5	†	(3)	1		(4)

Estimates (SEs). *p<.05, **p<.01, ***p<.001

kindergarten, and that year-round students have school during part of the 9-month summer.

Our model of test score growth is

$$Y_{msct} = \alpha_0 + \alpha_1 AgeStartKind9_c + \alpha_2 Kind9_{ct} + \alpha_3 Summer9_{ct} + \alpha_4 First9_{ct}$$
$$+ YR_s(\beta_0 + \beta_1 AgeStartKind9_c + \beta_2 Kind9_{ct} + \beta_3 Summer9_{ct} +$$
$$\beta_4 First9_{ct}) + ... + f_m + r_s + u_{sct}$$

where Y_{sct} is the reading or math score of child c in school s and stratum m on test occasion t. On that occasion, $Kind9_{ct}$, $Summer9_{ct}$I, and $First9_{ct}$ are the number of months that the student has been exposed to 9-month kindergarten, 9-month dummer, and 9-month first grade. The coefficients $\alpha_2, \alpha_3, \alpha_4$ of these exposures are the average monthly learning rates during each period for children in 9-month schools. YR_s is a dummy for year-round schools, and the coefficients $\beta_2, \beta_3, \beta_4$ are the differences between the average learning rates of year-round and 9-month learning students during each period.

The model includes several terms to adjust for confounders and auto-correlation. The ellipsis (...) indicates inclusion of all of the school, teacher, classroom, and child covariates in Table 1, which are mean-centered and interacted with YR_s. In addition, the model includes a stratum fixed effect f_m which controls for unobserved stratum-level variables and limits the comparison to schools in the same stratum. The model also includes a school random effect r_s which accounts for the correlation among students from the same school, as well as a residual u_{sct} with a spatial power structure that accounts for the correlation between tests taken by the same student on different occasions.[3]

Many quantities of interest can be calculated as linear combinations of the model parameters. For example, the average learning rates for children in year-round schools are $\alpha_2 + \beta_2$ during 9-month kindergarten, $\alpha_3 + \beta_3$ during 9-month summer, and $\alpha_4 + \beta_4$ during 9-month first grade. These learning rates are estimated in Table 2.

Table 2 also estimates average monthly learning rates for the 1.2 months between the start of year-round kindergarten (on July 18, 1998) and the start of 9-month kindergarten (on August 25, 1998). Nine-month students are not in school during this period, so to estimate their learning rate, we exploit the fact that children vary in age at kindergarten entry. $AgeStartKind9_c$ is the child's age in months (mean-centered) at the start of 9-month kindergarten, so we interpret its coefficient α_1 as the monthly rate at which 9-month students learn just before the start of 9-month kindergarten.[4] For year-round students, the situation is different; they are in kindergarten for 1.2 months before the start of 9-month kindergarten, so during that period we assume that they learn at their kindergarten rate $\alpha_2 + \beta_2$.

We can now estimate students' ability levels at baseline. The coefficients β_0 and α_0 represent the average ability of year-round and 9-month students on the first day of 9-month kindergarten, but that is not the baseline date for year-round students. To calculate a common baseline before anyone has started school, we have to extrapolate back an additional 1.2 months to the first day of year-round kindergarten. During those 1.2 months, year-round children learn at a rate of $\alpha_2 + \beta_2$ and 9-month children learn at a rate of α_1, so on the first day of year-round kindergarten, year-round students have an average ability of $\beta_0 - 1.2(\alpha_2 + \beta_2)$ and 9-month students have an average ability of $\alpha_0 - 1.2\alpha_1$. Estimates of these baseline abilities appear in Table 2.

The final quantities in Table 2 are estimates of 12-month gains. Since 9-month kindergarten lasts 9.34 months and 9-month summer lasts 2.66 months, average gains over the 12 months after the start of 9-month kindergarten are $9.34\alpha_2 + 2.66\alpha_3$ for 9-month students and $9.34(\alpha_2 + \beta_2) + 2.66(\alpha_3 + \beta_3)$ for year-round students. Likewise, for the 12 months after the start of 9-month summer, average gains are $2.66\alpha_3 + 9.34\alpha_4$ for 9-month students and $2.66(\alpha_3 + \beta_3) + 9.34(\alpha_4 + \beta_4)$ for year-round students.

Alternatives

We considered two alternative ways to estimate the effects of the year-round calendar. These are not reported in our chapter, but we describe them here for readers who are thinking about other ways to approach these data.

One alternative is to match year-round to 9-month schools using propensity scores estimated from the variables in Table 1—both the school-level variables and school-level averages of student and teacher/classroom variables. The results are similar to those reported in Table 2 and Figure 1, suggesting that year-round students learn faster in the summer but do not learn more over periods of 12 months.

Propensity score matching works best when the matched units are in the same local area, so we also tried matching year-round schools to 9-month schools in the same survey stratum. When we tried this, though, we found we could not achieve good matches because, within strata, year-round and 9-month schools differed too much in enrollment.

Because the decision to adopt a year-round calendar is often driven by crowding, we also considered a regression discontinuity design where the forcing variable was a measure of crowding—either enrollment or the subjective crowding scale in Table 1. This approach also ran into difficulties, since although the probability of using a year-round calendar increases with both crowding and enrollment, there is no threshold where the probability increases discontinuously. Looking for such a discontinuity, we also considered using the ratio of enrollment to the number of rooms in the school. But this ratio was not strongly related to use of the year-round school, probably because the number of rooms was not measured well in the ECLS-K.

NOTES

1. The ECLS-K began with 21,260 kindergartners attending 1,018 schools. Table 13.1 uses a smaller subsample that excludes private schools because none of the year-round schools in the ECLS-K, and only 2% of year-round schools nationally, are private (National Association for Year Round Education, 2007). Table 13.1 also excludes schools with missing or contradictory calendar information. For example, it excludes two schools that were flagged as year-round but had fewer than 300 days between the first and last day of kindergarten or 1st grade.

2. IRT ability scales may seem strange to some readers because they can take negative values, and annual gains can be less than 1 point per year. In fact, IRT ability scales are used routinely by all modern test vendors, which typically rescale ability scores to be positive and show annual progress in tens or hundreds of points. The Northwest Evaluation Association, for example, multiplies ability scores by 10 and adds 200.

3. Under a spatial power structure, the residual correlation between two tests taken by the same student is $\square d$, where $\square < 1$ is a parameter estimated from the data, and d is the number of months elapsed between the tests (Littell, Milliken, Stroup, Wolfinger, & Schabenberger, 2006). We also tried an AR(1) structure, which yielded very similar estimates but ran more slowly.

4. This interpretation depends on the assumption that age at kindergarten entry is exogenous to ability. But for some students age at entry is endogenous; low-ability students are more likely to delay or repeat kindergarten, while high-ability students are more likely to enter kindergarten early. Endogenous entry may bias the estimated effect of age on ability, but the bias is not large in the ECLS-K (Elder & Lubotsky, 2009) .

REFERENCES

Adcock, C. (2010, December 22). Year-round learning. *Oklahoma Gazette*. Retrieved from http://npaper-wehaa.com/oklahoma-gazette/2010/12/22/#?article=1120034

Alexander, K. L., Entwisle, D. R., & Olson, L. S. (2001). Schools, achievement, and inequality: A seasonal perspective. *Educational Evaluation and Policy Analysis, 23*(2), 171–191.

Association of Independent Camps. (2008). Form 990-EZ: Short form return of organization exempt from income tax. Retrieved from http://990s.foundationcenter.org/990_pdf_archive/043/043299041/043299041_200908_990EO.pdf

Ballinger, C. (2000). Changing time, improving learning. *High School Magazine, 7*(9), 5–8.

CBS News Chicago. (2013, January 18). *CPS plans to eliminate year-round calendar next school year*. Retrieved from http://chicago.cbslocal.com/2013/01/18/cps-plans-to-eliminate-year-round-calendar-next-school-year

Chaker, A. M. (2005, August 3). Backlash grows as some schools begin next week. *The Wall Street Journal*.

Cook, T. D., Shadish, W. R., & Wong, V. C. (2008). Three conditions under which experiments and observational studies produce comparable causal estimates: New findings from within-study comparisons. *Journal of Policy Analysis and Management, 27*(4), 724–750.

Cooper, H. M., Valentine, J. C., Charlton, K., & Melson, A. (2003). The effects of modified school calendars on student achievement and on school and community attitudes. *Review of Educational Research, 73*(1), 1–52.

Cumming, D. (1993, November 28). Year-round schools draw fire from summer camps. *The Atlanta Journal-Constitution.*

Dempster, F. N. (1988). The spacing effect: A case study in the failure to apply the results of psychological research. *American Psychologist, 43*(8), 627–634.

Depro, B., & Rouse, K. (2015, December). The effect of multi-track year-round academic calendars on property values: Evidence from district imposed school calendar conversions. *Economics of Education Review, 49*, 157–171.

Donovan, J. J., & Radosevich, D. J. (1999). A meta-analytic review of the distribution of practice effect: Now you see it, now you don't. *Journal of Applied Psychology, 84*(5), 795–805.

Downey, D. B., von Hippel, P. T., & Broh, B. A. (2004). Are schools the great equalizer? Cognitive inequality during the summer months and the school year. *American Sociological Review, 69*(5), 613.

Education Commission of the States. (2011). *Learning time in America: Trends to reform the American school calendar: A snapshot of federal, state, and local action.* Retrieved from www.ecs.org/clearinghouse/78/24/7824.pdf

Elder, T. E., & Lubotsky, D. H. (2009). Kindergarten Entrance Age and Children's Achievement Impacts of State Policies, Family Background, and Peers. *Journal of Human Resources, 44*(3), 641–683. http://doi.org/10.3368/jhr.44.3.641

Graves, J. (2010). The academic impact of multi-track year-round school calendars: A response to school overcrowding. *Journal of Urban Economics, 67*(3), 378–391.

Graves, J. (2011). Effects of year-round schooling on disadvantaged students and the distribution of standardized test performance. *Economics of Education Review, 30*(6), 1281–1305.

Graves, J. (2013). School calendars, child care availability and maternal employment. *Journal of Urban Economics, 78*, 57–70.

Graves, J., McMullen, S., & Rouse, K. (2015). *Teacher turnover and quality effects of year-round schooling.* Unpublished manuscript.

Haug, J. (2010, April 9). *Majority of year-round schools will return to 9-month programs.* Retrieved from www.reviewjournal.com/news/majority-year-round-schools-will-return-9-month-programs

Indianapolis Public Schools. (2010, November 23). *Balanced calendars: What you need to know.* Retrieved from www.balcal.ips.k12.in.us/

Janofsky, M. (2005, August 6). As more schools open earlier, parents seek to reclaim summer. *New York Times*, p. 1.

Jepsen, C., & Rivkin, S. (2009). Class size reduction and student achievement: The potential tradeoff between teacher quality and class size. *Journal of Human Resources, 44*(1), 223–250.

Kane, T. J., & Staiger, D. O. (2008). *Estimating teacher impacts on student achievement: An experimental evaluation* (Working Paper No. 14607). Cambridge, MA: National Bureau of Economic Research.

Koretz, D. (2009). *Measuring up: What educational testing really tells us.* Cambridge, MA: Harvard University Press.

Lauer, P. A., Akiba, M., Wilkerson, S. B., Apthorp, H. S., Snow, D., & Martin-Glenn, M. L. (2006). Out-of-school-time programs: A meta-analysis of effects for at-risk students. *Review of Educational Research, 76*(2), 275–313.

Littell, R. C., Milliken, G. A., Stroup, W. W., Wolfinger, R. D., & Schabenberger, O. (2006). *SAS for Mixed Models* (2nd ed.). SAS Institute.

MacFarquhar, N. (1995, July 22). Two Trenton schools begin an experiment with year-round classes. *New York Times,* p. 21.

McCabe, F. (2015, March 6). *11 more Clark County schools will become year-round.* Retrieved from www.reviewjournal.com/news/education/11-more-clark-county-schools-will-become-year-round

McMillen, B. J. (2001). A statewide evaluation of academic achievement in year-round schools. *Journal of Educational Research, 95*(2), 67–74.

McMullen, S. C., & Rouse, K. E. (2012a). School crowding, year-round schooling, and mobile classroom use: Evidence from North Carolina. *Economics of Education Review, 31*(5), 812–823.

McMullen, S. C., & Rouse, K. E. (2012b). The impact of year-round schooling on academic achievement: Evidence from mandatory school calendar conversions. *American Economic Journal: Economic Policy, 4*(4), 230–252.

McMullen, S. C., Rouse, K. E., & Haan, J. (2015). The distributional effects of the multi-track year-round calendar: A quantile regression approach. *Applied Economics Letters, 22*(15), 1188–1192.

National Association for Year Round Education. (2007). *Statistical summaries of year-round education programs: 2006–2007* (Report No. R43588). Washington, DC: Congressional Research Service.

North Carolina State Legislature. Session Law 2012-145, Senate Bill 187, Section 7A.11 (2013).

Ohio 129th General Assembly. *Ohio House Bill 191 (2011).* Retrieved from https://legiscan.com/OH/bill/HB191/2011

Peercy, M. A., & McCleary, K. W. (2011). The impact of the year-round school calendar on the family vacation: An exploratory case study. *Journal of Hospitality & Tourism Research, 35*(2), 147–170.

Singer, J. D., & Willett, J. B. (2002). *Applied longitudinal data analysis: modeling change and event occurrence.* New York, NY: Oxford University Press.

Skinner, R. R. (2014). *Year-round schools: In brief.* Washington, DC: Congressional Research Service.

Steiner, P. M., Cook, T. D., Shadish, W. R., & Clark, M. H. (2010). The importance of covariate selection in controlling for selection bias in observational studies. *Psychological Methods, 15*(3), 250–267.

Stenvall, M. (1999). *A checklist for success: A guide to implementing year-round schools.* San Diego, CA: National Association for Year-Round Education.

Texas Association of School Boards. (2012). *School start date.* Austin, TX: Texas Association of School Boards.

Tourangeau, K., Le, T., Nord, C., Sorongon, A. G., & Chapman, C. (2009). *Early childhood longitudinal study, kindergarten class of 1998-99 (ECLS-K) eighth-grade methodology report* (NCES 2009-003). Washington, DC: National Center for Education Statistics, Institute of Education Sciences, U.S. Department of Education.

von Hippel, P. T. (2007). Regression with missing Ys: An improved strategy for analyzing multiply imputed data. *Sociological Methodology, 37,* 83–117.

Year Round Calendar Study Group. (2007). *Final report.* Las Vegas, NV: Clark County School District.

CHAPTER 14

Summer Learning and Programming in Rural Settings

Judy B. Cheatham and Doris T. Williams

More than 10 million public school children in the United States attend schools and districts in rural places. While rural America is vastly diverse, many rural places are struggling with the challenges of increased student population, diversity, and poverty in the face of dwindling support for already vastly underfunded schools. Public policy, philanthropy, and research lend little attention to the unique challenges of rural places and therefore do little to bridge the "opportunity gaps" to bring about more equitable educational outcomes between rural and nonrural children. Instead, they have opted for "scale" and urban-centric "research-based" reform strategies that do not fit, benefit, or sustain rural children and communities. As a result, rural children often have less opportunity to succeed during the school year and experience greater "summer slide" in the academic-year gains that they do make. In this chapter, we review three promising models of rural summer learning, decoded for their effective characteristics and codified to make clear research, policy, and practice recommendations.

In the fall of 2013, nearly 10 million children entered the doors of public elementary and secondary schools in rural America. Some entered small, remote schools with fewer than 50 students in grades K–12; others entered consolidated, regional schools with upward of 1,200 of their peers. Almost half of them (47.9%) entered schools marked by persistent and concentrated poverty, indicated by a free and reduced-price lunch eligibility rate of 50% or higher. More than 72% of rural African American students were in high-poverty schools, as were 66.3% of Hispanics, 63.2% of Pacific Islanders, and 77.9% of American Indians/Alaskan Natives. In some of the schools, virtually all of the students were children of poverty, children of color, or both (NCES, 2014). Such is the diversity of rural schools.

The communities from which rural students come are just as diverse as the schools they attend. Some are high-amenity, highly resourced destination spots; others are resource-starved crossroads with no local businesses, no libraries, and no places to gather for work, worship, or play. Most present challenges that educators, philanthropists, and policymakers have not united adequately to address. The plights of rural children and communities have been largely ignored or, at best, only marginally acknowledged, in the public discourse and on the national school reform agenda. Rather, rural schools and students have been forced to adopt and implement, "with fidelity," urban-centered, "research-based" "best practices" that give little to no consideration to the unique challenges, cultures, and assets of their local place.

A call to action appeared in a seminal study published in *Journal of Research in Rural Education* in 2005, "A Look at the Condition of Rural Education Research: Setting a Direction for Future Research" (Arnold, Newman, Gaddy, & Dean, 2005). The authors declared that rural education had been seriously neglected by researchers, that research in rural education has been scant at best, and that not a single randomized control trial had been completed in rural school settings: "Rural schools face a unique set of challenges, largely due to their geographic isolation," but without a base of research conducted in rural settings from which to build, "identifying . . . interventions is difficult." In addition, they concluded, "Relatively few scholars are studying rural education issues, and almost no funding is available to conduct education research in specifically rural contexts." A decade later, the state of research in rural education remained mostly unchanged, though the landscape identified as "rural" has been changing rapidly, increasingly becoming less homogeneous and more diverse (Johnson, Showalter, & Klein, 2012). While authentically rural education innovators are few, The Rural School and Community Trust recognizes an emerging body of innovators who are committed to authentic partnerships with rural schools and communities to ensure the success of rural children and families. These innovators recognize the importance of rural people and places in the American landscape, acknowledge and build on their assets, and see their challenges as opportunities to strengthen the social, economic, and political fabric of American society. They recognize the importance of extended learning time outside of the normal school academic year and have brought opportunities to rural children in spite of the voids and challenges around transportation, resources, leadership, and politics.

Among those innovators, to name a few, are Reading Is Fundamental (RIF), New Mexico StartSmart, Parents as Teachers, and Targeted Reading Intervention (TRI). Their innovations all have an early literacy focus. Perhaps the greatest thread through them, though, is the recognition that rural and low-income children can achieve at levels at least as high as their nonrural and more affluent counterparts *if* given the resources, opportunity, and time. They have approached the notion of scale, not as the number of students or schools they rotate through their programs but as a matter of the depth and breadth of collaboration and the capacity of local people to effect the change they need. They recognize the value of high-quality summer learning experiences, especially for disadvantaged children, and intentionally aim to provide those opportunities in the most challenged places, where such opportunities are quite often not available.

This chapter focuses on RIF as a comprehensive model that encompasses the key principles and components deemed essential for early literacy acquisition and educational equity in rural communities—access to resources, professional development for teachers, summer learning experiences for children, and parent and community engagement. Important in its own right, RIF's Read for Success model is an inexpensive, easily scalable and replicable intervention that shows promise for those students from lower socioeconomic communities scoring below the 50th percentile on standardized tests in reading. More importantly, given the lack of a substantial knowledge base about summer reading interventions in rural areas, this chapter presents important lessons learned regarding rural schools and school districts during RIF's 2 years of administering the Read for Success study in rural communities.

READING IS FUNDAMENTAL (RIF)

Over its 49-year history, Reading Is Fundamental (RIF) has provided more than 412 million books to children who need them most. The nation's oldest and largest nonprofit children's literacy organization, RIF has also worked with families to provide activities that motivate children to read and families to read together. Much of RIF's work is based on research indicating that motivation plays a major role in learning (e.g., Deci & Ryan, 1985; Dweck & Elliott, 1983; Lindsay, 2013; McCombs, 1989). Reading motivation, as Morrow (1992) and Wang and Guthrie (2004) found, has been linked to the development of lifelong readers. Children's choice in the selection of reading materials, too, has traditionally been a hallmark of RIF's philosophy and is supported by research underpinning the Universal Design for Learning, which values choice as beneficial to student motivation (Allington & McGill-Franzen, 2013a, 2013b; Biggs & Collis, 1991; Deci & Ryan, 1985; Lindsay, 2013; Patell, Cooper, & Civey Robinson, 2008).

As reading scores have not improved nationally in recent years and as subgroups on the National Assessment of Educational Progress (NAEP) show great gaps across socioeconomic lines, researchers and organizations like RIF have taken a hard look at innovative strategies to help close the gap in reading achievement. On the most recent NAEP, a higher percentage of rural students at grades 4 (36%) and 8 (33%) scored proficient or higher than their counterparts in cities (32% and 31%, respectively) and towns

(32% and 30%, respectively). Still, 64% of rural 4th graders and 67% of rural 8th graders scored below proficient in reading (NAEP, 2015).

Contrary to prevailing assumptions, not all struggling readers come from low-income schools or families. Nor is reading failure limited to a single race or ethnic group, although some groups are more negatively affected than others. For example, 4th-grade reading proficiency rates on the 2015 NAEP ranged from 18% for African American students to 57% for Asian students. One group of struggling readers is composed of mostly low-wealth children who enter school without the prerequisites to achieve high levels of early literacy from most whole class literacy instruction (Snow, Burns, & Griffin, 1998; Vernon-Feagans, Cox, & Conger, 2013). Many other struggling readers come from middle- to upper-middle-class families. These students tend to enter school with adequate oral language skills but have trouble comprehending the relationship between the spoken and the written word (Torgesen, 1999). Researchers have found that these students, like their low-wealth counterparts, are at risk of failure even when they have high-quality literacy instruction (Foorman & Torgesen, 2001; Whitehurst & Lonigan, 1998). Both of these groups of students are at risk of reading failure, but students in rural and low-wealth schools and communities are at greater risk due largely to summer learning loss.

Summer learning loss has been well documented for over a century (Alexander, Entwisle, & Olson, 2007; Allington & McGill-Franzen, 2003, 2013a, 2013b; Heyns, 1975; Luftig, 2003; Malach & Rutter, 2003; White, 1906). The summer losses among underprivileged students are cumulative over time and can be attributed largely to limited literacy activity (Storch & Whitehurst, 2001; Vernon-Feagans, Hammer, Miccio, & Manlove, 2001) and the absence of appropriate educational material in the homes during the summer months (Conger & Donnellan, 2007; Neuman, Celano, Greco, & Shue, 2001). But neither access to books alone nor extended learning time alone is sufficient to achieve and sustain early literacy proficiency. Instructional strategies and interventions must be appropriately matched to individual needs and interests.

Related but often not connected to summer learning loss is the national emphasis on science, technology, engineering, arts, and mathematics (STEAM). Any current discussion related to reading should also include the creation of a context or schema focusing on what Cummins (1984) identified 30 years ago as Cognitive Academic Language, that content-specific, unfamiliar vocabulary that Calderon (2011) and Beck, McKeown, and Kucan (2002) say must be taught intentionally, explicitly, and with frequent repetition (e.g., Calderon, 2011). Cognitive Academic Language Proficiency (CALP) includes Tier Three words in Common Core, those vocabulary words specific to content like biology, ecology, or mathematics. Academic vocabulary is not the vocabulary used in basic interpersonal speech, the lexicon that typically developing babies acquire (Fromkin, Rodman, & Hyams,

2013), and it is not common in a typical dinner conversation in the home (e.g., *obelisk, continent, hydrocarbon, obtuse angle*). If a reader does not know those Tier Three or content words, often he or she cannot understand informational texts or answer questions on assessments, even if the student can perform the task at hand, because the questions often test reading and content vocabulary. On the most basic level, the Tier Three lexical unit or word is harder to decode, much less understand.

The RIF Read for Success Model

RIF launched its Read for Success model in 2012 with funding from a U.S. Department of Education Innovative Approaches to Literacy (IAL) grant. Read for Success was designed to determine how schools and communities in the poorest and/or most rural areas across the country could address summer learning loss if provided with (a) access to opportunity for enrichment, (b) lots and lots of good, current books for both the classroom and for children's choice and ownership, all of which had STEAM themes or content-connections and almost all of which were informational texts, (c) expertly created learning resources that linked activities to the classroom books and to State or Common Core standards, and (d) professional development for teachers.

The Students, Their Schools, and Their School Districts

The RIF Read for Success model served 33,000 2nd-, 3rd-, and 4th-grade students from 173 public schools in 41 school districts across 16 states. Of the 41 school districts, 24 (60%) were classified as rural by the National Center for Education Statistics (NCES). These 24 rural school districts, all sparsely populated, contained 70 schools, or 40% of the total number of schools in the study. Seven of the 24 districts each had only one elementary school serving an entire school district; another six districts had only two elementary schools per district. Geographically, the 70 schools serving rural areas were located on American Indian reservations, in coal mining regions in the Appalachian Mountains, in the Mississippi Delta, on the Mexican border, and among the cotton fields in the South, the corn fields in the Midwest, and other farming areas in the Northwest.

To illustrate one difference between rural and urban school districts in the Read for Success study, in the two most sparsely populated school districts in rural settings, one county had a total population of 4,508, with an estimated 24 inhabitants per square mile; another, the most sparsely populated and remote in the study, had a total population of 9,882 people residing in a county that covers 1,388 square miles and had an estimated 6.9 inhabitants per square mile. One urban school district, by contrast, had 23 schools located in a city that covered 15.97 square miles and had an average of 9,029 inhabitants per square mile (U.S. Census Bureau, 2010 data). Explained another way, 24 school districts combined contained 70 schools, an average of not quite three schools per district; the remaining 17 school districts combined contained a total of 103 schools, an average of six schools per district.

According to the data reported to the U.S. Department of Education, of the 173 schools in the study, over three-quarters (77%) were characterized as high poverty, 22% as mid-high, and 1% as mid-low. Families of the student population self-identified as 34% Hispanic, 28% White, 19% Black, 14% other, and 5% American Indian. Importantly, the one characteristic shared by all 173 schools—rural, urban, or other—was low socioeconomic status across the student population, across the community, and across the school district at large. Each of the schools met the federal guidelines for a high-need LEA (i.e., at least 25% of the students aged 5–17 in the LEA were from families with incomes below the poverty line).

From the studywide 33,000 eligible participants, Lexile reader measures were obtained each spring and fall over the 2-year period of the study. For children to participate in the summer book distribution, parents were required to give permission, which included an hour's testing four times over the course of the study. Approximately 77% of parents did so. At the end of year 2 of the study, 3,745 participants attending rural schools had "linked" spring and fall 2014 test scores on the reading portion of the Iowa Test of Basic Skills (ITBS). The 3,745 rural participants—approximately 21% of the total population of 18,058 participants—had at least two linked ITBS scores at the end of the 2 years.

The Research Question and Hypothesis. The Read for Success 2-year study posed this research question: By providing (1) access to books in the classroom (the classroom "collections" of 80 titles that RIF asked teachers to use as read-alouds once a week for at least 10 weeks for each of 2 years), (2) teaching materials developed specifically for teacher use of each book in the two collections, (3) children's choice of 16 books for summer reading and for building home libraries, (4) an enrichment opportunity for school children during the year, (5) professional development for teachers, and (6) involvement of families, could a 2-year intervention cut in half the percentage of poor children who suffer reading loss over the summer? Guided by the research of Kim and White (2008) and Wilkins et al. (2012), the RIF Read for Success model used the student scores on four administrations of the reading portion of the Iowa Test of Basic Skills to measure results.

Given all the research (e.g., Allington & McGill-Franzen, 2013a) estimating that more than 80% of children from economically disadvantaged communities lose 1 to 3 months of reading skills over the summer because they lack access to reading materials, the hypothesis of the study was this: The RIF intervention would reduce by half the percentage of children who suffer summer learning loss, so that only 40% of the participants would show loss after 2 years instead of the more typical 80%.

The Intervention. The elements in the Read for Success intervention were all related to access: to new, vetted, informational texts for the elementary-school classroom; to colorful, engaging, informational books for children to choose to take home to keep and read over the summer; to activities and auxiliary teaching materials aligned with national and state standards and competencies designed to help teachers and parents better and more substantially use the new classroom books; and to enrichment opportunities for students. To those four elements were added parent involvement and staff development for teachers, who might or might not have had formal training on the use of children's literature as informational texts. Each of the 173 schools received funds to provide a STEAM-related enrichment opportunity (e.g., field trip, guest author, traveling science center) and to provide a stipend for a local, school-based RIF project coordinator. This coordinator—usually a school media specialist—was the local contact for the project. The RIF team felt that the local coordinator position was critical to the success of the project, especially since the sites, though poor and typically underserved, presented diverse situations across and within school districts. A local point of contact maintained the RIF place-based tradition of working with local individuals who know the issues in their particular schools and communities.

Books for the Classroom. Read for Success presented every 1st-through 5th-grade classroom and every school media center with a collection of 40 titles per year. Teachers were asked to use one book a week in a read-aloud for at least the last 10 weeks of the spring semester and document it, aligning and integrating the book with the curriculum for the given week. The purpose was to allow for another way—specifically, the picture book—for students in the classroom to connect with the content of the classroom curriculum.

All the books in both collections had content connections in science, technology, engineering, arts, and mathematics as reflected in state and national standards across grade levels. The goal was to identify books to support learning; for example, rocks are usually studied in 4th-grade science and the water cycle in 3rd, so reviewed, new books on both topics were placed in the collections (*All the Water in the World*, Lyon; *Rocks and Minerals*, Green; *Volcano Rising*, Rusch). RIF's literacy services and expert training teams and two national advisory boards comprised of experts in the field carefully vetted the 80 titles. The books were chosen from a much longer list of approximately 1,000 titles, all having been reviewed by reputable publications (e.g., *Horn Book*, *School Library Journal*, *Booklist*), listed on various "best" lists or lists from national councils like National Council of Teachers of Mathematics, and/or recognized as award winning (e.g., *The Eye of the Whale*, O'Connell, a 2014 recipient of the Green Earth Book Award). No book was chosen more than 5 years after publication so as to keep current with STEAM content.

The RIF Read for Success expert training team and two RIF national advisory committees looked at the following criteria for a book to be considered: Realistic illustrations with a purpose of (a) creating schema or background knowledge and that (b) depict children and adults as they are reflected throughout society, with heterogeneity in presentation, with (c) respectful representation of all human beings. Specifically, RIF sought books that showed males and females in nonstereotypical roles (e.g., women in the sciences, athletics, engineering); children and adults involved in the scientific method; explanations that provided appropriate schema for more complex ideas or processes; contributions to society made by minorities or people new to the United States; and biography or historical fiction that featured a broad base of subjects from diverse backgrounds (e.g., *The Boy Who Harnessed the Wind*, Kamkwamba and Mealer; *The Soda Bottle School*, Kutner and Slade; *Pierre the Penguin*, Marzollo; *Flying Solo: How Ruth Elder Soared into American's Heart*, Cummins). For the purposes of the Read for Success study, books in which setting or place is important were among those selected: for example, *Grandpa's Garden*, by Stella Fry, is set in a rural area; *Ballet for Martha*, by Greenberg and Jordan, tells the story of Copeland's *Appalachian Springtime* and Martha Graham's ballet set to it; and *Buffalo Song*, by Joseph Bruchac, has a mountain setting among Native people.

As Dr. Debbie Reese, a Nambe Pueblo, member of the RIF Multicultural Advisory Committee, and an expert in writing for and about American Indians in children's literature, noted,

> For generations, children in minority and economically disadvantaged groups have not seen themselves reflected in the books they read. Without those images, minority children are deprived of something that children in the majority demographic see as a matter of course: the opportunity to imagine themselves in a wide range of careers, including ones in math, science, and technology. (personal communication, July 3, 2014)

RIF's expert team and national advisory boards deemed all 80 titles developmentally appropriate for young children, 2nd through 4th grades, though many award-winning books were not chosen. Though excellent, they may have presented material too sensitive or controversial about topics regarding or implying a stand on politics or religion. Still others did not relate to the STEAM themes and thus did not contain vocabulary and illustrations that could create a context or schema for those topics. Books that needed to be read with parents were also not chosen.

Choosing the books for the collections seems simple, but it was an ongoing process that took months. During both years of the study, RIF identified, reviewed, and recommended books from diverse and varied authors and illustrators, working with 31 different publishers, including lesser-known and smaller presses, to do so. The particular challenges involved finding books that ran the gamut of subject matter and then, once a title was confirmed, finding sufficient numbers (2,000 or more copies) of that title. Because a print-run on a book for children is often small (typically 3,000 or fewer), the process related to the books—from start to finish—took about 8 months. Steps included researching titles, obtaining review copies and reviewing them, deciding how they might fit into a 2nd- to 4th-grade curriculum, selecting a short list of about 200 titles, pricing the titles, confirming that titles were in print or were being reprinted, selecting a second shorter list of about 50, taking bids for mass distribution, waiting for second printings, shipping to sites, and then confirming that all the books per collection were included in all the books shipped (about 2,000 collections per year). For RIF's IAL Read for Success book list, please see Appendix A.

Books for Ownership. From a selection of more than 6,500 titles, RIF chose 670 to use for the summer reading books. These 670 titles spanned eight Lexile levels. Participants were to choose eight books each summer, based on choice within a Lexile band, using the scores from the reading portion of the ITBS administered in late spring of both years. Inexpensive but high-quality paperback books were placed on tables by Lexile bands in 100-point spans (except for Lexile I, which began at 40L and reached 299L); the Lexile band was indicated only by the color of the tablecloth on the table. For each Lexile band, 20 to 40 titles were available from which the student could choose 8. These summer books were almost all informational texts, and they too had STEAM themes. As one principal indicated, he felt that the teacher-led discussions with the classroom titles had introduced students to informational texts, serving as a kind of scaffold to prepare them by the end of school to choose and accept nonfiction texts as opposed to books featuring cartoon or super-hero characters.

All told, the Read for Success model provided more than 750,000 books to 173 schools over a 2-year period: Each classroom grades 1 through 5 and each media center received a collection of 40 titles per year (80 titles total); each student participating in the actual study, grades 2 through 4, chose eight paperback books to own and to read over the summer for each of two summers (16 titles per child).

Implementation varied across the 173 schools, even within the same district. Teachers, administrators, and parents expressed their gratitude for the reading material and for the quality of the reading material in targeted interviews, surveys, and letters of support. Responses from LEA administrators were varied. In a very rural farm community without a traffic sign or street light, a principal of a one-building school housing nine grades fought back tears; she could not imagine how the children would feel when they had to return the books in the classroom, they had never seen books like these, and she needed to know what she could do to keep them on the shelves. Another principal said the books had actually made it possible for her to evaluate her teachers on the state evaluation of teacher quality. One evaluation standard called for the classroom teacher to use informational texts in the classroom and feature literature for, by, and about women and other minorities.

> "That is impossible to do," this principal said, "when the school has not received any new books for the classroom in the last 20 years. We don't have bookstores anywhere close to look at new books we might use. We don't have money to spend on books that we order only to find that they are not what we needed. The RIF books have helped teachers show their students the world these children know nothing about."

The recognition that emerged was that, with professional development and grade-level or school-level leadership, the picture books all of a sudden, according to one superintendent, "leveled the playing field" for these children raised in rural and often remote areas—children who had never seen a beach or a zoo animal, who had never seen the inside of a library, who did not have school buses in their county or a store closer than an hour away. Suddenly, the unknown, like the "mysteries of the amethyst quartz," according to one child, could be explained through good books with clear, colorful, engaging illustrations.

Professional Development for Teachers. The RIF expert training team conducting professional development on this project were all college professors, with advanced or terminal degrees in Elementary Education, Reading, Special Education, Linguistics, Rhetoric and Composition, Birth through Kindergarten, and Curriculum and Instruction. The trainers held at least two sessions in every one of the 41 school districts except one (because of weather), one a year, with at least monthly contact by telephone or email with the local RIF school coordinators.

The training team modified the professional development trainings within the first month (January 2013) for two reasons. First, for such a large project, the RIF team felt that a hands-on delivery system would be key for successful implementation, which would ultimately be dependent on the classroom teachers. The six trainers divided responsibilities, and each identified those school districts for which they would be the point of contact for the local RIF coordinators, although some urban districts were so heavily populated that two or three trainers were needed for multiple days because of the number of schools. Second, travel to the rural schools was more complicated than anticipated. None of the rural school districts was within an hour's drive of an airport, for example, and of the 24 rural school districts, lodging was not available in 15 of them. For eight districts, lodging was not available within a 30-mile radius.

Teaching Materials. Each of the 80 books in the RIF classroom collections had four or five "teaching" sheets to accompany it, created by RIF's literacy services team and professionally designed. To support teachers in their use of the classroom books as well as their commitment to Common Core, these teaching sheets contained—for each book—a lesson plan, a family page, a vocabulary scaffold based mostly on Tier Two vocabulary (i.e., "school" vocabulary words like *analyze, summarize, amble, scurry*), and a "Think-Tac-Toe" set of 9 to 12 assignments that were already modified to show differentiation in instruction and activities that allowed for differences in student strengths. Of the assignments in Think-Tac-Toe, for example, one might ask for a letter, another for research, a third for a list, and a fourth for a map with computation. (See Appendix B for samples.)

Enrichment Opportunity. The RIF IAL grant provided each school with $1,000 to do something "different" related to STEAM. Each school had the autonomy to use that money however it wanted, as long as the project addressed STEAM content and included all the 2nd, 3rd, and 4th graders, the target group of the study. Thus, for example, an LEA that was located an hour away from the ocean used the money to see the aquarium at the ocean. Across the board, schools brought in authors, illustrators, scientists, or ecologists, tapping into their state museums or travelling exhibits. One of the more isolated LEAs had to import a travelling program from a neighboring state—a 6-hour drive. One school, surrounded by field after field of cotton, chose to take its students on an hour field trip to the county's public library. This school, serving prekindergarten through 8th grade, housed 120 students whose families all farmed, working from sun-up until sun-down. Those families and many others like them could not themselves visit a library during regular hours, nor could they afford the gas to travel there.

Results. The hypothesis was accepted after each year's analysis. The results of the reading section of the Iowa Test of Basic Skills showed no significant difference either year between the rural and the urban areas, with over half of the students who participated in the Read for Success model improving their reading proficiency over the summer, each summer. On average, 61% of the sample saw no loss: 57% of those students tested showed statistically significant gains in reading proficiency from spring to fall each year; 4% stayed the same; and 39% saw loss. Of the three grades in the actual study, the 3rd graders made the greatest gains. Significantly and importantly, students in each grade who were performing at the 10th percentile or below—those children often categorized as having "special needs"—showed the greatest increase in scores: 74% of 2nd graders, 81% of 3rd graders, and 72% of 4th graders made or exceeded target gains, based on Lexile Reader Measures as well as Standard Scores on the ITBS. Of those students reading at the 90th percentile, 30% showed gains. For participants in rural schools, the spring 2014 and fall 2014 Lexile Reader Measures and Standard Scores are presented in Table 14.1, with average changes, percent achieving an increase, and percent achieving an increase or no loss.

Beyond the hard data, the RIF Read for Success team collected qualitative data from which this article quotes extensively. First, Policy Studies Associates, the external evaluation team, conducted focus groups and administered surveys of targeted participants. Second, the RIF Read for Success team was committed to formative assessment and thus consistently reached out to participants at the schools. The team applied for a second grant, which was not funded, but during the application process collected written assessments in the form of letters from teachers, administrators, and parents who expressed their gratitude for the reading material and for the quality of the program. As they wrote, they described their own situations, which are used in this article. Finally, the RIF team was so impressed by the kinds of work schools and parents were doing in their own local areas that practitioners were brought to RIF's Washington, DC, offices to come together as the real "experts" and to share with each other, with the training team, with the Summer Learning advisory board, and with authors and illustrators. Thus, RIF convened two IAL Summits, at which each part of the model and its implementation in their districts was discussed. Of the participants who attended the Summits, parents of children involved in the research model were present. At the second summit, the time frame was expanded to a day and

Table 14.1. Results of Iowa Test of Basic Skills, Reading Participants from Rural Schools, Spring and Fall 2014

Grade	Mean Spring Scores	Mean Fall Scores	Mean Change	% Achieving Increase	% Achieving Increase or No Loss
Lexile Reader Measures					
2	533L	560L	+26.3L	58%	62%
3	635L	683L	+48.1L	61%	64%
4	749L	772L	+22.5L	57%	59%
Standard Scores					
2	170	173	+3.2	58%	61%
3	183	189	+6.4	61%	63%
4	198	202	+3.5	57%	58%

a half, with the second day devoted to using literature in the classroom and featuring Dr. Debbie Reese, expert on books by and for Native Americans; Dr. Anne McGill-Franzen, nationally recognized researcher in reading; Dr. Karl Alexander, nationally recognized researcher in summer learning loss; Samantha Vamos and Kelly Starling Lyons, both writers of award-winning books for children; and R. Gregory Christie, nationally known illustrator.

Discussion. From a national perspective, for this study, RIF was interested in geographic diversity, especially in light of the recent discussions about different kinds of needs in education in rural areas. Surprisingly, according to "A Look at the Condition of Rural Education Research" (Arnold et al., 2005), as well as *Why Rural Matters*, a series of biennial reports from the Rural School and Community Trust (Johnson, Showalter, & Klein, 2012; Johnson et al., 2014; Johnson & Strange, 2005), studies on reading among school children in rural areas are scant, with not many that could be considered experimental, and no known completed randomized control trials. (The StartSmart K–3 Plus Project, which uses a randomized control trial focused on extended learning time and early literacy in urban and rural settings in New Mexico, was not complete at the time of publication of this book, although preliminary data are available. The study period ends in 2016.)

Several areas identified in the research and corroborated by experts, practitioners, teachers, and families informed RIF's work in the rural LEAs, allowing for differentiation between rural and nonrural school settings. For rural and/or remote areas, the lack of access to opportunity caused by geographic isolation was complicated by issues that stem from socioeconomic needs.

First is transportation—long cited as a barrier to education of children and their families and a formidable challenge to every part of the administration of the grant. According to a 2014 report by the National Center for Education Evaluations and Regional Assistance (NCEE), "A Focused Look at Rural Schools Receiving School Improvement Grants," the lack of transportation affects classroom attendance and parental involvement and engagement. Since rural schools serve broader geographical areas, students, parents, and faculty generally live farther from the school, making student participation in extracurricular activities or parental involvement in the education process of the child more difficult. The distance between home and school and limited or no public transportation available in many rural areas can deter parents from actively participating in school-related activities, including parent-teacher conferences or volunteering in the classroom. Impediments to parent participation are not unique to rural schools, but sheer distance and lack of public transportation are a consistent challenge. Some parents, teachers, and administrators feel that distance also indirectly impedes parent involvement by eroding the sense of community. The RIF team found all of this to be true and more.

Of the 24 rural school districts participating in the IAL RIF initiative, among other places, children lived on reservations or in trailers on the hillside or down hollows between mountains or amid fields of cotton or corn. These communities and their children lacked access to multiple services that research indicated would affect reading ability. Many had no public transportation and two did not provide school buses for the children; in these two systems, children either walked or were brought to school by parents or others. Some sites had school buses but any trip back to school or back to town posed a struggle, as the distance could be 30 miles one way. One superintendent in North Carolina said, "[Our county] is small and rural, with no industry, and with one primary and one intermediate elementary school right next to each other, serving children throughout the whole county. Most families have to commute great distances to get to the school or the library." Another superintendent from Alabama stated, "Many of our students have no opportunities for reading and no access to reading materials outside of the school day—because of a lack of resources in the home and the issue with transportation to get back to the school." In winter, especially in the IAL RIF schools in South Dakota and Eastern Kentucky, roads were often impassable because of snow and ice; the superintendents in two of the Kentucky school systems talked about "winter learning loss," as their schools were shut down for over 3 weeks.

Transportation played a critical part in the summer book distribution plan. Initially, all students who had permission to participate in the program chose five books in their Lexile band during a book distribution held at some point during the last month of school. The original plan in year 1 called also for a mid-summer book distribution: Families were to come back to school so that children could choose three more books at their particular Lexile levels. Schools were asked to set the mid-summer book distribution times over 2 or 3 days and to include "after work" time slots on at least 1 day.

That plan was scrapped for year 2: feedback delivered during the formative assessment after year 1 overwhelmingly indicated that transportation—and the multiple other barriers associated with it—precluded students returning in the summer. As one parent said, "I can't afford the gas or the time to drive 23 miles one way to get three books." This was true for the teachers as well, the RIF team heard anecdotally.

For the very few successful mid-summer distributions in year 1, schools made the book distribution accommodate the place instead of the other way around. These schools either paired the event with other services (e.g., a foodbank) or took the books to the children. One LEA used Title I monies to hire a bus driver familiar with the most rural routes and send him and the school's media specialist—usually the RIF local coordinator—into those rural areas, stopping the bus at the traditional bus stops. Another LEA used a similar strategy but assigned the bus driver to stop at different rural churches at which community children gathered during the summer. Still another school held its summer book distribution at the time the workday ended (after noon) in a particular crabbing community, where 100% of the families had at least one member who worked as a crabber. Sadly, as one superintendent described it, even when there are resources available like free books to choose and keep for the home library, if the parents cannot access them, the family cannot take advantage: "Our county library, which serves as the library for our high school, does offer computer and Internet services. But many families do not have access to transportation to get them there."

A second issue related to transportation also relates to parent employment, certainly not unique to rural America but its effects can take different forms. Parents do not have the money to provide access to opportunity—and in rural and remote areas, opportunity is often harder to find. As a principal wrote about her school located in a rural, remote area,

> Our town has a population of about 450 and our school serves 160 students. The majority of our families earn their living as agricultural laborers . . . working in our fruit orchards or the food processing plants in a nearby town. Nearly one-third of our students live in a subsidized-rent apartment complex provided by Catholic Families Charities. Another third . . . reside in one of three campgrounds . . . , year round, in campers or trailers. 94% of our children . . . qualify for free or reduced price school meals. Many of our students are home all summer alone or with older siblings and with very little stimulation while their parents work in the fields and orchards.

Her conclusion was that "summer learning loss has been a huge challenge for our students. . . . Our kids desperately need exposure" to books, resources, and learning opportunities. Another principal wrote, "Many of our kids do not have the ability to own their own books. . . . We are in rural communities that have limited hours at our public libraries. Our students can fund little on their own."

Impediments to parent participation are not unique to rural schools, but sheer distance and lack of public transportation are a consistent challenge (NCEE, 2014). The RIF Read for Success documents submitted by administrators at the school or district level cited a lack of reliable family transportation as many times as they did a lack of public transit. Families with children involved in rural reading programs that require parents coming to the school are not always appropriately served through approaches designed with urban and suburban schools in mind.

As principals and school superintendents told us on two occasions, though rural communities are themselves diverse in terms of income and culture, the challenges that arise from travel remain relatively consistent.

Rural schools serve less dense populations; correspondingly, travel from children's homes to and from the school site can be difficult, time consuming, and expensive for parents, students, and teachers. In low-income communities, with parents working or looking for work and with the price of gas as it is, where the school may be located 20 to 30 miles from the home, transportation to school, to a library if there is one, or to extracurricular activities can preclude participation by many families.

During the school year, even rural children have access to the resources of books, instruction, and food; however, according to the National Summer Learning Association, during the summer, 95% of those poor children are cut off from these resources (i.e., the "faucet" effect—during the school year, the "faucet" is open, with food and resources provided at school; during the summer, however, the faucet is turned off and children in poverty lose their access to resources). And even if these resources are offered at school, because of the looming issue of transportation, it is difficult for a child and family to take advantage.

In rural areas, the ability to serve children with special needs during the school year—not to mention summer—becomes more challenging. Though schools located in rural areas typically have fewer children to serve, they also have fewer teachers, a smaller tax base from which resources come, and fewer programs to serve those children. As the number of children with special needs and the number of different special needs increase, it becomes more difficult for a limited trained and licensed faculty—often a faculty of one—to serve the children. How too can one teacher with licensure in exceptionalities support inclusion for the classroom teachers across all grade levels?

When Policy Studies Associates, RIF's external evaluation team, shared the results of the ITBS testing with the school leadership—principals, curriculum coordinators, and superintendents—the RIF Summer Learning Advisory Board as well as the expert training team asked them to speculate about the 61% of the study's participants who saw no loss. Because the study was not set up as a randomized control trial and because RIF agreed not to share some of the information about the school districts, several questions cannot be answered. But almost to a person, LEA personnel reported that the classroom collections and the student books served as an inexpensive intervention that helped serve the needs of all children, especially those testing below average and especially those at the 25th to 10th percentile. A curriculum director said, "The classroom teachers were able to enhance their lessons, involving our students in interesting and diverse activities." Two principals said, "Many of our parents could never afford books like those." And a school superintendent declared that the books were the "only variable in a school equation"; she explained that the Read for Success model worked with trained teachers, in schools, with limited resources. What none of the 173 schools had in place before the intervention were these specially chosen, well-recognized, new informational texts for use in the classroom and the supplemental books for each participating child.

Because children who participated were tested using the Iowa Test of Basic Skills, which generates a Lexile level that can be used in identifying student-level, appropriate reading material, and because the selection of the books was heavily vetted by literacy experts with credentials in elementary education, linguistics, reading, exceptionalities (mild and moderate, severe and profound disabilities), and second language acquisition, participating students theoretically should have been able to read the books they selected for summer. Theoretically, auto-didacticism would be possible. The results of the RIF intervention suggest that may have been what happened: The RIF intervention—numerous, attractive, high-interest, content-heavy informational texts at the child's reading level—allowed the child to read the book, share it with friends and family, and participate in the multiple processing required to understand text and vocabulary, as Calderon (2011) suggests. Whatever happened, the intervention for each of the 2 years resulted in stemming learning loss in 61% of the sample, producing gains in 57%, and producing the greatest gains for the bottom 10th percentile.

CONCLUSION: IMPLICATIONS FOR POLICY, PRACTICE, AND FURTHER RESEARCH

Currently, no research available offers broad applicability for schools in rural or remote areas. While studies on rural schools exist, few are representative enough and large enough to support strong general conclusions applicable to all rural schools. The RIF Read for Success model itself did not include and did not gather and analyze other kinds of data that would prove useful at this point. RIF also promised not to share some of the data gathered. Because of the constant feedback among the RIF training team and discussions with our Summer Learning Advisory Board as well as key personnel across the 41 school districts, there is a substantial amount of qualitative and descriptive data that should help in informing future study, which is clearly needed.

A central issue that a research team must overcome is a school district's fear of scrutiny; "bad" test scores can produce brutal press. Another is funding. Based on RIF's best estimates, after pricing the 2-year initiative, a study as described below might cost close to $16 million. As the key advisors on the RIF Summer Learning Advisory Board and the external evaluators stressed, the Read for Success model is ripe for further research that should involve a 4-year, randomized control trial that features a 2-year control with a large enough sample to identify the effects of the intervention, to look at the sample by student, to study the effects of implementation across classrooms and schools, and to tease out nuances. The consensus among the training team and the advisory board was to randomize by school, not by classroom. The Read for Success model described above served approximately 11,000 students in each grade, 2nd through 4th, which should prove sufficiently large.

The RIF Read for Success intervention offers promising evidence that resources appropriately identified and used as well as professional development and sustained support make a difference. RIF data show important gains for children who have access to books during the summer months, but access to books alone may not be enough. Access to books must be paired with effective teaching strategies that (a) address the specific needs of the individual child; (b) provide extended learning time for students who need it; (c) bridge effectively regular school and external learning strategies aligned with appropriately developed standards; and (d) give students some choice in the selection of reading materials. Further study is needed to add the specifics above.

By contrast, policymakers at state and federal levels who often default to urban models assume that the only difference between the two would be size of the population or sample. While all communities are different, the comparative isolation of many rural schools makes an understanding of the unique circumstances of particular communities even more important in the rural context. Many programs ignore the unique sense of place rural communities can draw on, relying on generic and universal materials and avoiding engagement with place (Waller & Barrentine, 2015).

Frankly, it is a scandal that in this day of educational research, children in schools across rural America have been largely ignored. One would hope that within the next 5 years, there will be research that actually can inform policy and practice.

APPENDIX:
READING IS FUNDAMENTAL'S MULTICULTURAL BOOK COLLECTION
(RECOMMENDED AGES: KINDERGARTEN THROUGH FIFTH GRADE)

2013–2014

A Balloon for Isabel by Deborah Underwood, illustrated by Laura Rankin
A House in the Woods by Inga Moore
Ballet for Martha: Making Appalachian Spring by Jan Greenberg and
    Sandra Jordan, illustrated by Brian Floca
Blackout by John Rocco, illustrated by John Rocco
Buffalo Song by Joseph Bruchac, illustrated by Bill Farnsworth
Bull Trout's Gift by Confederated Salish and Kootenai Tribes Cloudette by
    Tom Lichtenheld

Diego Rivera: His World and Ours by Duncan Tonatiuh

Dreaming Up by Christy Hale

First Peas to the Table by Susan Grigsby, illustrated by Nicole Tadgell

Flying Solo: How Ruth Elder Soared Into America's Heart by Julie Cummins, illustrated by Malene Laugesen

Iggy Peck, Architect by Andrea Beaty, illustrated by David Roberts

It Jes' Happened: When Bill Traylor Started to Draw by Don Tate, illustrated by R. Gregory Christie

Lucky Ducklings by Eva Moore, illustrated by Nancy Carpenter

Memoirs of a Hamster by Devin Scillian, illustrated by Tim Bowers

My First Day by Steve Jenkins and Robin Page, illustrated by Steve Jenkins

National Geographic Book of Animal Poetry, ed. by J. Patrick Lewis

No Monkeys No Chocolate by Melissa Stewart and Allen Young, illustrated by Nicole Wong

Philip Reid Saves the Statue of Freedom by Steven Sellers Lapham and Eugene Walton, illustrated by R. Gregory Christie

Rachel Carson and Her Book That Changed the World by Laurie Lawlor, illustrated by Laura Beingessner

Rosie Revere, Engineer by Andrea Beaty, illustrated by David Roberts

Round Is a Tortilla by Roseanne Greenfield Thong, illustrated by John Parra

S Is for Scientists by Larry Verstraete, illustrated by David Geister

Scholastic Discover More: Rocks & Minerals by Dan Green

Snow School by Sandra Markle, illustrated by Alan Marks

Tea Cakes for Tosh by Kelly Starling Lyons, illustrated by E.B. Lewis

The Barefoot Book of Earth Tales by Dawn Casey, illustrated by Anne Wilson

The Beetle Book by Steve Jenkins

The Boy Who Harnessed the Wind by William Kamkwamba & Bryan Mealer, illustrated by Elizabeth Zunon

The Cazuela That the Farm Maiden Stirred by Samantha R. Vamos, illustrated by Rafael López

The Day the Crayons Quit by Drew Daywalt, illustrated by Oliver Jeffers

The Eye of the Whale: A Rescue Story by Jennifer O'Connell

The Favorite Daughter by Allen Say

The Honeybee Man by Lela Nargi, illustrated by Kyrsten Brooker

The Nowhere Box by Sam Zuppardi

The Patchwork Garden / Pedacitos de huerto by Diane de Anda, illustrated by Oksana Kemarskaya

The Secret Pool by Kimberly Ridley, illustrated by Rebekah Raye

Touch the Sky: Alice Coachman, Olympic High Jumper by Ann Malaspina, illustrated by Eric Velasquez

Track That Scat! by Lisa Morlock, illustrated by Carrie Anne Bradshaw

Volcano Rising by Elizabeth Rusch, illustrated by Susan Swan

2012–2013

10 Things I Can Do to Help My World by Melanie Walsh
A Full Moon Is Rising by Marilyn Singer, illustrated by Julia Cairns
All the Water in the World by George Ella Lyon, illustrated by Katherine Tillotson
Amelia to Zora, Twenty-Six Women Who Changed the World by Cynthia Chin-Lee, illustrated by Megan Halsey, Sean Addy
Balloons over Broadway by Melissa Sweet
Boy + Bot by Ame Dyckman, illustrated by Dan Yaccarino
City Dog, Country Frog by Mo Willems, illustrated by Jon J. Muth
Dave the Potter by Laban Carrick Hill, illustrated by Bryan Collier
Eight Days Gone by Linda McReynolds, illustrated by Ryan O'Rourke
Grandpa's Garden by Stella Fry, illustrated by Sheila Moxley
How Did That Get in My Lunchbox? by Chris Butterworth, illustrated by Lucia Gaggiotti
How Many Seeds in a Pumpkin by Margaret McNamara, illustrated by G. Brian Karas
If You Lived Here by Giles Laroche
Ish by Peter H. Reynolds
Just a Second by Steve Jenkins
Kunu's Basket by Lee DeCora Francis, illustrated by Susan Drucker
Math-terpieces by Greg Tang, illustrated by Greg Paprocki
Miss Lady Bird's Wildflowers by Kathi Appelt, illustrated by Joy Fisher Hein
National Geographic Little Kids First Big Book of Animals by Catherine D. Hughes
Neo Leo by Gene Barretta
Newton and Me by Lynne Mayer, illustrated by Sherry Rogers
North: The Amazing Story of Arctic Migration by Nick Dowson, illustrated by Patrick Benson
Owen & Mzee: The True Story of a Remarkable Friendship by Isabella Hatkoff, Craig Hatkoff; Paula Kahumbu, photography. Peter Greste
Pierre the Penguin by Jean Marzollo, illustrated by Laura Regan
Pop! The Invention of Bubble Gum by Megan McCarthy
Riparia's River by Michael J. Caduto, illustrated by Olga Pastuchiv
Summer Birds by Margarita Engle, illustrated by Julie Paschkis
Super Science: Feel the Force! by Tom Adams, illustrated by Thomas Flintham
The 5 Senses by Núria Roca, illustrated by Rosa M. Curto
The Busy Body Book by Lizzy Rockwell
The Day-Glo Brothers by Chris Barton, illustrated by Tony Persiani

The Mangrove Tree by Susan L. Roth and Cindy Trumbore, illustrated by Susan L. Roth

Through Georgia's Eyes by Rachel Rodriguez, illustrated by Julie Paschkis

Up, Up, and Away by Ginger Wadsworth, illustrated by Patricia J. Wynne

Weird but True by National Geographic

We're Roaming in the Rainforest by Laurie Krebs, illustrated by Anne Wilson

What Color Is My World? by Kareem Abdul-Jabbar and Raymond Obstfeld, illustrated by Ben Boos and A.G. Ford

What in the Wild? by David Schwartz and Yael Schy, photography by Dwight Kuhn

What Will I Be? by Nicola Davies, illustrated by Marc Boutavant

Z Is for Moose by Kelly Bingham, illustrated by Paul O. Zelinsky

REFERENCES

Alexander, K. L., Entwisle, D. R., & Olson, L. S. (2007). Lasting consequences of the summer learning gap. *American Sociological Review, 72*, 167–180.

Allington, R. L., & McGill-Franzen, A. (2003). The impact of summer setback on the reading achievement gap. *The Phi Delta Kappan, 85*, 68–75.

Allington, R. L., & McGill-Franzen, A. (2013a). Children will read during the summer if we provide access, choice, and support. In C. Cahill, K. Horvath, A. McGill-Franzen, & R. Allington (Eds.), *No more summer-reading loss* (pp. 16–42). Portsmouth, NH: Heinemann.

Allington, R. L., & McGill-Franzen, A. (2013b). Summer reading loss. In R. Allington & A. McGill-Franzen (Eds.), *Summer reading: Closing the rich/poor achievement gap* (pp. 1–19). New York, NY: Teachers College Press.

Arnold, M. L., Newman, J. H., Gaddy, B. B., & Dean, C. B. (2005). A look at the condition of rural education research: Setting a direction for future research. *Journal of Research in Rural Education, 20*(6). Retrieved from http://jrre.psu.edu/articles/20-6.pdf

Beck, I. L., McKeown, M. G., & Kucan, L. (2002). *Bringing words to life: Robust vocabulary instruction.* New York, NY: Guilford Press.

Biggs, J., & Collis, K. (1991). Multimodal learning and the quality of intelligent behavior. In H. Rowe (Ed.), *Intelligence: Reconceptualization and measurement* (pp. 57–76). Hillsdale, NJ: Erlbaum.

Calderon, M. E. (2011). *Teaching reading and comprehension to English learners, K-5.* Indianapolis, IN: Solution Tree.

Conger, R. D., & Donnellan, M. B. (2007). An interactionist perspective on the socioeconomic context of human development. *Annual Review of Psychology, 58*, 175–199.

Cummins, J. (1984). *Bilingual education and special education: Issues in assessment and pedagogy.* San Diego, CA: College Hill.

Deci, E. L., & Ryan, R. M. (1985). *Intrinsic motivation and self-determination in human behavior.* New York, NY: Plenum.

Dweck, C. S., & Elliott, E. S. (1983). Achievement motivation. In P. H. Mussen & E. M. Heatherington (Eds.), *Handbook of child psychology: Socialization, personality, and social development* (pp. 643–691). New York, NY: Wiley.

Foorman, B. R., & Torgesen, J. K. (2001). Critical elements of classroom and small-group instruction promote reading success in all children. *Learning Disabilities Research and Practice, 16*(4), 203–212.

Fromkin, V., Rodman, R., & Hyams, N. (2013). *An introduction to language.* Boston, MA: Cengage Learning.

Heyns, B. (1975). *Summer learning and the effect of school.* New York, NY: Academic Press.

Johnson, J., Showalter, D., & Klein, R. (2012). *Why rural matters 2011-12: The condition of rural education in the 50 states.* Arlington, VA: Rural School and Community Trust.

Johnson, J., Showalter, D., Klein, R., & Lester, C. (2014). *Why rural matters 2013-14: The condition of rural education in the 50 states.* Arlington, VA: Rural School and Community Trust.

Johnson, J., & Strange, M. (2005). *Why rural matters 2005: The realities of rural education growth.* Arlington, VA: Rural School and Community Trust.

Kim, J. S., & White, T. G. (2008). Scaffolding voluntary summer reading for children in grades 3 to 5: An experimental study. *Scientific Studies of Reading, 12*(1), 1–23.

Lindsay, J. (2013). Interventions that increase children's access to print material and improve their reading proficiencies. In R. Allington & A. McGill-Franzen (Eds.), *Summer reading: Closing the rich/poor achievement gap* (pp. 20–38). New York, NY: Teachers College Press.

Luftig, R. L. (2003). When a little means a lot: The effects of a short-term reading program on economically disadvantaged elementary schoolers. *Reading Research and Instruction, 42*, 1–13.

Malach, D. A., & Rutter, R. A. (2003). For nine months kids go to school, but in summer this school goes to kids. *The Reading Teacher, 57*, 5–10.

McCombs, B. L. (1989). Self-regulated learning and academic achievement: A phenomenological view. In B. J. Zimmerman & D. H. Schunk (Eds.), *Self-regulated learning and achievement: Theory, research, and practice* (pp. 51–82). New York, NY: Springer-Verlag.

Morrow, L. M. (1992). The impact of a literature-based program on literacy achievement, use of literature, and attitudes of children from minority backgrounds. *Reading Research Quarterly, 27*, 250–275.

National Assessment of Educational Progress (NAEP). (2015). *The nation's report card: 2015 mathmatics and reading assessments national results overview.* Retrieved from www.nationsreportcard.gov/reading_math_2015/#?grade=4

National Center for Education Evaluation and Regional Assistance (NCEE). (2014). *A focused look at rural schools receiving school improvement grants.* Washington, DC: National Center for Education Evaluation and Regional Assistance.

Neuman, S. B., Celano, D. C., Greco, A. N., & Shue, P. (2001). *Access for all: Closing the book gap for children in early education.* Newark, DE: International Reading Association.

Patall, E. A., Cooper, H., & Civey Robinson, J. (2008). The effects of choice on intrinsic motivation and related outcomes: A meta-analysis of research findings. *Psychological Bulletin, 134*(2), 270–300.

Snow, C. E., Burns, M. S., & Griffin, P. (Eds.). (1998). *Preventing reading difficulties in young children*. Washington, DC: National Academy Press.

Storch, S. A., & Whithurst, G. J. (2001). The role of family and home in the literacy development of children from low-income backgrounds. In P. Britto & J. Brooks-Gunn (Eds.), *The role of family literacy environments in promoting young children's emerging literacy skills* (pp. 39–52). San Francisco, CA: Jossey-Bass.

Torgesen, J. K. (1999). Assessment and instruction for phonemic awareness and word recognition skills. In H. W. Catts & A. G. Kamhi (Eds.), *Language and reading disabilities* (pp. 128–149). Needham Heights, MA: Allyn & Bacon.

Vernon-Feagans, L., Cox, M., & Conger, R. D. (Eds.). (2013). *The family life project: An epidemiological and developmental study of young children living in poor rural communities*. Malden, MA: Wiley-Blackwell.

Vernon-Feagans, L., Hammer, C. S., Miccio, A., & Manlove, E. (2001). Early language and literacy skills in low-income African American and Hispanic children. In S. B. Neuman & D. K. Dickinson (Eds.), *Handbook of early literacy research* (pp. 192–210). New York, NY: Guilford Press.

Waller, R., & Barrentine, S. J. (2015). Rural elementary teachers and place-based connections to text during reading instruction. *Journal of Research in Rural Education, 30*(7), 1–13.

Wang, J. H., & Guthrie, J. T. (2004). Modeling the effects of intrinsic motivation, extrinsic motivation, amount of reading, and past reading achievement on text comprehension between U.S. and Chinese students. *Reading Research Quarterly, 39*, 162–186.

White, W. (1906). Reviews before and after vacation. *American Education,* 185–188.

Whitehurst, G. J., & Lonigan, C. J. (1998). Child development and emergent literacy. *Child development, 69*(3), 848–872.

Wilkins, C., Gersten, R., Decker, L., Grunden, L., Brasiel, S., Brunnert, K., & Jayanthi, M. (2012). *Does a summer reading program based on Lexiles affect reading comprehension? Final Report (NCEE 2012-4006)*. Retrieved from http://ies.ed.gov/ncee/edlabs/regions/southwest/pdf/REL_20124006.pdf

An Introduction to Cost-Effectiveness and Cost-Benefit Analyses for Summer Learning Programs

Linda Goetze

Implementing a successful summer learning program involves planning, and successful planning involves a series of decisions to define the program and services that will be offered. The first step is to identify the goals the summer program will work to accomplish for students and families. Many programs focus on academic goals, including literacy and/or numeracy achievements for students. Other programs focus on social or other skills, health outcomes, or, for older students, work or vocational skills and experience. A second planning step is to decide which students (e.g., age or grade level, at-risk or all students, or specific geographic residency) will be the focus of the services. Another is to specify the budget and resources that will be available to deliver services. Effective planning requires data that describe, in as much detail as possible, the costs and outcomes for summer learning programs delivered and the characteristics of students and families served. These data then provide a foundation to compare costs and effects across similar summer learning programs—those that serve similar students and families and/or have similar intervention strategies and similar outcomes.

The two most commonly used methods for evaluating economic efficiency (defined, broadly, as the optimal allocation of resources) of education interventions are cost-effectiveness and cost-benefit analysis. These methods require evaluation of education costs as they relate to the following:

- The *effects* of education and related services on students measured in nonmonetary terms. Examples include the influence of summer learning on measures of academic outcomes such as reading or math scores.

- The *benefits* of education services measured in dollars. Examples include the cost savings from preventing grade retention or special education that result in reductions in future educational costs, increases in earnings due to increased education and graduation rates, and/or the broader economic value of improved long-term life outcomes such as reduced mortality and/or improved health outcomes from reduced obesity or smoking.

Economic evaluation is always a comparison of alternatives with respect to two goals: equity and efficiency.

- *Equity* is a matter of the *distribution* within society of the gains and losses from a program. Information on the distribution of gains and losses provides a basis for assessing the fairness of programs, policies, or interventions.
- *Efficiency* is a matter of society's *overall gains* from a program. For example, Program A is more efficient than Program B if Program A can make at least one person better off and no one worse off.

KEY DIFFERENCES BETWEEN COST-BENEFIT AND COST-EFFECTIVENESS ANALYSIS

Cost-benefit and cost-effectiveness analyses are two methods of comparing costs to program outcomes. Cost-benefit and cost-effectiveness analyses are often erroneously used as if they are synonymous when they are, in fact, very different measures of economic efficiency. The main difference between these two methodologies is in the treatment of outcomes. In a nutshell, program costs are measured in a similar way for both types of economic analysis, but the results of the treatment (i.e., intervention, program, or policy), described as either benefits or effects, are measured differently. These critical differences are highlighted below.

Cost-benefit analysis measures both the costs and the benefits in dollars. This type of analysis allows comparison of programs with similar or dissimilar outcomes. With cost-benefit analysis, it is possible to compare apples to oranges (inherently dissimilar outcomes) by valuating all outcomes in the common measure of dollars. It is also possible to compare apples to apples where outcomes are similar. For example, cost-benefit analysis may tell us that for every $1 invested in summer services, we are saving 50¢ in child-care costs and $1 in grade retention. This 50¢ net savings can be used to compare investments in either different or similar types of programs. Cost-benefit analysis is versatile because it translates the outcome variables into the common denominator of dollars.

Cost-effectiveness analysis measures only costs in dollars; effects are measured in some other nonmonetary way. For example, the measure may be the effect size difference on test scores in numeracy and literacy for students who attended summer programs or changes in obesity as measured by body mass index (BMI). Cost-effectiveness analysis typically is used to compare programs with *similar outcomes*. A summer learning program that focuses on reducing obesity would not be compared, using CEA, to a program focusing on academic outcomes because the measures of effectiveness could not be compared.

Steps Involved in Cost-Benefit Analysis

The steps in conducting a cost-benefit analysis based on experimental study are as follows:

1. Identify and estimate the amounts and itemized dollar values of all resources used in the program.
2. Sum the dollar values of all resources to obtain total program costs.
3. Determine whether there are significant differences in outcomes between the control and treatment groups.
4. Identify and estimate the dollar value of all outcomes to calculate benefits produced by the program.
5. Sum the dollar value of all benefits to obtain total program benefits.
6. Estimate the monetary value of the total resource and total benefits.
7. Adjust for inflation and calculate present value.
8. Aggregate present values in a way that meaningfully depicts the net economic value of the program to society as a whole.
9. Assess efficiency.
10. Examine the sensitivity of results of basic assumptions.
11. Consider whether any other limitations of the analysis might affect findings consider the qualitative residual.

Some of these steps are briefly discussed in the following sections.

IDENTIFYING AND DETERMINING A MONETARY VALUE FOR PROGRAM COSTS

Costs are defined as the dollar value of the resources used by a program. All component costs for a program must be identified to accurately calculate its entire costs. This is one of the most difficult and tedious parts of any economic evaluation.

The first step of cost analysis is to compile a complete description of services for each individual in the study. This will include education services provided by teachers, therapists, educational assistants, and administrators as well as any related services that might be influenced by the intervention that is under investigation. Services delivered to students in both comparison groups must be thoroughly described.

Typically, the major resources used in a program can be categorized as personnel, materials, equipment, and facilities. Some resources used by programs, such as volunteers, do not entail actual dollar expenditures but nevertheless represent costs because they could be used for valued alternatives. The dollar value of each resource must be estimated on *opportunity cost*, the value of a resource in its best alternative use. For example, volunteer time has a definite value, as volunteers could spend the time in paid work, in a productive activity at home, or volunteering elsewhere. Thus. the cost of a specific program or intervention is defined as the value of all the resources that it uses had they been assigned to their most valuable alternative use. In this sense, all costs represent the sacrifice of any opportunity that has been forgone. This notion of opportunity lost lies at the base of cost analysis in evaluation. By using resources in one way, we are giving up the ability to use them in another way, so a cost has been incurred (Levin, 1983).

This type of detailed accounting can be thought of as constructing an *ingredients model* wherein all ingredients that are required for any particular program or treatment are specified, and a value is place on each of them (Levin, 1983). The dollar values of all ingredients are then summed to establish the total cost of the treatment. This is a systematic and well-tested approach to determining the economic cost of any program.

It is also important to analyze the distribution of the cost burden. Costs may be borne by individuals, families, communities, or various levels of government. In measuring costs, it is first necessary to determine all contributors to program costs, and then it is useful to report the distribution of those costs among the contributors to understand who is contributing which proportion of the resources as measured in dollars. For example, costs may be borne by taxpayers or by individuals in their private capacities as students or family members.

Problems with Using Expenditure/Billing Data to Determine Education Costs

Since most education programs are funded by federal, state, and local governments, it may seem logical to simply use the expenditure or billing figures to determine program costs. The problem with this approach is that the amount billed may not accurately represent the costs or resources used to provide particular summer learning services. Many of the resources that are used in programs, such as volunteers or facilities, do not show up in school or district budgets or expenditures, but the use of these resources in the program does have identifiable cost. Further, the addition to cost from offering a summer learning program may differ from expenditures for other reasons.

For example, summer learning programs may rely on parent transportation. It may be determined that the addition to cost by adding a summer learning program doesn't include facilities or curriculum because the addition of a summer learning program doesn't add to those costs since those resources are fully funded for use during the 180-day school year. The key to success, therefore, is to use the ingredients model rather than simply relying on financial billing records.

The Need to Collect Data at All Administrative Levels for the Most Comprehensive Data on Service Costs

Many studies of education costs fail to incorporate all valued resources related to intervention services. For example, expenditure analysis is often based on state or district level data. A complete description of education services needs to include administrative and direct service costs at all levels—state, district, and school—to be complete. It is possible that the school is using economic resources, such as volunteers or support from private fund-raising, that don't show up in state or district budget data. Therefore, a complete cost study will collect cost and resource data at all administrative levels.

Estimating Uncertain Costs: The Use of Sensitivity Analysis

Sometimes it is necessary to estimate costs. However, there may be no reliable standard on which to base a cost estimate, or there may be a range of costs estimates for a particular ingredient. For example, the value of volunteer time may be estimated using the median wage rate for the nation, state, or locality or for women only. Alternatively, it may be more accurately estimated by each volunteer's wage rate (or potential wage rate if not in the labor force).

Each alternative has advantages depending on the situation. If the goal is to estimate national averages, the use of national prices avoids the effects of local idiosyncrasies. On the other hand, if the goal is to provide information on local variations in costs (e.g., a program might be expensive in one area of the country and not in another), a more detailed approach is required. Some regions of the country have much higher wage rates and real estate values. A technique known as *sensitivity analysis* can be used to evaluate the effect on results of using local vs. national prices or of a range of future prices when they are highly uncertain.

Sensitivity analysis is used "to estimate costs under different assumptions to see how the overall cost figures change and if such differences would change the rankings of alternatives" (Levin, 1983). As a relatively simple approach, worst case, best case, and most probable case cost scenarios can be created based on different types of assumptions. Each of the scenarios is then ranked with regard to cost-effectiveness. In some cases, the estimates will be highly robust with respect to the different cost scenarios, so that there is little reason to worry about variations in cost among localities or over time. Alternatively, if the ranking of projects changes in the different cost estimates, it may be necessary to choose different alternatives based on local differences or on the assumptions that seem most reasonable or likely at a particular time.

Incremental Costs: Comparing the Costs of Two Programs

Subtracting the cost of services provided to the control group from the cost of the treatment for the experimental group results in incremental cost. Incremental cost is necessary for proper evaluation and comparison to incremental benefits or effects. The additional (or reduced) cost of the control program in relation to the cost of the treatment program is the concern in this analysis. Total cost is sometimes inappropriately compared with incremental benefits. This may lead to conclusions that differ from those reached when making the proper comparison between incremental cost and incremental benefit.

IDENTIFYING, ESTIMATING, AND DETERMINING THE MONETARY VALUE OF PROGRAM BENEFITS

Benefits are the gains that accrue as a result of the program or intervention. In many instances, the major outcomes of a program can be valued in monetary terms, and adjustments can be made to take account of outcomes for which translation into monetary measures is problematic. As with costs, it is important to be as complete and accurate as possible in estimating the value of benefits. For example, a reduction in grade retention of students enrolled in a summer learning program as compared to grade retention rates for students not enrolled in a comparable summer learning program is one measure of the benefit of the program. If the monetary value assigned to the benefits (i.e., the savings) from the reduced grade retention exceeds the additional program costs of the comparison (i.e., a capitated system), there is a positive benefit. In other words, more was saved than spent. This means that the incremental costs of a summer learning program resulted in lower overall costs as measured by the reduced grade retention services. If the monetary benefit of summer learning program is less than the higher incremental costs of the summer learning program as reflected by grade retention, then there is a negative benefit of the program. That is, less was saved than was spent. This would mean that the more costly program was unsuccessful in lowering later education costs. Estimating additional savings from other education or life outcomes may add to benefits, pushing the benefits above the cost of the program over time. Generally, fewer or less expensive education or other services (such as health care in the case of a summer program that includes health goals for students or juvenile justice for one that could include goals related to reduced delinquency) for a student who received summer education services is calculated as a benefit.

As a rule, benefits of individual programs, interventions, or policies need to be calculated only in cases where the outcomes are statistically significantly positive in favor of the experimental group. For example, if two different programs result in the same level of later special education utilization for both the control and experimental groups, there is no reason to attach a dollar value to special education services since, in this case, the least expensive program would be selected as the most efficient. However, strictly speaking, it is possible for a program to produce a number of small effects that are not individually significant, but when their dollar values are summed, there is a significant difference in benefits. This is a matter of statistical power and possibility of diverse effects.

As with costs, it is also important to determine who receives the benefits. This is known as *distributional analysis*. Benefits may accrue to identifiable individuals, families, communities, government agencies, or to taxpayers or citizens generally. In measuring benefits, it is first necessary to determine all program benefits and then report the distribution of those benefits (measured in dollars) relative to the recipients.

Adjustments Made to Account for Changes in Dollar Value over Time

In conducting a longitudinal study, it is essential to account for the effect of time on the value of money. A dollar cost in 1990 is not completely offset by a dollar benefit in 2010. The costs of programs, and the benefits accrued later, may not be compared until adjustments are made for time. Two adjustments are required: inflation and discounting.

The Impact of Inflation on Monetary Values

To compare dollar figures from different years, such as the cost of a program in 2005 compared to benefits accrued in 2015, all dollars must be adjusted to have the same purchasing power. Simply adding up the nominal dollar values across years fails to account for the differing value of dollars in different years. Using a price index such as the Gross National Product deflator, the dollar figures from different years can be converted to a value at a specific point in time, thereby removing the effect of annual inflation. Not correcting for inflation can grossly exaggerate the value of a program when benefits are obtained long after the costs are incurred.

The Impact of Discounting on Monetary Values: Net Present Value

Discounting is necessary because even after dollar figures from different years have been adjusted for the effects of inflation, they are still not equivalent in value. Typically a dollar today is better than a dollar next year because of the opportunity cost of lost investment over time. Today's dollar can be spent or invested now, and the investment may appreciate from interest earned or other appreciation. The annual opportunity cost is the rate at which people willingly trade a dollar today for a dollar next year. This is called the *discount rate* (Barnett, 1986). Discounting converts all dollars to their "present value," which is typically their value in dollars when the project began. The calculation of net present value is central to cost-benefit analysis. If the net present value of a program is negative, then the program would not be a good investment over time if net present value is used as the investment criterion.

To illustrate the calculation of net present value, a hypothetical example is provided in Table 15.1. In this example, the discount rate is a real rate of 5%. By *real*, we mean that the figures have already been adjusted for inflation. The top part of the table shows the undiscounted, but the inflation-adjusted figures. The lower part of the table shows the discounted figures.

Table 15.1. A Comparison of Net Present Value Using Discounted and Undiscounted Values (real discount rate 5%)

Real Dollar Value	Year	Costs ($)	Benefits ($)
	1	$4,500	$0
	2		500
Undiscounted Value	3		500
	4		1,000
	5		3,000
Total		$4,500	$5,000
	1	$4,500 + 1.05=	$0
	2	$4,286	500/(1.05)=$476
Discounted Value	3		500/(1.05)=$476
	4		1000/(1.05)=864
	5		3000/(1.05)=2,468
Total		$4,286	$4,264
Net Present Value = $4,264−$4,286 = −$22			

The *undiscounted* figures in this table imply that the benefits of the program exceed the costs after 5 years. However, when the figures are *discounted* at a real rate of 5%, the net present value is negative, and this hypothetical program would not be a good investment at the end of 5 years using net present value as the investment criterion. Thus, the importance of adjustments for inflation and discounting are clearly illustrated by the example.

The Influence of Qualitative Residuals

Methods used to measure, quantify, and value costs and benefits is almost always incomplete. Thus, it is necessary to describe costs and benefits that have been excluded from the quantitative analysis so that decision makers can consider their potential effects on the analysis. For example, summer learning programs delivered provide a broad array of services and may improve long-term outcomes in ways that are difficult to value monetarily. While positive outcomes for students, such as better quality of life, may not be measurable as dollar benefits, they are important positive results of the intervention that should not be overlooked. A thorough description of what is included and excluded in the analysis is critical. Omitting this step can bias an economic evaluation and potentially weaken its credibility because evaluators may argue that important outcomes have been excluded from the analysis.

COST-EFFECTIVENESS ANALYSIS

The methodology for determining costs in a cost-effectiveness analysis is the same as for cost-benefit analysis, and many of the steps necessary for a cost-benefit analysis, such as discounting, examining equity, and conducting sensitivity analysis, are also part of cost-effectiveness analyses. However, the effects of the program, policy, or intervention are not converted into dollar values. Cost-effectiveness analysis is appropriate, for example, when a program is trying to decide whether adding summer services in kindergarten will improve early literacy skills. A comparison of different summer literacy interventions can be designed, and costs and effects compared to assist in making a decision. In this case, the same outcome measures, such as measures of literacy including reading comprehension and expressive and receptive vocabulary, are measured for each of the competing interventions that may vary in intensity (4 versus 6 weeks), setting (home versus school based), or person delivering the services (certified teachers versus college student volunteers).

Cost-effectiveness analysis is used *primarily* to determine which of several programs with similar outcomes is most worth the costs (as opposed to cost-benefit, which can be used to determine either which of several programs with similar outcomes is most worth the costs or which of several programs with different outcomes is most worth the costs). This type of analysis is appropriate "as long as the type of problem is that of attempting to choose from among competing alternatives for accomplishing a similar goal" (Levin, 1983).

However, it is not always the case that the program with the highest ratio of effects to costs should be chosen for implementation. For example, suppose $2 million is appropriated for summer services. A cost-effectiveness evaluation of two school districts with $1 million budgets finds that District A is the most cost-effective option. It is not known whether it will be the most cost-effective option when the services in District A are expanded to include additional students. Doubling the appropriations for summer educational services does not guarantee that the positive outcomes from those programs also will double. The choice of which project to implement should take into account the cost, benefits, and effects given the planned program expenditure and size of the program and target population served. It is possible that none of the alternative programs is worth implementing or that the theoretical "best" of all the alternatives (arguably the program with the highest ratio of effects to costs) may not be the best on efficiency grounds. Moreover, if one option is to adopt none of the alternatives, then cost-effectiveness analysis does not eliminate the need to value program effects. Rather, it shifts the responsibility for valuing the economic value of effects from the evaluator to the decisionmaker.

AN ILLUSTRATION OF COST-EFFECTIVENESS DATA OF THE K-3 PLUS PROGRAM

Consider a real-life cost-effectiveness comparison of students in two school districts that participated in a New Mexico school-based summer learning program. K-3 Plus extends the school year by 25 days for New Mexico students in high-poverty schools in kindergarten to 3rd grade. Data from a randomized control trial of kindergarten students enrolled in K-3 Plus is used to illustrate the data obtained in a rigorous randomized control trial of a state-legislated school-based summer learning program. The comparison students received no school-based summer program.

Students also received district-provided transportation and food services, and many engaged in additional art, music, and physical education opportunities during the school day. The cost estimates for K-3 Plus services

Table 15.2. State K-3 Plus Average Cost per Student

Average Cost Per Student for	District A 2,682 Students		District B 323 Students		Average Cost A & B
Direct Service Personnel	$875	72%	$613	53%	$847
Administrative Personnel	$86	7%	$74	6%	$85
Transportation	$23	2%	$135	11%	$35
Materials & Supplies	$11	1%	$75	6%	$18
Food	$78	6%	$107	9%	$81
Operations & Maintenance	$66	5%	$121	10%	$72
Facilities	$77	6%	$58	5%	$75
Total	$1216	100%	$1183	100%	$1.213

are shown in Table 15.2 for Districts A and B with the average cost of K-3 Plus across both districts estimated in the final column. Families of control group students reported that their students received little or no academic services during the summer. Many received formal and informal child-care services. Thus, the cost of summer academic services for the control group is assumed to be zero in contrast to an average K-3 Plus summer services cost of $1,213 per student. These costs were estimated after district staff completed a detailed survey that described the resources used across the categories shown in Table 15.2.

The focus of the outcome evaluation was on reading, math, and writing. Students in both groups were assessed on these outcomes prior to and after the 25-day summer learning program was delivered using the Woodcock Johnson test; an analysis of these outcomes is shown in Table 15.3. The baseline data showed that the groups were equivalent on these outcomes prior to the delivery of the summer services. The beginning of kindergarten assessment showed significant effect size differences, in favor of the summer learning intervention group, in basic writing, reading, and math, as shown in Table 15.3 (Goetze, Cann, Tran, & Vargis, 2013).

Table 15.3. K-3 Plus Effect Sizes: Kindergarten

Woodcock Johnson Domain	Effect Size
Basic Writing	.365
Broad Reading	.352
Broad Math	.219

The question becomes whether this marginal improvement in test scores is worth the marginal cost of $1,213 per student. The decision concerning the efficiency and equity of a program requires value judgments by the stakeholders because no dollar values are attached to the effects. Stakeholders may decide to defer that determination until after all 4 years of the K-3 Plus summer intervention have been delivered and analyzed.

Table 15.4 shows how the costs and effects data can be combined and analyzed—across all subjects or considering the data available for each of the outcome areas. This table shows the amount of time, out of the 6-hour school day, spent on each subject that is the focus of the outcome analysis. The third column shows the effect size difference, and the fifth column shows the cost-effectiveness ratio for each subject taking into account the portion of total cost spent on each subject estimated from the time spent on each subject and the total cost of the 25-day program. This cost-effectiveness ratio, $932 for reading, assumes that some cost is spent on nonacademic activities such as recess, lunch, and art and doesn't attribute those costs to the reading effect achieved. The final column assumes all costs were spent to achieve the three academic outcomes and allocates 100% of the cost of the program to the three subjects that were the focus of the outcome analysis. This increases the cost to achieve those outcomes. Since one of the stated goals, in the K-3 Plus New Mexico state legislation, is to achieve improvements in social skills, the cost-effectiveness ratios in column five may be the most relevant for policymakers in the state to consider.

Table 15.4. Cost-Effectiveness Analysis of New Mexico K-3 Plus Program

1	2	3	4	5	6	7
Subject	Time Spent	Effect Size	Cost: Time on Subject Only	Cost-Effectiveness Ratio: Cost of Time on Subject Only	Cost: All Costs Distributed Over 3 Subjects	Cost-Effectiveness Ratio: All Costs Allocated to Reading, Writing, and Math
Reading	1 hour, 23 min	.352	$328	$932	$542	$1540
Writing	32 min	.365	$182	$498	$294	$805
Math	1 hour, 5 min	.219	$230	$1,052	$376	$1,717
Total	3 hour, 39 min		$740		$1212	

AN ILLUSTRATION OF COST-BENEFIT ANALYSIS
OF THE K-3 PLUS PROGRAM

A final determination about the program's ability to reduce the achievement gap for high-poverty students may not be made until the dollar benefits of the K-3 Plus program can be achieved and estimated. Some initial benefit estimates include the value of child-care costs that were saved through the delivery of 25 full days of school-based summer services to students in the intervention group. At the time of the outcome analysis described in the previous section the five-star child-care value of K-3 Plus was estimated at $421 for the 5 weeks of K-3 Plus services per family. So if we assume this benefit for all intervention families, then $421 of the $1,213 cost of the program is immediately offset. Some of this benefit accrues to taxpayers because most K-3 Plus families were eligible for child-care subsidies.

While the long-term benefits have not been estimated for the randomized control sample of students enrolled in K-3 Plus, 2009 data from the statewide New Mexico Public Education Department (NMPED) database for 3rd-grade academic outcomes provides some useful information. One potential source of benefit for the early childhood summer learning programs is through the reduction of later grade retention. New Mexico is one of several states where 3rd-grade retention legislation for those that don't achieve reading proficiency has been introduced although it has not passed. One year of grade retention in New Mexico was estimated to cost $6,858 per student in 2009. Based on analysis of 3rd-grade state performance data in 2009–2010, 11,769 total students, including 1,640 who had K-3 Plus at least one year immediately prior to 3rd grade and 10,129 who did not, K-3 Plus students gained 7.5 points in reading, 43.8 points in writing, and 12.4 points in math (Goetze & Cann, 2013). Based on these data, it was estimated that 234 students in every 1,000 students who participated in K-3 Plus achieved reading proficiency but would not have done so without the program.

Table 15.5 illustrates one cost-benefit estimate that was done for the K-3 Plus program based on the analysis of the statewide 3rd-grade assessment data. Cost data for 2009 is not available, but we know program costs were estimated at $1,213 per student in 2012. Adjusting for inflation, this would be valued at $1,133 in 2009. Therefore, the cost of serving 1,000 students in K-3 Plus in 2009 was approximately $1,133,000. In addition, the child-care benefits discussed earlier that significantly reduced the net cost of the K-3 Plus program, estimated as $421 per student in 2012 dollars, would be $393 in 2009 adjusted for inflation. If we assume that 50% of these 1,000 students would have been enrolled in child care without the K-3 Plus program, then the total benefit for child care was $196,500. The average cost of 3rd grade in New Mexico was estimated at $6,858 per student. Based on these numbers, grade retention for these 234 students would have

Table 15.5. Cost-Benefit Analysis of K-3 Plus, 2009 Dollars

Variable	Cost and Benefit per Student	1,000 Students Served by K-3 Plus and 234 Achieved 3rd-Grade Reading Proficiency
K-3 Plus Cost	$1,133	$1,133,000
Child-care Benefits (assume 50% of K-3 Plus students would have received paid child care)	$393	$196,500
Grade Retention	$6,858	$1,604,772
Remediation (assume half the district estimate)	$1,028	$240,552
Mandatory Summer School	$522	$122,148
Total Benefits		$2,163,972
Total: Net Benefit		$1,030,972
Benefit Cost Ratio		$1.91

cost $1,604,722. Mandatory summer school was estimated to cost $522 per student in New Mexico in 2009, or $122,148 for 234 students (not including materials or transportation). Remediation services were estimated at approximately $2,057 per student in Albuquerque and $2,079 per student in Las Cruces in 2009. However, some legislative analysts questioned whether the districts inflated the cost of remediation. Sensitivity analysis allows us to make a more conservative assumption, perhaps 50% of this cost, or to exclude it from this analysis. If we assume that remediation cost $1,028 per student, then the total savings for 234 students would be $240,552 instead of $481,338. Based on these benefit estimates, it was cost-beneficial to provide K-3 Plus services to high-risk students in New Mexico in comparison to the alternatives of retaining students in grade and offering 3rd-grade summer school and remediation services. The net benefit was estimated at over $1,000,000 for the 1,000 students in this analysis. That translates into a benefit-cost ratio of about $1.91, which means that every $1 invested in K-3 Plus generated about 91 cents in benefits. This cost-benefit analysis is very simplified and is presented to illustrate the ingredients and assumptions that go into a cost-benefit analysis and to show the difference between cost-effectiveness and cost-benefit analyses. It is not presented to make a determination about the costs and benefits of the K-3 Plus program. A more complete analysis would factor in, for example, the cost of more than 1 year of service and the different benefits from attending in multiple years versus one or no summer service. It would also consider other benefits, such as special education services and the benefits attributable to improvement in other academic subjects such as math or improvements in social skills.

RELATIVE USEFULNESS OF COST-BENEFIT AND COST-EFFECTIVENESS ANALYSIS

In 2011, Americans spent an average of $11,841 per full-time equivalent student on elementary and secondary education services (NCES, 2015), yet stakeholders had very little information about what outcomes were positively influenced by these expenditures. Using evaluation methods, causal effects of education and related services can be difficult to evaluate without a prospective, randomized experimental design where one group of students receives one treatment and a different group another. This type of study requires careful design and analysis, adequate funding, and time, a combination that is not always available. As a result of the challenges involved in rigorously measuring and evaluating the efficacy of various treatments, much of what is currently considered effective service has not been scientifically tested. Furthermore, one intervention may affect academic outcomes, while another may affect quality of life. How can economic analysis accommodate such a wide variety of comparisons?

When many outcome variables are involved, such as effects of an education program on students, parents, teachers, and society, it has been argued that cost-benefit analysis may tend to be more useful to policymakers than cost-effectiveness analysis (Barnett, 1986). Since the outcome variables in a cost-benefit analysis are expressed in monetary terms, an evaluator can aggregate across outcomes and determine the intervention with the greatest financial benefit, which, realistically, is sometimes the bottom line in education programs.

Conversely, cost-effectiveness has some advantages over cost-benefit analysis that may recommend it for program evaluation. For example, the measures used to determine effectiveness can be the same measure that evaluators would normally use, such as student test scores. Only the actual cost of those programs must be added to an otherwise standard program evaluation to derive a measure of economic efficiency. In addition, cost-effectiveness evaluation may take less time and cost to complete, providing that the measures of effectiveness can easily be gathered during or at the end of a program. Cost-effectiveness analysis is particularly useful in early childhood education when dollar benefits may be limited because of the age of the students served. It has been argued that cost-effectiveness is a natural analysis for many program evaluations because it lends itself readily to the traditional evaluation approaches and to the types of outcomes that are often considered by decisionmakers (Levin, 1983).

As with any research methodology, economic evaluation has its limitations. Economic evaluation can only be as good as the underlying evaluation of program operation and outcomes. Most economic evaluations imperfectly account for program outcomes, and they tend to be better at quantifying costs than benefits. Sometimes, uncertainty regarding economic assumptions significantly limits the evaluation's precision. Future benefits are difficult to estimate accurately (Barnett, 1986). Evaluators are challenged to determine how far into the future the benefits of an intervention program are likely to continue to influence the subjects of a study.

The generalizability of a particular study to broader populations may be questionable. Local cost figures measured against local benefit figures may or may not be applicable to the broader national population depending on whether the relative expenditures on intervention costs and benefits are consistent across the country. The underlying estimates of program effectiveness may have significant weaknesses such as poor reliability and/or validity of the measures of outcome that are used. Failure to consider discounting, inflation, and opportunity costs, or to conduct appropriate sensitivity analyses will serious affect the accuracy of the evaluation. Despite these limitations, many education policymakers believe that economic evaluation can provide a key piece of the puzzle to improve public policy decisions.

CONCLUSION

As with other types of program evaluation, economic analysis has its strengths and limitations. It translates resources sacrificed to implement a program into dollar values. Cost-benefit analysis converts resources that are used for an intervention, as well as resources that are saved because of an intervention, into the common denominator of dollars. Since all of us have some understanding of what it means to exchange dollars for goods, this conversion into dollars in universally understood and therefore facilitates interpretation of program benefits and costs. "Cost-benefit analysis is a framework for organizing thoughts, or considerations: nothing more, and nothing less" (Gramlich, 1990).

However, not all costs and benefits are readily convertible to dollar amounts, thus forcing assumptions to be made.

> For any real world choice, there will always be some considerations that cannot easily be enumerated or valued, and where the analysis becomes quite conjectural. The sensible way to deal with uncertainty about some aspects of a benefit or cost is to quantify what can be quantified, to array and rank no-quantifiable factor, and to proceed as far as possible. (Gramlich, 1990)

Much may be omitted in economic analysis, and necessary assumptions may force a simplification of many issues. Nevertheless, many economic analyses succeed in their goal of reducing the uncertainties faced by decisionmakers.

Economic analysis does not claim to be a panacea, nor does it purport to be the only way to make difficult choices. It is simply one more tool that may contribute to wise decisionmaking when difficult questions are posed, and tough choices have to be made.

REFERENCES

Barnett, W. S. (1986). Methodological issues in economic evaluation of early intervention programs. *Early Childhood Research Quarterly, 1*, 249–268.

Goetze, L., & Cann, D. (2013, February). *Cost, effects and benefits: New Mexico's StartSmart K-3 Plus validation study.* Presentation to the Cost-Benefit Association Meeting, Washington, DC.

Goetze, L., Cann, D., Tran, H., & Vargas, Y. (2013, April). *StartSmart K-3 Plus: Making summer count by increasing kindergarten readiness.* Paper presented at the American Educational Research Association Meeting.

Gramlich, E. M. (1990). *A guide to benefit-cost analysis* (2nd ed.). Englewood Cliffs, NJ: Prentice Hall.

Levin, H. M. (1983*). Cost effectiveness: A primer* (New Perspectives in Evaluation Series, 4). Thousand Oaks, CA: Sage.

CHAPTER 16

A Review and Analysis of Evaluations of Summer Programs

Marc L. Stein and Ean Fonseca

Every year across the United States, thousands of programs work to provide children with opportunities to have academically enriching and healthy summers. Despite the large number of programs in existence, relatively little is known about what makes programs effective. In part, this is due to a dearth of rigorous empirical evaluations of these programs that could provide insights on program effectiveness generally and effective program elements specifically. Given these points, the purpose of this chapter is three-fold. First, we discuss the unique aspects of summer learning programs that must be considered in rigorously evaluating them. Second, from a sample of summer program evaluations, we examine the current state of practice in evaluating summer programs and analyze how these evaluations address the unique aspects of summer learning programs. Finally, the chapter concludes with suggestions for improving evaluations for summer learning programs that could be used by both evaluators and program providers.

The lack of rigor in summer program evaluations has been commented on in the academic literature. In 2000 Harris Cooper and colleagues conducted the most general and extensive meta-analytic review of the literature on the effect of summer learning programs on summer learning loss. While most readers may be familiar with the findings of this meta-analysis, the methodological recommendations made in the concluding section of the manuscript may be less well known and are rarely discussed. These recommendations focus on clear ways to address the authors' concern that "the generally weak designs" of summer program evaluations were potentially "the single greatest threat to the conclusions we have drawn from the summer school database"

The Summer Slide: What We Know and Can Do About Summer Learning Loss, edited by Karl Alexander, Sarah Pitcock, and Matthew Boulay. Copyright © 2016 by Teachers College, Columbia University. All rights reserved. Prior to photocopying items for classroom use, please contact the Copyright Clearance Center, Customer Service, 222 Rosewood Dr., Danvers, MA 01923, USA, www.copyright.com.

(Cooper, Charlton, Valentine, Muhlenbruck, & Borman, 2000, p. 103). This concern stems from the fact that approximately two thirds of the effect sizes (n=81) that were examined in the main analyses came from single-group pretest/posttest designs that have limited ability to provide evidence of program effects. Only 11 of the 125 effect sizes included in the analyses were derived from studies that used random assignment, which is considered the "gold standard" in evaluating the impacts of social programs.

The number of summer program evaluations using random assignment rigorously has increased in the 15 years since the Cooper et al. meta-analysis. While these studies have improved our knowledge about what works in summer programs, they are still relatively few in number. Further, many of these evaluations have been conducted under the auspices of individual researchers or as a part of large-scale studies specifically designed to estimate the impact of summer programs on student academic achievement. They are not generally conducted by summer program providers or their evaluators.

To better understand the current state of reporting and evaluation practices, we conducted an extensive search for summer program evaluation reports outside of the academic literature. We began with a pool of summer programs that had applied to the National Summer Learning Association's (NSLA) annual Excellence in Summer Learning Awards programs in 2013 and 2014. We supplemented this pool through a broad-based Internet search that attempted to locate publically available evaluations of summer programs. This task proved to be much more difficult than we anticipated. While most summer programs provide evaluative statements about the effects of their programs on their websites or in promotional materials, the analyses that generated those statements are not publicly available or accessible. The most important result of this review was that we found a continued and widespread use of what appears to be the "generally weak designs" to evaluate summer programs that Cooper et al. commented on in 2000.

We believe that in order to accelerate the accretion of knowledge about what works in summer programs and to expand the evidence base "to provide providers a variety of research-proven and replicable summer programs from which to choose" (Borman, 2000, p. 125), the quality of summer program evaluations and the reporting of those evaluations must and can improve. To contribute to this process, this chapter aims to improve understanding about summer program characteristics related to commonly used evaluation approaches, to illustrate the relative merits and pitfalls of different evaluation approaches, and to provide guidance on improving rigor in evaluative practice.

The chapter begins with an overview of the particular aspects of summer programs that generally threaten the validity of current statements of program effectiveness but simultaneously create the potential for more rigorous evaluation. Next we compare and contrast the common yet relatively weak one-group, pretest/posttest design with relatively uncommon but much stronger randomized control trial (RCT) design. This is followed by a brief discussion of alternative designs that can be used to evaluate summer programs. The chapter concludes with a summary discussion and recommendations.

CHARACTERISTICS OF SUMMER PROGRAMS

All summer programs share several characteristics that make them potentially difficult to evaluate, but these same characteristics simultaneously open the door for opportunities to rigorously evaluate them. In this section we briefly discuss those characteristics that are most salient to evaluation.

Programs Are Voluntary

By their nature most summer programs are voluntary—that is, families and children choose whether they wish to participate. This programmatic characteristic can lead to what researchers commonly refer to as *selection bias*. Selection bias occurs when a characteristic of an individual or family is related to the likelihood than an individual will be in one program-related group or another (i.e., people participating in the program vs. people not participating in the program). Selection becomes problematic when the characteristic that leads to participation is also related to the outcome of interest—for instance, when those most likely to participate are also more likely to have stronger achievement. When selection bias is not accounted for through design or methods, analyses can lead to biased estimates of the program effects, estimates that are systematically too high or too low.

Condliffe (2014) provides a clear example of potential selection bias in summer program participation. She finds variation within low-income Baltimore families in both their knowledge about the importance of summer for their children's continued academic growth and their ability to support continued academic growth in the summer, either in the home or through enrolling their child in a formal summer program. This commonly unobserved characteristic of students' home environments and parenting approach could lead to better academic outcomes for those students during summer months regardless of their participation in a summer program. The academic outcomes for these students will likely differ significantly from students whose families did not have this characteristic. The problem of selection arises when this supportive aspect of families is also related to a higher likelihood of enrolling and participating in a summer program. The fact that students in the program tend to have the unobserved characteristic that is related to academic outcomes can make the program seem more effective than it actually is. Therefore, a program evaluation that does not observe or control for this family characteristic may erroneously conclude that a program had a positive effect on children when in truth the positive effect estimated is solely due to the selection of families into the program based on this unobserved characteristic.

Attrition

The voluntary nature of summer programs introduces another concern to evaluation referred to as *attrition*. Attrition occurs when children who enroll in a program decide to stop participating in the program before its end. Like the problem of selection bias, attrition likely functions through a mechanism whereby those who choose not to continue participation share a common, often unobserved, characteristic that is related to that decision and to their academic outcomes. To the extent that children who complete the summer program are systematically different (e.g., higher achieving, more support in family) from those who do not, a naïve analyses will be biased and lead to faulty conclusions about the effectiveness of the program.

Limited Seats

With the exception of extended-year programs for special education students, the supply of seats in summer programs is not mandated. Additionally, the supply of seats is generally believed to be insufficient when compared to the number of students who need or wish to enroll. For example, a survey of the summer learning landscape in Baltimore conducted by the Family League and the National Summer Learning Association (2015) identified a total of 229 programs with approximately 22,000 seats during the summer of 2013. These seats were distributed across a range of participant ages and grade levels (kindergarten through 12th grade) and program types or focuses ranging from district-provided academic programs and summer jobs programs for high school youth to recreational and enrichment programs provided by the city Recreation and Parks Department. To put these numbers in perspective, the number of available seats represented approximately 25% of the number of students enrolled in city schools and is considerably lower if one considers the number of all school-age children (5–19 years old) living within Baltimore City.[1]

When the demand for program seats outstrips the supply of seats, program operators must decide on a mechanism to apportion those seats. More often than not, programs enroll children on a first-come, first-served basis. While this is a pragmatic way to fill seats, it can have a significant impact on the evaluation design decisions and the strength of inferences that can be drawn from an evaluation. Specifically, first-come, first-served enrollment is a probable pathway for selection to occur as those students and families who apply early are likely to be different from those who apply late in observed and unobserved ways. Thus, as discussed earlier, naïve analyses are likely to produce biased estimates of program effects under those conditions.

The undersupply of seats, however, provides an opportunity for the use of random assignment as the mechanism for enrolling students into a program, which in turn can lead to much stronger inferences about program effects, as will be discussed in the next section. Random assignment allows for stronger inferences because, generally speaking, bias associated with selection is negated by design. When random assignment is used, no individual or family characteristics determine who does or does not receive a seat in the program. Thus selection is a random process and is not based on those characteristics of children and families discussed previously that could cause concern.

Comparison Groups

When we wish to determine the potential effects of a summer program on children's outcomes, we must pay careful attention to the comparisons that form the basis of any evaluative statements we may make. To illustrate this point, consider this example of a typical statement made by summer programs about their effectiveness: "90% of participants improved or maintained their reading proficiency levels over the course of the summer."

Crucial to judging this claim is understanding the unspoken "compared to what" comparison being made. On their face, statements of this type imply that had they not participated in the summer program, these students would have experienced summer learning loss. As the forgoing discussion highlights, selection and attrition processes may be driving the observed "effect" rather than any true effectiveness of the program in stemming summer learning loss. Said another way, individual and family characteristics could have led the same students to experience the very same gains or maintenance in reading achievement in the absence of the program.

This is precisely the threat to inferences about summer programs identified by Cooper et al. that we began the chapter with—weak evaluation designs that do not account for unobserved student characteristics and do not attempt to answer the "compared to what" question. Next we will illustrate the differences in strength of inference between an evaluation design that does not account for unobserved student characteristics, the one-group pretest/posttest design, and an evaluation design that does, the randomized control trial.

COMPARISON OF TWO DESIGNS

In our review of summer program materials, we found that one of the commonly used designs for estimating program effects is the one-group pretest/

posttest design. In these designs a pretest is given to program participants before or shortly after the summer program begins. Near or at the end of the program, a second test, the posttest, is administered to the same group of participants. The pretest score for each student is subtracted from the post-test score to calculate a "gain," and then the average gain for the group of participants in calculated. This calculated average is treated as the "effect" of the program. These designs are quite weak as they do not provide the ability to disentangle or see distinctly changes due to the program from all the other things that might cause change in achievement during the summer. We will illustrate this point through an example that is reflective of common one-group pretest/posttest practices used in the field.

Suppose that a 5-week summer program that focuses on supporting children's summer reading and provides a range of enrichment experiences and other activities during the day enrolls 100 3rd-grade children. In the 1st week of the program, the children take a test that measures their read-ing achievement; the group average on the pretest is 100. At the end of the program, the same reading test is administered as a posttest; the group average is 104. Therefore the mean difference between pretest and posttest for the group is 4 points (illustrated by the bold solid line in Figure 16.1). The program conducts a dependent sample t-test of the means and found that the 4-point difference was statistically significant and represented an effect size of 0.2.

What can the program sponsors say about their finding? What inference can they make about the effectiveness of their program to support children's reading during the summer? The short and pithy answer is: Almost nothing. While the program providers would like to say that the program is the rea-son behind the gain, the only truly valid statement that the program can say from this finding is, "Students who participated in the program on average gained 4 points in achievement over the course of the summer program, but we cannot say with certainty that the program caused this gain."

Figure 16.1. Typical Figure Illustrating Program "Effects" Estimated from One-Group Pretest/Posttest Designs

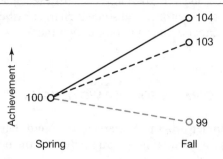

As we have noted already, these designs are unable to link gains to program effects because they do not provide the "compared to what would have happened without the program" contrast, which is necessary to be able to say that a program caused the observed gain in achievement. In fact the observed gain in achievement could be solely or primarily due to the natural growth of the students, illustrated by the bold dashed line in Figure 16.1. Comparing the bold solid and dashed lines, we can see that the hypothetical 4-point gain observed by the program is better understood to be composed of 1 point of gain potentially due to the program and 3 points of natural gain unrelated to the program.

Lacking a direct "what would have happened otherwise" comparison, providers are often compelled to supply the missing contrast from sources external to their evaluation. In many cases these contrasts come from the results of prior empirical studies such as the well-known summer learning loss estimates from the Cooper et al. meta-analysis (2000) or from the Beginning School Studies conducted in Baltimore (illustrated with the light grey dashed line in Figure 16.1). This is problematic as this naïve approach is likely to result in an inappropriate apples-to-oranges comparison. In order for the comparison to be appropriate, we must believe that the children of Baltimore in the 1980s and 1990s (in the case of a BSS-based comparison) and the summer learning losses they experienced are interchangeable for program participants *had they not participated in the program*. In the absence of evidence to support the appropriateness of this comparison, it is impossible for the end user of the evaluation to judge the validity of the claim being made.

One-Group Pretest/Posttest Simulation

On average, one-group pretest/posttest comparisons will yield varying degrees of mistaken inferences of program effects depending on the true program effect and on the distribution of unobserved characteristics in the sample of students in the summer program. To demonstrate and make this point more concrete, we created a model of the real world of summer learning loss by simulating a population of students where the relationships between student characteristics and summer learning loss is known. In our simple model, students have only two characteristics, one that is observed (racial group) and another that would normally not be observed by an evaluator or analyst but potentially influences summer learning growth and likelihood of enrolling in a summer program. Both of these characteristics affect the observed spring and fall achievement scores of the students in our simulated world but are otherwise unrelated to one another.

We designed our simulated world to contain 2,000 students. We started by assigning each student to one of two observed racial groups (Black or White) so that 60% of the students were White and 40% were Black.

We then generated a spring test score for each student, which was defined as a function of the student's race variable and some normally distributed random noise or error. Mirroring the relationship between test scores and race that has been demonstrated in previous research, we set Black students' spring achievement to be on average 1.5 points below White students.

We then generated our variable for the students' unobserved characteristics. We created this unobserved characteristic to represent some factor of a student's home environment that could cause students to perform better during the summer months than students whose families did not have this characteristic. We then generated a fall test score for each student as a function of their spring test score, their race variable, and their unobserved variable.

From this population we simulated a one-group pretest/posttest design and analysis while varying the true program effect (–2.5 points, 0 points, + 2.5 points) and the percentage of the participants who have the unobserved characteristic (0%, 50%, 100%). For each of the nine combinations of true program effect and participant composition, we conducted 1,000 simulations selecting 100 students from the population. For each simulation we captured the average pretest/posttest difference in achievement score.

Figure 16.2 summarizes the results of these simulations by presenting the distribution of estimates of the average pretest/posttest differences under the three participant composition scenarios. For the sake of presentation, Figure 16.2 shows the distributions of estimates for the scenario of no true program effect (0 points) as the results are similar for the other two program effect scenarios (negative and positive). Bar heights reflect the number of simulations that had estimated effects at the given value. Moving from across the panels, the reader should notice that the distribution of estimates

Figure 16.2. Distribution of Estimated "Effects" from One-Group Pretest/Posttest Simulations Across Varying Participant Composition

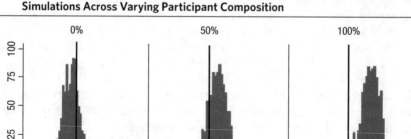

moves from averages of slightly negative values (mean = −.3) to averages of decidedly positive (mean = 1.3).

The figure illustrates that it is impossible to disentangle a program effect from the underlying natural growth of the participants. In fact, over many replications, the expectation for the mean pretest–posttest difference is simply the sum of the true program effect and the underlying average nonprogram-related growth of the participant group. In the real world, both of these values are unknown to the analyst, and any attempt to interpret the pretest-posttest difference as a program effect is invalid.

We turn now to the "gold standard" in treatment effect estimation, the randomized control trial (RCT). The randomized control trial holds this high status among treatment effect estimation techniques because it is, by design, capable of accounting for all unobserved characteristics of program participants. In a randomized control trial, participants are randomly assigned to one of two conditions: the treatment condition (summer program) or an untreated control condition (no summer program). The key here is that the only reason a child is assigned to the treatment condition is pure chance. By randomly assigning individuals to groups, we expect that, on average, the distribution of both observed and unobserved characteristics that are related to the outcome of interest will be equally represented in both groups. When these two groups are compared, therefore, the only expected difference between the two groups is the presence or absence of the treatment. A comparison of the group scores, therefore, will result in an unbiased estimate of the treatment effect.

Here it is important to clarify the meaning of "unbiasedness" in effect estimation. An unbiased estimate is one that on average will yield the correct value of the true program effect. This does not mean that an estimate from a given RCT will automatically be "correct." In fact we would generally expect that any given estimate would contain some error and would be different from the true effect. The magnitude and direction of the error would be unrelated to the observed and unobserved characteristics of the sample. When we average the estimates of a number of RCTs from random samples from the same population, the average treatment effect would therefore be equivalent to the true treatment effect.

To demonstrate this principle, we conducted another series of simulated trials using the same population of 2,000 students we generated earlier. As before, 1,000 simulations were run across each of three conditions, one in which the true treatment effect was set at –2.5, one in which it was set at 0, and one in which it was set at +2.5. For each simulation 200 students were randomly drawn from the population. Of these students 100 were randomly assigned to receive treatment and 100 to receive no treatment. The average fall score for each group was obtained and the difference between the two groups, the treatment effect estimate, was calculated and stored. Figure 16.3 presents the distribution of the treatment effect estimates for all 1,000 trials

Figure 16.3. Distribution of Estimated Effects from Randomized Control Trial Simulations Across Varying True Program Effect

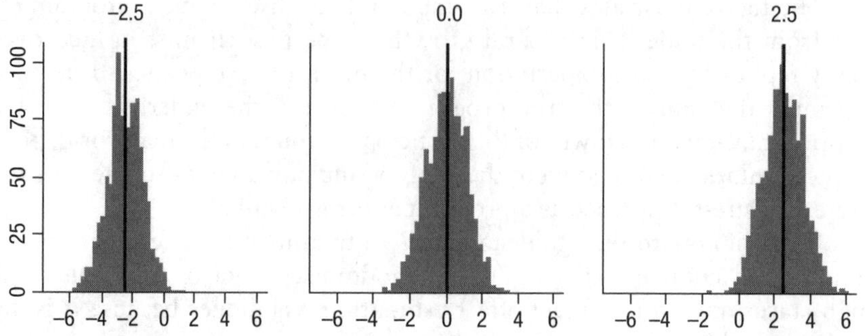

for each condition. The figure demonstrates that the estimates center on the true program effect specified regardless of the level of that effect.

Random assignment by design accounts for the unobserved characteristic compared to the one-group pretest/posttest design that leaves this uncontrolled for and thus suffers from bias and may lead to faulty inferences about program effectiveness.

ALTERNATIVE DESIGNS

Having demonstrated that simple one-group pre/post comparisons can yield biased estimates of summer program effects, we now hope to demonstrate the relative merits and limitations of another commonly used procedure for estimating program effects, ordinary least squares regression (OLS). While, on average, regression analyses of this type do a better job of accounting for "natural growth," they are still subject to bias from unobserved characteristics of students. The basic idea of OLS regression is that the scores of students who have received a treatment are compared to the scores of students who have not received the treatment, after accounting for other observable characteristics.

We demonstrate this using only one "trial" from our population of 2,000 students. We therefore needed to model the selection mechanism by which students would enroll in the program. Each student was assigned a probability of program enrollment that was a function of their spring score (an observed characteristic correlated with race), their unobserved characteristic, and some random noise. Adding the random noise allowed us to avoid the problem of having two students with the same spring score and the same unobserved characteristic have the same probability of enrollment.

After assigning each student a probability of enrollment, we then set a cut score. Students whose probability of enrollment was above the cut score were "enrolled into the program," and students whose probability of enrollment was below the cut score were not. We designed it so that students who enrolled in the program experienced an average treatment effect of 2.5 points.

We estimated a series of simple regression models attempting to extract the true program effect (see Table 16.1). With each iteration, progressively more students' characteristics are accounted for in the regression model. The reader will notice that with the inclusion of more characteristics that are related to the outcome of interest, the effect estimate begins to move closer to the true effect.

A simple regression of the fall score on a variable indicating whether the student enrolled in the program yields an estimated treatment effect of 7.8 (Table 16.1, Model 1). This value can be interpreted as the difference in the average scores of those who enrolled in the program and those who did not. As would be expected, this effect is substantially larger than the true treatment effect. This is because we have not accounted for the other student characteristics that are related to the outcome. To illustrate this, we ran a second regression in which we now account for a variable that would reasonably be expected to be related to a student's fall score, their spring test score. The effect of the treatment is now estimated to be 3.8 (Table 16.1, Model 2). This is closer to the true score but is still an overestimate of the treatment effect because we have not accounted for all student characteristics that are related to the outcome. One can see that if we now add another variable to the regression that is related to the outcome, student race, we still obtain a biased estimate because it does not account for the unobserved factor, which we know is related to the outcome. Because students who have the unobserved characteristic perform better over the summer and because these same students are also more likely to enroll in the program than other students, the estimate of the program effect will always be upwardly

Table 16.1. Simulated Estimates of Program Effects Using OLS Regression

	Model 1	Model 2	Model 3	Model 4	Model 5
Program Effect	7.8	3.8	3.8	2.6	2.5
Spring Score		0.8	0.8	0.8	0.8
Black			-0.9	-0.9	-1.3
Unobserved Characteristic				1.4	1.3
Noise term					1.0
Constant	198.2	41.0	41.6	39.8	40.0

biased (given our true model) when we do not account for the unobserved characteristic.

In order to obtain the true program effect, we would need to run a final regression in which we accounted for all of the unobserved characteristics that influences both the likelihood of enrolling in the program and outcomes (Table 16.1, Models 4 and 5). In a real-world context this would, of course, not be possible to do as we cannot account for student characteristics that we do not observe.

For the sake of simplicity we have chosen to illustrate OLS by comparing program participants with all other students in the simulated population who did not participate. While it is beyond the scope of this chapter to discuss to any depth, it should be noted that there are several methods for creating a comparison group of nonparticipants that could be employed to attempt to account for the bias induced by the unobserved characteristics. Principal among these methods is propensity score matching. At a minimum careful attention should be paid to the characteristics of program participants, and attempts should be made to find the most comparable group of nonparticipants to include in analyses.

CONCLUSION

Improvements in the reporting of summer program evaluations and the methods used to generate program effect estimates remain important tasks that need to be taken up more widely in the summer learning community. Better reporting

> would ensure that rather than informing only the immediate decision by a particular school district, the evaluation effort will inform other similar decisions that follow. Reciprocity would occur because all school districts would find an adequate database provided by others to help inform their next decision. (Cooper et al., 2000, p. 103)

Improved reporting is insufficient to increase our knowledge base unless it is combined with improved evaluation methods that can generate valid estimates of program effectiveness. Even a modest increase in the number of programs that implement these two recommendations could have a dramatic impact on our collective knowledge about what works in summer programs.

Better and more transparent evaluation of summer programs can and will benefit all stakeholders, not just researchers and program evaluators. For children and youth, better evaluation can lead to the creation and spread of proven effective whole programs and program components; for providers, better evaluation can lead to new ideas for improving existing programs and can be used to generate support for those programs; for policymakers, better evaluation can support summer learning policymaking and marshal more support for that work; for researchers, better evaluations can lead to a richer set of studies that can form the basis for the next generation of meta-analytic and research synthesis work.

NOTE

1. There were approximately 85,000 students enrolled in Baltimore City Public Schools in 2013. From the American Community Survey 5-year estimates 2009–2013, there were approximately 111,000 children and youth between the ages of 5 and 19 residing in Baltimore City.

REFERENCES

Borman, G. (2000). The effects of summer school: Questions answered, questions raised. *Monographs of the Society for Research in Child Development, 65*(1), 119–127.

Condliffe, B. (2014). Summer learning in the city: How schools, families, and neighborhoods influence urban elementary school students' opportunities and achievements. Unpublished doctoral dissertation, Baltimore, MD: Johns Hopkins University.

Cooper, H., Charlton, K., Valentine, J., Muhlenbruck, L., & Borman, G. (2000). Making the most of summer school: A meta-analytic and narrative review. *Monographs of the Society for Research in Child Development, 65*(1), i–127.

Family League of Baltimore & National Summer Learning Association. (2015). *Investments and opportunities in summer learning: A community assessment of Baltimore, Maryland.* Retrieved from http://familyleague.org/wp-content/uploads/2015/08/investments-and-opps-in-summer-learning.pdf

Facilitating Policymakers' Use of the Evidence on Summer Loss and Summer Programs

Emily Ackman, Thomas G. White, and James S. Kim

Though there is in hand compelling research evidence on the problem of summer loss and also on promising and relatively cost-effective programs that could help to ameliorate it, district, state, and federal policymakers rarely make effective use of this knowledge base. There are a number of possible explanations for inaction, some of which are obvious and some of which are more subtle and illustrative of the reasons why social science and educational research in general is underutilized. Drawing from the literature on evidence use, we offer some suggestions for facilitating policymakers' use of the evidence on summer loss and summer programs aimed at combatting it.

As this volume amply illustrates, the currently available evidence on summer learning and summer loss is compelling and well supported by theory. There is also a substantial body of research and evaluation data on the effectiveness and costs of programs that could boost summer learning and help to ameliorate summer loss. Further, there are signs of a dawning of awareness among policymakers, as the book's editors suggest in the Introduction. Still, the kind of impact on policy that many researchers dream of has yet to materialize.

This chapter has three goals. The first is to help readers arrive at a deeper understanding of how the current policy context evolved. Second, we want to explain why we (and the editors) believe there are grounds for optimism in the current policy context. Third and most important, we would like to offer some suggestions for facilitating policymakers' use of the evidence in the future.

Toward the first of the goals we present, in the next two sections, a historical analysis of research on summer learning and summer loss and its impact on policy and practice. We divide our analysis into two periods—what we call "The Age of Enlightenment," defined as the 38-year span of time between 1969 and 2007, and "The Instrumental Age," which began in 2007 and continues to the present. This sets the stage for the final section of the chapter where we will make our recommendations in hopes that they will help to accelerate the rate of progress, perhaps by encouraging more direct forms of evidence use than the ones that have characterized the past.

THE AGE OF ENLIGHTENMENT, 1969–2007

Beginning with Hayes and Grether in 1969, our "Age of Enlightenment" is characterized by higher-quality studies,[1] including the study of Atlanta schools by Barbara Heyns in 1978, the Baltimore-based Beginning School Study (BSS), and the ECLS-K studies based on a nationally representative sample. Chapter 2 describes the data, methods, and results of these studies, and they are cited throughout this book.

The articles and books that resulted from the Heyns, BSS, and ECLS-K studies generated considerable interest among academics, particularly sociologists, psychologists, and faculty in schools of education. To assess the level of interest in this research, we searched Google Advanced Scholar using the phrases "summer learning," "summer loss," "summer setback," and "summer slide." The search was restricted to publications containing at least one of the words "achievement," "school," or "students." Table 17.1 displays, in rank order by number of citations, the 10 most frequently cited articles or books, all of which were published between 1969 and 2007. Nine of the 10 publications were either based on the Atlanta, Baltimore, or ECLS-K studies or were meta-analyses or reviews that devoted considerable attention to one of these seminal studies.

Considering that the average article published in the *American Sociological Review (ASR)* receives just over 5 citations in a 5-year period (Jacobs, 2011), the publications in Table 17.1 appear to have had significant impact in academic circles, each with citation rates in the hundreds. An article on summer learning loss by Downey, von Hippel, & Broh (2004) is among the 50 most frequently cited articles in *ASR*, which is the top-ranked journal in sociology in terms of its ISI impact factor (Thomson Reuters, 2014).

We reference the number of citations to show the significant impact these studies have had on research and scholarship, but we are also exploring to what extent the research that is represented in Table 17.1 has influenced nonacademic audiences such as state and federal legislators, practicing educators, and the general public. In seeking to answer this question, we rely on: (a) interviews with Sarah Pitcock, Karl Alexander, and Harris Cooper; (b) a general Google search using the terms "summer learning in the news" and "summer loss in the news"; and (c) insights from the literature on evidence use.

Table 17.1. Most Frequently Cited Articles or Books on Summer Learning or Summer Loss

Rank	Author and Title	Number of Citations[1]
1.	Cooper et al. (1996), *Review of Educational Research*	680
2.	Heyns (1978), *Summer Learning and the Effects of Schooling*	679
3.	Entwisle & Alexander (1992), *American Sociological Review*	495
4.	Downey et al. (2004), *American Sociological Review*	472
5.	Alexander et al. (2001), *Educational Evaluation and Policy Analysis*	470
6.	Alexander et al. (2007), *American Sociological Review*	406
7.	Cooper et al. (2000), *Monographs of the Society for Research in Child Development*	356
8.	Kim (2004), *Journal of Education for Students Placed at Risk*	199
9.	Burkam et al. (2004), *Sociology of Education*	188
10.	Heyns (1987), *Child Development*	149

[1] Based on a search in Google Advanced Scholar, September 25, 2015

Part of our answer to the question of influence is that the researchers who conducted the studies in Table 17.1 either had no intention of influencing policy or, if they did, held no expectations that their work would have direct or immediate impact once published. Several of the authors did not discuss policy implications or make policy recommendations at the end of their work, where such recommendations are typically found. However, all of the articles by Karl Alexander and his colleagues, as well as both of the meta-analyses by Harris Cooper and his colleagues did make explicit recommendations for policy and, importantly, did call for programs that target low-income students specifically.

For instance, writing for *Educational Evaluation and Policy Analysis,* Alexander et al. (2001) suggested extending the school year through year-round schooling, high-quality summer programs, and home-school partnerships. Cooper et al. (2000) offered "guidelines for policy makers" that included continuing to fund summer programs, directing a significant proportion of summer school funding to mathematics and reading instruction, setting aside funds to encourage participation in summer programs, allowing for local control of program delivery, and requiring rigorous formative and summative evaluation of program outcomes. Additionally, Cooper et al. (2000) made suggestions for program implementers, such as "Running Start" summer programs that end just before the school year begins and are staffed with teachers who will teach the participating students in the upcoming year.

It is not our intention to lay blame on those who made no policy recommendations or promote the work of those who did. We understand that the research was driven in large part by broad scholarly questions or emerging methods arising from each scholar's discipline. For example: What is the role of schooling and home environments in social stratification? Or, summarizing the results of many studies, what are the overall effects of summer school, and what characteristics of students or programs are associated with more or less effective summer programs?

Further, we are keenly aware of the fact that academics have little incentive to simplify and "translate" their research into language and forms of publication that are more easily understood and accessible by a nonacademic audience and thus more likely to be used as evidence by policymakers (Firestone, 1989; Hird, 2005). This is one of many reasons why there is a gap between what policymakers want from research and what academics produce (Caplan, 1979; Davies, 2000; Postlethwaite, 1986; Weiss, 1982).

Policymakers need to receive research in a truncated time frame (Davies, 2000; Firestone, 1989; Schwartz & Kardos, 2009), presented in a way that is contextually relevant (Davies, 2000; Nelson, Leffler, & Hansen, 2009; Schwartz & Kardos, 2009) and jargon-free (Kirst, 2000; McCarthy, 1990; Postlethwaite, 1986), because they are balancing many issues and constituent concerns (Caplan, 1979; Lutz, 1988; Weiss, 1989). In contrast, academic research tends to be produced slowly (Davies, 2000; Firestone, 1989; Labaree, 2003) and without concrete solutions (Banfield, 1980; Davies, 2000; Weiss, 1977) because that is the type of research other scholars deem important (Firestone, 1989; Kirst, 2000; Postlethwaite, 1986; Rigby, 2005; Schwartz & Kardos, 2009).

Apart from the lack of impetus for academics to translate their research into usable forms, there is little incentive for academics who are seeking tenure to demonstrate the influence of their research on policy (Firestone, 1989; Hetrick & Van Horn, 1988). Academics are incentivized to write up their studies for publications that are read and, importantly, respected by other academics (Kruzel, 1994; Schwartz & Kardos, 2009). In short, the scholars whose work is highlighted in Table 17.1 (and others whose good work has had less time to be recognized) were unlikely to have had policy impact in mind as their primary aim.

When we interviewed Harris Cooper, he explained that in his view, "Policy research doesn't engender debate [among policymakers]"; instead "research waits to find a policy debate."[2] Thus, many times researchers find themselves "sitting on the riverbank" patiently waiting for the policymakers to come to them. Nowadays, Cooper finds his phone ringing frequently, most often in the spring as the school year is ending, because an education policymaker has discovered his research and has questions about summer programs.

Cooper, in referring to how scholars wait for policymakers to come to them, is describing what Carol Weiss (1979), a leading scholar on evidence use, calls a "problem-solving" model of policymakers' use of research evidence. In this model, policymakers are the sole players in defining a problem, and once the problem is identified, they seek research-based information in order to solve it. Next, the researcher provides information that is interpreted by the policymakers. Finally, the policymakers formulate logical policy choices and act upon them. In a sequence like this, research can have "direct and immediate applicability" and can be "used in decision-making" (Weiss, 1979, p. 428).

Weiss goes on to make an insightful, multidimensional, and plainly pessimistic assessment of the problem-solving model. She writes that:

> Even a cursory review of the fate of social science research . . . suggests that these kinds of expectations are wildly optimistic. . . . It probably takes an extraordinary concatenation of circumstances for research to influence policy decisions directly: a well-defined decision situation, a set of policy actors who have responsibility and jurisdiction for making the decision, an issue whose resolution depends at least to some extent on information, identification of the requisite informational need, research that provides the information in terms that match the circumstances within which choices will be made, research findings that are clear-cut, unambiguous, firmly supported, and powerful, that reach decisionmakers at the time they are wrestling with the issues, that are comprehensible and understood, and that do not run counter to strong political interests. Because chances are small that all these conditions will fall into line around any one issue, the problem-solving model of research use probably describes a relatively small number of cases. (1979, p. 428)

Cooper—and we suspect all of the readers of this chapter—are apt to resonate with Weiss's view of the limitations of the problem-solving model. So if that model of evidence use is, for the most part, unproductive, which model or models provide the still dreaming and forever sanguine researcher with more hope of influencing policy?

When we interviewed Karl Alexander, he suggested that while summer loss research currently "has legs," there seemed to be no single "pivotal moment" where the media started picking up on the research. He and others simply went about their business of writing for traditional academic journals, and "along the way [the research] started to filter through" to educators and the general public. Like Cooper, he has consistently been receiving inquiries from the media for over a decade.

The picture that Alexander paints is consistent with the ideas in Carol Weiss's classic 1977 article, *Research for Policy's Sake: The Enlightenment Function of Social Research*. In this article, Weiss argues that policymakers do not use research to make decisions in a logical fashion but instead "use research less to arrive at solutions than to orient themselves to problems" (p. 70). She further argues that, over time academic research is slowly diffused into popular thought, thus impacting the beliefs of constituents who eventually make their preferences known to policymakers. This is what she calls "the enlightenment function" of social science research.

Similarly and more recently, Nutley, Walter, and Davies identified a form of evidence use that they labeled "conceptual." Conceptual use is:

> a much more wide-ranging definition of research use, comprising the complex and often indirect ways in which research can have an impact on the knowledge, understanding, and attitudes of policy makers and practitioners. It happens where research changes ways of thinking, alerting policy makers and practitioners to an issue or playing a more general "consciousness-raising" role. (2007, p. 36)

The enlightenment model best captures what occurred in the period from 1969 to 2007, as published research on summer loss started to appear in nonresearch media. To better understand how, we conducted a Google search using the terms "summer learning in the news" and "summer loss in the news." For each of these terms, we followed the links to the first 25 items that were identified, eliminating overlap and erroneous "hits" (e.g., an article on a basketball team that lost a lot of games in the summer). Our aim was to show that diffusion into the public sphere has indeed occurred and to gauge the extent of the diffusion.[3]

One indication of the spread of ideas that may have originated with research is the diversity of media outlets in which the ideas appear. Among the 50 items in the search results, we found references to summer loss or summer learning in articles and videos that appeared in newspapers, websites, and televised media.

In reviewing the 50 news items, we were particularly interested in whether research evidence was being "used," at least in a general way. We coded two types of use, general and specific. The general use code was assigned if any of the following words appeared in the text: "research," "researchers," "experts," "evidence," "study," "studies," or "researched." The specific use code was assigned if (a) a specific study was cited or referred to; (b) there was a link to a specific study; (c) one of the authors listed in Table 17.1 was mentioned; (d) a summer learning/loss researcher was interviewed; or (e) an academic (e.g., faculty at a College of Education) was interviewed in a discussion of summer learning/loss that made reference to research findings. We combined "summer learning" and "summer loss" because the results were essentially the same.

There is no mention of research in about half (52%) of the cases examined, as shown in Table 17.2. In these cases, it is at least plausible that past research efforts and publications played an "enlightenment" (Weiss, 1977) or "conceptual" (Nutley et al., 2007) role. We also find that just under half (48%) of the identified information sources do include either a general reference or specific reference to research. In the general reference category, the sources contain phrases like "research shows," "studies have shown," or "all the research says." It is apparent that in these cases, the reporters or authors knew that some research had been done, and they were using that fact to stimulate interest in their topic or bolster their arguments for some form of intervention. Most of the specific uses involved one of the studies listed in Table 17.1 or an author of one or more of the Table 17.1 studies. Also, one of the national advocacy organizations, the National Summer Learning Association (NSLA), made specific use of the evidence by citing several of the studies in Table 17.1 in materials published on its website.

It seems likely that through the media outlets we identified (and likely others we did not identify) findings from summer learning/loss research have entered the consciousness of a growing number of people, including educators, reading experts, child advocates, a slew of local advocacy organizations, and members of the general public. Thus we conclude that academic research conducted between 1969 and 2007 served in an enlightenment function (Weiss, 1977). We further suggest that it was more successful than some people might think. It defined an important social problem, focused the public's attention on said problem, and left an imprimatur of scientific credibility.

Table 17.2. General and Specific Uses of Research on Summer Learning and Summer Loss as Revealed in Media Outlets

	N of Sources Identified	Percent
Specific use of research evidence (specific studies and/or researchers)	9	18
General use of research evidence	15	30
No mention of research	26	52
Total	50	100

Note: Based on a Google search, October 5, 2015. See detailed definitions of general use and specific use in the text.

THE INSTRUMENTAL AGE, 2007–PRESENT

A distinctively different policy context emerged in 2007. This next era, which we call the "Instrumental Age" is named for the increased instrumental use of evidence on summer learning and summer loss. The concept of using research in an "instrumental" fashion comes from Nutley, Walter, and Davies. They describe instrumental research use as "the direct impact of research on policy and practice decisions" (2007, p. 36). The Instrumental Age is marked by three important developments: (1) burgeoning summer loss advocacy organizations, (2) methodologically rigorous studies of summer interventions that took student poverty into account, and (3) attention paid to the problem of summer loss at the highest levels of the federal government.

The idea for summer loss advocacy stems from the methodologically rigorous summer loss research published in the 1990s. By then, Cooper's meta-analysis was instrumental in building a strong consensus among researchers that summer learning loss was very real and very problematic for students from low socioeconomic backgrounds. With that, researchers and others who were interested in ameliorating summer loss started to look for ways to solve this problem. In 1992, undergraduates and researchers at Johns Hopkins started a program in Baltimore to "prevent summer learning loss and promote academic achievement among early elementary school students" (Healthy Communities Network, n.d.). The driving force behind this program was college students who were trying to translate summer loss research into actionable policy. Karl Alexander describes the program that was created, Teach Baltimore, as being "instrumental in trying to take the insights of this research and put it to practical use by building summer programs to help poor kids."

Fortunately, in the Instrumental Age research on summer loss has progressed from just identifying the problem, as was done during the Age of Enlightenment, to testing interventions that offer potential solutions, by focusing research on students living in high poverty. Importantly, in many cases the interventions studied have been evaluated with rigorous research designs.[4] Some examples of studies that used a rigorous experimental design include Borman and Dowling's (2006) study of Teach Baltimore, the 2014 RAND study of voluntary summer programs in five urban districts (see McEachin, Augustine, & McCombs this volume), and studies of voluntary summer reading programs by Allington et al. (2010) and James Kim and colleagues (e.g., Kim & White, 2008; White, Kim, Kingston, & Foster, 2014).

In order to stay true to the underlying principles from summer loss research, Teach Baltimore targeted the program to low-income students and made sure that it was rigorously evaluated, all while continuously growing and improving on its mission. In November 2004, Teach Baltimore released a report of its rigorous longitudinal study of the impact of its Summer Academy program on the reading performance of students over a 3-year period. Results of the independent study showed that getting kids to attend voluntary programs was the first hurdle toward improving students' reading skills. With Teach Baltimore's research-based success at helping to slow summer learning loss, program administrators decided that they wanted to start sharing some of their good news and get into advocacy. Sarah Pitcock, CEO of the NSLA, said, "There was enough attention and interest they felt that there needed to be a center on this issue. And then a few years later, it became the Center for Summer Learning. . . . That really helped build political will." Teach Baltimore grew into the Center for Summer Learning at Johns Hopkins University (CSL). There, the team was able to continue the work of helping local students in Baltimore, but also start a national advocacy component, citing relevant summer loss research and translating findings to use in media coverage.

By 2008, the CSL had put out a comprehensive guide of media[5] (newspapers, TV, radio, Associated Press, podcasts, and blogs) with more than 50 individual stories about the negative impact of summer loss for low-income students and the importance of summer learning programs to combat the problem. Due to the success of its advocacy work, the CSL left Johns Hopkins in 2009 to become the National Summer Learning Association in 2009, with a sole focus on using research in lobbying, at both the state and federal level, for summer learning programs.

Individuals who translate research for a policymaking audience, as one needs to do for lobbying, are referred to in the research use literature as "research brokers." Brokers are primarily responsible for translating and synopsizing ideas uncovered through research into a format that is useful to policymakers. The concept of a research broker is attributed to James L. Sundquist in a chapter titled "Research Brokerage: the Weak Link" in 1978. In the policymaking realm, the research broker is an essential link in ensuring academic research is available to policymakers when they need to make policy decisions.

The primary task of the research broker is to acquire scholarly research (in this case, on summer loss) and present it in a user-friendly format to the "consumer," who is the policymaker. Sundquist delineates a clear vision of the place for research in the policymaking process: Information produced by scholars is gathered by academic intermediaries, then synthesized by research brokers, who in turn use it to inform policymakers. "The research broker . . . is responsible for serving as the conduit for the flow of social science information into the policymaking process" (Sundquist, 1978 p. 131).

Sundquist's vision of the research dissemination process is outlined in Figure 17.1. Applying his model to summer loss research, the "researchers" are scholars who published the methodologically rigorous studies

Figure 17.1. Sundquist's (1978) Model of the Research Dissemination Process

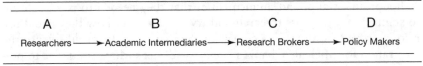

in Table 17.1. "Academic intermediaries" are Karl Alexander and Harris Cooper; academics who are willing to discuss summer loss research with nonacademic audiences. The "research broker" is the CLS-turned-NSLA. Finally, the "policymakers" are politicians and local education officials who learned about the problem of summer loss through the synthesized research that was brokered.

While the CLS and NSLA were garnering increased attention to the cause of summer learning loss, the Instrumental Age was being ushered in through legislation as well. In 2006, a synopsized version of the findings on summer learning loss made it into the hands of Barack Obama, then a U.S. Senator from Illinois. He found the research to be compelling enough that he proposed a bill in 2007 called the Summer Term Education Programs for Upward Performance Act of 2007, or the "Step Up Act of 2007." The Step Up Act proposed to spend $100 million to help remedy the problem of summer learning loss through a series of federal education grants. The bill referenced some of the most influential scholarship in the field of summer learning loss. Language from the bill states:

1. Analysis by Professor Karl Alexander and his colleagues demonstrates that summer learning differences during the elementary school years substantially account for achievement-related differences later in students' lives, including rates of secondary school completion.
2. This summer slide is costly for American education. Analysis by Professor Harris Cooper and his colleagues demonstrates that over 2 months of instruction is lost each school year due to re-teaching material from the previous year.

While the bill was introduced in Congress and made it out of committee, it was never passed (U.S. Government, 2007). Despite this, we argue that Senator Obama's introduction of the Step Up Act of 2007 ushered in the Instrumental Age of policymakers' research use on summer loss because it made clear that as a policymaker, he was using research on summer loss instrumentally in his policy decisions.

While it was not funded at the federal level, Senator Obama's instrumental use of findings from summer loss research in this bill, as well as his decision to champion the cause of summer loss (as is evidenced by an interview he did on *The Today Show* on September 27, 2010), was a signal to nonprofits, states, and municipalities that they needed to pay attention to summer learning loss research and try to figure out how they could use it to improve educational outcomes for their students. It was likely also the inspiration for Michelle Obama's "Let's Read! Let's Move" initiative to prevent reading loss over the summer and keep kids healthy (Bumpus, 2015).

The financial crisis of 2008 and election of Barack Obama as president cemented the Instrumental Age of policymakers using summer loss research instrumentally through the American Reinvestment and Recovery Act of 2009. Of the programs that came out of that bill, Race to the Top encouraged applicants to have robust summer learning programs, even offering a specific grant for summer programs in the third round of grant proposals, called RT3. The Investing in Innovations (i3) grants that were issued by the federal Office of Innovation and Improvement gave tens of millions of dollars to a series of research projects that studied summer learning loss as some or all of a strategy to help improve educational outcomes for low-income students. These studies were inspired by and produced academic research. Policymakers are paying attention to summer learning loss and are providing money to experts to try and find solutions. That is the Instrumental Age of summer loss research use.

WHAT ARE STEPS RESEARCHERS CAN TAKE TO ENSURE THEIR WORK HAS AN IMPACT ON POLICY?

Actionable ways that scholars can broker research for policymakers are:

- Consider all the aspects of a policymaker's decisionmaking process. For example:
  » Cost
  » Timing
  » Constituent concerns
- Build ongoing relationships with policymakers.
- Be an advocate *for* research and *through* research.
  » Craft research studies on topics that are relevant to policymakers in your area.
  » Write opinion pieces for local newspapers.
  » Be willing to be interviewed about your research.
  » Lobby a policymaker.

Policymakers are busy by profession. When crafting education policy they are balancing many issues, including constituent concerns and program costs (Lutz, 1988; Weiss, 1989).

One of the ways that the Center for Summer Learning (and later, the NSLA) was able to get policymakers to consider research in their policymaking decisions was advocacy or lobbying. This instrumental way of using research is off-putting to many scholars, but it is often necessary in order to engage and navigate with policymakers. When working in an advocacy or lobbying capacity, actionable items that can be quoted directly from research findings are key. This is even more effective if an easy-to-remember phrase is incorporated in discussions with policymakers. For example, summer loss advocates have coined the phrases "summer slide" and "summer setback." For scholars who want to get policymakers to consider research, the policymaker must easily understand the research. Often, published recommendations from academic findings will provide a framework to translate research generalizations into concrete examples policymakers can use.

Policymakers want to obtain answers in shorter turnaround times than those which scholars are typically accustomed to working under for purposes of publication (Firestone, 1989; Schwartz & Kardos, 2009). This is a difference that those who provide policymakers with research understand. "Policymakers need immediate answers and do not often have the time or the resources to disprove all the options available to them" (Lutz, 1988, p. 126).

The way that research brokers use timing has a strong impact on their relationship with policymakers, one that they actively cultivate. Brokers make a concerted effort to provide research in a timeframe and format that is useful to policymakers (Davies, 2000; Firestone, 1989; Postlewaite, 1986; Schwartz & Kardos, 2009). In doing so, they build relationships by fostering policymakers' trust (Ackman, 2013; Hetrick & Van Horn, 1988; McDonnell, 1988; Rigby, 2005).

One aspect of maintaining a trusted relationship with policymakers is their perception that the research provided is credible and coming from an expert who is either politically neutral (Lynn, 2001; Stone, 2002; Sundquist, 1978) or shares their values (Weiss, 1989). Policymakers "assume that academics, like everyone else, are pushing their own political values, but since they don't know what these are, they can't compensate for them" (Weiss, 1989, p. 420). This is why anyone who works to translate and broker research needs to build relationships and provide research in a bipartisan fashion. Doing so combats policymakers' natural suspicions, lending credibility to the work that research brokers provide.

Research brokers understand that their ongoing relationships and their credibility are their ticket to policy influence (Ackman, 2013; Kirst, 2000; Schwartz & Kardos, 2009). It is important to them that policymakers consider scholarly research when making decisions about education policy, even though it might not always be important to the policymakers themselves.

NOTES

1. The beginning of what we refer to as the "Age of Enlightenment" is marked by Hayes and Grether (1969) because it was the only study published prior to 1975 that examined the relationship between socioeconomic status and summer loss, according to Cooper, Nye, Charlton, Lindsay, and Greathouse, 1996.

2. This is referred to as "the policy window" in John Kingdon's 1983 book *Agendas, Alternatives, and Public Policies*.

3. We did not attempt to determine when diffusion occurred and note that the news items we identified all appeared in 2015.

4. Of course, there is always room for improvement (see Stein and Fonseca, Chapter 16).

5. http://www.thehatchergroup.com/doc/CSL_summer08coverage.pdf

REFERENCES

Ackman, E. R. (2013). Getting scholarship into policy: Lessons from university-based bipartisan scholarship brokers. Doctoral dissertation, Arizona State University.

Alexander, K. L., Entwisle, D. R., & Olson, L. S. (2001). Schools, achievement, and inequality: A seasonal perspective. *Educational Evaluation and Policy Analysis*, 23, 171–191.

Alexander, K. L., Entwisle, D. R., & Olson, L. S. (2007). Lasting consequences of the summer learning gap. *American Sociological Review*, 72, 167–180.

Allington, R. L., McGill-Franzen, A., Camilli, G., Williams, L., Graff, J., Zeig, J., & Nowak, R. (2010). Addressing summer reading setback among economically disadvantaged elementary students. *Reading Psychology*, 31(5), 411–427.

Banfield, E. C. (1980). Policy science as metaphysical madness. In R. A. Goldwin (Ed.), *Bureaucrats, policy analysts, statesmen: Who leads?* Washington, DC: American Enterprise Institute for Public Policy Research.

Borman, G. D., & Dowling, N. M. (2006). Longitudinal achievement effects of multiyear summer school: Evidence from the Teach Baltimore randomized field trial. *Educational Evaluation and Policy Analysis*, 28, 25–48.

Bumpus, K. (2015, January 23). *Let's read! Let's move! At the White House*. Retrieved from www.letsmove.gov/blog/2015/01/22/lets-read-lets-move-white-house

Burkam, D. T., Ready, D. D., Lee, V., & LoGerfo, L. F. (2004). Social-class differences in summer learning between kindergarten and first grade: Model specification and estimation. *Sociology of Education*, 77, 1–31.

Caplan, N. (1979). The two-communities theory and knowledge utilization. *American Behavioral Scientist*, 22(3), 459–470.

Cooper, H., Nye, B., Charlton, K., Lindsay, J., & Greathouse, S. (1996). The effects of summer vacation on achievement test scores: A narrative and meta-analytic review. *Review of Educational Research*, 66, 227–268.

Cooper, H., Charlton, K., Valentine, J. C., Muhlenbruck, L., & Borman, G. D. (2000). Making the most of summer school: A meta-analytic and narrative review. *Monographs of the Society for Research in Child Development*, 65(1), 1–127.

Davies, P. (2000). The relevance of systematic reviews to educational policy and practice. *Oxford Review of Education*, 26(3&4), 365–378.

Downey, D. B., von Hippel, P. T., & Broh, B. A. (2004). Are schools the great equalizer? Cognitive inequality during the summer months and the school year. *American Sociological Review, 69*, 613–635.

Entwisle, D. R., & Alexander, K. L. (1992). Summer setback: Race, poverty, school composition, and mathematics achievement in the first two years of school. *American Sociological Review, 57*(1), 72–84.

Firestone, W. A. (1989). Educational policy as an ecology of games. *Educational Researcher, 18*(7), 18–24.

Hayes, D. P., & Grether, J. (1969). *The school year and vacations: When do students learn?* Paper presented at the Eastern Sociological Association Convention, New York, NY (Eric Document ED 037 322).

Healthy Communities Network. (n.d.). *Teach Baltimore: An evidence based practice.* Retrieved from www.healthysanbernardinocounty.org/index.php?controller=index&module=PromisePractice&action=view&pid=134

Hetrick, B., & Van Horn, C. E. (1988). Educational research information: Meeting the needs of state policymakers. *Theory into Practice, 27*(2), 106–110.

Heyns, B. (1978). *Summer learning and the effects of schooling.* New York, NY: Academic Press.

Heyns, B. (1987). Schooling and cognitive development: Is there a season for learning? *Child Development, 58*(5), 1151–1160.

Hird, J. A. (2005). Policy analysis for what? The effectiveness of nonpartisan policy research organizations. *Policy Studies Journal, 33*(1), 83–105.

Jacobs, J. A. (2011). *Journal rankings in sociology: Using the H index with Google Scholar.* Population Studies Center, University of Pennsylvania, PSC Working Paper Series, PSC 11-05. Retrieved from http://repository.upenn.edu/psc_working_papers/29

Kim, J. S. (2004). Summer reading and the ethnic achievement gap. *Journal of Education for Students Placed at Risk, 9*, 169–188.

Kim, J. S., & White, T. G. (2008). Scaffolding voluntary summer reading for children in grades 3 to 5: An experimental study. *Scientific Studies of Reading, 12*, 1–23.

Kingdon, J. W. (1983). *Agendas, alternatives, and public policies* (Longman classics edition). London, England: Longman.

Kirst, M. W. (2000). Bridging education research and education policymaking. *Oxford Review of Education, 26*(3&4), 379–391.

Kruzel, J. (1994). More a chasm than a gap, but do scholars want to bridge it? *Mershon International Studies Review, 38*(1), 179–181.

Labaree, D. F. (2003). Peculiar problems of preparing educational researchers. *Educational Researcher, 32*(4), 13–22.

Lutz, F. W. (1988). Policy-oriented research: What constitutes good proof. *Theory into Practice, 27*(2), 126–131.

Lynn, L. E. (2001). The making and analysis of public policy: A perspective on the role of social science. In D. L. Featherman & M. Vinovskis (Eds.), *Social science and policy-making: A search for relevance in the twentieth century* (pp. ix, 228 p.). Ann Arbor: University of Michigan Press.

McCarthy, M. M. (1990). University-based policy centers: New actors in the education policy arena. *Educational Researcher, 19*(8), 25–29.

McDonnell, L. M. (1988). Can education research speak to state policy? *Theory into Practice, 27*(2), 91–97.

Nelson, S. R., Leffler, J. C., & Hansen, B. A. (2009). *Toward a research agenda for understanding and improving the use of research evidence.* Portland, OR: Northwest Regional Educational Laboratory.

Nutley, S. M., Walter, I., & Davies, H. T. O. (2007). *Using evidence: How research can inform public services.* Bristol, UK: Policy Press.

Postlethwaite, T. N. (1986). Policy-oriented research in education. *Oxford Review of Education, 12*(2), 135–151.

Rigby, E. (2005). Linking research and policy on Capitol Hill: Insights from research brokers. *Evidence & Policy, 1*(2), 195–213.

Schwartz, R. B., & Kardos, S. M. (2009). Research-based evidence and state policy. In J. D. Bransford, D. J. Stipek, N. J. Vye, L. M. Gomez, & D. Lam (Eds.), *The role of research in educational improvement* (pp. 47–66). Cambridge, MA: Harvard Education Press.

Stone, D. (2002). Using knowledge: the dilemmas of 'bridging research and policy.' *Journal of Comparative and International Education, 32*(3), 285–296.

Sundquist, J. L. (1978). Knowledge and policy: The uncertain connection. In L. E. Lynn (Ed.), *Assembly of behavioral and social sciences (U.S.). Study project on social research and development.* (pp. vii, 183 p.). Washington, DC: National Academy of Sciences.

Thomson Reuters. (2014). *2014 journal citation reports.* Retrieved from http://asr.sagepub.com/reports/most-cited

U.S. Government. (2007, January 4). *S. 116 (110th): STEP UP Act of 2007.* Retrieved from www.govtrack.us/congress/bills/110/s116

Weiss, C. H. (1977). Research for policy's sake: The enlightenment function of social research. *Policy Analysis, 3*(4), 67–81.

Weiss, C. H. (1979). The many meanings of research utilization. *Public Administration Review, 39*(5), 426–431.

Weiss, C. H. (1989). Congressional committees as users of analysis. *Journal of Policy Analysis and Management, 8*(3), 411–431.

White, T. G., Kim, J. S., Kingston, H. C., & Foster, L. (2014). Replicating the effects of a teacher-scaffolded voluntary summer reading program: The role of poverty. *Reading Research Quarterly, 49*, 5–30.

CHAPTER 18

Forging a Path Ahead

A Summer Learning Agenda for the 21st Century

Matthew Boulay, Karl Alexander, Sarah Pitcock, and Marc L. Stein

Almost 40 years have passed since the 1978 publication of Barbara Heyns's seminal book, *Summer Learning and the Effects of Schooling.* The logic underlying Heyns's novel approach is still persuasive today—by disentangling the summer months from the school year, researchers are potentially able to isolate the unique contributions of each season, school year versus the summer months. As the chapters in this volume instruct us, the problem of summer learning loss is well documented and has generated significant interest among researchers, policymakers, educators, and, not insignificantly, parents. While much progress has been made, the findings reported in these pages identify a number of lines of inquiry in need of further research. The contributions in this volume offer guidance for policy and practice as well. This chapter discusses priority "next steps," including the need to examine the extent of summer learning loss among particular subgroups of students who have been largely overlooked and the need to better understand the contextual factors that contribute to summer learning loss.

INVESTIGATING SUMMER LEARNING LOSS AMONG SUBGROUPS OF STUDENTS

The literature provides overwhelming evidence of summer learning loss, particularly among low-income students. Chapter 2, by Alexander and Condliffe, and Chapter 3, by Atteberry and McEachin, offer compelling overviews of this research across locales, grade levels, and demographic groups. That said, three subgroups of students have been largely overlooked.

Chapter 14, by Cheatham and Williams, discusses the unique experiences of one of these subgroups, the 10 million public school children living in rural America. As they conclude, the extent to which these students have been ignored by educational research, including studies that examine summer learning, is both surprising and disturbing. Given the extent of poverty in rural America, these children merit particular attention from researchers interested in summer learning loss and the achievement gap. Cheatham and Williams's observation regarding the implementation challenges facing rural summer programs is an important first step, but much work remains to be done in overcoming those challenges.

Students learning English as a second language also have been overlooked in the research literature to date, and this population is both growing rapidly and struggling to close the achievement gap. Given the possibility that their exposure to written and spoken English is limited when away from school, we might expect that English language learners are likely to experience extreme summer slide in verbal skills. However, there are virtually no seasonal studies that inform the question. As with rural students, there is some urgency around the need to take a closer look at the learning needs of these students.

A third gap in the literature on seasonality of learning concerns the summer experiences of children with intellectual, developmental, and behavioral disabilities. While evidence suggests that these children may learn at different rates and in different ways than their classmates without disabilities, little is known about how they and their parents navigate the months away from schooling. Nor, for that matter, do we know whether children with disabilities experience summer learning loss at rates greater than their classmates without disabilities. Further, while extended school year services can be provided during the summer as part of a child's individualized education program (IEP), to our knowledge summer learning research has not focused on these services and their potential impact on children's summer learning outcomes.

Prior research has largely centered on low-income children and has established that as a group they are more susceptible to summer learning loss. Such a focus is understandable as a first step, but as the field of summer learning research matures, it will need to take up the needs of other at-risk student populations. The three groups mentioned require particular attention, as their families—not all, but many—likely have limited resources during the summer months.

New Sources of Data

As researchers and policymakers continue to investigate the extent and effects of summer learning loss in specific locales and among particular subgroups of students, the emergence of "big data" may provide a unique opportunity. *Big data* is a popular term used to describe very large sets of data that are typically generated by users of digital services or web-based programs. Online, proprietary programs enroll millions of unique users through contracts with schools and school districts. Many of these contracts cover a 12-month period, meaning that student usage and growth rates can be tracked across periods of schooling and nonschooling.

A second source of new data on seasonal learning may be hiding in the field of neuroscience. Using newly developed brain mapping technologies, researchers working on diseases such as Alzheimer's have developed methods to trace brain activity, including the brain's ability to learn—and unlearn. These are the scans that light up in "reds and yellows" during memory and cognition tests. A persistent question for seasonal researchers is what it means when children appear to have "forgotten" material during the summer months. What type of knowledge is forgotten, and is the process of relearning faster or in any way different than the ways students initially learned the material?

Another crucial question might be, if children come back to school in September scoring less, how long does it take for them to recover what has been lost? In their 1996 meta-analysis, Cooper, Nye, Charlton, Lindsay, and Greathouse, for example, suggest that factual knowledge is more susceptible to summer loss than conceptual knowledge, and Chin and Phillips (2004) explore the possibility of a "carryover" effect in which pedagogical choices influence how much learning is retained or forgotten. It is possible that collaborations between social scientists and our friends in neuroscience may help answer some of these questions.

A third source of "new data" is actually not new at all. Thousands of programs, both school district and community based, operate every summer. The range and scale of summer programs represents an important opportunity to learn about what works and for whom in summer programs. However, given that relatively few of these programs are evaluated rigorously or are widely available publically, this opportunity is in large measure unrealized. Cooper, Charlton, Valentine, and Muhlenbruck (2000) made two recommendations, still relevant today, that if implemented would dramatically increase the knowledge base on summer learning loss and programs designed to stem those losses. First, improving the methodological rigor of evaluations will lead to stronger inferences about program effectiveness. Second, the improvement of reporting standards and availability of evaluation reports will lead to stronger and more informative research syntheses. This second recommendation, while improving research on summer learning loss, has greater potential to improve the summer program practices. As Cooper et al. powerfully state, and the contributions in this volume underscore,

> [improved reporting] would ensure that rather than informing only the immediate decision by a particular school district, the evaluation effort will inform other

similar decisions that follow. . . . All school districts would find an adequate database provided by others to help inform their next local decision. (p. 103)

As Stein and Fonseca argue in Chapter 16 on program evaluations, accumulating insights from the work of individual programs should be a goal of the field in the years to come, but that will require coming together around common standards and procedures for assessment.

Translating Research Evidence into Policy and Practice

Finally, continued effort is needed to translate research evidence into summaries and recommendations that can be easily understood by a general audience of parents, educators, and policymakers. Indeed, though the evidence surrounding summer learning loss is compelling, and though, as Ackman and her colleagues point out, practitioners and policymakers have begun to take notice, this work is far from done. For one, very few federal dollars are dedicated to summer programming. And as Borman and his colleagues point out in Chapter 6, there is considerable confusion at the state level around best practices for summer programs. Schools of education rarely include mention of summer learning in their curricula for aspiring teachers and school leaders, and while a few foundations have made significant investments around summer learning issues, most have yet to realize the connection between summer learning loss and the achievement gap. In short, while the field has come a long way in the last few decades, future research is more likely to be supported and funded if greater emphasis is placed on the dissemination of evidence to a broader audience that includes parents, educators, and policymakers at all levels of government. The National Summer Learning Association is leading that effort already, and one of our hopes for this volume is that it will encourage others to join us in this important mission.

EXPLANATORY FACTORS

Despite general agreement about the extent of social stratification during the summer months, previous research provides little clear evidence of the mechanisms that drive learning during the summer months and differences in summer learning across social lines (Alexander & Entwisle 1996; Phillips & Chin 2004; Burkam et al., 2004). Why is it that better-off students gain, or at least hold steady, during the summer months while poorer students experience significant loss? The logic underlying seasonal comparisons points to home and neighborhood influences as the key determinant of summer achievement, yet previous studies have largely ignored the question of whether class-based seasonal variation in parents' expectations and practices are related to the class-based gap in students' summer learning. This section suggests three lines of inquiry ripe for further research: the role of parents, the neighborhood context, and the role of teachers and other school personnel.

The Role of Home Influence and Parenting Logics

Researchers have advanced several models to describe the ways in which home and parenting influences may affect children's cognitive development. Some models focus primarily on the effects of parental involvement in their children's schooling (Epstein, 1992) or the ways in which parental attitudes and expectations shape children's learning (Yamamoto & Holloway, 2010). Others take an ecological approach, directing attention to the environmental context that influences parenting practices (Kotchick & Forehand, 2002; Luster & Okagaki, 2005), while still others focus on the ways in which class-based resources provide home advantages not uniformly available to all children and families (Reay & Lucey, 2003; Lareau, 2000; also Chapters 1 and 7 in this volume). These models, of course, are not mutually exclusive, and some have emphasized the simultaneity of home influences acting in concert with school and community influences (Bierman, 1996; Epstein & Sanders, 2000).

The logic underlying seasonal comparisons points to home and parental influences as the key determinant of summer achievement, yet class-based seasonal variation in parents' expectations and practices, and their relevance for class-based learning gaps, have yet to be plotted.

Another possible explanation for social stratification in summer learning centers on parents' beliefs and values. Phillips and Chin (2004) found that parental expectations were linked to their 1st-graders' summer math performance: Holding family background and children's academic skills constant, those children whose parents expected them to graduate from college or attend graduate school after college experienced the greatest summer gains in math computation and concepts. However, Borman, Benson, and Overman (2005) found that parental expectations—as measured by survey responses concerning the frequency with which parents spoke with their child about academic goals, their expectations for their child's grades, and the importance they place on getting a good education—did not explain much of the variation in summer achievement in their sample of 300 early elementary school students from high-poverty schools.

Two issues—one conceptual, the other methodological—limit our understanding of the nature of parental influences during the summer months. First, seasonal comparisons conceptualize home influence as a constant and continuous influence throughout the year, yet there is little empirical evidence to support this. While it is certain that home influence is *present* throughout the year, particularly in contrast to the temporal nature of the

9-month school year, it does not necessarily follow that home influence acts in a *constant or continuous* way throughout the year.

Downey and his colleagues (2008) caution that the assumption that "non-school influences on learning are similar during the school year and during summer vacation" is debatable for the "obvious reason that during the school year, children spend less time in their non-school environments" and thus we could expect that nonschool effects may be smaller during the school year than during the summer (p. 257). Chin and Phillips (2004) also raised the possibility of class-based seasonal variation in parenting practices by suggesting the possibility that

> families' child-rearing philosophies change seasonally, with middle-class families engaging in more concerted cultivation during the school year and less during the summer and working-class families engaging in less concerted cultivation during the school year (because they expect the school to play that role) and more in the summer. (p. 204)

We suggest that a distinction be made between the *presence* of home influences throughout the calendar year and the observation, yet to be made, that home influences exert a *constant* effect throughout the calendar year. By conceptualizing home influence as present yet not necessarily constant, we allow for the possibility of seasonal variation in parenting logics and influence. This distinction has implications for the methodology employed by seasonal comparisons, for our understanding of home influence and parents' role in their children's learning, and for explanations regarding how and why summer learning loss occurs.

A second constraint on our understanding of home and parental influences during the summer months centers on the way parental involvement data has been collected and measured. As has been pointed out, large data sets like ECLS-K and the National Longitudinal Survey of Youth 1979 do a better job reporting the *frequency* of parental activities than the *nature* of those activities (Burkam et al., 2004) because measurements of parental involvement are often blunt and dichotomous, thus blurring the "distinction between parents who regularly participate in school activities and those who do so infrequently" (Domina, 2005).

An ideal data set would provide information about the context and motivations for parental involvement activities, would include measures from not only parents but also students and teachers, and would include more nuanced forms of parental involvement, such as informal discussions between parent and child (Burkam et al., 2004; Domina, 2005). While qualitative studies have generated richer data sets that provide more detail and context about the nature of parental involvement activities (Lareau, 2003; Luster & Okagaki, 2005; Yamamoto & Holloway, 2010), none has employed a seasonal perspective to examine variation across periods of schooling and nonschooling.

Seasonal comparisons have tended to employ overly broad conceptualizations of home environment. For instance, using data on 1st graders from the nationally representative Prospects sample, Phillips and Chin (2004) investigated whether a range of parents' expectations, parenting practices, and children's activities were associated with summer gains. Specific measures included parents' expectations that their 1st graders would graduate high school and then attend a vocational school or a 2- or 4-year college; the degree to which parents were permissive or authoritarian in their rulemaking in the home; the frequency of family trips to the library and museums; and parents' actions to enroll their children in art and dance classes, organized sports activities, or summer school; the amount of time parents read to their children and children read to themselves or watched television; and finally, the presence in the home of books, newspapers, magazines, and computers.

Although such a broad conceptualization of the home environment can be useful when constructing lists of possible mechanisms that influence learning, when it is driven by the availability of data to be crunched, rather than a strong connection to analytical or theoretical reasoning, we risk missing potentially key elements of family life and family resources. Consider, for instance, Heyns's (1978) finding that students who reported owning a bike experienced less summer learning loss. It is difficult to know what, if anything, should be made of such a relationship. Is bike ownership a proxy for higher-class status? Is there any reason to believe that students who own bikes are more likely to read over the summer or engage in more formal or frequent learning activities?

Without providing the kind of context called for by Domina (2005) and Burkam, Ready, Lee, and LoGerfo (2004), an overly broad conceptualization of the home environment does little to advance our understanding of the mechanisms that produce the class-based differential in summer learning. Indeed, Chapters 1 and 7, by Downey and Pallas, respectively, as well as the discussion of shadow learning by Merry and his colleagues in Chapter 8, help narrow our conceptualization of the home environment by prodding us to think more deeply about the mechanisms through which social class exerts its influence during periods of schooling and nonschooling.

The Neighborhood Context

From a seasonal perspective, the anxieties produced by economic insecurity manifest themselves year-round but seem to take on increased importance during the summer months when parents are responsible for structuring all of their children's free time. As Pallas discusses in Chapter 7 on social class and summer learning, the seasonal perspective suggests that neighborhood influence may be greater during the summer months when children have more unstructured free time and, hence, engage more with the social and physical structures of the neighborhood. By providing a safe and nurturing environment on a daily basis, the presence of schooling mitigates, at least partially, the anxieties of economic insecurity. In other words, a "bad" neighborhood can feel worse when school is not in session because children's *exposure* to the neighborhood increases as they spend more time at home during the summer months. And crime tends to spike during the summer months, as does children's exposure to violence.

The Role of Teachers and Spillover

A third possible explanation for the linkage between summer learning loss and economic disadvantage centers on the notion of "spillover," or the interaction between teachers' school-year practices and summer learning. In Chapter 9, Condliffe highlights the role that teachers and principals play as information brokers. Previously, Phillips and Chin (2004) used nationally representative data from the Prospects study to explore whether teachers' education, experience, or teaching practices might influence children's achievement gains in the summer following 1st grade. Their results suggest that students assigned to new teachers (those with less than 3 years of teaching experience) for the school year experienced greater amounts of summer learning loss in mathematics than those with more experienced teachers and that students whose teachers assigned project work involving reading, writing, and research skills during the school year gained slightly more during the summer months.

However, Phillips and Chin's (2004) findings of a modest "spillover" effect in the Prospects data conflict with two other studies that relied on ECLS-K data: Georges (2003) found no relationship between kindergarten teachers' practices and summer learning, and Downey, von Hippel, and Hughes (2008) found that rates of summer learning between kindergarten and 1st grade were not affected by the assignment of summer book lists by kindergarten teachers or by schools sending home preparatory "packages" before the beginning of the 1st grade. As McEachin and his colleagues discuss in Chapter 12, James Kim's evaluations of voluntary and at-home literacy programs found promising or significant short-term effects but less evidence of longer-term effects.

A subsequent look at ECLS-K data in kindergarten mathematics achievement by Georges and Pallas (2010) yielded mixed results: Summer learning among low-SES students was positively associated with teaching practices that emphasized analytical and reasoning skills, but only modestly. Specifically, they found that teachers' use of manipulatives to read graphs, learn measurement, and estimate probabilities and quantities provided a modest advantage in summer learning compared to those students whose teachers relied more heavily on worksheets and collaborative instructional grouping. The authors suggest that teaching practices in kindergarten may be a weak treatment, given the limited amount of time and uneven quality of mathematics instruction in kindergarten. If they are correct and absent strong spillover, or carryover, then some portion of summer learning loss could reflect the fadeout effect of a weak school-year treatment.

The Seasonal Perspective Beyond Academics

The line of inquiry discussed in Chapters 10 and 11 are exciting in that they point to the promise of applying the seasonal perspective to issues beyond academics. While most seasonal comparisons investigate questions of cognitive development and academic achievement, one team of researchers led by Doug Downey and Paul von Hippel has extended the seasonal lens to examine patterns in children's health and weight gain (von Hippel, Powell, Downey, & Rowland, 2007) and to critique traditional methods for evaluating schools (Downey et al., 2008). Using ECLS-K data that reported the body mass index (BMI) of 5,380 kindergarten and 1st grade students in 310 schools nationwide, von Hippel and his colleagues used a seasonal research design to disentangle the effects of school and nonschool environments on weight gain in much the same way that prior research examined seasonal gains in cognitive achievement. They found that growth in BMI was faster and more variable during the summer months than during the school year and that the seasonal differences were especially large for three at-risk student groups: Black children, Hispanic children, and children who were already overweight at the beginning of kindergarten (von Hippel et al., 2007).

Downey et al. (2008) applied a seasonal perspective to the study of school evaluation methods. Using seasonal data from the ECLS-K study, they show that the traditional and most widely used method for evaluating schools— the achievement model that relies on annual tests to gauge students' levels of proficiency—fails to separate school from nonschool effects on children's learning, thereby "blaming" schools for the nonschool factors that also influence achievement (Downey et al., 2008). They suggest an alternative measure, the "impact" measure, which makes use of seasonal data to at least partially remove nonschool factors from school evaluation methods: by subtracting students' summer learning rate from their school-year learning rate, their impact measure, they contend, provides a more accurate estimate of how much a school contributes uniquely to its students' cognitive development.

CONCLUSION

As Ackmann and her colleagues demonstrate in Chapter 17, the recent history of the research on summer learning and its impact on policy and practice offer reasons for optimism. Now more than ever, a sizable and growing number of educators, policymakers, and, importantly, parents, are familiar with the problem of summer learning loss and engaged in the search for effective interventions. Now looking ahead, what additional advances might we anticipate over the next few decades?

If Ackmann and her colleagues are correct that we have entered the Instrumental Age—and their argument is persuasive—then we have reason to be optimistic that this important issue will attract even more attention. It is our hope that the contributions in this volume will help guide the committed community of parents, educators, researchers, and policymakers in their efforts to achieve a deeper understanding of the problem of summer learning loss and to work toward even more effective solutions. As this volume makes clear, much hangs in the balance, especially for our lost vulnerable children.

REFERENCES

Alexander, K. L., & Entwisle, D. R. (1996). Schools and children at risk. In A. Booth & J. F. Dunn (Eds.), *Family-school links: How do they affect educational outcomes?* (pp. 67–88). Mahwah, NJ: Erlbaum.

Bierman, K. L. (1996). Family-school links: An overview. In A. Booth & J. F. Dunn (Eds.), *Family-school links: How do they affect educational outcomes?* (pp. 275–287). Mahwah, NJ: Erlbaum.

Borman, G. D., Benson, J., & Overman, L. T. (2005). Families, schools, and summer learning. *The Elementary School Journal, 106,* 131–151.

Burkam, D. T., Ready, D. D., Lee, V. E., & LoGerfo, L. (2004). Social-class differences in summer learning between kindergarten and first grade: Model specification and estimation. *Sociology of Education, 77,* 1–31.

Cooper, H., Charlton, K., Valentine, J. C., & Muhlenbruck, L. (2000). Making the most of summer school: A meta-analytic and narrative review. *Monographs of the Society for Research in Child Development, 65*(1), i–127.

Cooper, H., Nye, B., Charlton, K., Lindsay, J., & Greathouse, S. (1996). The effects of summer vacation on achievement test scores: A narrative and meta-analytic review. *Review of Educational Research, 66*(3), 227–268.

Domina, R. (2005). Leveling the home advantage: Assessing the effectiveness of parental involvement in elementary school. *Sociology of Education, 78*(3), 233–249.

Downey, D. B., von Hippel, P. T., & Hughes, M. (2008). Are "failing" schools really failing? Removing the influence of non-school factors from measures of school quality. *Sociology of Education, 81*(3), 242–270.

Epstein, J. L. (1992). School and family partnerships In M. C. Alkin (Ed.), *Encyclopedia of Educational Research.* (pp. 1139–1151). New York, NY: Macmillan.

Epstein, J. L., & Sanders, M. G. (2000). Connecting home, school and community: New directions for social research. In M. T. Hallinan (Ed.), *Handbook of the sociology of education* (pp. 285–306). New York, NY: Kluwer Academic/Plenum.

Georges, A. (2003). *Explaining divergence in rates of learning and forgetting among first graders.* Paper presented at the American Sociological Association Annual Conference, Atlanta, GA.

Georges, A., & Pallas, A. M. (2010). New look at a persistent problem: Inequality, mathematics achievement, and teaching. *The Journal of Educational Research, 103*(4), 274–290.

Heyns, B. (1978). *Summer learning and the effects of schooling.* New York, NY: Academic Press.

Kotchick, B. A., & Forehand, R. (2002). Putting parenting in perspective: A discussion of the contextual factors that shape parenting practices. *Journal of Child and Family Studies, 11*(3), 255–269.

Lareau, A. (2000). *Home advantage: Social class and parental intervention in elementary education.* New York, NY: Rowman & Littlefield.

Lareau, A. (2003). *Unequal childhoods: Class, race, and family life.* Los Angeles: University of California Press.

Luster, T., & Okagaki, L. (2005). Introduction. In T. Luster & L. Okagaki (Eds.), *Parenting: An ecological perspective* (Monographs in Parenting Series, Kindle Edition, location 212–213). Abingdon, England: Taylor and Francis.

Phillips, M., & Chin, T. (2004). How families, children, and teachers contribute to summer learning and loss. In G. D. Borman & M. Boulay (Eds.), *Summer learning: Research, policies, and programs* (pp. 255–278). Mahwah, NJ: Erlbaum.

Reay, D., & Lucey, H. (2003). The limits of 'choice': Children and inner city schooling. *Sociology 37*(1), 121–142.

von Hippel, P. T., Powell, B., Downey, D. B., & Rowland, N. J. (2007). The effect of school on overweight in childhood: Gain in body mass index during the school year and during summer vacation. *American Journal of Public Health 97*(4), 696–702.

Yamamoto, Y., & Holloway, S. D. (2010). Parental expectations and children's academic performance in sociocultural context. *Educational Psychology Review, 22*, 189–214.

About the Contributors

Emily Ackman studies the way that politicians and policymakers make decisions about education—specifically when and how they use research in making policy decisions. She completed her PhD in Education Policy & Evaluation from Arizona State University in 2013 and won an Outstanding Dissertation Award from a Special Interest Group at the American Educational Research Association's 2014 annual meeting. She lives in metro-Boston, where she was born and raised, and is a die-hard Boston sports fan.

Karl L. Alexander is Director of the Thurgood Marshall Alliance, which provides technical support to schools in Baltimore, Maryland, that are committed to socioeconomic and racial/ethnic diversity. He also is the John Dewey Professor Emeritus of Sociology, having retired from the Johns Hopkins University faculty in 2014 after 42 years of service, 15 as chair of the Department of Sociology. Beginning in 1982 and continuing for more than a quarter century, he and colleague Doris Entwisle directed the Baltimore-based Beginning School Study, which tracked the life progress of 790 Baltimore children from first grade into mature adulthood. The culminating work of that project is *The Long Shadow: Family Background, Disadvantaged Urban Youth and the Transition to Adulthood* (Russell Sage Foundation, 2014), recipient of the 2016 Grawemeyer Prize in Education. He and his colleagues also have published extensively on summer learning loss in Baltimore.

Allison Atteberry is Assistant Professor in Research and Evaluation Methodology at the University of Colorado Boulder's School of Education. She recently completed a two-year IES Postdoctoral Fellowship at the Center of Education Policy and Workforce Competitiveness at the University of Virginia. Her academic interests center on policies and interventions that are intended to help provide high-quality instructional and schooling opportunities to the students who need them most, including the role of summers in understanding achievement disparities.

Catherine Augustine (PhD, Education, University of Michigan) is a Senior Policy Researcher at RAND. Her work focuses on improving educational outcomes for students in large urban school districts. Dr. Augustine both evaluates implementation of reforms and assesses their impact. She is co-leading a randomized controlled trial evaluation on the impact of five urban districts' (Boston, Dallas, Duval County, Pittsburgh, and Rochester) summer learning programs on elementary students. She is leading a randomized controlled trial on implementing restorative practices as a disciplinary alternative in an urban district. She is also part of a team evaluating the implementation of The Bill and Melinda Gates Foundation's effort to improve teaching effectiveness in urban sites across the country. Past research focused on the impact of policy coherence on school leadership; community collaboration in arts education; school district governance; and postsecondary education scholarship assistance.

Janice Aurini is an Associate Professor in the Department of Sociology and Legal Studies at the University of Waterloo. She received her PhD at McMaster University and was a postdoctoral fellow at Harvard University. Her research examines education policy, education inequality, private education, and parenting. Her recent articles can be found in Sociology of Education, Canadian Journal of Sociology, Canadian Public Policy, and Sociological Forum. She is currently the primary investigator on a 5-year Social Sciences and Humanities Research Council funded project on summer learning inequality and recently coauthored an advanced qualitative methods book.

Amy Bohnert, PhD, is an Associate Professor of Clinical and Developmental Psychology at Loyola University Chicago. Her research focuses on examining how various contexts, particularly out-of-school time, serve a protective role in psychological and health-related outcomes for youth, including obesity and obesogenic behaviors. Her work on out-of-school time has focused on both the after-school hours as well as summertime as well as a variety of outcomes. In particular, she is interested in whether organized activity involvement may facilitate better adjustment for at-risk individuals and across important developmental transitions. She has also investigated the most relevant determinants of activity participation at the community, family, and individual level. Recently, she has focused on examining associations between urban, low income, minority youth's out-of-school time and obesity and obesogenic behaviors, such poor dietary practices and physical inactivity. Her work has been published in the top educational, pediatric and youth development journals, including Journal of Developmental and Behavior Pediatrics and Review of Educational Research.

Geoffrey D. Borman is the Vilas Distinguished Achievement Professor of education policy and sociology, and Director of an Institute for Education Sciences funded Predoctoral Interdisciplinary Research Training Program at the University of Wisconsin-Madison. He has had a longstanding interest in summer learning and published, with coauthor Matthew Boulay, a 2004 edited volume, *Summer Learning: Research, Policies, and Programs*. In addition, he has conducted several experimental evaluations of summer school programs, including a study of the longitudinal achievement effects of a multiyear summer school intervention. Based on both regional and national data, he has also explored how family and neighborhood contexts relate to students' summer learning outcomes. Professor Borman was the recipient of a 2002 National Academy of Education/Spencer Postdoctoral Fellowship Award, the 2004 Raymond Cattell Early Career Award from the American Educational Research Association, the 2004 American Educational Research Association Review of Research Award, and the 2008 American Educational Research Association Palmer O. Johnson Award. In 2009, his significant contributions to the field of education research were recognized by his nomination and selection as a Fellow of the American Educational Research Association.

Matthew Boulay is the founder of the nonprofit National Summer Learning Association and coeditor of *Summer Learning: Research, Policies, and Programs*. A former elementary school teacher in New York City, Boulay earned a PhD in Sociology and Education from Columbia University's Teachers College and was recently named one of the 25 most influential people in out-of-school-time learning. He lives in Oregon with his wife and two children.

Claudia Buchmann is professor and chair in the Department of Sociology at the Ohio State University. She is coauthor of *The Rise of Women: The Growing Gender Gap in Education and What It Means for American Schools* (2013, Russell Sage Foundation). Her research on gender, race, and class inequalities in higher education has been published in many journals. She has investigated race and class inequalities in access to SAT test preparation and their impact on subsequent college admission and achievement gaps between immigrant and native-born students in industrialized countries. Buchmann has served as deputy editor of the *American Sociological Review* and as chair of the Sociology of Education Section of the American Sociological Association.

Judy B. Cheatham, Provost and Vice President of Academic Affairs at Martin Methodist College, was formerly the Vice President of Literacy Services at Reading Is Fundamental, in Washington, D.C., where she served as author and project director of a $9.4 million Innovative Approaches to Literacy grant, funded by the U.S. Department of Education. She began her academic career at Eastern Kentucky University, in central Appalachia, where she also worked with the Kentucky Literacy Commission and Kentucky Humanities Council on two National Endowment for the Humanities place-based projects. Since then, her focus as author, professor, trainer, speaker, program developer, editor, and consultant has always been on rural or mountain families, communities and schools, curriculum and instruction, and their relationships to economic development.

Barbara F. Condliffe is a Research Associate in the K-12 Education Policy Area at MDRC. Condliffe received her PhD in sociology from Johns Hopkins University (JHU), where she was also an IES Predoctoral Training Fellow. While at JHU, Condliffe worked with the National Summer Learning Association and the Baltimore Education Research Consortium. Prior to attending JHU, Condliffe was a middle school and high school English teacher in Brooklyn, NY. Condliffe's recent research has been published in the *American Education Research Journal* and *Teachers College Record.*

Dennis J. Condron is Associate Professor of Sociology at Oakland University in Rochester, Michigan. His research, which examines primarily unequal educational opportunities and outcomes along the lines of social class and race/ethnicity in the United States, has appeared in journals such as *Sociology of Education, Social Problems,* and *Social Forces.* He also has published on the role of economic inequality in international comparisons of achievement (*Educational Researcher, Sociological Spectrum*) and the impact of siblings on children's social and behavioral skills (*Journal of Marriage and Family, Journal of Family Issues*). His article "Social Class, School and Non-School Environments, and Black/White Inequalities in Children's Learning" (*American Sociological Review,* 2009) received the 2011 James Coleman Award for best article in the sociology of education published in the prior two years.

Scott Davies is Canada Research Chair and Professor of Policy and Leadership in Education at the University of Toronto. He previously taught sociology for 20 years at McMaster University. With Dr. Janice Aurini, he is the lead researcher for Ontario's Summer Learning Project, the largest on summer learning research ever conducted outside of the United States. He has published many articles on educational inequality, politics, and organizations in journals such as *American Journal of Sociology, Social Forces, Sociology of Education, Social Problems, European Sociological Review,* and *Research in Stratification and Mobility.* Recently he has coauthored articles on summer literacy learning in *Canadian Public Policy* and the *Canadian Journal of Sociology* and now is preparing papers on numeracy and on the long-term effects of summer interventions.

Douglas B. Downey is Professor of Sociology at the Ohio State University. He is motivated by the classic stratification question, "Who gets what and why?" In addition to researching the way family structure conditions children's school performance, he has studied race and gender dynamics in the stratification system. His current interests center on the role that schools play in shaping inequality. With Joseph Merry and Joseph Workman, he is assessing whether schools' compensatory role changed between 1998 and 2010. And with Paul von Hippel and Joseph Workman, he is testing whether schools exacerbate or reduce socioeconomic, racial/ethnic, and gender-based gaps in social and behavioral skills.

Ean Fonseca is a doctoral student in the School of Education at the Johns Hopkins University. His research interests include investigating the relationships between teacher turnover, school workplace conditions, and measures of teacher effectiveness. He has worked as a Senior Research Assistant at the Center for Social Organization of Schools, analyzing quantitative data relating to the whole-school reform organizations Diplomas Now and Talent Development Secondary. He has an MSEd from the University of Pennsylvania Graduate School of Education, and he has worked full time as a chess instructor in public elementary and middle schools in New York City.

Linda Goetze, PhD, was the Codirector for the New Mexico StartSmart K-3 Plus i3 Validation Grant and was the lead author of the successful Innovations in Education grant proposal. For over 20 years, Dr. Goetze has successfully collaborated with various state leaders to implement significant public policy changes in early childhood education intervention and finance. She has successfully completed state and local studies of child and family outcomes, cost and finance related to early childhood special education, summer learning, and state-funded preschool. Dr. Goetze has experience with national and state randomized control trials and regression discontinuity design—overseeing child and classroom assessment and cost data collection and analysis. Dr. Goetze has served on a variety of technical advisory boards such as the Technical Workgroup for IDEA assessment design and the National Early Intervention Longitudinal Study.

Kathryn Grant, PhD, is a Professor of Clinical Child Psychology at DePaul University. Her research is focused on two related areas. The first is basic research designed to reveal the effects of stressful life experiences on young people as well as processes that explain or influence stress effects. As part of her basic research agenda, Dr. Grant and collaborators are working to develop a taxonomy of stressors that will provide a conceptual and empirical framework for linking specific types of stressors with specific processes and outcomes. Dr. Grant's second area of research is applied research designed to translate basic research findings into effective interventions for youth exposed to severe and chronic stressors (e.g., youth residing in urban poverty). As part of this research, Dr. Grant and collaborators are developing two interventions that scaffold youth coping efforts through connections to supportive adults and protective settings (Cities Mentor Project and Cities Mother Daughter Project). Dr. Grant received her PhD from the University of Vermont and completed her clinical internship at Stroger Hospital in Chicago.

Amy Heard is a doctoral student in clinical psychology at Loyola University Chicago. Her research focuses on the environmental, biological, and social determinants of overeating and obesity in children and adolescents. As a National Science Foundation Graduate Research Fellow, Amy is pursuing work on the impact of food marketing on self-regulation and eating behaviors and is interested in the intersection between research and public policy.

Michelle K. Hosp, PhD, is Associate Professor of Special Education at the University of Massachusetts Amherst. Dr. Hosp's research focuses on reading and data-based decision making within multitiered systems of support. A nationally known trainer and speaker on problem solving and the use of progress monitoring data, she has served as Director of the Iowa Reading Research Center and as a trainer with the National Center on Progress Monitoring and the National Center on Response to Intervention and is currently on the technical review committee for the National Center on Intensive Intervention. She has published numerous articles, book chapters, and books.

James S. Kim is currently an associate professor of education at Harvard Graduate School of Education. He studies the effectiveness of literacy reforms and interventions in improving student outcomes. He leads the Project for Scaling Effective Literacy Reforms, a research-based collaborative initiative to identify and scale adaptive solutions for improving children's literacy learning opportunities and outcomes. He serves on the editorial boards of *Reading Research Quarterly* and the *Journal of Educational Psychology* and was the program chair for the 2014 annual meeting of the *Society for Research on Educational Effectiveness*.

Heather Marshall is a doctoral student in clinical psychology at DePaul University in Chicago. Her research interests include the mental health effects of chronic, uncontrollable stressors and trauma experienced by children and adolescents living in urban environments. Her thesis will explore the impact of chronic stress on physiological arousal and functioning in urban adolescents and address the role social support may play to moderate these effects.

Jennifer McCombs is a Senior Policy Researcher and Director of the Behavioral and Policy Sciences Department at RAND. She also serves as a professor at the Pardee RAND Graduate School. Her research focuses on evaluating the extent to which public policies and programs improve outcomes for at-risk students. Her studies combine implementation and outcome data to provide practitioners and policymakers guidance on how to improve programs and promote student outcomes. She currently leads a five-district, longitudinal study of voluntary summer learning programs for low-income elementary youth that includes extensive primary data collection, including classroom observations, interviews, surveys, and student testing. She is also conducting a developmental evaluation of cities' efforts to fully institute a measurement framework to strengthen their after-school systems. Over the course of her career, she has studied strategies to improve teacher effectiveness (through professional development, coaching, and education); development of systems for out-of-school-time programs; implementation and impact of test-based promotion policies; and effects of federal accountability policies on schools, classrooms, and students. McCombs earned her PhD in public policy from The George Washington University.

Andrew McEachin is a Full Policy Researcher at the RAND Corporation. He received his PhD in Education Policy and MA in Economics from the University of Southern California and his AB in History from Cornell University. The unifying goal of his research is to generate rigorous policy-relevant evidence to help educators and policymakers in their efforts to raise student achievement and narrow achievement gaps. His research agenda focuses on the determinants of persistent achievement gaps, including summer learning, as well as evaluating the effect of popular responses by policymakers and educators to reduce these gaps.

Dorothy McLeod is a doctoral student in clinical psychology at Loyola University Chicago. Her research interests lie in the etiology and prevention of physical/mental health disparities among children. Her thesis examines acculturation factors, their measurement, and their relation to obesity among Latino children. In preparation for this project, she conducted a systematic review of acculturation and obesity among Latino youth which is featured in Obesity Reviews.

Joseph J. Merry is Assistant Professor of Sociology at Furman University. His research investigates class-based and racial/ethnic inequalities in education. In particular, previous work examines educational influences from three major areas: the family, schools, and the realm of academic-oriented activities that occur outside of formal schooling, such as private tutoring. His work has appeared in journals such as *Sociology of Education, Annual Review of Sociology,* and *Journal of Family Issues.* His article "Tracing the U.S. Deficit in PISA

Reading Skills to Early Childhood: Evidence from the U.S. and Canada" received awards from the American Sociological Association and the American Educational Research Association. He holds a BA degree from John Carroll University and MA and PhD degrees from the Ohio State University.

Emily Milne recently joined the Department of Sociology at MacEwan University as an Assistant Professor. She received her PhD in sociology from the University of Waterloo and was a Postdoctoral Fellow at the University of Waterloo School of Pharmacy. Her research focuses on social inequality, education, Indigenous peoples, health, and policy. She is involved in projects that examine family/school relationships, student achievement, the effectiveness of university learning models and curricular programs, and barriers to health care access. She was involved with Ontario's Summer Learning Project for seven years.

Aaron M. Pallas is the Arthur I. Gates Professor of Sociology and Education at Teachers College, Columbia University. A former editor of the American Sociological Association journal *Sociology of Education*, he is a Fellow of the American Educational Research Association and an elected member of the Sociological Research Association. His most recent projects examine the interplay between education policies and the distribution of resources across schools in New York City.

Sarah Pitcock joined the Center for Summer Learning in 2006 and held progressive leadership roles prior to being appointed CEO of the National Summer Learning Association (NSLA) in 2013. Pitcock is a leading expert on summer learning research, practice, and policy. She has championed summer learning through testimony and presentation to legislative and policymaking bodies and has authored white papers, practice guides, op-eds, and blogs on the subject. Her major work includes the development of the Comprehensive Assessment of Summer Programs (CASP) and leadership of Smarter Summers, a $15.5 million investment from the Walmart Foundation to deliver summer learning programming to 28,000 middle school students in 16 major school districts. She proudly shared a podium with First Lady Michelle Obama at the U.S. Department of Education to celebrate National Summer Learning Day in 2014. Pitcock holds a master's degree in public policy from Johns Hopkins University and bachelor's degrees in public relations and political science from the University of Florida.

Alex Schmidt is a PhD student in the Department of Sociology at the University of Wisconsin-Madison. He received his master's degree from the department, with his thesis examining the behavioral impacts of a brief psychological writing intervention in middle schools. His research interests include educational inequality, the justice system, and program evaluation.

Marc L. Stein is an Associate Professor in the School of Education at the Johns Hopkins University. Dr. Stein is also an Affiliated Researcher with the Baltimore Education Research Consortium and a Faculty Affiliate with the Center for Social Organization of Schools. Dr. Stein has conducted quasi-experimental and mixed-methods research on school choice that has investigated the instructional conditions of charter public schools, parent involvement in charter public schools, and the effect of choice on student sorting by race and academic achievement. Other areas of research interest include neighborhood and school effects on student academic achievement and summer learning loss. Currently Stein is working on an Institute of Education Sciences (IES) funded randomized control trial that is investigating the efficacy of a 9th-grade Early Warning Indicator intervention in sample of high schools in a southern state, projects investigating summer learning loss in Baltimore City and a project to support schools to implement continuous improvement.

Paul von Hippel is an Associate Professor at the University of Texas, LBJ School of Public Affairs. He studies educational inequality and the relationship between schooling, health, and obesity. He is an expert on research design and missing data, and a three-time winner of best article awards from the education and methodology sections of the American Sociological Association. Before his academic career, he was a data scientist who developed fraud-detection scores for banks including JP Morgan Chase and the Bank of America.

Thomas G. White, PhD, is a Senior Research Scientist at the University of Virginia's Center for Advanced Study of Teaching and Learning. Throughout his career, he has focused his research on early reading, but he has become very interested in the utilization of research knowledge after serving as Co-Principal Investigator on IES and i3 (Investing in Innovation) grants in the past 5 years. He has published studies of vocabulary development, phonics instruction, and reading comprehension in *Journal of Research on Educational Effectiveness, Reading Research Quarterly, Scientific Studies of Reading, Journal of Educational Psychology*, and *The Reading Teacher*.

Doris Terry Williams has attained national prominence as a thought leader, visionary, and practitioner in rural, pre-K–12, adult, and higher education; youth and indigenous leadership development; and nonprofit organizational development and management. Her unique set of skills and expertise makes her a sought-after speaker, trainer, expert panelist, consultant, and facilitator for community-based, faith-based, governmental, and institutional clients. She is committed to developing the capacity of struggling schools, communities, and families to identify, strengthen, and leverage their assets, build strategic partnerships, and articulate and reach their individual and collective goals. Most recently, she was Executive Director of The Rural School and Community Trust and currently serves as a Senior Fellow to that organization. Approaching her work through a social justice and equity lens, she has founded and led major nonprofit organizations, obtained and managed grants totaling more than $35 million, taught multiple generations of youth and adults, contributed to groundbreaking policy and research initiatives and authored multiple articles, manuals, book chapters, and books.

Nicole Zarrett, PhD, is an Associate Professor in the Psychology Department at the University of South Carolina. She is a developmental psychologist whose research examines contextual affordances of key youth settings for promoting healthy physical, psychosocial, and achievement-related developmental pathways from childhood through adolescence. She has developed and implemented several interventions within schools and other youth settings to facilitate long-term behavior change and to promote positive health and adjustment among underserved youth. She is currently the Principal Investigator on a National Institutes of Health funded study—*Connect Through Positive Leisure Activities for Youth (PLAY)*—that tests the usefulness of an innovative motivational afterschool intervention for promoting social skill development and positive social connections among underserved adolescents.

Index

References for figures are followed by the letter *f* and tables are followed by the letter *t*.